Zimbabwe

WORLD BIBLIOGRAPHICAL SERIES
General Editors:
Robert G. Neville (Executive Editor)
John J. Horton

Robert A. Myers   Ian Wallace
Hans H. Wellisch   Ralph Lee Woodward, Jr.

John J. Horton is Deputy Librarian of the University of Bradford and currently Chairman of its Academic Board of Studies in Social Sciences. He has maintained a longstanding interest in the discipline of area studies and its associated bibliographical problems, with special reference to European Studies. In particular he has published in the field of Icelandic and of Yugoslav studies, including the two relevant volumes in the World Bibliographical Series.

Robert A. Myers is Associate Professor of Anthropology in the Division of Social Sciences and Director of Study Abroad Programs at Alfred University, Alfred, New York. He has studied post-colonial island nations of the Caribbean and has spent two years in Nigeria on a Fulbright Lectureship. His interests include international public health, historical anthropology and developing societies. In addition to *Amerindians of the Lesser Antilles: a bibliography* (1981), *A Resource Guide to Dominica, 1493-1986* (1987) and numerous articles, he has compiled the World Bibliographical Series volumes on *Dominica* (1987), *Nigeria* (1989) and *Ghana* (1991).

Ian Wallace is Professor of German at the University of Bath. A graduate of Oxford in French and German, he also studied in Tübingen, Heidelberg and Lausanne before taking teaching posts at universities in the USA, Scotland and England. He specializes in contemporary German affairs, especially literature and culture, on which he has published numerous articles and books. In 1979 he founded the journal *GDR Monitor*, which he continues to edit under its new title *German Monitor*.

Hans H. Wellisch is Professor emeritus at the College of Library and Information Services, University of Maryland. He was President of the American Society of Indexers and was a member of the International Federation for Documentation. He is the author of numerous articles and several books on indexing and abstracting, and has published *The Conversion of Scripts, Indexing and Abstracting: an International Bibliography* and *Indexing from A to Z*. He also contributes frequently to *Journal of the American Society for Information Science, The Indexer* and other professional journals.

Ralph Lee Woodward, Jr. is Director of Graduate Studies at Tulane University, New Orleans, where he has been Professor of History since 1970. He is the author of *Central America, a Nation Divided*, 2nd ed. (1985), as well as several monographs and more than sixty scholarly articles on modern Latin America. He has also compiled volumes in the World Bibliographical Series on *Belize* (1980), *Nicaragua* (1983), and *El Salvador* (1988). Dr. Woodward edited the Central American section of the *Research Guide to Central America and the Caribbean* (1985) and is currently editor of the Central American history section of the *Handbook of Latin American Studies*.

VOLUME 4

Zimbabwe

Revised and Expanded Edition

Deborah Potts

Compiler

CLIO PRESS

OXFORD, ENGLAND · SANTA BARBARA, CALIFORNIA
DENVER, COLORADO

British Library Cataloguing in Publication Data

Zimbabwe. – (World bibliographical series; vol. 4)
I. Potts, Deborah.   II. Series
016.96894

ISBN 1–85109–195–5

Clio Press Ltd.,
55 St. Thomas' Street,
Oxford OX1 1JG, England.

ABC-CLIO,
130 Cremona Drive,
Santa Barbara,
CA 93116, USA.

Designed by Bernard Crossland.
Typeset by Columns Design and Production Services Ltd, Reading, England.
Printed and bound in Great Britain by
Bookcraft (Bath) Ltd., Midsomer Norton

THE WORLD BIBLIOGRAPHICAL SERIES

This series, which is principally designed for the English speaker, will eventually cover every country (and many of the world's principal regions), each in a separate volume comprising annotated entries on works dealing with its history, geography, economy and politics; and with its people, their culture, customs, religion and social organization. Attention will also be paid to current living conditions – housing, education, newspapers, clothing, etc.– that are all too often ignored in standard bibliographies; and to those particular aspects relevant to individual countries. Each volume seeks to achieve, by use of careful selectivity and critical assessment of the literature, an expression of the country and an appreciation of its nature and national aspirations, to guide the reader towards an understanding of its importance. The keynote of the series is to provide, in a uniform format, an interpretation of each country that will express its culture, its place in the world, and the qualities and background that make it unique. The views expressed in individual volumes, however, are not necessarily those of the publisher.

VOLUMES IN THE SERIES

To Aislinn

Contents

Contents

Contents

Contents

Introduction

Zimbabwe finally joined the ranks of independent African nations in 1980, after fourteen years of an increasingly bitter civil war. The war, waged by the guerilla armies of the African liberation movements, the Zimbabwe African National Union (ZANU) and the Zimbabwe African People's Union (ZAPU), against Ian Smith's unrepresentative white settler government established by the illegal Unilateral Declaration of Independence, was the culmination of nearly a century of African resistance to colonial rule and oppression. This resistance was most direct and active at the beginning and end of the colonial era, which began in 1891 with the entry of the Pioneer Column into the territory now known as Zimbabwe. The Column was an instrument of the expansionist ambitions of the British imperialist and mining magnate, Cecil Rhodes. His aims in bringing Zimbabwe under British control included the desire to foil rival Portuguese and Boer expansion in the region, his plan for a Cape-to-Cairo railway running the length of Africa through British territory, and the mistaken hope that the colony would provide a 'Second Rand' – a mineral-rich reef to rival the Witwatersrand area in South Africa. Initially administered under a British crown charter by Rhodes' British South Africa Company, the colony was named Southern Rhodesia after him.

The first decade of British occupation of Zimbabwe was characterized by terrible violence and general disregard for the rights of the indigenous peoples by the colonialists. It is only in recent decades that an Africanist perspective on this period has become widely reflected in the literature on Zimbabwe: early publications tended to depict it as a glorious period of courageous European exploits against treacherous African tribes, during which the seeds of 'civilization' were sown, and peace imposed. A notable exception to this trend was Olive Schreiner's indictment of her old friend Rhodes and the British South Africa Company in her novel *Trooper Peter Halket of*

Mashonaland. The belief that Southern Rhodesia benefitted from a
'pax Britannica' rested on the idea that the country's main ethnic
groups, the Shona and the Ndebele (then sometimes called the
Mashona and the Matabele), were natural enemies and that since the
Ndebele had first entered the southern part of the country in the late
1830s they had terrorized and exploited the less aggressive Shona.
Although such a conception of pre-colonial inter-ethnic relationships
was convenient for the colonialists, it has been challenged by modern
historians who have charted a far more complex and varied set of
interactions between the different groups. The tendency to present
the Shona-speaking people of Zimbabwe as a cohesive ethnic group
with a long tradition of a single cultural identity is also no longer
accepted, and has been re-evaluated in terms of the theory that
ethnicity and tradition were often invented by colonial administrators
and missionaries. This re-interpretation of ethnic relations and of
ethnicity itself has resonances for the modern period where political
divisions and conflict are often analysed in starkly simplistic ethnic
terms, particularly in the mass media. Again contemporary studies of
Zimbabwean politics providing more nuanced discussion of the role
of ethnicity in modern politics are now available.

The first colonial war was fought against the Ndebele in 1893, and
resulted in a calamitous defeat for them and their king, Lobengula.
Their cattle-based economy had been located on the southern high
veld, the band of elevated land running through Zimbabwe from the
south-west to north-east. The Europeans confiscated their cattle and
relocated them to agro-ecologically marginal 'reserves' in the low
veld. Thus began a process of land alienation and eviction which was
one of the most significant aspects of Southern Rhodesia's colonial
experience. The Ndebele war was swiftly followed by uprisings by
both the Ndebele and the Shona in 1896 and 1897. These events have
been subjected to much re-evaluation and academic debate in recent
decades, with particular attention paid to the role of the Shona in
this, their first Chimurenga – the Shona term for resistance or
rebellion which is also applied to the liberation war for independence
in the 1960s and 1970s. The significance of such debates is not
confined to the halls and libraries of academe, particularly in a newly
emergent nation like Zimbabwe. New school curricula are gradually
being developed which reflect the African experience of colonial rule,
in which colonialist versions of historical events, which had played a
fundamental role in fostering a culture of white supremacy and had
dominated colonial education, are challenged and placed in perspective. Of equal, if not greater, significance in this process of building a
more balanced and African-focused school literature is a much-

needed shift in emphasis towards pre-colonial history. The achievements and socio-economic bases of the civilizations and cultures which had flourished in the region, such as the Munhumatapa kingdom, are now firmly part of the history curriculum, drawing on recent academic writings by local historians such as Beach, Bhebe and Mudenge. The most notorious example of the inaccuracies which developed from European bias is that of the early writings on the stone zimbabwes found all over the country, and particularly the massive ruins at Great Zimbabwe near Masvingo. These were often depicted as the work of non-Africans who had travelled to the area, reflecting European reluctance to accept that there had been any local civilization capable of such sophisticated architectural feats. These debates and developments are reflected in the publications cited in the history sections of this bibliography.

Southern Rhodesia's political and economic development reflected the dominant interests of the British South Africa Company up until its administration ended in 1923, and thereafter the tiny minority of white settlers who had opted for 'responsible self-government'. The British Colonial Office retained, in theory, responsibility for many major aspects of government, including 'native affairs', but rarely exercised its powers. The colony's mineral wealth had attracted many hopeful European prospectors, but although Zimbabwe has a variety of mineral resources, there was no Second Rand to exploit, and from early in the 20th century the settlers were also encouraged to farm, eventually occupying half of the country's agricultural land. The demands of these farmers were very influential in Rhodesian politics throughout the colonial period, and were sometimes in conflict with other capitalist sectors. The particular nature of settler colonialism in Rhodesia is much debated in scholarly literature, sometimes in comparison with other settler colonies like Kenya. Institutionalized racism, which hugely disadvantaged the indigenous people, was a central characteristic, affecting almost every sphere of their social, political and economic life from education to residential rights. One highly significant aspect of the state's response to the demands of settler interests was the development of policies aimed both at creating an African migrant labour force and undermining African agricultural competitiveness. Such policies have been analysed in detail in the literature from a variety of theoretical perspectives. The alienation of African land on a massive scale and a process of evictions of African households from 'white' land were major elements of these policies, and the repercussions of this for African livelihoods later fueled peasant support for the guerilla armies during the liberation war, and inspired post-colonial policies directed at directed at addressing glaring inequalities in land ownership and agricultural commercial opportunities. These policies have been the subject of much controversy and the land question, associated agrarian issues, and government land and agricultural policies, have been subjected to intense analysis by academic writers, as indicated in the sections on these topics in this bibliography.

An issue related to the unequal land division and subsequent overcrowding in many of the African reserves is that of environmental conservation. The physical resources of many of the communal lands, as the old reserves are now known, have been under intense pressure from increasing populations of people and livestock for many decades. The colonial tendency to blame environmental problems in the reserves on peasant techniques or ignorance was often reflected in, and partly a product of, contemporary academic analysis, but some of the more recent academic literature not only challenges the assumptions behind such views, but also calls into question the 'scientific', technocratic approach to agricultural development which still characterizes this sector in Zimbabwe. The debates are potentially of great importance since the 'traditional' views on peasant modes of agricultural production are frequently used by both large-scale commercial farming interests and external funding bodies as an argument against land redistribution.

Southern Rhodesia came to the forefront of international politics in 1965, when the white minority illegally declared a Unilateral Declaration of Independence (UDI) from Britain. The circumstances surrounding this decision, and its ramifications, have been exhaustively covered in the literature from many different perspectives. In the period immediately preceding UDI, Southern Rhodesia had been the dominant partner in the Federation of Rhodesia and Nyasaland, which included the territories of Northern Rhodesia and Nyasaland (later Zambia and Malawi). Beginning in 1953, the federal period had experienced some easing of the racially discriminatory practices which characterized Southern Rhodesian society. New patterns of economic development emerged in the post-war period, with significant increases in urbanization and industrialization. Racial separation remained a fundamental feature of the Southern Rhodesian state however, and the African populations of its two federal partners opposed the Federation from the start. Much was published on both political and economic aspects of Federation before it collapsed in 1963, with Zambia and Malawi both becoming independent a year later. However most of the white population of Southern Rhodesia was not prepared to allow the African majority to vote in independent elections as Britain desired, and the UDI was the result. At this time the country became known simply as Rhodesia. The international community responded by imposing theoretically mandatory economic sanctions. However the international political machinations surrounding Rhodesia for the next fifteen years were generally characterized by ambiguity and self-interest, as Cold War diplomacy, economic demands and, many would argue, blatant and covert racism, took their toll. Whilst there was no reason why Rhodesia's Africans should settle for anything less than elections with universal suffrage and the participation of all political parties, the British and American governments made various attempts to introduce compromise internal settlements which fell short of this objective. The South Africans, and the Portuguese in neighbouring Mozambique, ensured that 'sanctions-busting' was made easy, and that the all-important fuel, without which the economy would have foundered, was delivered. Transnational companies happily broke the embargoes; the Americans chose to exclude chrome from sanctioned Rhodesian exports because it was deemed a strategic mineral; and little was done to rescue and assist landlocked Zambia which, in its attempt to honour its commitment to sanctions and oppose white minority rule, found itself held doubly to ransom by Rhodesia and the Portuguese colonies which controlled its essential access to the sea.

Internal resistance to Ian Smith's government was eventually the major factor in the régime's downfall, and by the later 1970s it became apparent that the government could not survive. However the exact mix of international leverage, regional political pressures, economic problems eventually induced by sanctions, and the impact of the guerilla war, which finally brought all parties involved to the negotiating table in 1979 remains a matter of debate amongst experts. Whilst it appears that the black guerilla armies could have won the war, it is clear that their regional backers – Zambia, and Mozambique which had supported the liberation cause after its own independence in 1975 – put strong pressure on the liberation movements' political leadership to bring the conflict to a swift, even if not altogether satisfactory conclusion. This was because the strain of supporting the Zimbabwean struggle was becoming too much for their fragile economies and polities to bear. Smith and his supporters were similarly confronted with the threat of the withdrawal of crucial South African backing: the apartheid state judged that their attempts to prop up a white 'buffer' state against black majority rule had failed, and that every further delay in an internationally recognized settlement might well have political outcomes of an increasingly radical nature.

The Lancaster House agreement which was negotiated between the various parties in London laid down the ground rules for independent Zimbabwe's short-term political future, and, as it has turned out, also the structures of its medium and perhaps long-term economic development. As with the process of UDI itself, the circumstances and nature of the agreement have been subjected to detailed analyses and interpretation. Key elements included the retention of guaranteed parliamentary seats for whites in the first six years, a gesture which turned out to be of largely symbolic significance, although very irksome to the newly independent government, and strict constraints on the nature of future land redistribution – the cause which had led many to participate in the liberation struggle. These included the conditions that land could only be acquired on a willing-seller willing-buyer basis, and that the purchase price must be payable in foreign exchange.

The main parties contesting Zimbabwe's independence elections were ZANU (Patriotic Front or PF), ZAPU, ZANU (Sithole), the United African National Council (UANC) led by Bishop Abel Muzorewa, and Ian Smith's Rhodesian Front. The development of African nationalism and the emergence of the various different political movements has been written about extensively, but including a number of usually autobiographical accounts by political participants, many of whom went on to hold key positions in post-independence governments, which are particularly revealing. ZAPU, led by Joshua Nkomo, formed the main opposition to continued white rule in the 1960s until ZANU, led by Reverend Ndabaningi Sithole, broke away from it in 1963. These parties were banned almost from their outset, and their leaders soon imprisoned or driven into exile. Robert Mugabe, who was to become independent Zimbabwe's first Prime Minister and then Executive President, replaced Sithole as ZANU's leader in 1970 while both of them were still in jail. Released in 1974, he played a key role in organizing ZANU's guerilla war from Mozambique, which was ZANU's main regional backer. For ZAPU and Joshua Nkomo, this regional role was played by Zambia. Little financial or logistical support for the liberation movements had been forthcoming from the west, and both ZANU and ZAPU had eventually obtained important support from the communist superpowers, with the Soviet Union backing ZAPU and China aiding ZANU. Both ZANU and ZAPU operated guerilla armies: ZANU's was known as the Zimbabwe African National Liberation Army (ZANLA) and ZAPU's as the Zimbabwe People's Revolutionary Army (ZIPRA). There is now a range of literature on the various strategies adopted by these forces, although ZANLA, which adopted mass mobilization techniques amongst the peasantry, has received the most attention. There are also a number of publications on the nature of relationships between the guerilla armies and the peasantry, and associated issues relating to the particular historical experience of the Rhodesian peasantry under colonialism and the role of traditional religion in resistance. Published analyses and accounts, from widely different perspectives, are also available on the strategies and experiences of the Rhodesian armed forces, and there is a growing body of war fiction.

The independence elections were monitored by independent observers, including the Commonwealth Observer Group, and administered by the British through the governorship of Lord Soames. It is now widely believed, as is clear from various published sources on the independence process, that the British were not even-handed in their treatment of the various parties contesting the elections, and that Robert Mugabe and ZANU (PF) were deliberately hindered in their election campaign since they were perceived as being the most radical party, with a stated commitment to Marxism-Leninism. Nevertheless, ZANU (PF) won a convincing majority, with ZAPU as the main opposition party. These two parties had come together in a political alliance known as the Patriotic Front in 1976, but after the Lancaster House agreement Mugabe decided that ZANU should contest the elections as a separate entity. The other main African parties, Ndabaningi Sithole's ZANU (Sithole) and Abel Muzorewa's UANC received very little support, both leaders having become increasingly discredited in the eyes of most African Rhodesians in the late 1970s because of their decisions to negotiate with the Smith regime. In 1979 this had led to an internationally unrecognized internal settlement and elections (in which neither ZANU nor ZAPU participated), after which the country was re-named Zimbabwe-Rhodesia and Muzorewa became Prime Minister in a short-lived new government.

Zimbabwe's route to independence was intensely painful. It also inherited the legacies of the harsh racial discrimination suffered during the colonial period. These factors, combined with the first government's public commitment to socialist transformation and its opportunity to learn from twenty years of post-colonial experience in the rest of Africa, made it one of the most intensely studied and analysed societies in the developing world in the early years of independence. Every aspect of the economic and social inheritance, and of the early changes and developments which occurred were researched and debated in a rapidly growing literature. Thus there is a wide range of published material on Zimbabwe for the later 1970s and early 1980s. This was particularly welcome in the field of economics, which before this was a rather neglected area in the published literature. The new publications included a very useful series of social and economic surveys sponsored by the Catholic Institute of International Relations, sometimes in association with the

Introduction

Catholic Bishops' Conference on Justice and Peace in Zimbabwe – an important local monitor of human rights; a two-volume collection by UNCTAD; a wide-ranging series by the local Whitsun Foundation which contain excellent data; and a number of edited volumes in which both local and foreign academics provide overviews of various social and economic issues, and assess the prospects for change.

A major area of debate amongst academics has been the issue of socialist transformation. Shortly after independence it became quite clear that neither the fears of the right, nor the hopes of the left, were to be realized and that Prime Minister Mugabe was going to tread a cautious path. Great efforts were made to achieve reconciliation in the new society and to allay the fears of the whites; there was no compulsory nationalization, and the economy remained essentially capitalist in nature, albeit with many government restrictions and interventions (many of which mirrored colonial practice). There were early significant increases in minimum wages but inflation has eroded the value of these. The worst excesses of racial discrimination in terms of access to public services (but not to productive resources) were swiftly removed, and very impressive improvements in health and education have been achieved, including a halving of the infant mortality rate in less than ten years. But fundamental structural change has not yet been achieved, and even land redistribution has progressed only very slowly.

Analysts identify two major sets of reasons why Zimbabwe has taken this path of limited structural change. First, the African political élites who led the liberation movements and are now in government are often claimed to be essentially petty bourgeois, with no real commitment to restructuring the nature of the inherited economy. In this Zimbabwe has mirrored the experience of many other African nations after independence. Second, are a range of constraints emanating from external sources. The nature of the Lancaster House Agreement was one such factor, but it was also significant that Zimbabwe's first decade of independence coincided with the rising tide of economic liberalization which the International Monetary Fund (IMF), World Bank and aid donors have encouraged and sometimes forced African governments to accept. Zimbabwe's policies of foreign exchange and import controls, and protection of its industries, which had assisted the diversification of its economic base in the past, were now glaringly out of fashion. A large increase in the national debt, combined with a crippling drought in the early years of independence, lead to some internal structural adjustment in the early 1980s, although major components of interventionist economic policy were retained. The economy recovered, but further droughts in the later 1980s led to more economic setbacks, compounded by the huge expense of fighting South African-backed destabilization in Mozambique, Zimbabwe's natural transit route to the sea. Certain aspects of government economic policy were also imposing serious constraints on economic development and the parastatal sector was bedevilled by corruption and mismanagement. External prescriptions for the Zimbabwean economy essentially embraced the standard IMF package of devaluation, trade liberalization and massive cutbacks in government expenditure and intervention in the economy – all of which would render any transformation of the inherited economic structures impossible. Such policies have particularly harsh implications for the country's industrial sector, which is relatively advanced by African standards and the main contributor to GDP. Two leading industrial analysts, Riddell and Stoneman, have demonstrated that World Bank reports on Zimbabwean industry ignored many achievements and prescribed quite inappropriate policies: however, the pressures to accept the standard liberalization package became too much, and in 1990 the country embarked on its Economic Structural Adjustment Programme (ESAP), which is still in progress. As elsewhere in Africa the impact on the poor was very negative as inflation rose, and the advances in health and education have been halted or even reversed. Unfortunately any economic improvements which the programme might encourage are not yet apparent, since the initiation of the ESAP coincided with a two-year drought in 1990-91 and 1991-92. This drought was the worst on record and devastated the agricultural and energy sectors, overwhelming most underlying economic trends. Medium-term economic development patterns however will quite clearly eschew any hint of socialist transformation.

In the international arena, Zimbabwe is a member of the non-aligned movement, and a leading member of the Front Line States which have lobbied for effective international pressure on South Africa to bring an end to apartheid. It has suffered from South African destabilization throughout the 1980s, which has affected the whole of Southern African and is one of the most significant factors hindering social and economic development in that region. Whilst Zimbabwe has not suffered to the same degree as Mozambique or Angola where South Africa backed anti-government forces throughout the 1980s to devastating effect, there is no doubt that its economic and political freedom of choice has been curtailed. Its landlocked position makes it vulnerable, and only in 1993 was it able to withdraw its forces from guarding one of its railway exit routes to Beira, on the Mozambiquan coast. Peace in Southern Africa is a *sine qua non* for the management and planning of real human development. However the recent re-start of war in Angola, where the anti-government forces are still supported by elements within the South African defence forces, does not bode well for the hoped-for return to political normality in Mozambique, which has negative implications for Zimbabwean development too. A major regional economic issue is the future role of a post-apartheid South Africa. The present regional economic grouping, the Southern African Development Community (SADC), excludes South Africa and has emerged from a grouping which aimed to reduce dependence on the apartheid state. If South Africa becomes part of such a grouping, this could have pros and cons for Zimbabwe, which has had the potential to dominate SADC economically but would have to yield that role to South Africa, potentially damaging its regional exports and industries. On the other hand, greater regional stability should yield enormous economic benefits.

In the internal political arena, ZANU (PF) has increased the dominant position it gained at independence in later elections. Dreadful conflict in Matabeleland occurred in the early and mid-1980s when ZAPU dissidents, partly responding to a perceived government failure to deliver on the causes for which the war had been fought, including land, returned to the bush to fight the government. The South Africans also played a role in this destabilization. The repercussions for the civilian population, some of whom initially supported the dissidents' cause, were very serious. Development initiatives in the region came to a halt, and they suffered at the hands of the dissidents, particularly those supported by South Africa, and from many atrocities committed by the government's Fifth Brigade, an élite army unit which had been trained by the North Koreans and was sent to put down the unrest. The ramifications of this period in the country's post-independence political experience are very much alive today, for although a political pact (usually known as the Unity Accord) was struck at the end of 1987 which essentially amalgamated ZAPU into ZANU, and peace was achieved, there is now a strong political lobby for the government to recognize publicly and in some way atone for the Fifth Brigade's activities.

Despite ZANU (PF)'s continued electoral victories, it has lost its former popularity. The economic difficulties of the 1980s, and now the suffering caused by the ESAP, are major causes of dissatisfaction, with few of the population perceiving an improvement in their financial circumstances since independence. Many do recognize that there have been major social welfare benefits, but it appears that people are generally becoming more cynical about the political process which they feel is not meeting their aspirations, and many ZANU (PF) victories are won today on extremely low electoral turnouts. Concerns about corrupt behaviour by politicians, some of whom, along with other members of a new black élite, now own large tracts of land as well as other productive resources, fuel this cynicism. This issue has been an important element in a number of confrontations between university students and staff, and the government, and the independence of the university has now been severely compromised by new government legislation. These experiences all mirror, rather depressingly, patterns familiar from other African nations. One important political difference however is that despite a strong desire by Mugabe for a one-party state, this was generally opposed by the Zimbabwean people, including members of Mugabe's cabinet, and after much heated debate the decision has been taken to remain a multi-party democracy. The lack of an effective opposition party is generally agreed to be an important reason why ZANU (PF)'s power has not been seriously challenged – although a number have emerged in recent years, none have had an effective leadership or convincing policy platform. This situation may have changed recently with the development of the Forum Party of Zimbabwe (FPZ) in 1993. Nevertheless, although the generally conservative economic policies associated with this group may appeal to urban constituencies which may hope that these will improve economic performance, it is hard to see what the mainly rural populace stand to gain. The re-emergence of ZAPU as a separate political entity has also been mooted, if the government fails to satisfy Matabeleland's urgent demands for action on its acute water shortages. These new political factors, combined with economic uncertainties as Zimbabwe struggles to emerge from the combined impact of drought and the ESAP, make its future unpredictable, and fraught with both problems and opportunities.

Guide to the bibliography

This bibliography on Zimbabwe is part of a World Bibliographical Series which aims to provide interpretations of individual nations through selected, annotated bibliographies which express each nation's culture, its place in the world, and the qualities and experiences which make it unique. The coverage is therefore very broad and multidisciplinary. Since Zimbabwe has attracted and produced a wealth of serious academic research and analysis, there can be no comprehensive coverage of any topic or area of interest, although an effort has been made to indicate some of the major foci and debates of various disciplines via the items selected and the accompanying annotations. The arts have also flourished since independence, with major new writers emerging in fiction and drama, and theatre has become an important part of community education.

Shona sculpture has established itelf as one of the most important new genres of sculpture in the world. In these fields, the selections for the relevant sections of this bibliography have been chosen in an attempt both to identify important writers and themes, and to indicate the breadth and variety of literature available.

The bibliography is aimed at the informed general reader looking for information on virtually any aspect of Zimbabwean society. For this reason items have occasionally been included which are not of great academic or literary value, but which cover topics or research directions where there are few, if any, other available publications. Many of the items cited are published books, and these have been given preference in the selection process, but quite often it has been necessary to draw upon articles in journals in order to reflect the breadth of research available on particular issues. Journal articles are also sometimes included if they provide a useful introduction to a topic covered in great detail in a book, or are likely to be more easily found than a locally-published book, some of which may be hard to find outside Zimbabwe. Items have also been selected in an attempt to exemplify the range and diversity of opinion and lines of inquiry into different aspects of the country's society and history, including some indication of how these have changed over time. Some of the publications are blatantly racist but have been included because of their historical significance. The serious scholar will be familiar with the items in his or her own particular discipline, but may find the bibliography a useful guide to publications and research in another field. The bibliography is also aimed at helping librarians to answer queries about the nature, and strengths and weaknesses, of publications on particular topics about Zimbabwe. Only works in English are covered.

The bibliography is organized into chapters covering topics from history and geography to literature and recreation. Some chapters are sub-divided. In the case of History this is done by chronological period; in other cases issues have been subsumed into the most relevant discipline – thus environmental issues are dealt with under Geography. Technical and scientific publications which have no direct social significance are not covered – an exception, for example, is the material on rural sanitation technology in which Zimbabwe is a world leader. The items are numbered chronologically, and are organized alphabetically by author within chapters. Within many of the annotations other relevant publications are mentioned – these may be subsidiary to the main item, or give an indication that other publications on a similar theme have been produced. Of particular note is the Rhodesiana historical series of sixty reprinted white settler accounts of Southern Rhodesia and the region, which have been grouped together in one item and cross-referenced with other items and chapters where appropriate. The bibliography also provides a guide to research materials with coverage of selected bibliographies and journals on Zimbabwe, and an indication of the availability and nature of statistical sources. Cross references are found at the end of each chapter and may sometimes refer to chapters on that topic within an edited volume entered in another section. Three indexes are provided: a subject index; an author index covering all authors mentioned including those within the annotations and editors of volumes from which an article is cited; and a title index which includes all titles mentioned with the exception of journal articles subsumed within an annotation.

Zimbabwe is fortunate in having a well-established publishing industry, and many of the books in this bibliography are locally published. Mambo Press, which is located in Gweru, is of particular significance and has a long tradition of publishing local fiction and academic research. Other significant local publishing houses include the Zimbabwe Publishing House, Baobab Books, the Harare Publishing House, and Books of Rhodesia. In most cases the country of publication is cited when the place of publication is not a capital city, but this has been dispensed with in the case of the large number of books published in Gweru and Bulawayo.

The University has its own publishing house, the University of Zimbabwe Press. A number of important local journals are based at the University also, although in many cases their appearance is sporadic. *Zambezia*, the journal of the University of Zimbabwe, is extremely wide-ranging in its coverage, and also produces excellent substantial supplements on specific research topics, many of which are included in the bibliography. Many of the academic departments produce their own excellent research paper series – because of the difficulty of acquiring such publications these are not usually mentioned in this bibliography. However some are cited – where for instance there is no other publication on the topic, or the item is particularly noteworthy. A number of items from the Centre for Applied Social Research (CASS) are covered for example. Another research institution, the Zimbabwe Institute of Development Studies (ZIDS), also produces useful research papers, and these have been similarly treated.

A very large number of place name changes occurred at and after independence and it is not possible to list them here. Lists are available from time to time from the Surveyor-General, PO Box 8099, Harare, Zimbabwe. However it does seem appropriate to mention a few changes which might help to clarify some items listed in this bibliography. The country was called Southern Rhodesia up

Introduction

until 1965, Rhodesia until 1979, Zimbabwe-Rhodesia in 1979, and Zimbabwe from 1980. The capital city was called Salisbury until 1980, and then renamed Harare although a number of government and other publications still cited Salisbury as place of publication for a year or two after independence. The important provincial capitals of Fort Victoria and Umtali were renamed Masvingo and Mutare. These are referred to throughout the bibliography according to the appropriate context. Gweru was called Gwelo before independence, and where this is the place of publication it is spelt as in the book cited.

The research for this bibliography was mainly conducted in the libraries of the University of Zimbabwe, and the School of Oriental and African Studies, University of London. It draws heavily upon the Zimbabweana collection held in the former library, which has excellent coverage of books published on any aspect of the country. Other sources include various other University of London libraries, and, particularly for the less academic titles and topics, the bookshops of Harare. A useful source on the Zimbabwean media was the Britain-Zimbabwe Society's Review of the Press.

Acknowledgements

My thanks go to Jacob Kufa, the librarian for the Godlonton collection at the University of Zimbabwe within which the Zimbabweana collection is housed, for allowing me free access to the collection. I would also like to thank Professor Terence Ranger and Dr. Colin Stoneman for commenting on certain items in the bibliography. All errors of inclusion, omission or interpretation are my own. I would like to dedicate this work to my daughter, Aislinn, whose arrival delayed its completion but her birthday is particularly appropriate – Zimbabwean independence day.

Selected theses and dissertations on Zimbabwe

Major theses are cited in the main bibliography.

Jennifer Adams. 'Economic differentiation and wage labour in rural Zimbabwe: with particular reference to Masvingo Province', PhD thesis, Cambridge University, 1989.

Kofi Akwabi-Ameyaw. 'Government agricultural resettlement policy and the responses of farmers in Zimbabwe', PhD thesis, University of Florida, 1988.

J. Beza. 'The Organization of African Unity and Rhodesia', PhD thesis, University of Illinois, 1971. 195p.

Golden Dzimba Chekenyere. 'Primary and secondary school education dilemmas in Rhodesia and Zimbabwe: analysis of dilemmas emerging from educational policies, goals, plans and their implementation from 1965 to 1983', PhD thesis, University of Wisconsin, 1984. 387p.

Robert J. Chelliss. 'Foundation of the racially segregated education system in Southern Rhodesia 1890-1923 with special reference to the education of Africans', PhD thesis, University of Zimbabwe, 1982. 487p.

Theresa Chimombe. 'The role of banks and financial institutions in the accumulation and re-investment of capital in Zimbabwe', MPhil thesis, University of Zimbabwe, 1983.

Tapera O. Chirawu. 'The African National Congress of Zimbabwe 1914-59', PhD thesis, Howard University, 1984. 238p.

E. M. Chiviya. 'Land reform in Zimbabwe: policy and implementation', PhD thesis, Indiana University, 1982.

Emmanuel M. Chiwome. 'The poetics of Shona song and verse', MPhil thesis, University of Zimbabwe, 1987. 472p.

I. Dube. 'Market gardening in Chinamora communal lands, Goromonzi district', MSc thesis, University of Zimbabwe, 1989.

Allan Borje Gustafsson. 'Economy-wide implications of resettlement in Zimbabwe', PhD thesis, University of Stanford, 1987.

H. Hamandawana. 'The social and economic impact of small-holder irrigation schemes on development in communal areas of Zimbabwe: a case study of Nyanyadzi irrigation scheme', MSc thesis, University of Zimbabwe, 1989.

D. T. Hatendi. 'The political impact of foreign based capital (multinational corporations) in Rhodesia', PhD thesis, Oxford University, 1987.

Charles J. G. Hove. 'The economic and policy implications of government investment in water and irrigation development in Zimbabwe', PhD thesis, London School of Economics, 1983.

Susie Jacobs. 'The effect of agricultural policies on women in Zimbabwe', PhD thesis, University of Sussex, 1983.

M. P. Kanyepi. 'Public urban transport in Harare: a critique of the proposed Harare-Chitungwiza rail link', MSc thesis, University of Zimbabwe, 1987.

T. J. G. Kufakwemba. 'Tractor tillage programmes in the communal lands: a comparative analysis with special reference to organization and management', MSc thesis, University of Zimbabwe, 1989.

John Wesley Zvomunondita Kurewa. 'Towards an African concept of the church: the self-consciousness of the United Methodist Church in Rhodesia 1897-1972', PhD thesis, Northwestern University, 1973. 237p.

A. Ladley. 'Courts and authority: a study of a Shona village court in rural Zimbabwe', PhD thesis, University of London, 1985.

V. E. M. Machingaidze. 'The development of settler capitalist agriculture in Southern Rhodesia with particular reference to the role of the state 1908-39', PhD thesis, School of Oriental and African Studies, University of London, 1980.

Peter K. Mavunga. 'Understanding crime and social control in Zimbabwe', MPhil thesis, University of London, 1985.

C. Mazobere. 'Racial conflict in Rhodesia', PhD thesis, University of Boston, 1973. 309p.

David Moore. 'The contradictory construction of hegemony: politics, ideology and class in the formation of a new African state', PhD thesis, York University, Toronto, 1990.

Olivia N. Muchena. 'Women, subsistence farming and extension services in the Tribal Trust Lands of Rhodesia', MSc thesis, Cornell University. 147p.

Jane Mutambirwa. 'Shona pathology, religio-medical practices, obstetrics, paediatrics and concepts of growth and development in relation to scientific medicine', PhD thesis, Harare, 1984. 318p.

Elias Ncube. 'An analysis of the farming perceptions of small farmers at Gwabhila and Silalabuhwa irrigation scheme in Matabeleland', PhD thesis, Kansas State University, 1984. 164p.

Welshman Ncube. 'The matrimonial property rights of women during and after marriage in Zimbabwe: a study of property relations, domestic labour and power relations within the family', MPhil thesis, University of Zimbabwe, 1986. 489p.

Caiphas T. Nziramasanga. 'African immigration to Southern Rhodesia 1890-1945', PhD thesis, Oklahoma State University, 1978.

J. Rennie. 'Christianity, colonialism and the origins of nationalism among the Ndau of Southern Rhodesia 1890-1935', PhD thesis, Northwestern University, 1973. 660p.

Norman Reynolds. 'A socio-economic study of an African development scheme', PhD thesis, University of Cape Town, 1969. 360p.

David Deems Rohrbach. 'The growth of smallholder maize production in Zimbabwe: causes and implications for food security', PhD thesis, Michigan State University, 1988. 335p.

Abel F. Sana. 'A critical examination of primary teacher education program changes in Zimbabwe', EdD thesis, University of Washington, 1985. 204p.

Sipho Sibanda. 'The political economy of land tenure, decision-making and change in Zimbabwe 1890-1980 and lessons from comparative experience', PhD thesis, University of Wisconsin, 1983. 1062p.

Tatiana Sillem. 'South African destabilization of the Front Line States: the case of Zimbabwe', MPhil thesis, University of Cambridge, 1988. 114p.

Alice Stewart. 'Women and the urban economy in Harare, Zimbabwe', PhD thesis, University of Keele, 1985.

M. O. West. 'African middle class formation in colonial Zimbabwe, 1890-1965', PhD thesis, Harvard University, 1990.

T. Yoshikuni. 'Black migrants in a white city: a social history of African Harare, 1890 to 1925', PhD thesis, University of Zimbabwe, 1990.

Lovemore Mondiwa Zinyama. 'Growth and location of manufacturing industry in Rhodesia 1890-1953', MPhil thesis, University of Rhodesia, 1978.

The Country and Its People

1 **A decade of development :Zimbabwe 1980-90.**
Diana Auret. Gweru: Mambo Press in association with Catholic
Commission for Justice and Peace in Zimbabwe, 1990. 161p.

This overview of development in Zimbabwe during the first ten years after
independence focusses on popular participation in development processes in the
communal areas. It includes chapters on education, health, agriculture, women, water,
drought and irrigation, and roads, transport and housing. Major advances that have
been achieved in the fields of education, health and sanitation are acknowledged and
discussed. Various problem areas are also identified, including environmental
conservation and insufficient land redistribution. The volume contains very useful
concise information on many aspects of the economy, including marketing, farmer
organizations, credit and extension services in the agricultural sector. However much
of the data pertains to the early and mid, rather than the late, 1980s. Another general
assessment of the first ten years of Zimbabwean social and economic development is
*Perspectives on independent development in Southern Africa: the cases of Zimbabwe
and Namibia*, by the German Development Institute (Berlin: German Development
Institute, 1980).

2 **The politics of reconciliation: Zimbabwe's first decade.**
Victor de Waal. London: Hurst; Cape Town: David Philips, 1990. 146p.

De Waal is an Anglican priest and former Dean of Canterbury who spent six months in
Zimbabwe in 1988, and interviewed a wide cross-section of people to obtain a picture
of the problems and successes experienced during the early years of independence. His
findings were largely positive, and he suggests that Zimbabwe provides a model for
others to learn from. The discussion of issues raised in interviews is wide-ranging and
includes colonialism, peace, the elections, moral values, the churches, the impact of
war, the unity accord, and views on socialism.

1

3 **Historical dictionary of Zimbabwe.**
R. Kent Rasmussen, Steven C. Rubert.   Metuchen, New Jersey;
London: Scarecrow Press, 1990. 2nd ed. 502p.

This useful reference work builds on the first edition compiled by Rasmussen, with new material and revisions prepared by Steven Rubert. Its main contents are an annotated alphabetical listing of people, places, events, historical periods and objects which are necessary to an understanding of Zimbabwean history up to the present day. Over a thousand entries are included. The volume can be used for information on such diverse topics as the details of the major features and settlements of a specific district, to the major novels and literary themes of local writers or the explanation of specific racist concepts developed by the colonial state. A valuable multidisciplinary subject bibliography is included (although it is weak on economics) and a chronology of historical events.

4 **Socio-economic review of Zimbabwe 1980-85.**
Ministry of Finance, Economic Planning and Development.   Harare:
Ministry of Finance, Economic Planning and Development, 1986. 221p.

This very useful survey of Zimbabwean society and the economy five years after independence is packed with data, supported by analysis and discussion. It was particularly welcome because the Ministry had published nothing since the Annual Economic Review in August 1981. The socio-economic review was primarily carried out as background research for the *First Five Year National Development Plan*. It contains eighteen chapters covering basic facts, international co-operation, general economic indices, trade and balance of payments, resource allocation, the budget and public sector, inflation and incomes, pricing and subsidies, employment, earnings and labour productivity, money and finance, agriculture; rural development and resettlement, mining, manufacturing, construction, distribution, hotels and restaurants, transport and communications, energy and water, health, education and manpower. Each chapter is accompanied by text explaining the data and changes over the years. A further sixty-six tables are found in an annex at the end of the review.

5 **From Rhodesia to Zimbabwe: behind and beyond Lancaster House.**
Edited by W. H. Morris-Jones.   London: Frank Cass, 1980. 123p.
(Studies in Commonwealth Politics and History, no. 9).

This is one of a number of volumes on Zimbabwe published around the time of independence which reviewed various aspects of the country's past and its prospects for the future. This collection of essays by academics came out in January 1980, just before the end of colonial rule, and therefore reflects the hopes and uncertainties of the time. The editor was Director of the Institute of Commonwealth Studies at the time, and the essays had all originally appeared as a special issue of the *Journal of Commonwealth and Comparative Politics*, vol. 18, no. 1 (1980). The papers are: Roger Riddell, 'Zimbabwe's land problem: the central issue'; Colin Stoneman, 'Zimbabwe's prospects as an industrial power'; Duncan Clarke, 'Zimbabwe's international economic position and aspects of sanctions removal'; Richard Hodder-Williams, 'Political scenarios and their economic implications'; James Barber, 'Zimbabwe's Southern African setting'; A. R. Wilkinson, 'The impact of the war', and a paper by Day on ethnicity and politics (see item 385).

6 **Zimbabwe: a country study.**
Edited by Harold D. Nelson. Washington, DC: American University,
1983. 360p. (American University: Foreign Affairs Studies. Area
Handbook Series).
The Area Handbook Series from the American University is aimed at American
Foreign Affairs specialists and provides useful and detailed guides to the history,
geography, politics and economics of the countries covered.

7 **Zimbabwe since independence: a people's assessment.**
Andrew Nyanguru, Margaret Peil. *African Affairs*, vol. 90, no. 361
(1991), p. 607-20.
Ten years after independence a number of assessments of the achievements and
failures of independent Zimbabwe were published. This is one of the most interesting
in that it is based on interviews with 540 men and 272 women in Harare, Mutare, and
villages up to fifty kilometres from these cities. All the respondents were over sixty
years of age. They were asked to rate their perceptions of 'the progress of Zimbabwe
since independence', and 'the chances of getting ahead in Zimbabwe today', as well as
how access to health care and attitudes to the elderly had changed. The response to the
first issue was generally positive, although the economic problems of the 1980s meant
that many people felt that they had achieved little economic progress. Improvements in
social services were generally felt to be a major advance. The study is also very useful
for information on the elderly in Zimbabwe.

8 **Zimbabwe: a land divided.**
Robin Palmer, Isobel Birch. Oxford: Oxfam, 1992. 64p.
This is a useful short introductory text which concentrates on the record of the
independent government. The authors highlight the successes achieved in the fields of
health and education. On the more negative side they discuss the government's
faltering progress in land reform, and its ambiguous attitude towards political pluralism
and democracy. Other topics covered include Zimbabwe's contributions in the fields of
music, sport and art. Both authors work for Oxfam.

9 **Past and present in Zimbabwe.**
Edited by John D. Y. Peel, Terence O. Ranger. Manchester, England:
Manchester University Press in association with *Africa*, Journal of the
International African Institute, 1983. 120p.
This volume consists of seven substantive papers originally contributed to a special
issue of *Africa*, vol. 52, no. 3 (1982), which focussed on Zimbabwe. These papers
cover a very wide range of topics from history to the land issue to customary law, and
in the present bibliography are entered as separate items under relevant chapters.

10 **The political economy of Zimbabwe.**
Edited by M. Schatzberg. New York: Praeger, 1984. 276p.
This useful volume on political economic issues in early post-independence Zimbabwe
brings together contributions to a one-day conference held at Johns Hopkins
University's School of Advanced International Studies in 1983. The articles cover a
wide range of topics. Schatzberg provides an introduction, and the other papers are
'The political economy of state and party formation in Zimbabwe', by Leo Cokorinos;

The Country and Its People

'Race and the public service in Zimbabwe 1890-1983', by R. Murapa; 'Continuities in the politics of state security in Zimbabwe', by R. Weitzer; 'Developmental strategies and political divisions in the Zimbabwean state', by R. T. Libby; 'Political risk assessment: contrasting perspectives of Zimbabwe', by Pauline T. Baker; 'Housing the urban poor in the socialist transformation of Zimbabwe', by Diana Patel; and 'Zimbabwe in Southern Africa: from dependent development to dominance or co-operation', by Carol B. Thompson. There is also a useful multidisciplinary bibliography on the political economy provided by Jonathan Evans.

11 Zimbabwe: a country study.

Howard Simson. Uppsala: Scandinavian Institute of African Studies, 1979. 91p. (Research Report, no. 59).

This brief volume provides a useful, concise overview of the economy and society just before independence. Divided into two parts, the first part considers the country's history, the colonial economic system 1890-1978, and the transformation of health and education and other aspects of the social structure during UDI. The second part examines the prospects for the future, and includes a critical analysis of the colonial economic system.

12 Zimbabwe's inheritance.

Edited by Colin Stoneman. London: Macmillan, 1981. 234p.

Colin Stoneman is an economist at the Centre for Southern African Studies at the University of York. He is one of the primary economists outside the country who specialize in the economy of Zimbabwe, and more recently of South Africa. He has written and edited a number of books on Zimbabwe (see also items 13 and 14), and has conducted research there as an academic and as a consultant. He was largely sympathetic to the new order in Zimbabwe at independence, and has been critical of the changes in the late 1980s and 1990s as the country moved increasingly away from socialist ideals, and towards a market economy, although he stresses the role of external forces such as the British government and the IMF in these changes. This volume brought together papers from leading academics which provide a broad picture of the nature of the new society and the problems which it faces. Colin Stoneman provides an introduction and papers on the mining industry and agriculture, and with Rob Davies, an economic overview. The other papers are by Lionel Cliffe, 'Zimbabwe's political inheritance'; Coenraad Brand, 'The anatomy of an unequal society'; Mudereri Kadhani and Roger Riddell, 'Education'; Laurence Harris, 'The reproduction of inequality: taxation and the social order'; David Wield, 'Manufacturing industry'; and Rob Davies, 'Foreign trade and external economic relations'.

13 Zimbabwe's prospects: issues of race, class, state and capital in Southern Africa.

Edited by Colin Stoneman. London: Macmillan, 1988. 377p.

This volume is a useful and authoritative sequel to Stoneman's edited collection at independence, Zimbabwe's inheritance (see item 12). After eight years of independence the contributors are able to review the progress and setbacks which had occurred with reference to the expectations of 1980, and assess the literature which has emerged since independence. Many of the twenty-one papers adopt a political economy perspective, although some are more descriptive than analytical. Particular themes are the relative importance of external and internal influences on developments in Zimbabwe, and the relevance of its experience for the future of South Africa. The papers are divided into five sections. The introductory section sets the context of developments in the economic and political spheres, with papers by Ian R. Phimister on 'The combined and contradictory inheritances of the struggle against colonialism' and Stoneman on 'A Zimbabwean model?'. The second section contains eight papers analysing the first eight years of independence: Rob Davies, 'The transition to socialism in Zimbabwe: some areas for debate'; Joseph Hanlon, 'Destabilisation and the battle to reduce dependence'; Colin Stoneman, 'The economy: recognising the reality'; Daniel Weiner, 'Land and agricultural development'; Obert I. Nyawata, 'Macroeconomic management, adjustment and stabilisation'; Fay Chung, 'Education: revolution or reform?'; René Loewenson and David Sanders, 'The political economy of health and nutrition'; and Elinor Batezat, Margaret Mwalo and Kate Truscott, 'Women and independence: the heritage and the struggle'. Part three contains four papers on the world context of the late 1980s: Nelson Moyo, 'A hostile world economic climate?'; Raphael Kaplinsky, 'Technological change: the increasing costs of 'keeping up' in the microelectronics era'; Martin Fransman, 'What has Zimbabwe to learn from the Asian Newly Industrialised Countries?'; and Michael Evans, 'The security threat from South Africa'. Future prospects are considered in the fourth section: Carol Thompson 'Zimbabwe in SADCC: a question of dominance?'; Arnold Sibanda, 'The political situation'; Brian Wood, 'Trade-union organization and the working class'; Lionel Cliffe, 'The prospects for agricultural transformation in Zimbabwe'; and Logan Pakkiri, Peter Robinson and Colin Stoneman, 'Industry and planning in a small country'. The concluding section returns to the theme of whether there is a Zimbabwean model, addressed by the editor in his introductory paper. It contains two papers, Peter Robinson, on 'Relaxing the constraints', and a conclusion by Colin Stoneman.

14   **Zimbabwe: politics, economics and society.**
   Colin Stoneman, Lionel Cliffe.   London, New York: Pinter, 1989.
   210p. (Marxist Regime Series).

This major study of Zimbabwe towards the end of the first decade of independence was written as one of a series on Marxist regimes. However, as the authors readily admit, this was something of a misnomer, since Zimbabwe was an 'unequivocally capitalist economy'. The book is partly directed at students, and it is both readable and comprehensive in its coverage. A major theme is whether Zimbabwe's political economy exhibits identifiable elements which might indicate that some form of socialist future is still possible. A useful overview of other literature on this topic, including Mandaza, Astrow and Arrighi, is included in the first chapter. The book is divided into five sections which cover the general historical and political context of post-independence developments; social structures (class and race); the political system, government and mass organizations; the economy; and government policy in the fields of economics, health and education, employment, population, environment, urbanization and external relations. The important issue of land reform is dealt with throughout all of these sections. The authors concluded that whilst Zimbabwe had shown little evidence of socialist practice in the transition period prior to the book's publication, this did not necessarily deny the possibility of a socialist future. However the odds against the implementation of a socialist programme had been almost insuperable.

5

15 **Zimbabwe: towards a new order – an economic and social survey.**
UNCTAD, United Nations Development Programme. New York:
United Nations, 1980. 374p. (Working Papers, no. 1).

This United Nations survey of Rhodesia at independence is one of a number
undertaken at this time providing overviews and analyses of various elements of the
socio-economic and political situation. The survey is often referred to as the Chidzero
Report, after Bernard Chidzero who later became Minister of Finance, Economic
Planning and Development in Mugabe's government. It is divided into two sets of
working papers. This first volume provides a very comprehensive coverage of the
economy, dealing with some of the more technical aspects which do not feature in the
other edited volumes. The list of articles is impressive: Duncan Clarke, 'The monetary,
banking and financial system in Zimbabwe'; D. Jelenc, 'Assessment of the energy
sector of Zimbabwe and its position after independence'; Laurence Harris and Svogi
Wingwiri, 'Public finances and public debt'; Leonard Tsumab, 'Money, credit and
financial flows in Zimbabwe'; S. Mahlahla, 'A survey of the distribution industry of
Zimbabwe'; David Wield, 'Technology and Zimbabwean industry'; V. Nyathi-Mdluli, '
Manufacturing industry'; D. Jelenc, 'Assessment of the mining sector and policies for
the transition period'; and Mudziriri Nziramasanga, 'Agricultural sector in Zimbabwe:
prospects for change and development'.

16 **Zimbabwe: towards a new order – an economic and social survey.**
UNCTAD, United Nations Development Programme. New York:
United Nations, 1980. 506p. (Working Papers, no. 2).

This second collection of papers from the UNCTAD-sponsored survey of Zimbabwe is
much more strongly focussed on social issues than the first, although it also contains
economic assessments. The papers are by Daniel B. Ndhlela, 'The Rhodesian economy
in a historical perspective, part I'; Tonderai Makoni, 'The Rhodesian economy in a
historical perspective, part II'; G. Mandishona, 'A demographic estimate of the
indigenous population of Zimbabwe'; K. Moyana and A. ten Kate, 'Economic
structure, models and developing planning'; S. Wingwiri and Laurence Harris, 'Public
finance and public debt'; H. V. Moyana, 'The impact of the war on the use of land and
on the settlement of the rural population in Southern Rhodesia'; Duncan Clarke, 'A
review of skills problems and policies in Zimbabwe'; K. L. Dube, 'Education system in
colonial Zimbabwe: structure and politics'; Ibbo Mandaza, 'Education in Zimbabwe:
the colonial framework and response of national liberation movements'; David
Sanders, 'A study of health services in Zimbabwe'; S. Ncube, 'Nutrition and food
supplies in Zimbabwe'; and Grace Gono, 'Social services and social welfare: a need for
structural transformation'.

17 **Zimbabwe: at 5 years of independence: achievement, problems and
prospects.**
ZANU (PF), Department of the Commissariat and Culture. Harare:
ZANU (PF), Department of the Commisariat and Culture, [1985]. 265p.

This retrospective analysis of the first five years of independence was produced by the
ruling party, and is largely party propaganda. Its main value is in offering a
government perspective on the early years of independence. Its stated aim is to assess
how far 'economic and social justice have been achieved'. There are sections on wealth
production, the distribution of wealth, welfare services and social infrastructure, and
the nature of government (including local government), public services, the judiciary
and foreign affairs.

Inequalities in Zimbabwe.
See item no. 266.

Makers of history. Who's Who 1981-82. Nationalist leaders of Zimbabwe.
See item no. 403.

Geography

General

18 **Evolution of national boundaries in Zimbabwe.**
J. Best, Lovemore M. Zinyama. *Journal of Historical Geography*, vol. 11, no. 4 (1985), p. 419-32.

This article reviews the way in which the boundaries of modern day Zimbabwe were drawn up. The broad outlines are shown to have been delineated by 1891, only one year after the settlers arrived, and competing claims between the British and Portuguese affected these in minor details only. The later evolution of the boundaries is covered in detail, and the nature of the boundaries is also discussed. It is shown that there was a preference for determining borders according to geographical features, and some problems which have arisen from this are highlighted.

19 **Zimbabwe in maps: a census atlas.**
Central Statistical Office. Harare: Central Statistical Office, 1989. 30p.

This very useful publication is packed with information presented cartographically. Drawing on the 1982 census and the earlier censuses of the 1960s it presents information on population distribution and growth, household size, urban centres and rate of urban growth 1969-82, sex and age structure, migration, sex ratios and fertility ratios. The distribution of social and economic development is indicated by maps of surrogate indices: the distribution of schools and teachers and urban educational indicators, and surfaced roads per head of population and area.

20 **Rhodesia: a human geography.**
George R. Kay. London: University of London Press; New York: Holmes & Meier, 1970. 192p.

As a geography text suitable for undergraduates this has not yet been superseded in terms of its comprehensive coverage of the usual human geographical themes. However, a number of new school texts are available. This book's present usefulness is limited by the age of the data on subjects like population, urban growth and industrial production, although as a guide to settlement patterns and to the human geography of the UDI period it remains a standard work.

21   **The erosion surfaces of Zimbabwe.**
   L. A. Lister.   Harare: Zimbabwe Geological Survey Bulletin no. 90, 1987. 163p. map.
This is the definitive work on the geomorphology of the whole country, with detailed information on underlying geology and the processes which have shaped the landscape. The accompanying map is an excellent reference source.

22   **Southern Africa: a geographical study.**
   John H. Wellington.   Cambridge, England; New York: Cambridge University Press, 1955. 2 vols.
This is a standard and major reference work on the geography of the region which includes Zimbabwe. The human and economic volume is now too outdated to be of much interest, except for studies of economic and geographical history. However the volume on physical geography is still extremely relevant, very detailed, and an excellent source for information on Zimbabwean climate, geology and geomorphology.

23   **Zimbabwe. 1:1 000 000 relief layered.**
   Department of the Surveyor General.   Harare: Department of the Surveyor General, 1984. map.
This is the basic relief map of the country, which provides information on standard topographical features such as rivers and elevation, plus details on the urban and transport system, and the location of mines, game reserves, forests and national park lands. The Surveyor General's office provides an excellent selection of maps of Zimbabwe at very reasonable prices. There is very good topographic map coverage over the entire country at three scales: 1:50,000, 1:250,000 and 1:500,000. Also, at the 1:1,000,000 scale there are several single sheet maps providing very useful visual displays of information on natural agro-ecological regions, farming areas, geology, soils, hydrological zones, land classification, topography, and population density in 1969 and 1982. Rainfall and temperature maps are available at 1:250,000. About fifty per cent of the country is covered by detailed geological maps. Aerial photographs for the whole country can also be obtained at 1:80,000 and 1:25,000 at five-yearly intervals from 1963.

Zimbabwe: a country study.
See item no. 6.

Physical resources, geology and climate

24 Climate handbook of Zimbabwe.
Department of Meteorological Services. Salisbury: Department of
Meteorological Services, 1981. 222p. bibliog.

This is the most comprehensive reference book on Zimbabwe's climate. It covers the
usual range of climatic factors including the variation throughout the year of
temperature, wind strength and prevailing directions, average hours of sunshine, and
rainfall. Regional differentiation in these factors is also discussed. Data for the period
1935-80 are presented to indicate any changes over time.

25 Common veld grasses of Rhodesia.
Prepared by Christopher Lightfoot. Salisbury: Natural Resources
Board, 1975. 2nd ed.

This is a technical volume designed to aid range management in local conditions. One
hundred and six grass species are described, particularly in terms of their palatibility
and forage value, with information on good veld management and conservation. Also
see K. E. Bennet, *Kirkia: keys to Zimbabwean grass species* (Harare: Research and
Special Services Information Services, Government Printer, 1980), a handbook on
local grass species, with particular reference to their value as cattle feed, which is
reprinted from *Kirkia*, vol. 11, no. 2 (1980), p. 169-286. The toxicity of various
indigenous and introduced plants for sheep, cattle, pigs and fowl is reported in D. K.
Shone, 'Poisonous plants of Rhodesia', *Rhodesia, Zambia and Malawi Journal of
Agricultural Research*, vol. 4, no. 2 (1966), p. 81-94 and vol. 5, no. 1 (1967).

26 Seasonal rainfall fluctuations in Zimbabwe.
T. Ngara, D. L. McNaughton, S. Lineham. *Zimbabwe Agricultural
Journal*, vol. 80, no. 4 (1983), p. 149-50.

This short paper discusses the incidence and possible causes of fluctuations in expected
rainfall during the wet season in Zimbabwe.

27 Can the Zambezi irrigate the Kalahari?
Chris Nugent. *Zimbabwe Science News*, vol. 21, no. 5/6 (May 1987),
p. 68-69.

The possibility of using water from the Zambezi to ease water shortages in the region
has often been mooted. South Africa in particular is in need of water for its industrial
complex in the Transvaal. Nugent, who has done extensive research on the hydrology
and geology of the Zambezi catchment, discusses these projects and contends that they
would have serious implications for the production of hydro-electricity at Kariba.

28   **An outline of the geology of Rhodesia.**
     J. G. Stagman, with contributions from N. M. Harrison, T. J.
     Broderick, V. R. Stocklmayer.   Salisbury: Government Printer, 1978.
     126p. (Rhodesia Geological Survey Bulletin, no. 80).

This detailed discussion of Zimbabwe's geology and mineral resources is designed to be read in conjunction with the 7th edition of the Provisional Geological map of Rhodesia published in November 1977 (see item 23) on a scale of 1:1,000,000. The text is further illustrated with statistical tables, a map showing the stage of geological mapping reached at the end of 1976 and several photographic plates. Other general discussions of geology can be found in Wellington (item 22) and the Tabex encyclopedia (item 854).

29   **Gemmology.**
     J. Sweeney.   Salisbury: Mardon Printers, 1990. 2nd ed. 112p. (Bundu
     Series).

This books contains a discussion of the gems found in Zimbabwe, where they are located, and how they are treated before sale. A pocket size alternative is *The Bundu book of geology, gemmology and archaeology* (Salisbury: Mardon Printers, 1968), in which Sweeney provides the gemmology section, the geology section is by K. A. Viewing, and the archaeology chapter by the eminent scholar Peter S. Garlake.

30   **A guide to the soils of Rhodesia.**
     J. G. Thompson, W. D. Purves.   Salisbury: Rhodesia Agricultural
     Journal, 1978. (Technical Handbook, no. 3).

This is the most detailed and scientific guide on Zimbabwean soils for agricultural use. On other properties of local soils see *Soil mechanics and foundation engineering* (Rotterdam, Netherlands; Boston, Massachusetts: A. A. Balkema, 1984. [Proceedings of eighth regional conference for Africa, Harare, 1984]), edited by J. R. Boyce, W. R. Mackechnie, and K. Schwartz.

31   **Handbook and guide to Rhodesian waters**
     S. C. Trethowan.   Salisbury: Mardon Printers, [1974]. 192p.

This book provides information on all the lakes and rivers in Zimbabwe. The waterways are described in detail, and the types of boats suitable for different purposes are discussed, with the rules and regulations governing their use. The author was Shipping Adviser for the Ministry of Transport and Power before independence.

32   **Climatic change and variability in Southern Africa.**
     P. Tyson.   Cape Town: Oxford University Press, 1986. 489p.

The major droughts of the 1980s and early 1990s in Zimbabwe caused renewed interest and concern about the possibility that the country, and the region, is experiencing a shift in climate towards more arid conditions. In fact, the issue has been debated throughout this century in Southern Africa, and as this excellent regional study shows, there is no scientific evidence for such a long-term shift, although it is clear that there are cycles of wetter and drier periods. Drought periods have been experienced often in the past, which sometimes triggered off major socio-economic changes (see item 151). Two earlier publications which both asserted that real change was occurring are

Geoffrey Bond, *Past climates of Central Africa*: *inaugural lecture* (London: Oxford University Press, 1962) and Charles K. Brain, 'New evidence for climatic change during middle and late Stone Age times in Rhodesia', in *South African Archaeological Bulletin*, vol. 24, no. 95/96 (1969), p. 127-43.

33 **The Great Dyke of Southern Rhodesia.**
   B. G. Worst.   Salisbury: Geological Survey, 1960. 234p. maps.
   (Bulletin, no. 47).

The Great Dyke is one of the major geological and geomorphological features of Zimbabwe, formed by volcanic action. It is rich in minerals, chromite being of particular economic significance. This paper describes the geological and mineral characteristics of the dyke, which are illustrated with maps and diagrams.

Zimbabwe: a country study.
See item no. 6.

Pasture research in Zimbabwe 1964-84.
See item no. 736.

Environment and conservation

34 **Conserving soil in the native reserves.**
   Douglas Aylen.   Salisbury: issued by authority of the Ministry of
   Agriculture and Lands. [n.d.] (Reprinted from *Rhodesian Agricultural
   Journal*, vol. 39, no. 3 (May-June 1942), p. 152-60.)

One of the seminal papers on soil erosion by a colonial technical assistant for soil conservation in the pre-war era. It is a fascinating document today, of particular value as an example of early technocratic approaches to environmental issues. Aylen paints a gloomy picture of the African farmer's ability to conserve the soil, although his paper is self-contradictary, since he also states that many were eager to adopt techniques which might improve the soil. It was attitudes such as those represented in this article which led in part to the policies of de-stocking and changes in land tenure which were so unpopular that they had to be abandoned.

35 **The Save study: relationships between the environment and basic needs
   satisfaction in the Save catchment, Zimbabwe.**
   Edited by B. M. Campbell, R. F. du Toit, C. A. M. Atwell.   Harare:
   University of Zimbabwe, 1989. 119p. (Supplement to Zambezia, Journal
   of the University of Zimbabwe).

One of the most important environmental issues in Zimbabwe is the protection of upper water catchment areas to limit erosion and the siltation of water courses. The Save catchment area has extremely serious problems and under the Smith government these were usually blamed on the farming practices of the communal farmers in the upper catchment areas. This simplistic approach which ignores the socio-political context of land alienation and overcrowding in the former reserves is still current in independent Zimbabwe. This study, however, provides a welcome balance in its approach to the environmental problems of the Save. It addresses the whole range of issues which must be considered for an understanding of the causes of erosion and related environmental processes, including patterns of land use, local ecosystems and natural resources, and people's perceptions of the environment. It also attempts to estimate sustainable population densities, and propose social and environmental measures which might help to protect the environment and improve the satisfaction of people's basic needs. The study involved a collaborative, interdisciplinary approach and is an important contribution to the environment debate in Zimbabwe.

36   **Problems and progress in nature conservation in Rhodesia.**
      Graham Child. In: *Proceedings of a symposium on the state of nature conservation in Southern Africa.* Edited by G. de Graaff, P. T. van der Walt.   Pretoria: National Parks Board of Trustees, 1977, p. 116-37.

This paper provides a general discussion of the development of conservation policies in Zimbabwe's game reserve areas during the colonial period.

37   **The conservation issue in Zimbabwe.**
      Lionel Cliffe.   *Review of African Political Economy*, vol. 42, (1988), p. 48-57.

This is the best contextual introduction to the background on the debate over the issues of conservation and land reform in Zimbabwe. After a balanced consideration of the issues, Cliffe puts the case, in strong terms, for agrarian reform as the main solution to the environmental problems of the commmunal areas. He argues that any examination of these problems which ignores the inequality in land holdings in the country can only lead to inappropriate solutions, and that the scientific basis for prescriptions on environmental problems in the communal areas is frequently questionable. Such analyses are often the result of a reluctance to tackle the land redistribution issue. He stresses the degree of underutilization of land in the former white farming areas, and the inefficiency of leaving this land idle, and criticizes the 1985 National Conservation Strategy. His thesis directly challenges the argument that land reform would undermine the commercial export agriculture on which the Zimbabwean economy partly depends. Cliffe is Director of the Centre for Development Studies at the University of Leeds, and an authority on agrarian reform in Africa. He has been an important contributor to the debate about land reform in Zimbabwe and Southern Africa as a whole (see items 13 and 14).

38   **Soil erosion and conservation in Zimbabwe: political economy and environment.**
      Jenny Elliott.   PhD thesis, University of Loughborough, Loughborough, England, 1989.

The incidence of soil erosion in the communal lands has long been regarded as an environmental crisis, leading to a number of interventionary policies by the state, none of which has been very effective. The belief that this erosion was causing irreparable environmental degradation, and was in part due to poor agricultural techniques, was almost universally held amongst colonial planners, and many post-independence planners still adhere to it. In this study, Jenny Elliott questions this version of the soil erosion problem. She provides an overview of soil erosion and conservation in

Zimbabwe from 1900-80, and throws serious doubt on the wisdom of colonial conservation practices. An important element of these were contour ridges. These major earthworks were theoretically meant to slow down water flow and thus diminish the rate of the removal of top soil. They were extremely labour-intensive to construct and the African farming population was forced to build them with virtually no consultation. Elliott shows how this led to many political problems, and also that the ridges frequently actually worsened erosion. Excellent material on communal farmers' conceptions and understanding of soil erosion is included. Her thesis is partly based on a case study of Svosve communal land, and she demonstrates that soil erosion there has been largely stable for a number of decades. The political significance of studies such as this is considerable since environmental degradation is an argument used against land reform by vested interest groups in Zimbabwe. For another study questioning the incidence of soil erosion see Biot, Lambert and Perkins (item 50).

39 **Biomass resources assessment: measuring family fuelwood consumption in Zimbabwe.**
Brian S. J. MacGarry.   London: Commonwealth Science Council, 1987. 54p. (CSC Technical Publication, no. 217).
A major environmental concern in Zimbabwe is deforestation associated with fuelwood use. One technology often assumed to have potential to alleviate pressure on wood resources is the use of small stoves to replace the traditional open fires. In this research study, MacGarry brings this assumption into question. Two surveys were performed: one to test the possible benefits to low-income urban households of using charcoal stoves, and the other comparing the amount of fuelwood collected and used over a year between households with mudstoves, and those with open hearths. It was found that the charcoal stove offered no appreciable saving compared to the use of paraffin or wood, and that the mudstoves used roughly as much wood as the open hearths. Nevertheless people remain interested in any method which can decrease their fuelwood needs.

40 **Woodland resources, ecology, policy and ideology: an historical case study of woodland use in Shurugwi communal area, Zimbabwe.**
Jo-Anne MacGregor.   PhD thesis, University of Loughborough, Loughborough, England, 1991.
The consumption of wood for fuel and other household and agricultural uses in the communal land has frequently been blamed in local environmental conservation circles and literature for causing environmental degradation, as population pressure on communal resources has increased. However the simplistic approach to the ways in which local people perceive and use wood resources typical of these views is sharply challenged by this major study, based on field research in Shurugwi in the late 1980s, and historical research in the National Archives. Not only is it shown that the conservation of wood resources is recognized as an important concern, but also that the worst depredations on Zimbabwe's indigenous timber were perpetrated by settler farmers and the mining community. This work is an important reference for anyone interested in either modern woodland use and conservation issues, or in the history of timber exploitation in Zimbabwe.

41 **Zimbabwe's environmental dilemma: balancing resource inequities.**
Sam Moyo, Peter Robinson, Yemi Katerere, Stuart Stevenson, Davison Gumbo. Harare: Zero, 1991. 165p.

This book, produced by a team of practising local environmental professionals, provides a useful introduction and overview of environmental issues in Zimbabwe. The principal environmental issues are identified and relevant policies analysed and discussed, particularly the National Conservation Strategy. Topics covered include a resource inventory of vegetation, soil, water, wildlife and other natural resources, human settlement and land tenure, soil erosion, livestock, forestry, and legal and institutional aspects of resource management and environmental conservation. Recommendations for improved environmental management include more investment in the communal areas, decentralization of administration, and various agronomic practices including agroforestry. However the material does not reflect some of the most recent critical evaluations of environmental policy, and should be supplemented by reference to other studies such as items 39, 41, 616, 621, 611 and 634, and Biot (et al.) in item 50.

42 **A short history and annotated bibliography on soil and water conservation in Zimbabwe.**
Kingston W. Nyamapfene. Maseru: Co-ordination Unit, SADCC, Soil and Water Conservation and Land Utilisation Programme. 1987. 305p. (Report no. 12).

A brief history of soil and water conservation policy and practice, including pre-colonial conservation practices, the colonial period, issues in African and European areas, the various departments involved and conservation research. The bibliography is very extensive, annotated and a useful resource.

43 **Discourse and the discipline of historical context: conservation and ideas about development in Southern Rhodesia 1930-50.**
Ian R. Phimister. *Journal of Southern African Studies*, vol. 12, no. 2 (1986), p. 263-75.

This stimulating paper falls into the genre of studies of the development and politics of environmental conservationism in Southern Africa, and provides some historical perspectives on this issue in Zimbabwe. The discussion of the Native Land Husbandry Act does not add much to the wide literature on this subject; much more useful is the material on poor environmental practices amongst white farmers, the lack of a government response to this, and attempts to undermine black agricultural competition by the state.

44 **Whose heritage? The case of the Matobo National Park.**
Terence Osborn Ranger. *Journal of Southern African Studies*, vol. 15, no. 2 (1989), p. 217-49.

This stimulating article on the Matopos National Park in Southern Zimbabwe appeared in a special issue of the Journal of Southern African Studies on politics and conservation, and weaves together discussion of the environment, settlement history, a promise by Rhodes to the Ndebele, local agricultural practices, traditional religion, technocratic agronomists and the symbolic significance of this outstandingly beautiful area in the myths of both blacks and whites. The history of the decision to remove people from the area, which had been occupied for many thousands of years, forms a major part of the paper, and Ranger gives an account of the disastrous consequences for those removed. The fallacious arguments used to justify the depopulating of the park are described with reference to archival records. The story of the people's continued lobbying to be allowed to return to Matopos is described up to 1988, when the paper was written.

45 **The relationship of agricultural history and settlement to severe soil erosion in Rhodesia.**
Michael A. Stocking. *Zambezia*, vol. 6, no. 2 (1978), p. 129-45.
Stocking has carried out much significant technical research on the topic of soil erosion in Zimbabwe. In this paper he traces the relationships between land division and the country's agricultural history, and land degradation.

46 **Lake McIlwaine: the eutrophication and recovery of a tropical African man-made lake.**
Edited by J. A. Thornton. The Hague: Dr. W. Junk Publishers, 1982. 251p. bibliog.
Lake McIlwaine is a man-made lake near Harare, which provides the city with its water supply. This study contains twenty-seven papers describing its construction, and discussing its role as a water supply for domestic use, irrigation, recreation and fishing. A major focus of the papers is the gradual eutrophication of the lake due to increasing nutrient levels, and the management of its rehabilitation. There is also a major bibliography.

47 **A preliminary assessment of the environmental implications of the proposed Mupata and Batoka hydro-electric schemes (Zambezi River, Zimbabwe).**
R. F. du Toit, for the committee to advise on the environmental impacts of major projects. Zimbabwe: Natural Resources Board of Zimbabwe, 1982. 209p.
The development of new dams on the Zambezi is a controversial topic both within and outside Zimbabwe. This report is highly critical of the Mupata scheme because it would have a devastating impact on wildlife resources of international significance, but is more positive about the Batoka scheme, which would have limited impact on wildlife since it would mainly flood a basalt gorge and would have various economic spin-offs beyond energy generation. Companion reports on this topic, all from the Department of Land Management, University of Zimbabwe are *Appraisal of environmental and economic factors related to further hydro-electric development in the Zambezi valley* (1982), and an executive summary of that report, and M. J. Stanning, *Report on the economic impact to Zimbabwe of hydro-electric power development of Mupata and Batoka gorges, from an environmental viewpoint* (1982). A short paper on the schemes by du Toit is 'Some environmental aspects of proposed hydroelectric schemes on the Zambezi River, Zimbabwe', *Biological Conservation*, vol. 28, no. 1 (1984), p. 73-87.

48   **Household use of woodland resources in rural areas.**
Richard Whitlow.   Causeway, Salisbury: Natural Resources Board,
Department of Natural Resources, 1979. 24p.

This short report on the use of tree products in rural areas contains the result of a survey conducted by Whitlow for the Natural Resources Board. The usual concerns about the over-use of timber resources are expressed. The survey covers household uses of timber such as cooking, heating, beer brewing and construction. This research is also reported in Whitlow's 'Woodland resources in the communal areas of Zimbabwe: current status and future prospects', in *Geographical Perspectives on development in Southern Africa* (Australia: Commonwealth Geographical Bureau at James Cook University of North Queensland, [1986]), edited by Geoffrey Williams and Adrian Wood. A general discussion of the problems of deforestation is provided by Whitlow in *Deforestation in Zimbabwe: problems and prospects*, (Harare: University of Zimbabwe, 1980. [Supplement to Zambezia]).

49   **Land degradation in Zimbabwe: a geographical study.**
Richard Whitlow, report prepared on behalf of Department of Natural
Resources.   Harare: Geography Department, University of Zimbabwe,
1988. 62p.

This influential report focusses on soil erosion, and presents the results of the most extensive nationwide survey of sheet erosion, conducted via analysis of aerial photographs. The study covers the history of erosion in small and large-scale commercial farming areas, and communal areas (the former Tribal Trust Lands); the survey methodology; the general distribution of erosion in relation to land tenure, natural regions and cropping patterns; and the influence of physical and human factors. The report is of some political significance, since it highlights erosion problems in the communal areas, and Whitlow, amongst many others (including the Commercial Farmers' Union), has used this to argue against land resettlement policies. This viewpoint has been criticized for biased reporting and doubtful methodology with respect to soil erosion rates, and for neglecting the role of artificially high, politically-induced population densities in many communal areas in environmental degradation when making policy recommendations. A paper written by Whitlow with B. Campbell based on the research for this report, which is more easily accessible for those outside Zimbabwe is 'Factors influencing erosion in Zimbabwe: a statistical analysis', *Journal of Environmental Management*, vol. 19 (1989), p. 17-29.

50   **Soil erosion and conservation policy in Zimbabwe: past, present and future.**
Richard Whitlow.   *Land Use Policy* (Oct. 1988), p. 419-33.

In this paper Whitlow provides an overview of soil erosion and conservation in Zimbabwe which generally reflects the orthodoxies of the past. Whilst on the one hand accepting that racially discriminatory land policies are at the root of population pressure in the communal areas, and therefore of ensuing environmental problems, he nevertheless uses these problems to put a case against land reform, which in his view would damage the productivity of former white-owned land. For other papers on similar themes by Whitlow see 'Conflicts in land use in Zimbabwe: political, economic and environmental perspectives', *Land Use Policy*, (Oct. 1985), p. 309-22, and his influential report for the Natural Resources Board (item 49). Whitlow was born in Rhodesia, and educated at the University of Rhodesia in the Geography department. He became a senior lecturer in that department, before leaving for a post in the

Geography Department of the University of Witwatersrand in South Africa in 1991. For a rather different interpretation of soil erosion and conservation issues see Jenny Elliott (item 39), as well as some of the material in Macgregor, Scoones and Wilson (items 41, 621, 634). The whole methodological basis on which commonly cited estimates of rates of erosion in Zimbabwe's communal lands have drawn has been challenged by Lambert in his contribution to *What's the problem? An essay on land degradation, science and development in sub-Saharan Africa*, edited by Yvan Biot, Robert Lambert and Scott Perkin, Norwich: School of Development Studies, University of East Anglia, 1992. (Discussion Paper no. 222).

Guardians of the land: essays on Central African territorial cults.
See item no. 28.

Agroforestry for Shurugwi, Zimbabwe: report of an appraisal exercise for agroforestry research and extension.
See item no. 594.

The use of dambos in rural development, with reference to Zimbabwe.
See item no. 622.

Adaptation to marginal land amongst the peasant farmers of Zimbabwe.
See item no. 629.

Ecological dynamics and human welfare in Southern Zimbabwe.
See item no. 634.

Tourism, travel guides and travellers' accounts

51 **This is Zimbabwe.**
Gerald Cubitt, Peter Joyce.   London: New Holland, 1992. 160p.
This is a beautifully produced 'coffee-table' book, which contains 200 photographs of Zimbabwe's natural scenic splendours. The brief text provides a general profile of the country.

52 **Zambezi odyssey: a record of adventures on a great river in Africa.**
Stephen John Edwards.   Cape Town: Bulpin, 1974. 230p.
This is an account of the author's 1971 canoe trip on the Zambezi from the Lower Umfuli in Zambia, via Zimbabwe and Mozambique, to the Indian Ocean at Chindi. The trip took several months, and was undertaken at a time of considerable political strife in the region, making it all the more hazardous.

53 **Beneath a Zimbabwe sun.**
Graham Publishing Company.   Harare: Graham Publishing Company, 1990. 239p.
This is a popular book on the beauties of the Zimbabwean landscape aimed at the local and external tourist trade, which was first published in 1987. It contains attractive photographs illustrating each region's landscapes and tourist attractions.

54 **Proceedings of the conference on tourism and tourist areas in Zimbabwe 1985.**
Edited by Robin Heath. Harare: Geographical Association of Zimbabwe, 1986. 126p.

Tourism is an important source of foreign exchange in Zimbabwe, and the country has rapidly become a favoured destination for tourists attracted by its wildlife in particular, as well as sights such as Victoria Falls, Lake Kariba and the Zimbabwe ruins. It is not a mass-market destination, but caters to rather specific demands such as the desire to experience life in the African 'bush', backed up by high-quality hotels and service in urban areas. A number of sophisticated enterprises have moved into the marketing of this type of tourism. This conference discussed issues such as the need to expand tourism in a controlled fashion, and some of the conflicts which arise between local needs and those of the tourist. On wildlife areas and tourism see Graham Child's, 'Wildlife and protected area management in Zimbabwe', p. 27-51 in these proceedings, and his 'Tourism and the parks and wildlife estate in Zimbabwe', *Tourism and Recreation Research*, vol. 10, no. 2 (1985), p. 7-11.

55 **Africa calls: a handbook of Zimbabwe: tourist guide.**
Mark Igoe. Harare: Modus Publications, 1985. 176p.

This is a comprehensive guide for the tourist in Zimbabwe. It covers the country by region, listing and describing all the tourist attractions. It also provides a wealth of useful information for the visitor, including details of the national parks, accommodation, shopping, foreign missions and tourist organizations.

56 **Mosi-oa-tunya: a handbook to the Victoria Falls region.**
Edited by D. W. Phillipson. Salisbury: Longman Rhodesia, 1975. 222p. 3rd ed.

This substantial reference work on the Victoria Falls and its surroundings contains fifteen scholarly essays on different aspects of the physical and human environment including flora and fauna and environmental conservation, Stone Age and Iron Age human occupation, the region, traditional history and ethnography, the early history of Livingstone, traditional carving, the town of Victoria Falls and the geology and formation of the Falls. This third edition replaces earlier volumes edited by J. D. Clark and Brian M. Fagan respectively, entitled *The Victoria Falls: a handbook to the Victoria Falls, the Batoka Gorge and part of the Upper Zambesi River* (Lusaka: Commission for the Preservation of Natural History and Historical Monuments and Relics, Northern Rhodesia, 1952, 1964).

57 **Zimbabwe portrait.**
Dick Pitman. Harare: Modus Publications, 1986.

This is a glossy, pictorial introduction to Zimbabwe as a leading tourist attraction. There are over 300 colour photographs taken from *Africa Calls* and in-flight magazines, with the text by Pitman, who has long been involved in Zimbabwe's conservation movement. The main focus is the obvious tourist attractions which are dealt with by region, but there is also material on the main towns, and the economy. Another glossy guide with beautiful photographs is Mohamed Amin, I. Willetts and T. Duncan, *Journey through Zimbabwe* (Nairobi: Camerapix Publishers International, 1990).

58 **Historic Rhodesia.**
Oliver Ransford, Peter Steyn.   Salisbury: Longman Rhodesia, 1975.
70p. (Bundu series).

This useful little tour guide focusses on historical sites in Zimbabwe, and contains details on eighteen locations.

59 **Zimbabwe, Botswana and Namibia: a travel survival kit.**
Deanna Swaney, Myra Shackley.   Hawthorne, Australia: Lonely Planet Publications, 1992. 486p.

The Lonely Planet travel guides are mainly, but not exclusively, aimed at the young and fairly impecunious traveller. This guide provides the usual information on subjects of interest to travellers, from post office opening times to sites of interest, but also covers topics like police attitudes and the inappropriateness of single women visiting beer halls. The Zimbabwe section, provided by Deanna Swaney, is full of useful hints, and presents a reasonably balanced approach to local society.

60 **The Matopos.**
Edited by Sir Robert Tredgold.   Salisbury: Federal Department of Printing and Stationery, 1956. 114p. map.

This is a very comprehensive and detailed guide to the Matopos region of southern Zimbabwe, which is justly famed for its beauty and fascinating history. It is here that Cecil Rhodes was buried. There has been a long, and continuing struggle between local people and the state over their rights to residence in the Matopos, which is now a national park (see item 45). This guide was produced for and by Europeans and tends to ignore local issues. The topics covered are geology, archaeology and prehistory, fauna, flora, tourist sights, origins of the park, and history including its associations with Mzilikazi, Lobengula and the Mlimo cult.

Historical dictionary of Zimbabwe.
See item no. 3.

Wankie: the story of a great game reserve.
See item no. 78.

Wild places of Zimbabwe.
See item no. 81.

Mana Pools.
See item no. 82.

Gold regions of Southeastern Africa.
See item no. 122. (vols. 3, 4, 8, 9, 12, 25, 26, 28, 29, 33, 35; Silver Series: vols. 6, 24)

Settlers' and colonial guides

61 **Southern Rhodesia.**
Edited by Fergus W. Ferguson. Port Elizabeth, South Africa;
London: South African Publishing Syndicate, 1907. 328p.

This extensive general guide to Rhodesia is sub-titled 'an account of its past history, present development, natural riches and future prospects with special particulars for intending settlers, numerous illustrations and much general information'. Like most works of this period, the work is Eurocentric, with a discussion of Rhodes which is written with complete disregard for the African population, and only fourteen pages on the 'natives of Rhodesia'. This perspective is also apparent in the treatment of Rhodesian history. Some of the other topics and information are of potential interest to historical researchers. These include geography, railways, telegraphs, posts, geology, minerals and mining, agricultural outlook, sport, Victoria Falls and other tourist attractions, urban areas, potted biographies of other prominent white Rhodesians and South Africans beside Rhodes, and of British South Africa Company officers. The propaganda for settlers covers the land, professions, defence matters, and notable commercial and industrial undertakings. The text is well illustrated with photographs. Some extraordinarily inaccurate observations are made, including the belief that one should wear red because it helps to reduce the impact of the sun's rays.

62 **Rhodesia and Eastern Africa.**
Alistair Macmillan. London: W. H. L. Collingridge, 1931. 547p.

This is a beautifully-produced publication designed to encourage investment in the region, and to act as propaganda for British imperialism. It is sub-titled, rather curiously, 'Historical and descriptive, commercial and industrial facts, figures and resources', and this gives an indication of the breadth of subject matter. It contains valuable pictures of colonial buildings and enterprises. About half of the book is concerned specifically with Southern Rhodesia. Commercial and industrial history are well covered, with many details on business concerns in each town in Northern and Southern Rhodesia.

63 **Southern Rhodesia: a handbook for the use of prospective settlers on the land.**
Issued by direction of Minister for Agriculture and Lands. Salisbury:
Minister for Agriculture and Lands, 1930. 5th ed. 108p.

This handbook is of considerable historical interest, and also of use to the student of Rhodesian colonial land settlement. The information presented for prospective settlers is extremely wide-ranging. A few examples are topography, irrigation, insect pests, native labour, education, transport, and minerals. Of particular interest is the detailed guide to land acquisition, which includes data on land settlement schemes and prices. Other local associations and groups also tried to entice settlers into the region and published handbooks. The Rhodesian Publicity Association brought out *Rhodesia: the land for the settler and the tourist* (Bulawayo: Rhodesian Publicity Association, 1927), and the Beira and Mashonaland and Rhodesia Railways issued the *Guide to Rhodesia for the use of tourists and settlers with illustrations, maps and plans* (Bulawayo: Davis and Company, 1924). These both contain fascinating insights into the process of settler colonialism.

64   **The guide to Rhodesia.**
      Edited by George Henry Tanser.   Johannesburg, Salisbury: Winchester Press, 1975. 337p.

This guide to Rhodesia, published during UDI, covers the usual areas such as history, the economy and tourist attractions, and states that it is partly aimed at prospective settlers. Given the timing of publication this was rather wishful thinking.

Gold regions of Southeastern Africa.
See item no. 122. (Silver series: vol. 3).

Flora and Fauna

General

65 The fishes of Zimbabwe.
Graham Bell-Cross, John L. Minshall, illustrated by Hilda Jubb, Janet Duff.   Harare: Trustees of the National Museums and Monuments of Zimbabwe, 1988. 294p.

This is the major reference work on Zimbabwean fish species, which updates a previous 1976 work by Bell-Cross. In this study several new species are included, and new taxonomic approaches are incorporated. A useful bibliography is included. Another guide to local fish is *An illustrated guide to the freshwater fishes of the Zambezi River, Lake Kariba, Pungwe, Sabi, Lundi, and Limpopo Rivers* by Rex A. Jubb (Bulawayo: Stuart Manning, 1961). In the Bundu series, see *Fishes of Kariba* (Harare: Longman Zimbabwe, 1989. rev. ed.), which is designed for the layperson.

66 Rhodesian wild flowers.
H. M. Biegel, illustrated by Margaret H. Tredgold.   Salisbury: Trustees of the National Museums and Monuments of Rhodesia, 1979. 77p. (Thomas Meikle Series, no. 4).

This book replaced an older guide to local wild flowers of the same title by Robert Martineau (London: Longmans, Green, 1953), and is well illustrated with paintings of the flowers. The approach is fairly technical: a simpler guide for the layperson is the Bundu book on wild flowers by Drummond and Plowers, which is illustrated with photographs. For the serious scholar, a highly technical and detailed guide to the flora of the Zambezi valley is the ten-volume *Flora Zambesiaca: Mozambique, Federation of Rhodesia and Nyasaland, Bechuanaland Protectorate* (London: HMSO, 1960-71) by A. W. Excell, A. Fernandes and H. Wild.

67   **A Rhodesian botanical dictionary of African and English plant names.**
H. M. Biegel, S. Mavi.   Salisbury: Government Printer, [1972]. 281p.
This is an updated and much extended version of an earlier guide to local plant names:
A Southern Rhodesian botanical dictionary of native and English plant names by H.
Wild (Salisbury: Government Printer, 1952). The names of the various plant species
are given in Latin and English, and also where appropriate in Shona and its various
dialects, Tonga, Nguni, Ndebele and Lozi. Brief descriptions of the plants are also
given. Another source for African language names of plant species is Chief
Conservator of Forests, *Provisional checklist botanical and native names for
Mashonaland and Manicaland*, (Salisbury: Chief Conservator of Forests Office, 1952).

68   **Snakes of Zimbabwe.**
Donald G. Broadley, Everard V. Cock.   Harare: Longman Zimbabwe,
1989. Rev. ed. 152p.
This guide to snakes in Zimbabwe contains much more than the normal taxonomic
details, and description of habitats, habits and behaviour. Also covered are local myths
and legends about snakes, how to collect them and care for them, and information
about their venom, and what to do if bitten. Another useful reference is Vivian F. M.
Fitzsimons' *Snakes of Southern Africa* (Cape Town; Johannesburg: Purnell, 1962)
which is a standard, well-illustrated reference work on the region's snakes by the
Director of the Transvaal Museum. It includes scientific details on all of Zimbabwe's
snakes, a gazetteer, notes on habits, folklore and superstition, and a bibliography.

69   **Common trees of the highveld.**
R. B. Drummond, Keith Coates Palgrave, with water colour paintings
by Olive H. Coates Palgrave, photographs by Deric and Paul Coates
Palgrave.   Harare: Longman, 1973. 99p.
This is the standard reference on highveld trees, with detailed descriptions and
illustrations (both photographic and paintings) of fifty-four common indigenous trees,
and their leaves, flowers and fruit. It is organized alphabetically by major Latin family
names. Both English and Afrikaans common names are given, as well as some Shona
and Ndebele names. Medicinal uses of the trees' products are also described.

70   **The bundu book of flowers, trees and grass.**
G. L. Guy, B. D. Elkington.   Salisbury: Longman Rhodesia, 1965.
97p. (Bundu Series).
This title is one of the two original Bundu books, along with the volume on mammals,
reptiles and bees (see item 71). It is a very basic guide; later titles in the series
contained more details on specific types of vegetation. These include Kay Linley and
Bryan Baker's *Flowers of the veld* (Harare: Longman Zimbabwe, 1990. 2nd
impression); *A field guide to the aloes of Rhodesia* (Salisbury: Longman Rhodesia,
1974) by Oliver West; and *Trees of the Highveld* (Harare: Longman Zimbabwe, 1990.
3rd impression), and *Wild Flowers of Zimbabwe* (Harare: Longman Zimbabwe, 1990.
Rev. ed.) by D. Plowers and R. Drummond. These books are generally well
illustrated, usually with photographs, and are extremely suitable for the interested
layperson, although the specialist will probably need more scholarly guides.

71 **The Bundu book of mammals, reptiles and bees.**
G. L. Guy, B. D. Elkington. Salisbury: Longman Rhodesia, 1972.
(Bundu Series).

This is one of the original Bundu books which provide simple yet useful guides to Zimbabwean flora, fauna and natural resources. Bundu means 'bush', and the series was aimed initially at young, white Rhodesians interested in the local wildlife and vegetation. The series has been immensely successful and popular, and many of the old titles are regularly updated. Other titles in the series on local animals are *Wild mammals: a field guide and introduction to the mammals of Rhodesia* (Salisbury: Longman Rhodesia, 1975) by Dale Kenmuir and Russell Williams; *Birds of the Highveld* (Harare: Longman Zimbabwe, 1990. 3rd impression) and *Birds of the Lowveld* (Salisbury: Longman Rhodesia, 1972) by Peter Ginn; *Butterflies of Rhodesia* by Richard Cooper (Salisbury: Longman Rhodesia, 1973); and *Some well-known African moths* (Salisbury: Longman Rhodesia, 1975) by Elliott Pinley.

72 **The birds of Zimbabwe.**
Michael P. Stuart Irwin. Salisbury: Quest Publishing, 1981. 464p.

This is the major work on Zimbabwean birds. It updated the previous main study which was conducted by the Rhodesian Ornithological Society, and co-authored by Irwin, who is Director of the National Museum in Bulawayo. Information is provided on 635 species along with the areas in which they are found, and there is a gazetteer of localities mentioned at the end of the book. Colour plates of all the birds covered are provided. Another major, but rather old, reference for the professional ornithologist is *The birds of Southern Rhodesia* by Cecil Damer Priest (London: W. Roberts Clowes, 1933-36. 4 vols.). A complete set is located in the Godlington collection of the University of Zimbabwe library.

73 **Roberts' birds of Southern Africa.**
Gordon Lindsay Maclachlan, illustrated by Kenneth Newman, Geoff
Lockwood. Cape Town: John Voelcker Bird Book Fund, 1985. 5th ed.

This is the best guide to birds in the region, and is illustrated by numerous colour plates. The information on each species is very detailed, including a description and geographical distribution, habitat, voice, and feeding and breeding habits. Names for the birds are given in various languages, including Shona for birds commonly found in Zimbabwe. The original Roberts' guide was published in 1940.

74 **Newman's birds of Southern Africa.**
Kenneth Newman. Johannesburg: Macmillan SA, 1983. 461p.

This is a major reference work on birds in Southern Africa, which includes all the species to be found in Zimbabwe. It is organized by type of bird, with brief details on habits, a detailed description, a colour plate, and information on where each bird has been recorded, with illustrative maps. The region covered is the area south of the rivers Cunene and Zambezi.

75 **Trees of Central Africa.**
Olive H. Coates Palgrave, Keith Palgrave.   Salisbury: National
Publications Trust, 1956. 466p.

The Palgrave family are famous in Zimbabwe for their arboreal knowledge. This book
contains detailed information on 110 indigenous trees, mainly the more common
species. Each tree is illustrated by a colour painting, and with photographs taken by
Deric and Paul Palgrave. In addition to scientific details, there is information on local
names and local use of tree products.

76 **The mammals of the Southern African sub-region.**
Reay H. N. Smithers, with illustrations by Clare Abbott.   Pretoria:
University of Pretoria, 1983. 736p. maps. bibliog.

The author is Senior Research Officer at the Mammal Research Institute, University of
Pretoria. This is a major reference work on Southern African mammals, updating a
1951 work by Austin Roberts, and Reay's earlier works such as *The mammals of
Rhodesia, Zambia and Malawi* (London: Collins, 1966). All of Zimbabwe's mammal
species are covered, with English, Afrikaans, Latin and colloquial names; taxonomic
notes; description; and information on distribution, habitat, habits, food, reproduction, and skull formation. Maps are provided to show the area where each species is
found. The region covered is the area south of the rivers Cunene and Zambezi. There
are colour plates of each of the 291 species detailed, and a major bibliography is
provided at the end of the book containing over 2,000 entries. Three editions of this
work were produced: the special presentation, subscriber, and ordinary editions. Much
more manageable and transportable is Reay's *Land mammals of Southern Africa: a
field guide* (Johannesburg: Macmillan SA, 1986) which is based on the major text, and
intended for use in the field.

77 **Food plants of Zimbabwe: with old and new ways of preparation.**
Margaret H. Tredgold.   Gweru: Mambo Press, 1986. 121p.

This is a beautifully illustrated book by a leading local botanist on the huge variety of
local plants, including tree products and fungi, which are used for food. It includes
information on folklore, and other uses for medicine, magic and cosmetics.
Information on local foods is also found in Manel I. Gomez, 'A resource inventory of
indigenous and traditional foods in Zimbabwe', *Zambezia*, vol. 15, no. 1 (1988), p. 53-
74. This is essentially a listing of food products, with their scientific, Shona and
Ndebele names, and very brief notes on preparation and use. The nutritive values of
commonly eaten foods in Zimbabwe, including exotic products, are analysed in detail
in Irene C. Chitsiku, 'Nutritive values of foods of Zimbabwe', *Zambezia*, vol. 16, no. 1
(1989), p. 67-97, which provides data for each food on calorific values, vitamins,
minerals, protein, fats and carbohydrates.

**A preliminary assessment of the environmental implications of the proposed
Mupata and Batoka hydro-electric schemes (Zambezi River, Zimbabwe).**
See item no. 38.

Proceedings of the conference on tourism and tourist areas in Zimbabwe 1985.
See item no. 54.

Mosi-oa-tunya: a handbook to the Victoria Falls region.
See item no. 56.

The Matopos.
See item no. 60.

Gold regions of Southeastern Africa.
See item no. 122.

Some aspects of the Kariba hydroelectric project in the Central African Federation.
See item no. 645.

National parks and wildlife policy

78 **Wankie: the story of a great game reserve.**
Ted Davison.   Cape Town: Books of Africa, 1967. 211p.

Wankie game reserve is Zimbabwe's largest wildlife area, and contains a wealth of animal life. It is one of the country's greatest tourist assets. It has now been re-named Hwange. The author of this book was Wankie's first warden, serving in this capacity for thirty-four years. He provides an anecdotal version of the park's establishment and development. Another book on the reserve is *Wankie National Park* (Salisbury: Natural Resources Board, [1977]), by Graham Child and Boyd Reese, respectively the Director of National Parks and Provincial Warden of Wankie at the time. This was the first of a series which the National Parks Department planned to publish on Rhodesia's game parks. It has a brief history and description of the park, but the emphasis is on the fauna with brief guiding notes to all the mammals.

79 **Elephant management in Zimbabwe.**
Edited by Rowan B. Martin, A. M. G. Conybeare, a review compiled by the Department of National Parks and Wild Life Management. Harare: Department of National Parks and Wild Life Management, 1992. 2nd ed. 124p.

The fate of the elephant in Africa has attracted an enormous amount of publicity and media attention, and the topic is often emotionally charged. Zimbabwe's elephant population is healthy, and increasing. The government argues that this is because the populations are carefully managed, and that, in order to prevent elephant numbers growing to levels which would result in environmental damage, it is necessary to cull them. Further, the revenues from such culls help to provide the necessary wildlife management. This view has been criticized in some external wildlife circles, particularly those in Kenya, which support the current ban on ivory trading. The ban poses a major problem for Zimbabwe and other Southern African countries where elephants are officially culled. This is an excellent document on the Zimbabwean experience of elephant management, which assesses the various arguments about Zimbabwean-style management, and presents a wide range of technical information and analysis on elephant populations, the ecosystems which support them and management techniques. A similar document is available on rhinos, although it now appears that few of these large mammals will survive in the wild. See Ministry of Environment and Tourism, Department of National Parks and Wild Life Management, *Zimbabwe: black rhino conservation strategy* (Harare: Department of National Parks and Wild Life Management, 1992). For a listing of protected species see Department of National Parks and Wild Life Management, *Protected species of animals and plants in Zimbabwe* (Harare: Department of National Parks and Wild Life Management, 1991).

80 **Southern Rhodesian wildlife policy 1890-1953: a question of condoning game slaughter?**
Robin Mutwira.   *Journal of Southern African Studies*, vol. 15, no. 2 (1989), p. 250-62.

This is a valuable discussion of the development of wildlife policy up to the beginning of Federation. The incredible slaughter of game animals under various official policies, including anti-rabies and anti-tsetse campaigns, is highlighted. African resentment about wildlife policy was widespread, as it generally operated to their considerable disadvantage. The author contends that conservation had little to do with either the white settlers', or the government's, attitudes to game during this period, although some changes were beginning to emerge in the post-war period.

81 **Wild places of Zimbabwe.**
Dick Pitman.   Bulawayo: Books of Zimbabwe, 1980. 192p.

This guide covers all the main game reserves as well as some smaller parks. It includes details on Chizarira, Gona re Zhou, the Matopos, Wankie, Mana Pools and Matusadona.

82 **Mana Pools.**
Jan Teede.   Harare: Quest Publications, 1988. 216p.

Mana Pools is one of the most important wildlife areas in the world, and has been named a World Heritage Site. Located on the Zambezi, on the border with Zambia in Northern Zimbabwe, its riverine location allows the area to support a high density of animal population. Another unique feature is that visitors are allowed to walk in the park without a guide (but at their own risk). This guide to Mana Pools provides information on its ecology and history, descriptions of its flora, fauna and vegetation, and contains many colour plates.

83 **People, wildlife and natural resources – the Campfire approach to rural development in Zimbabwe.**
Zimbabwe Trust, Department of National Parks and Wild Life Management, Campfire Association.   Harare: Conlon Printers, [1990]. 24p.

Campfire stands for Communal Areas Management Programme for Indigenous Resources, Zimbabwe's pioneering approach to the management of wildlife and other natural resources. The theory behind the strategy is that if the people are given control over resources, they will tend to manage them sustainably. This approach contrasts with colonial wildlife policy, which almost always meant prohibiting the African population from exploiting wildlife resources, even if their livelihoods were being damaged by, for example, elephants raiding crops. In reality the present policy involves local communities benefitting from cash resources raised by hunting and tourism by other people, and the government is still the real manager. Much research on this topic is currently under way. As yet there is little published on Campfire's achievements, although wildlife and conservation magazines sometimes carry brief reviews. This booklet is produced by the three major organizations involved with Campfire, and describes the historical background of the project, its major components, and case histories taken from existing Campfire projects in various parts of Zimbabwe. The Zimbabwe Trust, a non-governmental organization, is a useful source for further information, and can be contacted at 4 Lanark Road, Belgravia, Harare, Zimbabwe. Management of wildlife in areas populated by humans is also discussed in R. D. Taylor, 'Buffer zones: resolving conflicts between humans and wildife interests in the Sebungwe, Zimbabwe', *Zimbabwe Agricultural Journal*, vol. 79 (1982), p. 179-84.

Problems and progress in nature conservation in Rhodesia.
See item no. 36.

Whose heritage? The case of the Matobo National Park.
See item no. 45.

Proceedings of the conference on tourism and tourist areas in Zimbabwe 1985.
See item no. 54.

The Matopos.
See item no. 60.

Evaluating the impact of NGOs in rural poverty alleviation: Zimbabwe country study.
See item no. 507.

Hunting and fishing

84 **National reviews for aquaculture development in Africa. 1: Zimbabwe.**
J. D. Balarin.   Rome: FAO, 1984. 69p. bibliog. (FAO Fisheries circular, no. 770.1).

One of a series of FAO publications on aquaculture in African countries, this study is based on an extensive literature review and information from research conducted in the early 1980s. Also on fish farming, see D. H. S. Kenmuir's 'Fish production prospects in Zimbabwe', *Zimbabwe Agricultural Journal*, vol. 79, no. 1 (1982), p. 11-17.

85 **Studies of fishing on Lake Kariba.**
Michael F. C. Bourdillon, Angela P. Cheater, M. W. Murphree. Gweru: Mambo Press, 1985. 185p. (Mambo Occasional Papers: Socio-Economic Series, no. 20).

A major study by three sociologists, this book describes the history of fishing on the lake, the different management policies on the southern and northern shores, and the practices of two different ethnic groups, the Shona and the Tonga. The role and importance of kapenta, the small fish which is found in great abundance in the lake, and which is usually dried before marketing, is also considered – this fish is a useful source of protein for many people in both urban and rural areas. The study concludes with discussion of policy issues and the direction of future research. On Kariba fishing co-operatives see Michael F. C. Bourdillon, *Inshore fishing co-operatives in the Kariba district*, (Gweru: Mambo Press, 1986).

86 **Commercial and safari hunting in Zimbabwe.**
D. H. M. Cumming. In: *Wildlife production systems: economic utilization of wild ungulates*. Edited by Robert J. Hudson, K. R. Drew, L. M. Baskin. Cambridge, England: Cambridge University Press, 1989, p. 132-56.

Safari hunting is a relatively recent phenomenon in Zimbabwe, dating back to the early 1960s. It is conducted under a variety of arrangements involving landowners, safari operators, hunters' associations or individual hunts. This reference explains the different types of operations, and the management of the wildlife involved. Hunting is presented as economically and ecologically attractive. The costs and benefits for the communal areas, safari areas and national foreign exchange reserves are also considered.

87 **Chivalry, social Darwinism and ritualised killing: the hunting ethos in Central Africa up to 1914.**
John M. Mackenzie. In: *Conservation in Africa: people, policies and practice*. Edited by David Anderson, Richard Grove. Cambridge, England: Cambridge University Press, 1987. p. 41-62.

In this article Mackenzie paints a most disturbing picture of the ideology prevalent amongst the early settlers which led to the massive slaughters, not only of animals, but also at times of the indigenous people. Much of the material deals directly with colonial and pre-colonial Rhodesia.

88 **Hunting: on safari in Eastern and Southern Africa.**
Aubrey Wynne-Jones, illustrated by André de Villiers. Johannesburg: Macmillan SA, 1980. 180p.

This handbook for trophy hunters covers every aspect of the hunting safari from the early planning stages to the hunt itself. Information is included on trophy animals with distribution maps, illustrations, and recommendations on suitable rifles. Hunting is presented as an important part of wildlife conservation.

Lake McIlwaine: the eutrophication and recovery of a tropical African man-made lake.
See item no. 47.

Southern Rhodesian wildlife policy 1890-1953: a question of condoning game slaughter?
See item no. 80.

Gold regions of Southeastern Africa.
See item no. 122 (vol. 29).

Prehistory and Archaeology

89 **Early Zimbabwe from the Matopos to Inyanga.**
Peter S. Garlake, illustrated by Zimbabwean Co-operative Craft
Workshop.   Gweru: Mambo Press, 1983. 34p.

Similar to Garlake's short guide on Great Zimbabwe (see item 91), this introduction to
Zimbabwe's cultural and economic history is simplified but lovingly produced. The
author describes the peoples who occupied the country and their cultures, from the
Stone Age to the time when the African civilization associated with the development of
Great Zimbabwe was at its height. With so many of the more accessible studies
focusing on Great Zimbabwe, this guide is a useful addition since it includes other
early societies, including the people who constructed the extraordinary terracing on the
mountains in the eastern highlands near Inyanga. Another valuable scholarly reference
on the Inyanga culture is Roger Summer, *Inyanga: prehistoric settlements in Southern
Rhodesia* (Cambridge, England: Cambridge University Press for the Inyanga Research
Fund, 1958).

90 **Great Zimbabwe.**
Peter S. Garlake.   London: Thames & Hudson, 1973. 224p. (New
Aspects of Antiquity Series).

Garlake is the leading authority on Great Zimbabwe and associated archaeological
sites, and has published extensively on the ruins, including popular guides (see item
91). This volume is the standard academic source on Great Zimbabwe, beautifully
illustrated and well written. The coverage is comprehensive, including discussion of the
cultures and economic patterns associated with Great Zimbabwe, as well as the
archaeology and history of exploration. Garlake provides a balanced account of the old
controversy about the origins of the ruins, and the obvious and overwhelming case for
indigenous origins. He outlines chronological stages of occupation from c. AD 1000-
1500, although in his 1982 guide the earliest phase is revised to the 13th century. The
development of the civilization of Great Zimbabwe is shown to have been gradual and
evolutionary, with trade contacts, including those to the coast at Kilwa, an important
aspect of the economy. This substantial study superseded a slightly earlier publication
which also surveyed the evidence and literature about the ruins, demonstrating its

Prehistory and Archaeology

indigenous origins, by Roger F. H. Summers, *Zimbabwe: a Rhodesian mystery* (Johannesburg: Nelson, 1965). Also by Summers on this topic are *Ancient ruins and vanished civilizations of Southern Africa* [Cape Town: T. V. Bulpin, 1971], and with Keith Radcliffe and A. Whitty, *Zimbabwe excavations, 1958* (Salisbury: National Museums of Southern Rhodesia, 1961. [Occasional Paper, no. 23A]). A short and accessible paper on this site which also highlights the importance of trade with the coast for the rise of Zimbabwe, and suggests that disruption of that trade combined with ecological degradation may have caused its decline is Thomas N. Huffman's 'The rise and fall of Zimbabwe', *Journal of African History*, vol. 13, no. 3 (1972), p. 353-66.

91 **Life of Great Zimbabwe.**

Peter S. Garlake, illustrated by Zimbabwean Co-operative Craft Workshop. Gweru: Mambo Press, 1982. 50p.

This very popular guide to the social history of the inhabitants of Great Zimbabwe is regularly reprinted, and is also available in Shona. It provides simple explanations, and is aimed primarily at tourists and children. The life and culture described are beautifully illustrated. Garlake states that the civilization associated with the ruins dates back to the 13th century. The cultural achievements of this civilization were at their peak in 1350, but had dwindled away by 1500. Possible causes of this decline are mooted including ecological and political factors. A short handbook on the ruins at Great Zimbabwe by Garlake is *Great Zimbabwe: described and explained* (Harare: Zimbabwe Publishing House, 1982). Another guide which focusses on technical and archaeological aspects is *Symbols in stone: unravelling the mystery of Great Zimbabwe* (Johannesburg: Witwatersrand University Press, 1987) by Thomas N. Huffman, of the Department of Archaeology at the University of Witwatersrand in South Africa.

92 **The origin of the Zimbabwean civilization.**

R. Gayre of Gayre, with appendices on some of the principal ruins of Rhodesia by E. Langland. Salisbury: Galaxie Press, 1972. 218p.

The controversy over the origins of the Great Zimbabwe ruins should have been firmly laid to rest by the 1970s, but the claim for a non-African origin was symbolically important to some white settlers, who refused to accept evidence that did not fit in with their prejudices. This large and glossy illustrated volume is probably the most detailed and determined example of its genre. It even contains maps showing wind directions to explain how 'cultured' immigrants could have sailed to African shores.

93 **Pre-historic Rhodesia.**

Richard Nicklin Hall. London: T. F. Unwin, 1909. 488p.

In this extensive work, which is well illustrated with photographs and maps, Hall goes to great lengths to dispute any idea that the ruins at Great Zimbabwe were of African origin, and specifically attacks the 1905 findings of Randall-Maciver (see item 97). This item is of interest as an example of the determination of some researchers of the period to ignore the evidence in pursuit of theories which fitted more closely into their frequently racist paradigms. The book closes with a section on ethnology and a gazetteer of medieval south-east Africa between 915 and 1760. Discussing his own excavations of 1902-04 in an earlier volume, *Great Zimbabwe* (London: Methuen, 1905), Hall postulated a link between the ruins and the Queen of Sheba. Similar beliefs are expressed in another publication written with W. G. Neal (see volume 23 in item 122). Shorter contributions from other exponents of non-African origins for the various stone zimbabwes, some of them vehement in their detraction of writers with alternative views, are Count Wilmot, FRGS, *The zimbabwes of southeastern Africa* (Cape Town: T. Maskew Miller, 1919), W. H. Tooke, 'Who built the Rhodesian ruins?', *South African Journal of Science*, vol. 15 (1918), p. 492-99, and Major Sir John C. Willoughby, *A narrative of further excavations of Zimbabwe, Mashonaland* (London: George Phillip & Son, 1893). The latter item is also notable for its ethnographic material, with much information and discussion about the Makalanga, and the origins of their name. In a similar vein to much later writings on Shona ethnicity (see item 252), he questions the existence of a Shona identity, and wonders at the 'word Mashonaland, the origins of which I am quite unable to account for, as there is no native throughout the country who calls himself a "Mashona"'.

94 **Southern African prehistory and palaeoenvironments.**
   Edited by Richard G. Klein.   Rotterdam: A. A. Balkema, 1984. 404p.
   bibliog.

This is a collection of scholarly and authoritative papers on the archaeology and associated fossil record of Southern Africa including Zimbabwe. It provides an up-to-date reference and summary for Southern African prehistory and related palaeoenvironmental studies. The papers address the topics of early man and evolution; climatic, vegetation and environmental change; Early, Middle and Later Stone Age peoples (from two million to 40,000-30,000 years ago); and the appearance of Iron Age mixed agricultural societies ca. 2,000 years ago. A massive bibliography of over 800 items is included.

95 **The later prehistory of Eastern and Southern Africa.**
   D. W. Phillipson.   Nairobi, Ibadan, Nigeria; Lusaka, London:
   Heinemann, 1977. 323p.

This study of regional prehistory covers the last 20,000 years, and together with Klein (item 94) provides useful coverage of general themes in Zimbabwe's prehistory to earliest times. It is based primarily on archaeological sources, but includes use of linguistic and ethnographic research, and oral and written historical records. The topics covered include material culture, crops and cultivation, rock art, early industry, and pastoralism.

96 **Settlement location in Northern Zimbabwe AD1250-1800.**
   Gilbert Pwiti.   MPhil thesis, University of Cambridge, Cambridge,
   England, 1985.

In this dissertation Pwiti examines the location of various stone zimbabwes in Northern Zimbabwe, and analyses the sites in relation to location theories which emphasize the significance of resource proximity. The conclusion of the discussion, therefore, is that their siting was ecologically determined.

97 **Mediaeval Rhodesia.**
   David Randall-Maciver.   London: Macmillan, 1906. 106p.

The investigations of the Greater Zimbabwe and other associated archaeological sites described here were carried out in 1905 with the support of the British Association and Rhodes' Trustees. The opinion expressed is that the ruins were not older than the 14th or 15th century and were of African origin; any ideas of Egyptian or oriental origins are firmly rejected. This authoritative interpretation was an important departure from earlier, and often amateur, analyses of the ruins which claimed external origins.

Prehistory and Archaeology

Similar opinions to Maciver's are expressed by Franklin White in his studies which detailed with great exactitude the form and measurements of various ruins, including photographic plates, in *Notes on the great Zimbabwe elliptical ruins* (London: Anthropological Institute of Great Britian and Ireland, 1905), and *On the ruins of Dhlo-dhlo in Rhodesia* (London: Anthropological Institute of Great Britian and Ireland, 1901). A later study in 1929 by Gertrude Caton-Thompson, *The Zimbabwe culture: ruins and reactions* (Oxford: Clarendon Press, 1931; reprinted, London: Frank Cass, 1970; Westport, Connecticut: Negro Universities Press, 1971) confirmed Randall-Maciver's opinions about the indigenous origins of the ruins, but, without the benefit of Carbon 14 dating techniques, incorrectly dated the occupation to the 8th or 9th century. The last serious academic contribution to the debate before the introduction of this technology, which also asserted African origins, is Heinrich Albert Wieschhoff, *The Zimbabwe-Monomotapa culture in Southeast Africa* (Menasha, Wisconsin: George Banta Publishing, 1941).

98 **The Stone Age archaeology of Southern Africa.**
    C. Garth Sampson.   New York: Andronicus Press & Academic Press,
    1974. 518p. bibliog.

Southern Africa, including Zimbabwe, has extremely important archaeological sites of pre-historic human occupation, which are of world significance. This major scholarly work is an excellent reference on Stone Age cultures in the region, technically detailed and well researched and illustrated. Both the archaeological sites and their remains, and the occupants' lifestyles and environment are examined. An excellent bibliography is included. Another solid and scholarly reference for Zimbabwean prehistory is John D. Clark's *The prehistory of Southern Africa* (Harmondsworth, England: Penguin, 1959), although this does not reflect recent research, for which see Klein (item 94).

Mosi-oa-tunya: a handbook to the Victoria Falls region.
See item no. 56.

Gold regions of Southeastern Africa.
See item no. 122 (vols. 5, 23; Silver Series: vol. 16).

History

General surveys and historiography

99 **The Zimbabwe controversy: a case of colonial historiography.**
David Chanaiwa. Syracuse, New York: Eastern African Studies
Programme, Syracuse University, 1973. 142p.

This is a study of the various scholarly interpretations of the origins of the civilization
associated with the Zimbabwe ruins. It reviews the literature from the perspective of
how the socio-political context of settler colonialism had influenced the historical
analysis and encouraged 'diffusionist' theories which insisted that the culture which
developed the site must have had outside roots. The author is a Zimbabwean who
earned his doctorate at the University of California at Los Angeles in 1971, taught in
the United States and Britain and then returned to Zimbabwe at independence.
Garlake, the pre-eminent authority on Great Zimbabwe has also written specifically on
the influence of ideology on interpretations of the ruins in 'Prehistory and ideology in
Zimbabwe', *Africa*, vol. 52, no. 3 (1982), reprinted in *Past and present in Zimbabwe*
(item 9). Another authoritative study is David Beach's 'The historiography of the
people of Zimbabwe in the 1960s', *Rhodesian History*, vol. 4 (1973), p. 21-30.

100 **Zimbabwe epic.**
Researched and compiled by P. C. Mazikena, I. J. Johnstone, edited
and designed by R. J. Douglas. Harare: National Archives, 1982.
280p.

This is a glossy, popular history of the African people of Zimbabwe from the beginning
of human settlement to the struggle for liberation from colonialism. It was produced as
a cooperative venture by the staff of the National Archives, with the aid of a UNESCO
grant. There is no attempt to cover the history of the European population of
Rhodesia: this aspect of the country's history is dealt with in an earlier volume
Rhodesian Epic, by T. W. Baxter and R. W. S. Turner (Cape Town: Howard
Timmins, 1966), which takes a negative view of African culture. Both volumes are
lavishly illustrated. A similar treatment to that in *Rhodesian Epic* is found in *All our*

yesterdays, 1890-1970: a pictorial review of Rhodesia's story from the best of 'Illustrated Life Rhodesia' (Salisbury: Graham Publishing, 1970).

101 **Rhodesian legacy.**
Ian Murphy, Alf Wannenburgh. Cape Town, Johannesburg: C. Struik Publishers, 1978. 30p.

This is essentially a photographic history of Rhodesia. The main part of the book consists of 187 colour plates taken by Murphy. The text by Wannenburgh provides a somewhat romantic, but fairly objective brief history of the country, in the form of captions to the illustrations. The photographs are organized by region.

102 **Zimbabwe: economic and social historiography since 1970.**
Ian R. Phimister. *African Affairs*, vol. 78, no. 311 (1979), p. 253-68.

This article provides a useful guide to the academic trends in historical interpretation of Rhodesia which occurred during the 1970s, supplemented by a comprehensive bibliography. These trends are identified and discussed through an extensive review of a number of relevant publications, including books and articles by Ranger, van Onselen, Clarke, Cobbing and Palmer. For a very different treatment of historiography in the region, which is written from a conservative perspective, and includes analysis of work on Rhodesia see Harrison M. Wright, *The burden of the present: liberal-radical controversy over Southern African history* (London: Rex Collings, 1988).

103 **The historiography of Southern Rhodesia.**
Terence Osborn Ranger. *Transafrican Journal of History* (Kenya), vol. 1, no. 2 (1971), p. 63-76.

This is a useful reference on developments in historical research on Rhodesia and changing approaches to the subject up to the beginning of the 1970s. The author is one of the most authoritative scholars of Rhodesian and Zimbabwean history. For a more specific consideration of the question of the pre-colonial relationship between the Shona and the Ndebele see Ranger's 'The rewriting of African history during the scramble: the Matabele dominance in Mashonaland', *African Social Research* (Zambia), vol. 4 (Dec. 1967), p. 271-82.

104 **The valiant years.**
Beryl Salt. Harare: Galaxie Press, 1978. 143p.

In this volume the story of Rhodesia from 1890 to 1978 is told entirely through the medium of facsimile reproduction of newspaper articles and headlines, with a brief, one-page introduction. This presentation of Rhodesian history is marvellously evocative of the attitudes and values which shaped events. It ends at what was thought, erroneously, to be the transition to majority rule with Sithole and Muzorewa.

105 **Zimbabwe: a new history.**
G. Seidman, David Martin, Phyllis Johnson. Harare: Zimbabwe Publishing House, 1982. 140p.

The re-writing of colonial school texts was of particular significance in the discipline of history. This book is aimed at upper primary schools, and is of interest as an indicator of the changed interpretation of the past which independence allowed. Emphasis is placed on early Zimbabwean civilization and the pre-colonial states such as the

Monomotapa and Rozvi empires. European colonialism is treated as one of many influences on Zimbabwean historical development and change, and the events of the first Chimurenga of 1896-97 are written from an African perspective. The significance of African protests against the colonial state are highlighted, and the development of nationalist politics from 1950 is given a high profile.

106   **The Zambesian past: studies in Central African history.**
Edited by Eric T. Stokes, Richard Brown.   Manchester, England: Manchester University Press; New York: Humanities Press, 1966. 427p.
This edited volume made a major contribution to the development of historical work on Central Africa when it was published. The contributions are derived from a Rhodes-Livingstone Institute conference in 1963. There are seven papers on Zimbabwe, contributed by K. R. Robinson, D. P. Abraham, P. R. Warhurst, Richard Brown, Terence O. Ranger, and G. Kingsley Garbett. Three deal with aspects of religion, including a discussion of the role of religious authorities in the 1896-97 rebellion. The others deal with archaeology, political succession and the development of modern politics, and the colonial scramble in Gazaland and Matabeleland.

107   **The road to Zimbabwe: the political economy of settler colonialism, national liberation and foreign intervention.**
C. Utete.   Washington, DC: University Press of America, 1979. 170p.
This discussion of the nature of settler colonialism falls into the underdevelopment school of economic analysis, and is widely used within the University of Zimbabwe. The author's examination of the socio-economic structure and development of settler colonialism is developed in the context of the need to understand how the economy and its institutions worked, in order to dismantle them and create a fairer society. This analysis of settler colonialism examines the Zimbabwe case within the context of the general experience of Southern Africa. The author contends that the nature of colonial development actively underdeveloped Rhodesia's potential for economic growth in the long term, and also discusses the endemic nature of conflict in settler societies.

108   **The road to Zimbabwe: 1890-1980.**
Anthony Verrier.   London: Jonathan Cape, 1986. 364p.
This excellent study focuses on the relationship between Britain and Rhodesia, and the attitudes of successive British governments to racism in Rhodesia. Verrier demonstrates that Britain never really took a liberal or even objective stance on Rhodesia, but always supported the whites against the black population. This position is carefully reasoned and well supported, although the text is not an in-depth academic study. Verrier had first-hand experience of both the Lusaka Commonwealth Conference and the Lancaster House Conference, and he uses his personal experience, information from many interviews, and secondary sources which include the Welensky papers and British cabinet papers to support his case. The section on the run-up to independence and the elections is of particular interest. He shows how the Thatcher government sympathized with the colonialist white establishment, but was forced to agree to a constitutional conference at the Lusaka Commonwealth Conference in 1979. Mugabe's election victory came as a shock to the British who, Verrier demonstrates, had tried to disadvantage his contingent at the Lancaster House negotiations for a ceasefire and eventual elections, and also hindered his election campaign in Zimbabwe in 1980. The Commonwealth Observer Group and monitoring force are shown to have been vital

instruments for maintaining basic security for the elections, and the crucial need for impartial observers in the process is stressed. Verrier is a journalist and lecturer, and wrote this whilst a Senior Associate Member of St. Antony's College, Oxford.

109 An introduction to the history of Central Africa.
Alfred John Wills.   London; New York: Oxford University Press, 1985. 4th ed. 556p.

This is a standard regional history text which covers Zimbabwe and its former partners in the Central African Federation, Zambia and Malawi (the former Northern Rhodesia and Nyasaland). It is aimed at history students and teachers in these countries. The fourth edition covers from pre-historic times to the early years of Zimbabwean independence. Serious historical research would require more detailed material than this useful, but general text can provide. Central African history is also the theme of a volume edited by Terence O. Ranger, which contains two papers specifically on Rhodesia, *Aspects of Central African history* (London: Heinemann, 1968).

Historical dictionary of Zimbabwe.
See item no. 3.

Zimbabwe: a country study.
See item no. 6.

Zimbabwe: a country study.
See item no. 11.

Zimbabwe: towards a new order – an economic and social survey. vol. 2.
See item no. 16.

White farmers in Rhodesia, 1890-1965: a history of the Marandellas District.
See item no. 376.

Precolonial history

110 Ndebele raiders and Shona power.
David N. Beach. *Journal of African History*, vol. 15, (1974), p. 633-51.

Whilst it was convenient for European settlers to believe that their colonization of Zimbabwe served to end the Shona's violent subjugation at the hands of the Ndebele, historical research has shown that the Ndebele's domination was not nearly as complete nor as brutal as supposed. This article is an accessible and focussed study explaining the complexities of Shona-Ndebele relationships, and dispelling the old myths. Further details and discussion are available in Ngwabi Bhebe's earlier article in the same journal, 'Some aspects of Ndebele relations with the Shona in the nineteenth century', vol. 4 (1973), p. 31-38.

111 **The Shona and Zimbabwe 900-1850: an outline of Shona history.**
David N. Beach. London: Heinemann; Gweru: Mambo Press, 1980.
422p.

Beach is a senior lecturer in history at the University of Zimbabwe and has been one of
the most important figures in the re-interpretation and re-evaluation of Shona history
in the past twenty years. His research output has been fundamental in building up a
picture of the complex culture and economy of the pre-colonial groups who spoke
Shona. His work is generally well written and easily accessible to the non-specialist.
This book provides a systematic analysis of Shona dynasties, and detailed examination
of development and change in the socio-economic base, the material culture, trade,
political forms and traditions of the various Shona-speaking states. Beach shows that
terms such as Korekore, Zezuru and Manyika which are applied to sub-groups of the
Shona did have a pre-colonial currency, but these did not necessarily refer to ethnicity
as they do today. Instead the terms could refer to the topography inhabited by a
community, or be a slang term for an enemy, for example. Thus although various
Shona-speaking communities did share some cultural traits, they were unaware of a
common cultural or political identity. A very useful shorter text by Beach is *Zimbabwe
before 1900* (Harare: Longman Zimbabwe, 1981; rev. ed. Gweru: Mambo Press,
1984). This is the original uncut version of a paper entitled 'The Zimbabwe plateau and
its peoples', published in *The history of Central Africa: volume I* (Harlow: Longman,
1983), edited by D. Birmingham and D. Martin. In this book Beach discusses historical
aspects of Zimbabwean society, economy and politics and provides a guide for students
and teachers to the differing schools of thought and interpretations which have been
applied to this period of Shona history.

112 **Trade and politics in a Shona kingdom: the Manyika and their
Portuguese and African neighbours 1575-1902.**
H. H. K. Bhila. Harlow, England: Longman; Salisbury: Longman
Zimbabwe, 1982. 291p. (Studies in Zimbabwean History).

The author lectures in history at the University of Zimbabwe, and this work draws on
his doctoral thesis. Bhila's study focusses on the Manyika of central Zimbabwe, one of
the Shona-speaking groups. He traces the social and economic development of their
small and wealthy kingdom, focussing on the central role played by trade in gold and
ivory. By careful manipulation and control of this trade the Manyika succeeded in
maintaining their position in relation to the Portuguese, the Changamire (Rozvi)
kingdom and Nguni. Only when the trade was dislocated did the kingdom break apart
and its people were absorbed by the colonial powers. The book contains a useful
examination of the various theories about the first Chimurenga. He discusses the work
of Ranger, Beach and Cobbing (see items 139, 123, 114) in the context of the debate
about the exact role of the Shona and their religious leadership.

113 **The Karanga empire.**
Aeneas Chigwedere. Harare: Books for Africa, [1983]. [n.p.].

This study of the origins of the Kalanga people is written by the headmaster of
Goromonzi High School, who was regional Chair of National Museums and
Monuments and a member of the Ministry of Education's History panel which
undertook to review history textbooks in Zimbabwe. Although not a deeply scholarly
work, this interpretation of Kalanga history provides an African perspective on their
culture and society. Chigwedere has also written *From Mutapa to Rhodes* (London:
Macmillan, 1980) in which he proposed that eighty-five per cent of today's black

Zimbabweans had a common ancestry which was united into one political complex until 1500. He suggests that fragmentation of this polity progressed particularly rapidly from the beginning of the 18th century.

114 The Ndebele under Khumalos, 1820-1896.

Julian Raymond Dennis Cobbing. PhD thesis, University of Lancaster, Lancaster, England, 1976.

A much-praised study, this thesis provides a thorough analysis of Ndebele politics and society from 1820 to the 1896 uprising, based on documentary sources and interviews with over eighty informants. In detailing dynasties, political linkages and social change and relationships with neighbouring groups, including raiding activities, Beach (see item 123) argues that 'in virtually every sphere of Ndebele history, radical changes to Ndebele historiography were proposed and in most cases convincingly proven'. Cobbing challenged Ranger's original interpretation of the 1890s which relied heavily on a spiritual leadership for coordinating the Ndebele and Shona uprisings (see item 139). He also argued against the view that the seeds of later African nationalism were to be found in the rebellion. This seminal work has never been published in full, but articles based on the research include 'The evolution of Ndebele Amabutho', *Journal of African History* (UK), vol. 15 (1974), p. 607-31, and 'The absent priesthood: another look at the Rhodesian risings of 1896-1897', *Journal of African History* (UK), vol. 18, no. 1 (1977), p. 61-84.

115 A political history of Munhumutapa c.1400-1902.

S. I. G. Mudenge. Harare: Zimbabwe Publishing House, 1988; London: James Currey; New Jersey, USA: Heinemann, 1989. 420p.

The author has lectured in history at a number of African universities, and at independence became Permanent Secretary in the Ministry of Foreign Affairs, then the Permanent Representative of Zimbabwe at the United Nations. This major study of the Munhumatapa kingdom was researched and written during the war years in Zimbabwe, and provides a comprehensive historical survey of the politics, religious and military structures, economic base and court institutions of this significant African state. The work is largely based on Portuguese documents, and tends therefore to be mainly a history of the Munhumatapa rulers and their interaction with outsiders, especially the Portuguese. This study provides a useful chronological framework to the study of Zimbabwean history, and is now the main synthesis of evidence on the Munhumatapa state. A brief survey of theses on other Zimbabwean polities is found in the first chapter. Much previous research on Munhumatapa was undertaken by D. P. Abraham, and although this never resulted in a major book, useful material can be found in 'The Monomotapa dynasty', *Nada*, vol. 36 (1959), p. 59-84. Further details on the dynasties are included in 'Dynasties of the Mutapa-Rozwi complex', *Journal of African History*, vol. 11, no. 2 (1970), p. 203-30 by Edward A. Alpers. Mudenge has also published a short study specifically on attempts to convert the Munhumatapa rulers: *Christian education of the Mutapa court: a Portuguese strategy to influence events in the empire of Munhumatapa* (Harare: Zimbabwe Publishing House, 1986), which focusses on the experience of the Mutapa princes taken to Goa to expose them to Christianity and western education. Another major study of the kingdom, originally published in French as *L'Empire du Monomotapa du XV au XIX siecle* (Mouton, Paris, The Hague: Ecole des Hautes Etudes en Sciences Sociales, Centre de Recherches Historiques, no.46), is *The Empire of Monomotapa from the fifteenth to the nineteenth century* (Gwelo: Mambo Press, 1979. [Series on Culture and Society in Central Africa, Zambeziana no. 7]) by W. G. L. Randles. This also made extensive use of the Lisbon archives and covers the origins of the empire, the intervention of the Portuguese in the 16th and 17th centuries, and the organization of the societies of the highveld including discussion of their agriculture, cattle, industry, politics, religion and trade.

116 **Dzimbahwe: life and politics in the golden age 1100-1500** A.D.
Ken Mufuka. Harare: Harare Publishing House, 1983. 58p.

This short historical study provides an interesting perspective on aspects of early history. The author has used both secondary sources and oral evidence to describe and analyse some of the old myths about this period in Zimbabwe's past. These tended to be colonial in origin and to denigrate the material and political achievements of indigenous peoples. Discussion of the newer approaches and evidence about this time provide a picture of societies which were much more complex and sophisticated than was previously thought.

117 **Mzilizikazi of the Ndebele.**
R. Kent Rasmussen. London: Heinemann Educational Books, 1977. 48p. (African Historical Biographies Series).

Mzilikazi was the first king of the Ndebele, and led their migration into the territory of modern-day Zimbabwe. This excellent, concise biography traces his life from birth in c.1795 to his death in 1868, and provides an introduction to the movement of the Ndebele to Zimbabwe. For a very detailed study of the Ndebele and Mzilikazi see Rasmussen's *Migrant kingdom: Mzilikazi's Ndebele in South Africa* (London: Rex Collings; Cape Town: David Philip, 1978), which focuses on the migration through South Africa. The author is an associate editor of the Marcus Garvey Papers Project at the University of California, Los Angeles, and has researched Zimbabwean history for over two decades.

118 **The shattered nation.**
J. G. Storry. Cape Town: Howard Timmins, 1974. 175p.

This is a non-academic general account of the Ndebele nation from around 1838 to 1894, Lobengula's defeat by the colonial forces, and the shattering of the Ndebele economy.

119 **The warriors.**
Roger F. H. Summers, C. W. Pagden. Cape Town: Books of Africa, 1970; London: White Lion, 1974. 181p.

This study of the Ndebele focuses on their military capabilities and history which held much fascination for many of the European settlers, and the authors admit to a romantic bias in their perspective of the Ndebele. Another study of the Ndebele army is David Chanaiwa's, 'The army and politics in pre-industrial Africa: the Ndebele nation, 1822-93', *African Studies Review* (USA), vol. 19, no. 2 (1976), p. 49-68. Also see Cobbing, item 114.

120 **Trade and the Rozwi Mambo.**
Nicola Sutherland-Harris. In: *Pre-colonial African trade*. Edited by
Richard Gray, David Birmingham. London, New York: Oxford
University Press, 1970, p. 243-64.

One of the debates about pre-colonial Zimbabwean polities is the extent to which they
owed their development and organization to religious or trade influences. This study
argues strongly for the importance of the trade factor for the Rozwi, with their ruler,
Mambo or Changamire, controlling regional gold trade. Mudenge has argued that this
overstates the trade factor for the Rozwi, and re-asserts the significance of religion and
military functions for the development of the state. See his 'The role of foreign trade in
the Rozwi Empire: a reappraisal', *Journal of African History*, vol. 15 (1974), p. 373-91,
which is based on his 1972 University of London doctoral thesis *'The Rozvi Empire and
the Feira of Zumbo'*. Other useful sources on trade in the Zimbabwean region in the
pre-colonial era which document Portuguese influences are J. M. Chirenje, 'Portuguese priests and soldiers in Zimbabwe, 1560-72: the interplay between evangelism
and trade', *International Journal of of African Historical Studies*, vol. 6, no. 1 (1973),
p. 36-48, and Ronald Gregson, 'Trade and politics in South-East Africa: the Moors,
the Portuguese and the Kingdom of Mwenemutapa', *African Social Research*, vol. 16
(Dec. 1973), p. 413-46. Also see Bhila, item 112.

Historical dictionary of Zimbabwe.
See item no. 3.

My friend Kumalo: sidelights on Matabele tradition.
See item no. 250.

**From spears to ploughshares: changes in the political structure of the
AmaNdebele.**
See item no. 370.

Pastoralism and Zimbabwe.
See item no. 618.

Colonization and early African resistance

121 **Firearms in South Central Africa.**
Anthony Atmore, J. M. Chirenje, S. I. Mudenge. *Journal of African
History*, vol. 12, no. 4 (1971), p. 545-56.

This article is the most specific and comprehensive reference on the impact of the
introduction of firearms on the peoples of Zimbabwe. First introduced in the 17th
century by the Portuguese, firearms were soon highly prized by the indigenous people.
The authors examine the different effects of the new technology on the Shona,
Ndebele and Tswana and also the reactions of the whites to the new power wielded by
the indigenous peoples. Firearms were also part of the deal known as the Rudd
Concession struck with Lobengula, and these are discussed by Julian Cobbing in 'The
unknown fate of the Rudd Concession rifles', *Rhodesian History*, vol. 3 (1972), p. 77-81.

122   **Gold regions of Southeastern Africa.**
Thomas Baines.   Bulawayo, Zimbabwe: Books of Rhodesia Publishing
Company, 1968. 240p. (Rhodesiana Reprint Library, no. 1); London:
Edward Stanford, 1877; Mystic, Connecticut: Lawrence Verry, 1968
(Rhodesiana Reprint Library Series, no. 1).

In the late 1960s, two white Rhodesian families who traced their ancestry back to the
original pioneer column of 1891 helped to fund the reprinting of some of the classic
books on Rhodesia and the region written by white settlers and travellers. Most of the
books date back to the end of the 19th and beginning of the 20th centuries. These
books covered a wide range of topics from archaeology and flora and fauna, to military
exploits, hunting and travel adventures. Stories or first-hand experiences of the
Ndebele, and various interpretations (almost invariably incorrect) of the Zimbabwe
ruins were popular themes, and the 1893 and 1896-97 uprisings against colonialism
were exhaustively described and discussed. Many accounts were biographical or
autobiographical. By the 1960s the vast majority of these books, which were
immensely popular with the local white population, were out of print. The reprint
series which was dedicated to the Rhodesian Pioneers' and Early Settlers' Society thus
had a ready audience. Eventually sixty titles were reprinted, thirty-six in the first series
and twenty-four in the following Silver Series, with the run ending in 1979. The books
provide fascinating insights into the psyche, culture and motivations of the early
settlers, and a wealth of material on contemporary economic and social conditions.
Hostile attitudes towards the African population are almost universal in these
accounts. This first title in the series contains an account of the travels of a Fellow of
the Royal Geographical Society who, like so many of his contemporaries, was tempted
to the region by its much vaunted gold wealth: his story did much to encourage
metropolitan interest in the region. The other titles are listed below in order of volume
number; in most cases the titles are sufficient guide to the contents. All are published
by Books of Rhodesia Publishing Company in Bulawayo, and the first date refers to
the date of publication by this publisher. Each book was simultaneously re-printed in
the USA by Lawrence Verry in Mystic, Connecticut in their Rhodesian Reprint
Library series. Where details are available on previous publishers, these are given as
well.
2. F. C. Selous, *Sunshine and storm in Rhodesia* (1968; London: R. Ward, 1896),
relates to his commission under Rhodes to lead the Pioneer Column into
Mashonaland; 3. Stanley Portal Hyatt, *The old transport road* (1969); 4. George
Pauling, *The chronicles of a contractor* (1969); 5. J. Theodore Bent, *The ruined cities
of Mashonaland, being a record of excavation and exploration in 1891* (1969; London:
Longmans, Green, 1892; Plainview, New York: Books for Libraries (Black Heritage
Library Collections); Saint Clair Shores, Michigan: Scholarly Press, 1976)); 6. Cullen
Gouldsbury, *Rhodesian rhymes* (1969. Reprinted 1977), a collection of white settler
poetry; 7. Lord Randolph Churchill, *Men, mines and animals in South Africa* (1969);
8. Rose Blennerhassett and Lucy Sleeman, *Adventures in Mashonaland: by two
hospital nurses* (1969; London: Macmillan, 1893); 9. C. E. Finlason, *A nobody in
Mashonaland* (1969); 10. Thomas Morgan Thomas, *Eleven years in Central South
Africa* (1970; London: John Snow, 1872; London: Frank Cass, 1971. [Library of
Missionary Research and Travels], distributed in the U.S.A. by International Scholarly
Services, Forest Grove, Oregon 1972)), a valuable description of Ndebele life in the
mid-nineteenth century by a former missionary; 11. Sheila Macdonald, *Sally in
Rhodesia* (1970) – a collection of letters home from a settler wife; 12. William Harvey
Brown, *On the South African frontier: the adventures and observations of an American
in Mashonaland and Matabeleland* (1970); 13. G. W. H. Knight-Bruce, *Memories of
Mashonaland* (1970); 14. F. C. Selous, *A hunter's wanderings in South Africa* (1970.

History. Colonization and early African resistance

Reprinted 1976; London: Richard Bentley, 1881); 15. H. N. Hemans, *The log of a native commissioner* (1971); 16. J. G. Macdonald, *Rhodes – a life* (1971); 17. W. A. Wills and L. T. Collinridge (editors), *The downfall of Lobengula: the cause, history and effect of the Matabeli war* (1971; London: African Review, 1894; Westport, Connecticut: Negro Universities Press, 1969); 18. M. Rorke, *Melina Rorke told by herself* (1971); 19. Ethel Tawsie Jollie, *The real Rhodesia* (1971; London: Hutchinson, 1924). Jollie was the first woman member to sit in the Rhodesian parliament. This book deals in general with colonial life but part is devoted to establishing the case for responsible self-government and the termination of company control; 20. Sir Edwin Alfred Hervey Alderson, *With the mounted infantry and the Mashonaland field Force, 1896*; (1971; London: Methuen, 1898); 21. Frank W. Sykes, *With Plumer in Matabeleland: an account of the Matabeleland Relief Force during the rebellion of 1896* (1972; London: Archibald Constable, 1897; Westport, Connecticut: Negro Universities Press); 22. J. P. R. Wallis, *One man's hand: the story of Sir Charles Coghlan and the liberation of Southern Rhodesia* (1972). A biography of the first prime minister of Rhodesia; 23. R. N. Hall and W. G. Neal, *The ancient ruins of Rhodesia (Monomotapa imperium)* (1972; London: Methuen, 1902); 24. Frank Johnson, *Great days: the autobiography of an empire pioneer* (1972; London: Bell, 1940); 25. F. C. Selous, *Travel and adventures in Southeast Africa* (1972; London: R. Ward, 1893; Plainview, New York, Books for Libraries, 1972 [Black Heritage Library Collection Series]); 26. Percy M. Clark, *The autobiography of an old drifter* (1972); 27. Hans Sauer, *Ex Africa* (1973); 28. Edward Mohr, *To the Victoria Falls of the Zambesi* (1973); 29. William finaughty, *The recollections of an elephant hunter 1864-75* (1973); 30. Hugh M. Hole, *The Jameson Raid* (1973); 31. H. F. Varian, *Some African milestones* (1973); 32. Major A. G. Leonard, *How we made Rhodesia* (1973); 33. Colonel J. G. Woods, *Through Matabaleland in a waggon* (1974); 34. *Kingsley Fairbridge: his life and verse* (1974); 35. Lionel Decle, *Three years in savage Africa* (1974); 36. D. C. de Waal, *With Rhodes in Matabeleland* (1974).
Silver Series: 1. J. Cooper-Chadwick, *Three years with Lobengula* (1975; London: Cassell, 1894); 2. *The '96 rebelllions: the British South Africa Company reports on the native disturbances in Rhodesia 1896-97* (1975). This reprint contains a foreword and illustrations by the historian, David Beach; 3. E. F. Knight, *Rhodesia of today: a description of the present conditions and the prospects of Matabeleland and Mashonaland* (1975; London: Longman, Green, 1895; Westport, Connecticut: Negro Universities Press), a good example of misleading propaganda designed to entice settlers from a pro-Rhodes journalist; 4. F. R. Burnham, *Scouting on two continents* (1975; Garden City, New York: Doubleday, Page, 1926); 5. Hylde Richards, *Next year will be better* (1975), on farming in the 1930s and 1940s; 6. S. P. Olivier, *Many treks made Rhodesia* (1975); 7. Alfred Bethell, *Notes on South African hunting* (1976); 8. H. M. Hole, *Old Rhodesian days* (1976; London: Macmillan, 1928. Reprinted, London: Frank Cass, 1968 [Library of African Studies]); 9. Elsa Goodwin Green, *Raiders and rebels in South Africa* (1976); 10. J. F. Macdonald, *The war history of Southern Rhodesia 1939-45, Volume I* (1976; Salisbury: Government Printer, 1947); 11. J. F. Macdonald, *The war history of Southern Rhodesia 1939-45, Volume II* (1976; Salisbury: Government Printer, 1950) – these two volumes comprise the most comprehensive survey of Rhodesia's role in the Second World War; 12. W. D. Gale, *One man's vision* (1976), on Rhodes and the first six years of Rhodesia; 13. Nancy Rouillard, *Matabele Thompson: his autobiography* (1977: Johannesburg: Central Africa News Agency, 1936. 2nd ed. 1957). The highlight of this account is the section on twenty-nine days of negotiation with Lobengula for the Rudd Concession; 14. Herbert Baker and W. T. Stead, *Cecil Rhodes – the man and his dream* (1977); 15. S. J. du Toit, *Rhodesia, past and present* (1977); 16. Dr. Carl Peters, *The Eldorado of the ancients* (1977); 17. Adrian Darter, *The pioneers of Mashonaland*

(1977); 18. E. P. Mathers, *Zambesia, England's El Dorado in Africa* (1977); 19. Friedrich Wilhelm Traugott Posselt, *Fact and fiction: a short account of the natives of Southern Rhodesia* (1978; Bulawayo: Rhodesian Printing and Publishing Company, 1935). This is a frequently criticized account of the Zezuru, with shorter sections on the Tonga, Tawara, Rozwi and Ndebele; 20. Hugh Marshall Mole, *The passing of the black kings* (1978). A Eurocentric account of the Ndebele; 21. Henri Rolin, translated by Deborah Kirkwood, *Rolin's Rhodesia* (1978); 22. Anthony P. D. Perna, *A right to be proud* (1978); 23. C. H. W. Donovan, *With Wilson in Matabeleland* (1978); 24. Frs. H. Depelchin and C. Croonenberghs, translated by Moira Lloyd, *Journey to Gubuluwayo: letters of Frs. H. Depelchin and C. Croonenberghs, S.J., 1879, 1880, 1881* (1979).

123 **War and politics in Zimbabwe 1840-1900.**
David N. Beach. Gweru: Mambo Press, 1986. 165p.

In this book, Beach addresses a wide range of issues affecting the central and southern Shona groups in the nineteenth century, the main themes being the changing relationship between the Ndebele and the Shona, and the impact of the onset of colonial rule. The 1896-97 first Chimurenga is examined in detail. Beach shows how the Shona were initially overwhelmed by colonialism, but as they managed to acquire guns, a more even military balance was struck. Useful maps are included to illustrate the direction of various military raids and the location of different Shona clans. Some different elements emerge in this interpretation of the uprising, in comparison to Ranger's analysis (see item 139). Much of the material on which the book is based had previously been published as articles. A useful brief discussion of the Shona role in the uprising is found in his '"Chimurenga": the Shona rising of 1896-97', *Journal of African History*, vol. 20, no. 3 (1979), p. 395-420.

124 **Lobengula of Zimbabwe.**
Ngwabi M. B. Bhebe. London: Heinemann Educational Books, 1977. 48p. (African Historical Biographies Series).

Much has been written about Lobengula, the last king of the Ndebele. Under him, and his predecessor Mzilikazi, the Ndebele were a force to be reckoned with, and the Pioneer Column and other settlers entered the territory in some trepidation about his reactions. The Europeans were prepared to accept Lobengula's role as an influential military force when it suited them, for example by treating agreements made with him as legitimizing their entry into Shona-speaking territories. However, settler mythology really preferred not to accept the indigenous peoples as equals, and this may in part explain the literature on Lobengula which casts him as merely an evil despot. Bhebe's booklet is an easily accessible source on Lobengula. It was originally designed for African secondary schools and avoids the problem of a Eurocentric approach to this controversial figure. He highlights the king's skills as a statesman and military leader, but shows how in the end he was unable to prevent Cecil Rhodes' forces from overwhelming his nation. Another biography of Lobengula is Per S. Hassing's, 'Lobengula', in *Leadership in Eastern Africa: six political biographies*, Boston, Massachusetts: Boston University Press (African Research Studies, no. 9); New York: Holmes & Meier, 1968, edited by N. R. Bennett, p. 221-60. Examples of early settler accounts which deal wholly or partly with Lobengula can be found in the Rhodesiana Reprint series (see item 122) and include publications by Colonel J. G. Woods, J. Cooper-Chadwick, Nancy Rouillard, Hugh Marshall Hole, and H. Depelchin and C. Croonenberghs (vol. 32; Silver Series: vol. 1, vol. 13, vol. 20, vol. 24). Hugh Marshall Hole also wrote a novel on the king, *Lobengula* (London: Philip Allen, 1929), and his treatment at the hands of Rhodes and other Europeans is the subject of another novel by Samkange (see item 770). Other studies include: Ian Henderson, 'Lobengula: achievement and tragedy', *Tarikh* (UK), vol. 2, no. 2 (1968), p. 53-68; Gustav S. Preller, *Lobengula: the tragedy of a Matabele king* (Johannesburg: Afrikaanse Pers-Boekhandel, 1963); and Cobbing (see item 114). A more recent and wide-ranging article is Tendai Mutunhu, 'Lobengula and the Matabele nation: his monarchial rise and relations with missionaries, Boers and the British', *Journal of Southern African Affairs*, vol. 5, no. 1 (1980), p. 5-22.

125 **First steps in civilizing Rhodesia, being a true account of the earliest white settlers – men, women and children, in Southern and Northern Rhodesia.**
Jeanne M. Boggie. Bulawayo: Philpott and Collins, 1940. 337p.
The title not only describes the contents of this book, but also gives an indication of the attitudes expressed towards the indigenous cultures. This book contains a wealth of detail on the pioneers and the conditions they encountered. On a similar theme, see Neville Jones' *Rhodesian genesis: the story of the early days of Southern Rhodesia compiled from the reminiscences of some of the pioneers* (Bulawayo: Rhodesian Pioneers' and Early Settlers' Society, 1953). This presents oral history from fourteen early settlers on the 1890s.

126 **The Pioneer Corps.**
Robert Cary. Salisbury: Galaxie Press, 1975. 141p.
This interesting book contains a definitive list of the members of the 1890 Pioneer Column sent by Rhodes to settle Rhodesia. A fairly detailed biography of each pioneer member is given, and a family tree. In addition a chronology of the main events on the march and early settlement is provided, along with a background chapter. The book is illustrated with photographs of contemporary scenes and people. The social characteristics of the Pioneer Column are also discussed in P. Stigger, 'Volunteers and the profit motive in the Anglo-Ndebele war, 1893', *Rhodesian History*, vol. 2 (1971), p. 11-23.

127 **The occupation of Southern Rhodesia: a study of economic imperialism.**
David Chanaiwa. Lusaka: East African Publishing House, 1981; New York: St. Martin's Press, 1974. 283p.
This historical study examines the background to the eventual settlement and colonization of Southern Rhodesia in the 1890s. Chanaiwa analyses the political, military and economic causes and influences which encouraged Rhodes and the British to claim the colony. He argues that the prime motivation was the economic advantages to be gained from colonial control. His study covers events in the period 1840-90.

128 **The life of Jameson.**
Ian Colvin. London: Edward Arnold, 1923. 2 vols.
This biography of Jameson (1853-1917) was written by a personal acquaintance and is far less critical than later assessments. Jameson was Rhodes' agent in his British South Africa Company's imperial activities, and played a key role in the early occupation of Southern Rhodesia and both the Ndebele War (1893) and the 1896-97 Shona and Ndebele uprisings. Jameson's most disastrous action was the Jameson Raid into Johannesburg, an ill-timed, ill-fated and utterly misconceived attempt to establish

British control in the Transvaal. Jameson's deceitful dealings with Lobengula are dealt with by Julian Cobbing in 'Lobengula, Jameson and the occupation of Mashonaland, 1890', *Rhodesian History*, vol. 4 (1973), p. 39-56. The essentially commercial purpose of the Jameson Raid is examined in 'Lost causes of the Jameson Raid', *Economic History Review*, 2nd series, vol. 18, no. 2 (1965), p. 350-66, by G. Blainey. See also Galbraith, item 132.

129   **The Victoria incident and the Anglo-Matabele war of 1893: a study of early colonization in Central Africa, and the African response.**
Anne Dovey.   Salisbury: Central African Historical Association, 1966. 23p. (Local series, no. 16).

This short paper provides excellent coverage of the event which probably finalized the deterioration in the relationship between Lobengula and the European settlers. The incident itself involved a Matabele attack on Shona groups around Fort Victoria (modern-day Masvingo), which brought the town to a standstill. After Jameson had insisted that the Matabele leave and return to Matabeleland, a patrol was sent to verify their departure. A skirmish ensued and nine Matabele were killed. Dovey's analysis is generally sympathetic to Lobengula's position. A very different perspective is found in another account of a specific military incident in the 1890s, which details the daring exploits of a Rhodesian army unit, the Mazoe patrol, which succeeded in bringing a number of women from Mazoe to the safety of Salisbury during the 1896 uprising against colonialism. As is frequently the case in colonial accounts of this period, the Shona are much reviled and it is asserted that they were pushed into the rebellion by the Ndebele. See Geoffrey Bond, *Remember Mazoe: the reconstruction of an incident* (Salisbury: Pioneer Head, 1973).

130   **Alfred Beit: a study of the man and his work.**
George Seymour Fort.   London: Ivor Nicholson & Watson, 1932. 221p.

Beit, a close associate of Rhodes, is mainly remembered in Zimbabwe today for the Beit Trust, an important philanthropic fund. Another biography which pays special attention to this Trust is *The will and the way: being an account of Alfred Beit and the trust which he founded, 1806-1956* (London: Longmans & Green, 1957), by his son, Sir Alfred Beit, and J. G. Lockhart.

131   **The occupation of Mashonaland.**
W. Ellerton Fry.   Bulawayo: Books of Rhodesia, 1982. maps. bibliog.

This is a fascinating visual record of the Pioneer Column and the original European settlement of Southern Rhodesia. The original book of photographs was published in 1891, and this modern version reproduces them, in a smaller format, from a copy which the publishers managed to obtain in 1972. The excellent additional material provided by Peter Mclaughlin sets the photographs in context. This consists of new text, captions, a bibliography, a biography of Fry who was a member of the Pioneer Column, and annotated maps indicating, for example, routes taken by the settlers.

132 **Crown and charter: the early years of the British South Africa
Company.**
John S. Galbraith. Berkeley, California: University of California
Press, 1974. 354p. (Perspectives on Southern Africa Series).

This is a major and authoritative study of the British South Africa Company, Rhodes'
tool for realizing his imperial dreams in what became Rhodesia. The book details the
machinations of the company's founder to obtain his charter from the British
government, and to implement his plans for the exploitation of Rhodesia through the
Company. It emphasizes the lack of control exercised by the British, which led to some
disastrous events. These included the Jameson Raid, which helped to trigger off the
1896-97 uprisings by the Ndebele and Shona, and the Boer War of 1899-1902. The
author taught at the University of California, Los Angeles from 1947, and was Smuts
Professor at Oxford 1968-89. A popular history of the Company up to the war against
Lobengula in 1893 can be found in Robert Cary's *Charter Royal* (Cape Town: Howard
Timmins, 1970).

133 **The Matabele war.**
Stafford Lancelot Dudley Glass. London: Longmans, Green; Atlantic
Highlands, New Jersey: Humanities Press, 1968. 308p.

Although flawed, this study is the most extensive and specific treatment of the 1893
war which led to Lobengula's downfall. It includes a strong account of the military
details of the various battles which are illustrated with figures, and several
contemporary documents are reproduced. However, the analysis of events surrounding
the war is unbalanced, being extremely Eurocentric. Cobbing (item 114) and Galbraith
(item 132) also cover the war, and should be used to supplement this account. For the
general reader, Robert Cary has used Glass's work to produce a less academic account
of the war, *A time to die* (Cape Town: Howard Timmins, 1968).

134 **Rhodes and Rhodesia: the white conquest of Zimbabwe 1884-1902.**
Arthur Keppel-Jones. Kingston, Montreal: McGill-Queen's
University Press; Pietermaritzburg, South Africa: University of Natal
Press, 1983. 674p.

This historical study examines the key period of British operations north of the
Limpopo and the establishment of Rhodesia. Keppel-Jones' fluent style makes this
well-researched and documented study a particularly accessible source on the period. It
draws on archival and library resources in Zimbabwe, Oxford, London and South
Africa. As with many of the earlier, colonial accounts of this era the focus is on the
white settlers, and on the actions and roles of individuals. Close attention is paid to the
British South Africa Company, the irregularities of its financial and political
operations, and the tensions between it and the white settlers. Chapters are also
devoted to the Rudd Concession, the pioneers, relationships with Portugal, Jameson
and the 1893 Ndebele War, and the 1896-97 uprisings. One unusual aspect of the
treatment of the latter is the attention given to the role played by black troops in
putting down the Shona and Ndebele revolts. Keppel-Jones also examines the role of
the maxim gun in defeating the Ndebele, and the early years of white society, including
local political affairs and the nature of racial prejudices. The author is Professor
Emeritus of History at Queens' University.

135 **Rhodes.**

John G. Lockhart, Christopher Montague Woodhouse.   London:
Hodder & Stoughton, 1963.

This important scholarly biography of Rhodes departed from previous uncritical
analyses of the famous imperialist, and is also significant for its extensive use of
reference material on Rhodes at Rhodes House, Oxford. Rhodesian archival sources
are less well represented. The work was also published as *Cecil Rhodes: the Colossus of
Southern Africa*, (New York: Macmillan, 1963. 511p.). For a critique of this biography
see Terence O. Ranger, 'The last word on Rhodes?', *Past and Present*, vol. 28 (1964).
Lockhart wrote several biographies (see item 130) and Woodhouse was general
director of the Royal Institute of International Affairs in London. Another significant
and competent biography is *Cecil Rhodes* (Boston: Little, Brown, 1974. [Library of
World Biography]; London: Hutchinson, 1976), by John E. Flint. An interesting
biographical treatment which also examines the lives of two of Rhodes' main
antagonists is *Against these three: a biography of Paul Kruger, Cecil Rhodes and
Lobengula* (Boston, Massachusetts: Houghton Mifflin, 1945), by Stuart Cloete, which
was also published as *African portraits: a biography of Paul Kruger, Cecil Rhodes and
Lobengula, last king of the Matabele* (London: Collins, 1946). A typical early treatment
is H. Baker and W. T. Stead (volume 14 in item 122). See also item 141.

136 **Thy beginning.**

Jessie Lovemore, edited by J. A. Hughes.   Salisbury: Rhodesian
Pioneers and Early Settlers Society, 1956, 83p.

The full title of this book is *'Thy beginning' being the recollections of Mrs. Jessie
Lovemore, daughter of the Rev. and Mrs. Charles Helm, of life in Matabeleland from
1875 until her marriage in 1900*. The Reverend Helm was one of the key figures in the
Europeans' dealings with Lobengula and the Matabele, and this account is therefore of
some historical interest. Not only does it provide information on Bulawayo before its
European occupation, and on Lobengula whom the author often visited, but also a
woman's perspective on this period of European contact and of the role of
missionaries.

137 **Birth of a dilemma: the conquest and settlement of Rhodesia.**

Philip Mason.   London: Oxford University Press, 1958. 366p.
(Institute of Race Relations Series).

A sensitive examination of the early history of colonialism in Rhodesia up to the
beginning of the 20th century, this study was written as part of a trilogy sponsored by
the Institute of Race Relations, London, and the Rockefeller Foundation (see also
items 263, 166). Mason was director of studies in race relations at the Royal Institute
of International Affairs in 1952, and became director of the Institute of Race Relations
in 1958.

138 **John Smith Moffat C. M. G.: a memoir.**

Robert U. Moffat.   London: John Murray, 1921; Reprinted,
Westport, Connecticut: Negro Universities Press. 388p.

Moffat was one of the most important missionary figures associated with Southern
Rhodesia, who played a special role amongst the Ndebele. He acted as an intermediary
between Lobengula and other Europeans, having established the Inyati mission
amongst the Ndebele in 1859. The 'Moffat treaty' signed by Lobengula paved the way

for the Rudd concession, and eventual British occupation of Zimbabwe. He was born into a famous missionary family in Bechuanaland in 1835, and after education in Cape Town and England, returned to Africa in 1858. He acted as an agent for the British from 1880 to 1896, and was British resident in Matabeleland from 1890 to 1892. This memoir, written by one of his sons, includes correspondence and diary extracts. It is a key historical source for the period, and particularly on the Ndebele. John Moffat's father, Robert, played an even more influential role in Ndebele history, becoming Mzilikazi's closest European friend both before and after the migration to Zimbabwe. His account of the Ndebele can be found in *The Matabele journals of Robert Moffat, 1829-1860* (London: Chatto & Windus, 1945, 2 vols), edited by John P. R. Wallis. Also see *The Matabele mission: a selection from the correspondence of John and Emily Moffat, David Livingstone and others, 1858-1878* (London: Chatto & Windus, 1945), also edited by Wallis. Another missionary record and an account of the infamous Rudd Concession is *Gold and the gospel in Mashonaland, 1888, being the journals of: 1. The Mashonaland mission of Bishop Knight-Bruce; 2. The concession journey of Charles Dunell Rudd* (London: Chatto & Windus, 1949), edited by Constance E. Fripp and V. W. Hiller.

139   Revolt in Southern Rhodesia 1896-97: a study in African resistance.
Terence O. Ranger.   London: Heinemann, 1979. 403p.

Ranger's work on African resistance to colonialism from the early settler period through to UDI is a significant contribution to the history of the period. The author successfully conveys the depth and nature of indigenous resentment and resistance to European economic and social domination. In this study he provides a very detailed examination of the 1896-97 uprising in which both the Ndebele and the Shona were involved. The colonial historical treatment of this war, and the 1893 Ndebele uprising, tended to portray the struggles as heroic European victories over treacherous and misguided African tribes. In addition, the Shona's role in military resistance has been downplayed. The re-interpretation of the historical evidence puts the struggle in the context of the disastrous socio-economic impact of colonialism on the indigenous peoples, and places them at the centre of the analysis. In this study, Ranger argues that the Shona played a central role in the 1896 revolt, and that previous analyses which suggested that Ndebele coercion was necessary to incite them to resist are incorrect. The Mwari cult of the Shona is suggested to have been a crucial co-ordinating factor in the rebellion, as it was also allied to the Ndebele aristocracy. This study was first published in 1967 (London: Heinemann; Evanston, Illinois: Northwestern University Press). Ranger's interpretation of the role of the Mwari cult and of the links between the uprisings and later African nationalist movements became matters of some debate by other historians (see items 114, 123, and 160). Ranger published a self-criticism in 'The people in African resistance: a review', *Journal of Southern African Studies*, vol. 4, no. 1 (1977), p. 125-46, and this 1979 re-issue of the 1967 book contains a new preface and modified interpretation which takes account of some of the new scholarship since the 1960s. Professor Ranger who went to Southern Rhodesia in 1957, lectured in history at the University, and was an active supporter of African nationalism, joining the Zimbabwe African People's Union. He was deported for his political activities in 1963, and went to Tanzania where he became chair of the history department at the University College of Dar es Salaam. He later taught at the University of California, Los Angeles, and was chair of history at the University of Manchester. He is currently Rhodes Professor of Race Relations at the University of Oxford.

140   **The Cape-to-Cairo dream: a study in British imperialism.**
Lois Alward Raphael.   New York: Columbia University Press, 1936.
514p. Reprinted, New York: Octagon, 1971.

Rhodes' imperial dream of a route for transport and communications through British territory which ran the length of Africa was one factor in British dealings in the 'Scramble for Africa'. This major study is based on the author's doctoral thesis for Columbia University, and considers the origins of the 'dream', and its impact on imperial territorial and transport strategy, including the territory of today's Zimbabwe.

141   **The founder: Cecil Rhodes and the pursuit of power.**
Robert I. Rotberg, with the collaboration of Miles F. Shore.   New York, Oxford: Oxford University Press, 1988. 800p.

This monumental work is the most comprehensive biography of Rhodes available. The result of eighteen years of exploration and research, and six years of writing, it covers every facet of Rhodes' life, both personal and public. Rotberg's collaborator in this task is a psychiatrist, and thus Rhodes' life is analysed through the methods of psycho-analysis, in addition to the examination of his extraordinary impact on the economic and political history of Southern Africa. Private and public archival and library resources in Zimbabwe, South Africa and Britain are fully utilized. The study emphasizes his imperialist drive, and also the complexities and contradictions of his personality. The account of the creation of Rhodesia is balanced and detailed. A major aim of this biography is to present a balanced account of Rhodes, where many previous studies have been clearly partisan. This comprehensive work may prove too ponderous for the general reader.

142   **The origins of Rhodesia.**
Stanlake John William Samkange.   London: Heinemann, 1969. 292p. maps.

The early years of colonial settlement are retold here by Samkange from an African perspective, focusing on the brutal and unprincipled behaviour of the British South Africa Company agents and settlers. The book, which is written in a popular style, draws on many historical sources. A particular feature is the reproduction in the text of verbatim reports of discussions with Lobengula, and extracts from many letters, memos and documents of Company officials.

143   **Pioneers of Rhodesia.**
Edward C. Tabler.   Cape Town: C. Struik; Mystic, Connecticut: Lawrency Verry, 1966. 185p.

This compilation of over 400 names and biographical details deals with individual 'pioneers' of all races who came to the Zimbabwe region from the south after 1836 but prior to the arrival of Rhodes' Pioneer Column. Also see Tabler's *The far interior*: *chronicles of pioneering in the Matabele and Mashona countries, 1848-1879* (Cape Town: A. A. Balkema, 1955).

144 **Shona reaction and resistance to the European colonization of Zimbabwe, 1890-98. A case against colonial and revisionist historiography.**
Madziwanyika Tsomondo. *Journal of Southern African Affairs*, vol. 2, no. 1 (1977), p. 11-32.

This article not only condemns the colonial historical interpretation of the Shona and their response to colonization, but also attacks 'revisionist' interpretations, specifically that of Ranger (item 139), with briefer consideration of Samkange (item 142). Thus whilst admitting that 'revisionist' historiography had made a contribution by demonstrating that the Shona were not totally dominated by Ndebele, nor weakly acquiescent to European colonization, Tsomondo contends that these interpretations still underplayed the nature and strength of Shona resistance before 1896. Apart from detailing some specific incidents of resistance, his criticisms do not shed much new light on this period, revolving to a large extent around the use of the term 'revolt' or 'rebellion' by Ranger, rather than 'uprising'.

145 **Anglo-Portuguese relations in South-Central Africa: 1890-1900.**
Philip R. Warhurst. London: Longmans for the Royal Commonwealth Society, 1962. 169p.

This is the most specific account of the drawing up of Rhodesia's boundaries during the scramble for Africa. It particularly deals with the failure to maintain access to the sea, which Rhodes attempted to secure. The Portuguese claim to Mozambique, then Portuguese East Africa, was recognized by the British government to meet its own diplomatic interests. The author was educated at the University of Witwatersrand in South Africa, and Oxford, and lectured in history at the University of Rhodesia. A briefer and more accessible account is found in his article in item 106. Also see Best and Zinyama, item 18.

Historical dictionary of Zimbabwe.
See item no. 3.

Trade and politics in a Shona kingdom: the Manyika and their Portuguese and African neighbours 1575-1902.
See item no. 112.

The Ndebele under Khumalos, 1820-1896.
See item no. 114.

Gold regions of Southeastern Africa.
See item no. 122 (vols. 2, 3, 9, 10, 12, 13, 15, 17, 20, 21, 24, 30, 32, 36; Silver series: vols. 1, 2, 12, 13, 14, 17, 18, 23, 24).

Rhodesia's pioneer women (1859-1896).
See item no. 358.

Mapondera: soldier of Zimbabwe.
See item no. 765.

Colonial period 1900-53

146 **The Rozwi in search of their past.**
David N. Beach. *History in Africa* (USA), vol. 10, (1983), p. 13-34.
This wide-ranging study of the Rozwi begins with an examination of the output of
Zimbabwean African historians up to the 1960s. The way in which these historians
interpreted the traditions of the Changamire Rozvi are then analysed, and the great
confusion over the details of the history of this great state is emphasized. Beach goes
on to discuss Rozwi revival movements in the 1950s, and the revival of the Mambo
title, through which the Rozwi attempted to re-build their identity and understand
their former position as a priestly clan in pre-colonial times. These movements were
also a minor feature of African nationalist mobilization. The article also contains a
bibliography on the Rozwi.

147 **The legend of Lomagundi.**
Colin Black. Zimbabwe: Northwestern Development Association,
1976. 88p.
This is a strictly colonial account of Lomagundi district, drawing on the anecdotes of
past and present settler residents to present a popular history of seventy-five years of
development in the district. A similar history of the European population in another
specific district is Shirley Sinclair, *The story of Melsetter* (Salisbury: M. O. Collins,
1971).

148 **A history of Rhodesia.**
Robert Blake. London: Methuen, 1977. 430p. bibliog.
This is a major scholarly text on Rhodesian history, from the 18th century until 1977.
The first section is devoted to a detailed survey of the development and expansion of
the Matabele kingdom from 1700 to 1886 but very little attention is paid to the pre-
colonial history of other indigenous groups, and the remainder of the book largely, but
not entirely, focuses on the European settlers. The treatment is chronological, with
other sections of the book considering the beginning of British colonialism 1889-95, the
British South Africa Company 1902-18, the two World Wars, the Federation of
Rhodesia and Nyasaland, and UDI up to 1977. The book has been criticized for not
fully utilizing available African scholarship, and for adding little to historical
knowledge about Rhodesian history, despite having access to the private papers of
Todd and Welensky.

149 **A history of Southern Rhodesia: early days to 1934.**
Lewis H. Gann. London: Chatto & Windus, 1965. Reprinted, New
York: Humanities Press, 1969. 354p.
The author of this volume gained a certain notoriety as an apologist for UDI in
Rhodesia, whose analyses of white settler society were generally favourable. Gann was
born in Germany, obtained his doctorate from Oxford University, and was employed
at the National Archives of Rhodesia. He left Rhodesia before independence and went
to the Hoover Institution, Stanford University, California. His perspectives naturally
colour this analysis of white settlers, which is the first scholarly work on the history of
settlers specifically in Southern Rhodesia.

150 **Lost chance: Southern Rhodesia 1945-58.**
Hardwicke Holderness, foreword by Garfield Todd.   Harare:
Zimbabwe Publishing House, 1985. 235p.

Born in Southern Rhodesia and trained as a lawyer in South Africa and Oxford, Holderness was elected to the Southern Rhodesian parliament in 1954, and was a leading supporter of the liberal prime minister, Garfield Todd. After Todd's defeat by Edgar Whitehead in 1958, heralding the end of a relatively liberal period of Rhodesian politics, Holderness continued to practice law until 1975 and always remained an advocate of constitutional reforms ending racial discrimination. In this book he provides a personal account of this post-war period which saw the beginning of reforms and change in Southern Rhodesia, a process reversed in 1958. The foreword by Garfield Todd describes this account as the 'inside story of those whites to whom Ian Smith was anathema'.

151 **Famine in Zimbabwe 1890-1960.**
John Illiffe.   Gweru: Mambo Press, 1990. 140p.

The hypothesis which led to the research for this book was that the high population growth rates recorded for the Rhodesian African population from the early colonial period could be explained by the introduction of colonial relief systems, which ended the 'famines that killed', assumed to be a regular occurrence amongst pre-colonial societies. Illiffe's research, based on the Harare archives, mission records, contemporary newspapers and secondary works, suggests, however, that the true picture of famine in Zimbabwe is rather different. A multitude of indigenous coping systems meant that pre-colonial deaths from famines were uncommon, although drought and scarcity were frequent. The colonial impact, which is analysed for the period for which official records were available, was mixed and is divided into three chronological phases. Some official relief was gradually introduced by 1922, and with relatively less interference in indigenous systems than was to occur in later periods, the only disastrous famine being the one caused by the 1896-97 uprisings. The second period, up to 1950, saw the beginnings of endemic malnutrition connected with land alienation, but also the control of famine by means of the Maize Control Board. The 1950s, however, saw more acute hunger as the agrarian crisis in the reserves worsened, and the need for government relief as the white farms could no longer absorb the available labour.

152 **Colonial policy and conflict in Zimbabwe: a study of cultures in collision 1890-1979.**
Dickson A. Mungazi.   New York: Crane Russack, 1991. 180p.

This is an interpretive study of the relevance of Paulo Freire's theory of cultural invasion and political domination to Zimbabwe's colonial experience from 1890 to 1979. Dickson contends that the conflicts of this period between the colonists and the African population stem from the fact that government policies were defined by whites who had little understanding or respect for African culture. Thus it is argued that the decision not to allow democratic rights to Africans was made on cultural, rather than political, grounds. Such decisions had immense political implications, and these are examined, with education a particular focus. The author gained his BA in the United States of America, then taught in Mutare from 1964 to 1974. He returned to the States and gained his doctoral degree from the University of Nebraska in 1977. He is currently associate professor of education and history at Northern Arizona University, Flagstaff. He has written extensively on education in Southern Africa.

153 **Islands of white: settler society and culture in Kenya and Southern Rhodesia 1890-1939.**
Dane Kennedy. Durham, North Carolina: Duke University Press, 1987. 272p. (Duke Centre for International Studies Publications).

Kennedy's study of settlers in Southern Rhodesia and Kenya is based on his doctoral thesis. The focus is on the settler's socio-economic backgrounds, their reasons for emigrating to Africa, and their responses to the new conditions they found there. The nature of settler culture and its evolution is explored, and Kennedy's lucid style makes this a useful source on this topic.

154 **The rise of settler power in Southern Rhodesia (Zimbabwe), 1898-1923.**
James A. C. Mutambirwa. Cranbury, New Jersey: Associated University Press, 1980. 245p.

The focus of this study is the rise of settler power during the era of the British South Africa Company, and the evolution of British policy towards Africans in Southern Rhodesia from 1898-1923. The author then draws on the nature of these events to help to explain how UDI occurred, and why Britain did not bring a swift end to Smith's rebellion. In his view the original settlers were pawns in a British strategy which aimed to use them against the Boers in South Africa, and were also used by the Company which hoped to make a fortune in the new colonies. Neither strategy succeeded when the settlers opted for responsible self-government, and refused to join the Union in 1923. Mutambirwa was an officer of ZANU from 1965-68, and the research for this book was conducted outside Zimbabwe whilst he was in exile.

155 **An economic and social history of Zimbabwe 1890-1948: capital accumulation and class struggle.**
Ian R. Phimister. Harlow, England: Longman, 1988. 336p.

This is probably the most important recent analysis of the economics of Rhodesian colonialism, and the first general social and economic history of Rhodesia. Throughout the book the author stresses the violent nature of the impact of colonial capitalism on the indigenous communities, and the significance of local struggles against the demands of the colonial state. The treatment is chronological, dealing with Rhodes and early settlement, economic reconstruction and the rise of domestic capital 1903-22, the compromise of the settler state 1923-29, the Great Depression 1930-38, and the growth of secondary industry 1939-48. Particular emphasis is placed on the 1948 Great Strike, and conflicts over developmental policies in rural areas as evidence of an emergent class struggle. An article on Zimbabwe's general economic history by the same author is 'Zimbabwe: the path of capitalist development' in History of Central Africa: volume II London, New York: Longman, 1983), edited by David Birmingham and Phyllis Martin, p. 251-290. Phimister gained his PhD from the University of Rhodesia in 1975, and has taught at the universities of Zambia, Rhodesia and Cape Town.

156 **The African voice in Southern Rhodesia: 1898-1930.**
Terence Osborn Ranger. London: Heinemann; Evanston, Illinois: Northwestern University Press; New York: International Publications Service; Nairobi: East African Publishing House, 1970. 252p.

In this book Ranger continues his analysis of Rhodesian history which focusses on the significance of African resistance to colonial rule and racial injustice, begun in his interpretation of the 1896-97 rebellion (see item 139). The African 'voice' is articulated in many different ways over the period here under study, but was never acquiescent to the racial domination and exploitation which characterized the European contact. Ranger's account ends in 1930 because archival evidence beyond that date was not available. For biographical details on the author, see item 139.

157 The way of the white fields in Rhodesia: a survey of Christian enterprise in Northern and Southern Rhodesia.

Edwin W. Smith.   London: World Dominion Press, 1928. 166p.

Livingstone's views on the need for European settlement in Central Africa were always that Christianity and commerce went hand-in-hand. This study is a straightforward Eurocentric description of the establishment and growth of Christian commercial enterprises in the Rhodesias. The data contained in a number of appendices are of interest to economic historians.

158 'Good boys', footballers, and strikers: African social change in Bulawayo, 1933-53.

Osmond Wesley Stuart.   PhD thesis, University of London, London, 1989. (Available from School of Oriental and African Studies, University of London).

This excellent study of historical social change in Bulawayo provides a number of challenges to, and re-interpretations of, previous analyses of social and political events in this city during the pre-federal period. The main focus of the study is long-term African urban residents, and the nature of African protests and strikes in Bulawayo, including the African general strike of 1948. Stuart contends that strike actions cannot be understood in the context of workplace events alone, but must be viewed in the context of the generally very poor quality of life suffered even by this section of the population. The view that long-term residents were becoming a labour aristocracy is directly challenged, as is the view that trade union development was accompanied by a weakening of ethnic affiliations. A major element of the study is discussion of the development of culturally distinct social and recreational African organizations, and in particular the evolution of autonomous African football clubs. The role of such organizations in challenging both employers and the hostile city council is examined. There is as yet so little published on African sport that this is also a prime source on African football. Another historical study which uses the medium of African sport to address wider issues is Terence Ranger, 'Pugilism and pathology: African boxing and the black urban experience in Southern Rhodesia', in *Sport in Africa: essays in social history* (New York: Africana Publishing Company, 1987) edited by W. J. Baker and J. A. Mangan.

159 An ill-fated people: Zimbabwe before and after Rhodes.

Lawrence Vambe.   London, Nairobi, Ibadan, Nigeria: Heinemann, 1972 (African Writers Series, no. 112); Pittsburgh, Pennsylvania: University of Pittsburgh Press, 1973. 254p.

This is one of the most widely read autobiographical accounts of traditional African life and the influence of westernization, which is also an indictment of European colonialism. Vambe was educated at Chishawasha Jesuit Mission, fifteen miles from Harare, and lived in Chishawasha until he was sixteen. In this book he provides an insight into the way of life of the VaShawasha, the people from this area, from the late 19th century to the late 1920s, drawing in part on oral history. The influence of commercial farmers, local government officials, mining activities and the missions are all dealt with. Vambe was educated as a priest and teacher, and worked in several fields including as a newspaper editor, and in public relations for Anglo-American. For a critical analysis of his writing see Veit-Wild, item 747. Vambe continued his autobiography with item 396.

160 **An African area in change: Belingwe 1894-1946.**
Per Zachrisson. Gothenburg, Sweden: Bulletin of Department of History, University of Gothenburg. 1978. 388p.

This is a major research study of colonialism, missionary activity and the African response in a specific area. Belingwe is between the Matopos and Masvingo, and whilst it has a large Shona population, administratively it is part of Matabeleland. The study is divided into three parts addressing different aspects of change which generated a response from the local population. The aspects are administrative and fiscal measures, the impact of capitalism, and social and religious change. Zachrisson argues that whilst in the earlier years Africans were mainly agents of response and the missionaries and colonial administrators agents of change, later on it was frequently the Africans who wished for change, whilst some Europeans became agents opposed to change. He places the responses into four categories: collaboration, acceptance or adaptation, passive resistance and active resistance. He specifically challenges Ranger's original interpretation of the 1896 rebellion on the basis that his local informants argued that the Ndebele, not the Shona, instigated the uprising in this area, although he does allow that the Shona also played an autonomous part. He also dismisses the importance of the Mwari cult as an influence on the rebellion, insisting that it was associated with no more than rain-making and fertility ceremonies. Excellent case study material on the local economy, land encroachment and alienation, migration and religion is presented. The study is extensively documented. Much source material was found in the Rhodesian National Archives, and the missionary records of the Swedish Lutheran Methodist Church, and some use was made of published academic work. In addition oral evidence from chiefs and elders is incorporated.

Historical dictionary of Zimbabwe.
See item no. 3.

Gold regions of Southeastern Africa.
See item no. 122 (vol. 19; Silver Series: vol. 22).

Down memory lane with some early Rhodesian women.
See item no. 352.

Federation of Rhodesia and Nyasaland 1953-63

161 **The anatomy of partnership: Southern Rhodesia and the Central African Federation.**
Thomas Richmond Mandell Creighton. London: Faber & Faber, 1960. 258p. Reprinted, Westport, Connecticut: Greenwood Press, 1976.

This study of the Federation of Rhodesia and Nyasaland argued strongly against its continuance, asserting that it had nothing to offer the African majority. It contains an appendix reproducing the African National Congress's inaugural programme of September, 1957. Anti-federation stances are also found in Edward M. Clegg, *Race and politics in the Federation of Rhodesia and Nyasaland* (London: Oxford University Press, 1960. Reprinted Westport, Connecticut: Greenwood Press, 1975), and Harry Franklin, *Unholy wedlock: the failure of the Central African Federation* (London: George Allen & Unwin, 1963). Both of these analyse the Federation primarily from a Northern Rhodesian perspective.

162 **Race and nationalism: the struggle for power in Rhodesia-Nyasaland.**
Thomas M. Franck. New York: Fordham University Press, 1960. 369p. Reprinted, Westport, Connecticut: Greenwood Press, 1973.

An assessment of political attitudes towards the Federation of Rhodesia and Nyasaland, this study was in part based on sample surveys of Europeans in Salisbury and Lusaka. Franck concludes that the federation is failing. African and European political movements and politicians are critically assessed. The author was a professor at the Graduate School of New York University, and the study was sponsored by the Ford Foundation and the Canadian Institute of International Affairs. For an analysis of the 1953 election, see Eugene P. Dvorin's 'Central Africa's first federal election: background and issues', *Western Political Quarterly*, vol. 7, no. 3 (1954), p. 369-90.

163 **Huggins of Rhodesia: the man and his country.**
Lewis H. Gann, Michael Gelfand. London: George Allen & Unwin, 1964. 285p.

Godfrey Huggins (1883-1971) was prime minister of Southern Rhodesia for twenty years, from 1933 to 1953, and prime minister of the Federation of Rhodesia and Nyasaland between 1953 and 1956. He was an exceptionally influential figure in Zimbabwe's political history. He was able to translate his advocacy of racial segregation, which he called the 'Two Pyramid' policy, into reality and was a prime mover of many pieces of racial legislation. In the 1950s with the emergence of the Federation he modified his position on race relations to 'partnership', although the substance of his views were little changed. This biography provides an adequate account of his life and role in Zimbabwe's historical development, although the fact that both authors were personal acquaintances of Huggins probably prevented them from adopting a sufficiently objective viewpoint.

164 **Rhodesia and Nyasaland: a survey of the Central African Federation.**
Compiled by James Andrew Gray.   London: Marshall Press, 1957.
80p.

This is a good example of pro-Federation propaganda. It contains eighteen essays, including two from the federal and Southern Rhodesian prime ministers, Roy Welensky and Garfield Todd. Other topics include the railways, the university, white immigration, and the press. The compiler was the editor of *South Africa*. A similarly laudatory volume, compiled by F. S. Joelson, editor of *East Africa and Rhodesia*, is *Rhodesia and East Africa* (London: East Africa and Rhodesia, 1958). Both of the prime ministers again contributed and were joined by former Southern Rhodesian and federal prime minister Huggins. Numerous other contributions include one by Lawrence Vambe giving an African perspective on the federation.

165 **Testimony of a Rhodesian federal.**
J. M. Greenfield.   Bulawayo: Books of Rhodesia, 1978. 259p. (Men of
Our Times, no. 1).

Greenfield established Rhodesia's Federal Supreme Court, and was a Queen's Counsel. This autobiography deals with his early life and history, but focusses in particular on the relationship between Rhodesia and successive British governments during the federal period, 1953-63. His view is that Britain broke faith with the white minority in Rhodesia by conceding the principle of majority rule, rather than the federal principle of racial partnership. The book contains many vignettes of key post-Second World War white Rhodesian figures. This book was the first of the publishers' series of memoirs and biographies of individuals who had influenced the course of Rhodesian history. The second, *The reluctant President: the memoirs of the Honourable Clifford Dupont, G.C.L.M., I.D.* (Bulawayo: Books of Rhodesia, 1978) by Clifford Dupont, deals with the life of Rhodesia's first President after the country became a Republic in 1970. The third volume, *Some recollections of a Rhodesian speaker* (Bulawayo: Books of Rhodesia, 1980) by A. R. W. Stumbles, deals with the long political life of Stumbles, the Speaker in Smith's House of Assembly during UDI and also the President of the Rhodesian Amateur Athletic Association.

166 **The politics of partnership.**
Patrick Keatley.   London: Penguin, 1963. 528p.

This is a journalistic account of the Federation of Rhodesia and Nyasaland by a *Guardian* reporter. It is a useful source for details on the British role during the federal years and the eventual collapse of the Federation, although it contains much unnecessary historical detail on the pre-federal period. Assessments based on interviews with key figures including Huggins, Welensky, and Nkomo are included. The author had the benefit of analysing the federation after it had ended. A number of other analyses published a few years earlier often suffered from being overtaken by events. Examples include Clyde Sanger's *Central African emergency* (London: Heinemann, 1960), Philip Mason's *Year of decision: Rhodesia and Nyasaland in 1960* (London: Oxford University Press, 1960), Channing Richardson's *The Federation of Rhodesia and Nyasaland: the future of a dilemma* (New York: American Committee on Africa, 1959), Cecil Phillips' *The vision splendid: the future of the Central African Federation* (London: Heinemann, 1960), and W. T. Blake's *Central African survey: facts and figures of Rhodesia and Nyasaland* (London: Alvin Redman, 1961). Only the first of these was unequivocal in its assertion that the federation would fail, and the latter two books were firmly in support of the federation.

167 **A new deal in Central Africa.**
Edited by Colin Leys, Cranford Pratt. London: Heinemann; New
York: Praeger, 1960. 226p.

Concerns over British responsibilities for the deteriorating situation in Central Africa
led to a conference in Oxford in 1959 to discuss and assess the Federation of Rhodesia
and Nyasaland. This volume includes the papers given at the conference, which
focussed mainly on Zimbabwe. The various contributions on the Federation, political
repression and racism, included items from Guy Clutton-Brock and Dr. Bernard
Chidzero. Pratt taught at the University of Toronto, Oxford University and Makerere
College, Kampala. For biographical details on Leys see item 457.

168 **Break up: some economic consequences for the Rhodesias and
Nyasaland.**
D. S. Pearson, W. L. Taylor. Salisbury: Unitas Press, 1963. 85p.

The break up of the title refers to the ending of the Federation of Rhodesia and
Nyasaland in 1953. The authors consider that this grouping had, in fact, had little
impact on economic development in the three countries involved, although there had
been some redistribution of wealth from Northern Rhodesia to Southern Rhodesia.
The report was produced under the auspices of the Phoenix Group, a Southern
Rhodesian economic research group formed in 1959. Another economic analysis of the
Federation is Arthur Hazlewood, 'The economics of federation and dissolution in
Central Africa', in *African integration and disintegration: case studies in economic and
political union* (London; New York: Oxford University Press, 1967), p. 185-250, edited
by Arthur Hazlewood, in which he argues that there were economic benefits derived
from the groupings' greater attraction for foreign investors. The official view, which
emphasized that economic advantages would accrue to all three federal partners is
presented in *Legacy of progress: achievements of the years of Federation, 1953-63*
(Salisbury: Federation of Rhodesia and Nyasaland, 1963).

169 **Welensky's 4000 days.**
Sir Roy Welensky. London: Collins, 1964. 383p.

This is an autobiographical account of Welensky's time as prime minister of the
Federation of Rhodesia and Nyasaland. Born in Salisbury, Welensky rose to political
heights from a background of working on the railways, and trade union activities in
Northern Rhodesia. Naturally enough, his perceptions of the causes of the federation's
collapse are rather different from those of many other analyses which cite African
opposition, in all three countries involved, to a political arrangement solidifying
European domination (see items 161, 162). Welensky blames the British and
specifically the Macmillan government, which he perceives as having withdrawn its
initial support for the federation in a dishonest and unprincipled way. Welensky's book
provides insights into the attitudes towards the federation of many of the whites in
Southern Rhodesia and the other countries involved. He opposed UDI, and eventually
left Zimbabwe for Britain in 1981. Two uncritical and laudatory biographies of
Welensky, one published just before he assumed his premiership in 1956, and the other
just before the collapse of the federation in 1963 are Don Taylor's *The Rhodesian: the
life of Sir Roy Welensky* (London: Museum Press, 1955) and Garry Allighan's *The
Welensky story* (London: Macdonald, 1962).

170 **The Welensky papers: a history of the Federation of Rhodesia and Nyasaland.**
J. R. T. Wood. Durban, South Africa: Graham Publishing, 1983. 1330p. bibliog.

This immense work provides an extremely detailed and scholarly account of the Federation of Rhodesia and Nyasaland from the viewpoint of the British Colonial Office and the Rhodesian government. The perspective is a function of the source of the research material. Welensky, who was the Prime Minister of the Federation, left a huge collection of papers which Wood has synthesized and analysed for this study, with the support of a research award from the Ernest Oppenheimer Memorial Trust. The research was conducted at the University of Rhodesia. A major bibliography is provided.

Historical dictionary of Zimbabwe.
See item no. 3.

Lost chance: Southern Rhodesia 1945-58.
See item no. 150.

Economic survey of the Federation of Rhodesia and Nyasaland, with special reference to the possibility of expanding its economy.
See item no. 487.

UDI

171 **Rhodesia: the road to rebellion.**
James P. Barber. London: Oxford University Press, 1967. 338p.

This study attempts to explain the course of political events and processes during the 1960s which led up to the Unilateral Declaration of Independence in 1965. The author was living in Rhodesia whilst writing the book in 1966 and was therefore very aware of the extreme tensions of the time. The detailed chronological history of the rise of the Rhodesian Front party is recounted in fluent style, and this is an accessible source on white Rhodesia's attempt to maintain white minority rule. Britain's increasing isolation, as it sought to establish a compromise between the whites and the African nationalists, is also highlighted.

172 **The quiet man: a biography of the Honourable Ian Douglas Smith, I.D., Prime Minister of Rhodesia.**
Phillipa Berlyn, with an appendix on the constitutional history of Rhodesia by J. Reid Rowland. Salisbury: M. I. Collins, 1978. 256p.

This biography of Smith makes little attempt to provide an objective analysis of his character and role in UDI, being unashamedly in favour of both the man and his aims in declaring illegal independence. The book is also very critical of Great Britain's stance towards Rhodesia during UDI. Another biography, which suffers from not having gained access to Smith, and which paints him as a man whose actions were the inevitable response to contemporary events, is Peter Joyce's *Anatomy of a rebel: Smith of Rhodesia, a biography* (Salisbury: Graham Publishing, 1974).

173 Under the skin: the death of white Rhodesia.
David Caute. Harmondsworth, England: Penguin & Allen Lane, 1983. 448p.

This study of the death throes of white Rhodesia during the closing years of the war was well received by academics and a wider audience. The author was formerly an academic at All Souls College, Oxford and in the United States who turned to journalism, becoming Literary Editor of the New Statesman. He began working on Rhodesian politics in 1978, and this study, which covers the years 1976-80, combines a historian's and journalist's approach. He graphically describes how the white élite fought to maintain its privileged position. The study covers the lifestyles of various sections of the white community including farmers under siege, missionaries in the Tribal Trust Lands, and white liberals. Profiles of various leaders including Smith and Mugabe are also provided. His account exposed the neuroses and obsessions of white Rhodesians at this critical phase in their history. Caute also published a novel dealing with the last year of white Rhodesia, *The K factor* (London: Michael Joseph, 1983). A later study of the experience of white Rhodesians in the independence war is Peter Godwin and Ian Hancock's *'Rhodesians never die': the impact of war and political change on white Rhodesia c. 1970-1980* (Oxford: Oxford University Press, 1993).

174 The April 1979 elections in Zimbabwe-Rhodesia.
Mick Delap. *African Affairs*, vol. 313, no. 78 (1979), p. 431-38.

The 1979 elections in Zimbabwe were held as the result of an unrecognized internal settlement, and Bishop Abel Muzorewa's victory was short-lived. Nevertheless, the elections attracted considerable attention. This article analyses three reports on the elections by Lord Boyd, Claire Palley and Lord Chitnis. Claire Palley's report, *The Rhodesian elections*, was published by the Catholic Institute of International Relations in London in 1979. The nature of support for the elections is considered in Tony Rich's 'The internal elections: differentiation of support in Zimbabwe-Rhodesia, April 1979', in *Conference on Zimbabwe*, June 21, 1980 (Leeds: University of Leeds, 1980), edited by the Department of Politics, University of Leeds.

175 Serving secretly: an intelligence chief on record. Rhodesia into Zimbabwe 1964 to 1981.
Ken Flower. London: John Murray, in association with Quest Publishing, 1987. 330p.

This is one of the key documents to be published after the liberation war, as it gives an extraordinary insight into the devious workings of the Rhodesian secret service by the man who headed the service from 1963. Flower provides detailed inside information about Rhodesian infiltration of the resistance and liberation movements, covert communication with Great Britain and other countries during sanctions, and Rhodesia's creation of the Mozambique National Resistance (RENAMO), a move which was to have appalling and far-reaching consequences. He also details his efforts to make the Smith government face reality, once he realized that there could only be a political solution to the war. Flower was born in England, and moved to Rhodesia to become a member of the British South African Police (BSAP) in 1937. From 1941 to 1948 he served in the British military administration in Ethiopia. Returning to Rhodesia he became a police corporal, and was then commissioned in 1949. By 1961 he was Deputy Commissioner of the BSAP, and in 1963 he was made Head of the new secret service in Rhodesia. Almost incredibly, but perhaps with the view that it was better to have him 'on the inside', Mugabe made him Head of Zimbabwe's secret service at independence, from which he retired in 1981. Evidence about secret Rhodesian military aid to help the Portuguese in Mozambique against FRELIMO is recorded in a book by a journalist who was jailed and then exiled by Ian Smith, Peter Niesewand, *In camera: secret justice in Rhodesia* (London: Weidenfeld and Nicolson, 1973).

176   **UDI: the international politics of the Rhodesian rebellion.**
Robert C. Good.   London: Faber; Princeton, New Jersey: Princeton University Press, 1973. 368p. bibliog.

This survey of the international background and involvement in Rhodesia's Unilateral Declaration of Independence was written in the midst of the machinations over the crisis. The author was American Ambassador to Zambia, and the unfortunate impact of UDI on that country is one theme. He is highly critical of Britain's role in events. Good went on to become dean of international studies at the University of Denver and president of Denison College, Granville, Ohio.

177   **Rhodesia: white racism and imperial response.**
Martin Loney.   Harmondsworth, England; New York: Penguin, 1975. 235p.

Loney's analysis of the British response to UDI is that, despite its public statements to the contrary, it was not fundamentally opposed to the white regime. His argument rests on his evaluation of British capitalist interests, which were not threatened by UDI. His study includes a consideration of the plight of the African majority. Loney was educated in Britain and Canada, and was politically active in anti-racist movements, and vice president of the National Association of Labour Students' Organizations.

178   **The past is another country: Rhodesia 1890-1979.**
M. Meredith.   London: Andre Deutsch, 1979. 383p.

Rather journalistic in style, this history of Rhodesia concentrates in particular on the 1960s and 1970s. Earlier historical periods receive much briefer attention. The book ends with discussion of the internal settlement which briefly brought Muzorewa to power.

179   **A short thousand years: the end of Rhodesia's rebellion.**
Paul L. Moorcroft.   Salisbury: Galaxie Press, 1979. 248p.

This is a contemporary account of UDI, written during the run up to the unrecognized internal settlement in 1979 when Bishop Abel Muzorewa was elected prime minister. Although the author had lectured at the University of Rhodesia, this is not primarily an academic account, but it is fairly objective in its consideration of events. The title is drawn from Smith's assertion that whites would rule for a thousand years. The text is illustrated with contemporary cartoons.

180 **Zimbabwe is free: a short history of the struggle for national liberation in Southern Rhodesia.**
Kimpton Ndlovu, Jan Flavell.   London: Liberation & Caledonian Road, 1980. 2nd ed. 20p.

This booklet provides short historical notes, from a pro-liberation standpoint, on the struggle for freedom and independence in Zimbabwe from the 19th century to independence. It was written just after Mugabe won the elections at independence, and is primarily aimed at students. The main focus is on the events of the 1960s.

181 **Rhodesia accuses.**
A. J. A. Peck.   Salisbury: Three Sisters Press; London: Johnson Publications, 1966. 170p.

The author, a Rhodesian-born farmer and solicitor who had stood for parliament in 1962, makes out a passionate case for supporting white minority rule and UDI in Rhodesia. As with many other publications in this genre, the ideological thrust behind the work combines a belief in the innate superiority of white 'civilization' and fears of encroaching communism. Britain's role is criticized, and the year after this book appeared Peck published *Rhodesia condemns* (Salisbury: Three Sisters Press; Chulmleigh, Devon, England: Britons Publishing, 1967). Other titles which also provide insights into local and South African white support for UDI are Morris L. Hirsch is *A decade of crisis: ten years of Rhodesian Front rule (1963-72)* (Salisbury: Peter Dearlove, 1973); Frederick R. Metrowich's *Rhodesia: birth of a nation* (Pretoria: African Institute of South Africa, 1969); Philippa Berlyn's *Rhodesia: beleaguered country* (London: Mitre Press, 1967); Richard C. Haw's *No other home: coexistence in Africa* (Bulawayo: Manning, 1961); Douglas Reed's *The battle for Rhodesia* (New York: Devin-Adair; London: A. Gibbs, 1967; London: Universal-Tandem, 1968); W. D. Gale's *The years between 1923-73: half a century of responsible government in Rhodesia* (Salisbury: H. C. P. Andersen, 1973); and Desmond Lardner-Burke's *Rhodesia: the story of the crisis* (London: Oldbourne, 1966).

182 **You must be new around here.**
Dick Pitman.   Bulawayo: Books of Rhodesia, 1979. 214p.

The author of this eye-witness account of events in the late 1970s first came to Rhodesia in 1977. He became a local journalist, and is now well known as a wildlife enthusiast. This book was based on his travels round the country in the last years of UDI, and his meetings with people from all shades of the political spectrum. The account is mainly sympathetic to white Rhodesians' viewpoints, and focusses on their reaction to the idea of the Muzorewa settlement in 1979. Many accounts of the ending of white rule were published. *The last days of white Rhodesia* (London: Chatto and Windus, 1981) was written by Denis Hills, who had already gained some notoriety by writing a personal account of post-independence Uganda which had led to him being imprisoned by Amin; he only escaped a firing squad through the intervention of the British. After lecturing at the University College of Rhodesia in 1976, he spent 1978 to 1980 travelling through Rhodesia and neighbouring territories. His book is an account of that journey and the people whom he met; but since he met few African nationalists it is a rather unbalanced account and an uneasy sympathy for the white position is evident. Hills also wrote *Rebel People* (London: George Allen and Unwin, 1978), an account of life in white Rhodesia in the 1970s and his own stay in Gwelo. Another examination of the last days of UDI is H. P. W. Hutson's *Rhodesia: ending of an era* (London: Springwood Books, 1978) which is unashamedly pro-settler, the author being a proponent of the idea that white rule was the only thing saving Africa from communism.

183 In defence of the Rhodesian constitutional agreement. A power promise.
Ndabaningi Sithole. Salisbury: Graham Publishing, 1978. 71p.

Sithole, who had been a key member of the African liberation movements, agreed to participate in the unrecognized internal settlement at the end of the 1970s, thereby losing much of his political credibility. This short tract describes his views on why the settlement should be accepted. For another view on this settlement see Chengetai Zvobgo's 'Rhodesia's internal settlement: a record, 1977-79', *Journal of Southern African Affairs*, vol. 5, no. 1 (1980), p. 25-38.

184 A bishop in Smith's Rhodesia: notes from a turbulent octave 1962-70.
Kenneth Skelton. Gweru: Mambo Press, 1985. 152p.

Skelton became Anglican Bishop of Matabeleland in 1962, but resigned in protest in 1970, returning to England to become Bishop of Lichfield from 1975 to 1984 when he retired. In this account he details his experiences during his time in Rhodesia, his anxieties about the country's developing racism, and the stand which he took against this, leading to him receiving death threats from racist whites. Other biographies on prominent church leaders in Rhodesia include *Archbishop Aston Chichester 1879-1962: a memoir* (Gweru: Mambo Press, 1978) by F. C. Barr, which details the life of Rhodesia's first Catholic bishop, and *Knight Bruce: first bishop and founder of the Anglican church in Rhodesia* (Salisbury: Christchurch & Borrowdale with the assistance of the Christian Literature Bureau in Rhodesia, [no date]) by R. R. Langham-Carter.

185 Strategic resettlement in Rhodesia.
Anna Katherina Hildegard Weinrich. *Journal of Southern African Affairs*, vol. 3, no. 2 (1977), p. 207-09.

Strategic resettlement was the process whereby the rural black population was removed from their homes, and settled in protected villages. This often amounted to little more than imprisonment during the night, and was immensely disruptive of their agricultural livelihoods since it restricted access to the fields. The motivation was to prevent the people from having contact with the guerilla fighters. In many cases the resentment caused by the enforced resettlement in fact pushed the peasantry towards supporting the guerilla forces, even when they had previously been opposed or antipathetic toward them. For biographical notes on the author see item 877.

186 Zimbabwe now.
Edited by S. E. Wilmer. London: Rex Collings; Nairobi: East African Publishing House, 1973. 141p.

This collection of ten papers published during the UDI years was derived from seminars on Rhodesia given at Oxford University between December 1971 and February 1972, the time of the Pearce Commission which found that African sentiment was strongly against the settlement proposals being put forward then by the British and Rhodesian governments. The volume is useful for its reflection of contemporary attitudes. Rhodesia's role in Southern Africa is also covered. Four of the contributors were Zimbabwean, and included Bishop Abel Muzorewa. Oxford-based seminars have led to other publications on Rhodesia (see items 167, 379), and research on Zimbabwe is strongly associated with that university.

Zimbabwe: a country study.
See item no. 11.

The African National Council and the Rhodesian situation: Rhodesia, mid-1974.
See item no. 373.

Sanctions

187 **Oilgate: the sanctions scandal.**
Martin Bailey.   London: Coronet Books & Hodder & Stoughton, 1979. 288p.
This is the most detailed and extensive published study of the methods Rhodesia and its allies employed to obtain oil illegally during sanctions. It covers the period 1965-78.

188 **Economic sanctions and Rhodesia.**
Timothy Roger Champion Curtin, David J. Murray.   London: Institute of Economic Affairs; Levittown, New York: Transatlantic Arts, 1967. 56p.
This early analysis of sanctions against the Rhodesian economy attempted to assess the likely outcome of the sanctions programme, and is of interest as an example of an economic evaluation which does not have the benefit of hindsight. The authors make a detailed input-output analysis of the economy, and argue that there was much potential for domestic industrialization to replace imports. In this they proved correct, but their belief that sanctions would be less damaging as time went on was not borne out by events. Another early publication is *Sanctions against Rhodesia: the economic background* (London: Africa Bureau, 1966), by Robert Sutcliffe, which was later updated by Guy Arnold in *Sanctions against Rhodesia 1965-72* (London: Africa Bureau, 1972).

189 **Portrait of an economy: Rhodesia under sanctions.**
John A. Handford.   Salisbury: Mercury Press, 1976. 204p.
The impact of sanctions on the economy are here analysed from the perspective of a supporter of UDI. The success of the economy in avoiding the worst impact of the embargoes, and the positive influence of the protection afforded to industry are discussed. A wide range of economic indicators for the mid-1970s are considered, including gross national product and employment, and productivity in manufacturing industry, mining, transport, and housing. Many useful statistical tables are provided. The author maintains that sanctions were immensely beneficial to Rhodesia. The tone of the book may be gauged from the title of the first chapter: 'A first blast of the trumpet against the monstrous regiment of academic economists'. Its main worth is as an indication of the views and level of commitment of white 'insiders' during UDI. The

book is alternatively titled *A portrait of the Rhodesian economy under sanctions 1965-78*.

190 **Sanctions double-cross: oil to Rhodesia.**
Jorge Jardim. Bulawayo: Books of Rhodesia, 1979. 154p.

The author of this fascinating account of the history of sanctions-busting is one of Southern Africa's most notorious characters. Jardim is Portuguese and had settled in Mozambique in 1952. He was a close colleague of Salazar's, and a great supporter of Ian Smith. At the end of Portuguese colonial rule he was a leading figure in the development of an internal resistance to FRELIMO, a fore-runner of the Rhodesian-backed Renamo. He left Mozambique in 1974 and became associated with anti-FRELIMO activities from outside the country, as well as assisting the white minority in Rhodesia in sanctions-busting.

191 **The United Nations and economic sanctions against Rhodesia.**
Leonard T. Kapungu. Farnborough, England: Teakfield; Lexington, Massachusetts: Lexington Books, 1973. 155p.

This study of the UN and Rhodesian sanctions was based on the author's London School of Economics thesis, and on research carried out while on the staff of the UN Institute for Training and Research in 1968-70. The range and level of enforcement of sanctions imposed by eleven countries against Rhodesia are assessed, including Scandinavian countries which had a good record of enforcement, and Italy and the Netherlands which aided evasion. The author felt that sanctions had failed to force Rhodesia to change.

192 **When sanctions worked: the case of Rhodesia re-examined.**
W. Minter, Elizabeth Schmidt. *African Affairs*, vol. 87, no. 347 (1988), p. 207-38.

As this study notes, scholarly analyses of sanctions on Rhodesia which emerged around the time of independence tend to argue that they produced only limited success (for example see Strack, item 194). However, more recent general studies on sanctions as a policy tool have concluded that they can be effective, citing the Rhodesian case as an example. The authors of this article contend that most analyses of Rhodesian sanctions have failed to recognize the complexity of the issue, which involves separating the effects of 'particular economic measures from other interacting economic factors, and the even more problematic estimation of the political effects of such economic results'. The importance of distinguishing between short-term and long-term effects, and recognizing that sanctions have multiple objectives, is stressed. The major question should be what would have happened in the absence of sanctions, which should not be evaluated in terms of their ability to induce the changes desired without other actions against the regime. The research for this article included interviews with businessmen who had operated under sanctions, and other Zimbabweans. The authors conclude that sanctions made a substantial contribution to the ending of UDI, as it became more difficult to maintain the war and the economy simultaneously in the 1970s. This article provides, in a fairly concise format, excellent coverage not only of the events relevant to the sanctions debate, but also a comprehensive review of the literature.

193 **The impact of international economic sanctions on the internal viability of Rhodesia.**
G. V. Stephenson. *Geographical Review*, vol. 65, no. 3 (1975), p. 377-89.

This geographer's perspective on how sanctions were affecting development patterns in Rhodesia includes consideration of how government subsidies were given to assist white agriculture. Black farmers therefore bore the brunt of sanctions. The under-utilization of farm land owned by whites is also examined, and the author argues that land redistribution could help to bring about national cohesion, and end the need for sanctions.

194 **Sanctions: the case of Rhodesia.**
Harry Strack. Syracuse, New York: Syracuse University Press, 1978. 296p.

This is an important and comprehensive contribution to the literature on sanctions against Rhodesia, covering the period 1965-77. Information on the legal steps taken to apply international sanctions is provided, followed by detailed discussion of the impact of sanctions on the Rhodesian economy. The many efforts and initiatives to avoid and minimize sanctions by the Rhodesian regime and its trading partners are described. The role of the UN is critically evaluated. A briefer report on the impact of sanctions on the Rhodesian economy published just before independence is Roger Riddell, *Sanctions and the Zimbabwe-Rhodesia economy* (London: Catholic Institute of International Relations, 1979).

195 **The United Nations and Rhodesia: a study in international law.**
Ralph Zacklin. New York: Praeger, 1974. 188p.

Zacklin argues that sanctions were failing because of the non-compliance of the white minority regimes in the Portuguese colonies and South Africa, who controlled Rhodesian access to the sea and deliberately helped the UDI regime. In addition, the Western European nations were guilty of a number of violations of the mandatory UN blockade. Appendices give a comprehensive list of UN actions on Rhodesia as well as statistics of exports to Rhodesia. Zacklin was born in England and earned degrees from the University of London and Columbia University, and was attached to the Carnegie Endowment from 1967-73. This study was published whilst he was with the UN Office of Legal Affairs. Another legal study of sanctions is John W. Halderman, 'Some legal aspects of sanctions in the Rhodesian case', *International and Comparative Law Quarterly* (UK), vol. 17, no. 3 (July 1968), p. 672-705.

From Rhodesia to Zimbabwe: behind and beyond Lancaster House.
See item no. 5.

War in the air: Rhodesian air force 1935-80.
See item no. 98.

The 'Tar Baby' option: American policy towards Southern Rhodesia.
See item no. 471.

Technological capability and industrialisation: effects of aid and sanctions in the United Republic of Tanzania and Zimbabwe.
See item no. 660.

Liberation war

196 Counter-insurgency in Rhodesia.

J. K. Cilliers. Beckenham, England; Sydney: Croom Helm, 1985. 266p.

This is an interpretative analysis of the counter-insurgency strategies adopted by the Rhodesian security forces in the critical period of the liberation war from 1972 to 1979. It is based on the author's Master's dissertation in Strategic Studies for the University of South Africa in Pretoria, and the information was drawn from secondary sources and interviews with expatriate Rhodesians in South Africa. Some official classified documents from former security force members were made available, and extensive use was also made of newspaper articles. After a brief historical introduction the book focusses on specific organizations or counter-insurgency strategies and includes discussion of the command and control structures of the Rhodesian security forces, the intelligence organizations of the Rhodesian state and the methods they employed, the use of 'protected villages' to try and limit contact between the guerillas and the rural population, border minefield obstacles, pseudo-insurgent activities, internal defence and development, external operations and the self-defence militia system. The book ends with an account of the security situation in 1979. There are also a number of other accounts and analyses of insurgency and counter-insurgency tactics in Rhodesia. In *The Rhodesian Front war: counter-insurgency and guerilla warfare* 1962-80 (Gweru: Mambo Press, 1989), H. Ellert, who served in the police force in Rhodesia from 1964-80, provides an account of the war from the police viewpoint. Although this is not an academic account, unlike many other published reminiscences of the war by whites who were actively involved, it does make an attempt to be reasonably scholarly and place events in a historical context. There are two articles by A. R. Wilkinson on insurgency: 'Political violence, counter-insurgents and change in Rhodesia', in *Southern Africa: research in progress* (York, England: Centre for Southern African Studies, 1974) edited by Christopher R. Hill and P. Warwick, which covers the period 1960-74, and *Insurgents in Rhodesia: 1957-73: an account and assessment*, (London: International Institute for Strategic Studies, 1973. [Adelphi paper no. 100]). Rhodesia is also covered in Michael Morris's *Terrorism: the first full account in detail of terrorism and insurgency in Southern Africa* (Cape Town: Howard Timmins, 1971).

197 The elite: the story of the Rhodesian Special Air Service.

Barbara Cole. Amanzimtoti, South Africa: Three Knights, 1984. 449p.

This is a general history of the unit which specialized in counter-insurgency operations, including many cross-border raids against the liberation movements in Zambia, Mozambique and Botswana. The unit is portrayed as a heroic defender of white Rhodesia. Another example of this genre is an account of the Rhodesian air force's bombing of ZAPU's base camps in Zambia in 1978, *Operation Zambia: the raid into Zambia* (Salisbury: Welston Press, 1979), by Peter Armstrong.

198 War in the air: Rhodesian air force 1935-80.

Dudley Cowderoy, Roy C. Nesbit. Alberton, South Africa: Galago, 1987. 248p.

This history of the Rhodesian Air Force concentrates on its role during the war for independence in the 1960s and 1970s. Details on the significant assistance rendered by the South African air force in defending the UDI state, and on sanctions-busting by air are included. The authors were both instructors for the Rhodesian Air Force and the perspective is totally in favour of UDI and the settler state.

199 The struggle for Zimbabwe: battle in the bush.
L. H. Gann, T. H. Henriksen. New York: Praeger, 1981. 155p.

Most of the scholarly studies of the war for independence in Zimbabwe have been generally sympathetic to the guerillas' cause. Gann's previous publications on Rhodesia have focussed on the white settlers, and his sympathies tend to lie with this section of the population. This study of the 1966-79 war deals competently with the events in a chronological fashion, but makes little attempt to analyse the liberation movements' problems and strategies in depth. The role of the spirit mediums in the war, for example, which has attracted great interest, is dismissed here as a 'corruption' of traditional 'folk' beliefs.

200 The effects of the war on the rural population of Zimbabwe.
T. J. B. Jokonya. *Journal of Southern African Affairs*, vol. 5, no. 2 (1980), p. 133-48.

This article discusses the impact of the violence of the guerilla war, particularly that of the Rhodesian security forces, on the rural population of the communal areas in the 1970s. The use of the 'protected villages' strategy to try and limit contact between the peasantry and the guerilla armies is discussed, and a major theme is the mass exodus of rural people to the urban areas, and their fate there as refugees. It is suggested that this was a first step on the way to proletarianization for these people. The refugees in surrounding countries are also examined.

201 Zimbabwe's guerilla war: peasant voices.
Norma J. Kriger. Cambridge, England: Cambridge University Press, 1992. 303p. (African Studies Series, no. 70).

This book has been developed from the author's PhD thesis from the Department of Political Science at MIT. She is currently Associate Professor in Political Science at Johns Hopkins University. The topic of the relationship between the guerilla fighters and the peasantry during the liberation war has been one which has attracted considerable attention. Kriger's study focussed on Mutoko communal area in north-eastern Zimbabwe. The research was mainly conducted in 1982. In contrast to the findings of Ranger and Lan (items 139, 202) whose research was conducted in different areas, she emphasizes the peasants' lack of support for the guerillas, and their fear of both them and the government forces. She feels that coercion was more important in persuading peasants to help the guerillas than others have found, and also stresses how this was in part because they were unable to offer any utilitarian benefits such as welfare services. These in fact tended to come under guerilla attack as symbols of the racist state. In her study she focusses on the significance of choices made by individual peasants, rather than the peasantry in general. She agrees, however, that most peasants wished for the end of the settler state. A shorter paper on the liberation war by the same author is 'The Zimbabwean war of liberation: struggles within the struggle', *Journal of Southern African Studies*, vol. 14, no. 2 (1988), p. 304-22.

202 **Guns and rain: guerillas and spirit mediums in Zimbabwe.**
David Lan. Harare: Zimbabwe Publishing House, 1985. 244p.

One of the most important analyses of the liberation war period and the relationship between the peasantry and the guerillas, this study is based on Lan's doctoral thesis for the London School of Economics. The research was conducted in Dande district at independence and covers the 1966-80 period in this former operational zone. It is an important contribution to historical and political analysis of the war, although the approach is anthropological. It describes the active support given to the guerillas by Shona religious leaders, and details the collaboration between the ancestors and their descendents, past and present, living and dead. It has been criticized for neglecting the significance of women in these interactions.

203 **American mercenaries in Rhodesia.**
Richard Lobban. *Journal of Southern African Affairs*, vol. 3, no. 3 (1978), 319-25.

White mercenaries from a number of Western countries were attracted to the Rhodesian war, where they usually justified their involvement in terms of countering a communist takeover. This article considers the American involvement in the latter years of the war from 1976-78. This theme is also considered by Cynthia Enloe in 'Mercenarization', in *U.S. military involvement in Southern Africa* (Boston: South End Press, 1978) edited by the Western Massachusetts Association of Concerned African Scholars, and Akbarali Thobhani in 'The mercenary menace', *Africa Today*, vol. 23, no. 3 (1976), p. 61-68. Enloe's paper looks at American mercenaries in Rhodesia in the Southern African context, and Thobhani considers white mercenaries in Rhodesia as well as other African countries.

204 **The struggle for Zimbabwe: the Chimurenga war.**
David Martin, Phyllis Johnson. London, Boston: Faber & Faber, 1981, 378p.

This well-documented book focusses on the role of ZANU during the war for independence. Chimurenga is the Shona word for rebellion and refers to the wars against colonialism in Rhodesia, including the 1896-97 war against Rhodes' forces. It is often asserted that ZANU's army ZANLA bore the brunt of the fighting in the 1970s. Martin and Johnson's analysis, however, does not focus solely on the armed forces and their activities and strategies, but also covers the party's political and diplomatic efforts to gain international and regional moral and logistical support. The authors are journalists who were covering Africa for the Observer and Canadian Broadcasting in the 1970s. This major study is based on their extensive knowledge of war events, and many interviews with nationalist leaders, diplomats and officials. The study focusses on the post-1972 period with a very detailed examination of the war from the nationalist perspective, although there is some discussion of the struggle from 1960 to 1972. There is also a section on recruitment and mobilization by the guerillas, including discussion of the role of the spirit mediums and mass mobilization techniques. The events surrounding Chitepo's assassination are covered, and the authors believe the evidence suggests that he was killed by the Rhodesian secret service (see item 386). The book is dedicated to the late Josiah Tongogara, who was a key informant.

205 **The fight for Zimbabwe: the armed conflict in Southern Rhodesia since UDI.**
Kees Maxey. London: Rex Collings, 1975. 196p.

This is a scholarly account of the war in Rhodesia, which covers the years 1964-75. There were few secondary sources to refer to at the time, and the author also used personal contacts. It is of interest as a contemporary account of the guerilla war and counter-insurgency, and has appendices of statements from the dock made by guerillas on trial.

206 **White man: black war.**
Bruce Moore-King. Harare: Baobab Books, 1988. 134p.

This vivid first-hand account of the war, written by a former Grey's Scout in the Rhodesian armed forces, drew much attention when it was first published, and was criticized by some whites who had also been involved in the war, who felt it showed them in a bad light. The reason for the work's notoriety is the candour with which the author portrays his role and experiences of the war, coupled with a strong sense of horror at the atrocities committed and the lies he was told to justify the actions of the much-feared Grey's Scouts. For a very different perspective of the equally notorious Selous Scouts see item 210. Another account of the war by a white soldier is 'The war in Rhodesia: a dissenter's view', *African Affairs*, vol. 76, no. 305 (1977), p. 483-94 by Barry Cohen, which details the nature of anti-guerilla operations from 1973 to 1977.

207 **Peasant consciousness and guerilla war in Zimbabwe: a comparative study.**
Terence O. Ranger. London: James Currey, 1985. 377p.

This important book is a major contribution to the analysis of the role of the peasantry in the Chimurenga wars against white domination. The contents are a revised version of the Smuts Commonwealth lectures given by Ranger at the University of Cambridge in which he argued that the experiences of African peasants in Zimbabwe have produced a specific form of political consciousness. This led the peasantry to participate actively in the liberation struggle in a way that was different from peasant participation in guerilla wars in other African countries. Comparisons are drawn with the experience of Kenya and Mozambique, and issues of ideology and class are considered. A case study of the peasantry in Makoni District is presented as a vehicle to the study of the changing nature of the peasantry in Zimbabwe from early colonial times to the 1980s. Some feel that Ranger has overstated the strength of the peasants' commitment to the guerillas (see item 201). An earlier article on this theme by Ranger is 'The death of Chaminuka: spirit mediums, nationalism and the guerilla war in Zimbabwe', *African Affairs*, vol. 324, no. 81 (July 1982), p. 349-69. The links between rural underdevelopment in Rhodesia, and the aims and causes of the guerilla war are discussed in Michael J. Bratton, 'Settler state, guerilla war, and rural underdevelopment in Rhodesia', *Rural Africana* (New Series), vols. 4-5 (1979), p. 115-29, an article which was originally published in *Issue*, vol. 1-2, 1979, p. 56-62.

208 **Mao Tse-Tung and Chimurenga: an investigation into ZANU's strategies.**
Paresh Pandya. Braamfontein, South Africa: Skotaville Publishers, 1988. 272p. bibliog. (History Series, no. 3).

The purpose of the study is to compare the operating tactics of ZANU's armed forces, ZANLA, with Mao Tse-Tung's three-phase strategy of guerilla warfare, and to determine whether such strategies had any influence on the conclusion of the war. However, even if the reader is not interested in this perspective, this book is still of much interest as a reference on the war. The author interviewed many key people, including Mugabe, Munangagwa, Nyagumbo, and Walls, and utilized secondary sources at the Institute of Commonwealth Studies in London and the Zimbabwean National Archives. A very significant degree of detail on operational aspects of the guerilla campaign are presented, including the nature of internal operational areas, recruitment, training, discipline, and the role of chiefs and spirit mediums. Problems of disease and hunger in guerilla base camps are considered, and detailed data on ZANLA deaths during the campaign are presented. Other aspects of the war are also examined including the protected villages' strategy, Chimurenga songs and poetry, and the role of the churches, foreign support and aid. Much emphasis is placed on the significance of ZANLA's mass mobilization techniques, including the use of pungwes and mujibas. The author concludes that there were certain parallels between ZANLA's military strategies and the theories of Mao Tse-Tung, and that these strategies were a factor which influenced the nature of the conclusion of the war.

209 **Exit Rhodesia.**
Pat Scully. Ladysmith, South Africa: Cottswold Press, 1984. 207p.

The main focus of this account of UDI and the immediate post-independence period up to 1983 is the Rhodesian armed forces and their counter-insurgency tactics. It is told from a strictly white Rhodesian viewpoint, and makes no attempt at objectivity. A brief historical introduction is included, and the main theme is placed in the context of political and economic events during UDI. The author had originally intended to write a biography of General Walls, the head of the Rhodesian armed forces, and much of that material is included in this book. See also John Lovett's *Contact: a tribute to those who serve Rhodesia* (Salisbury: Galaxie Press, 1977), a lavishly illustrated tribute to the Rhodesian security forces written in a eulogistic style. This book includes a record of honours and awards conferred before 31st March 1977, and a roll of honour. The liberation struggle is portrayed as 'an ideological war between East and West'.

210 **Selous Scouts: a pictorial account.**
Peter Stiff. Alberton, South Africa: Galago, 1984.

This pictorial record of the Selous Scouts' regiment is accompanied by text that is so biased that even though it was published after the war had ended, it almost conveys the impression that the Rhodesian army won. See also Peter Stiff and R. Reid-Daly's *Selous Scouts: top secret war* (Alberton, South Africa: Galago, 1982). Stiff has also written an account of his own involvement in the Rhodesian war in *See you in November: Rhodesia's no-holds-barred intelligence war* (Alberton, South Africa: Galago, 1985).

211 **Women and the armed struggle for independence in Zimbabwe (1964-1979).**
Leda Stott. Edinburgh: Centre of African Studies, Edinburgh University, 1990. 80p. (Occasional Papers, Edinburgh University, Centre of African Studies, no. 25).

This stimulating paper, based on the author's M.Sc thesis, applies a more rigorous analytical approach to the role of women in the liberation war, and their subsequent positions in post-independence society, than is usual in discussion of these often ideologically-loaded issues. Stott challenges the claim that women's status and roles during the war underwent a radical change, as is sometimes claimed, making their lack of progress since 1980 less surprising. Different groups of women experienced different types of changes, and she examines a number of groups including guerilla camp inmates, spirit mediums, and older women, as well as the active fighters who undoubtedly did undergo a radical re-evaluation of their roles and status. The traditional supportive role of women, albeit in changed circumstances, was, however, normally maintained, and she contends that the liberation movements had no real interest in improving women's status, being unable to afford any consequent dwindling of male support.

212 **Perhaps tomorrow.**
Tom Wigglesworth. Salisbury: Galaxie Press, [1979]. 206p.

Tom Wigglesworth became a farmer in Rhodesia after lengthy service in the British army. He farmed in the Eastern Highlands on the border with Mozambique, and in 1978 was abducted by ZANLA guerillas. In this book he tells of his capture, and the six months he spent with the guerillas in Mozambique, during which time he met Mugabe and Tongogara. He was eventually released into the care of Amnesty International. This is a fairly detached account of his experience, which is not without sympathy for the liberation fighters and their cause.

The politics of reconciliation: Zimbabwe's first decade.
See item no. 2.

Historical dictionary of Zimbabwe.
See item no. 3.

From Rhodesia to Zimbabwe: behind and beyond Lancaster House.
See item no. 5.

Zimbabwe: towards a new order – an economic and social survey. vol. 2.
See item no. 16.

Serving secretly: an intelligence chief on record. Rhodesia into Zimbabwe 1964 to 1981.
See item no. 175.

None but ourselves: masses versus media in the making of Zimbabwe.
See item no. 815.

Independence process and post-1980

213 The last colony in Africa: diplomacy and the independence of Rhodesia.
Michael Charlton.   Oxford: Basil Blackwell, 1990. 164p.

This study falls in the genre of analyses which attempt to identify the special conditions which facilitated the ending of the civil war and UDI by negotiations (see also Stedman, item 221). This book is valuable for the insights it affords by extensive use of verbatim reporting of interviews which the author conducted with individuals who had played key roles at the time of the 1979 Lancaster House settlement. The book therefore also provides an oral history of the settlement process. These interviews were conducted between November 1987 and January 1988 and many were originally broadcast on BBC Radio 3. Those interviewed included President Mugabe, President Joaquim Chissano of Mozambique, President Kenneth Kaunda of Zambia, Joshua Nkomo, Bishop Abel Muzorewa, Ian Smith, Pik Botha and Lord Carrington, and various other British Foreign Office officials.

214 From Rhodesia to Zimbabwe.
M. Clough. In: *Changing realities in Southern Africa: implications for American policy*. Edited by M. Clough.   Berkeley, California: Institute of International Studies, University of California, 1982, p. 1-60. (Research Series, no. 14).

This study of the process whereby Rhodesia became Zimbabwe examines the negotiations at the end of the 1970s, and attempts to identify the factors which brought them to a successful conclusion. It is argued that the key factor was that at this stage all of the parties involved believed that a negotiated settlement offered them an outcome preferable to continued conflict. Comparisons are made with conflicts in Algeria and Portuguese colonies, and the various earlier negotiations and settlement initiatives in Rhodesia.

215 Southern Rhodesian elections: the report of the Commonwealth Observer Group on elections leading to independent Zimbabwe.
Edited by Commonwealth Secretariat.   London: Commonwealth Secretariat, 1980. 351p.

The Commonwealth Observer Group monitored the Zimbabwean elections in 1980 which finally led to the country's independence. It reported that the process was sufficiently free and fair for the international community to recognize the result, which swept Mugabe's ZANU (PF) party into power, as a genuine reflection of the Zimbabwean people's wishes. There were, however, a number of transgressions of the democratic process by all parties involved, although some of these did not become public knowledge until after this report. The elections and the results were exhaustively analysed, from a wide range of different perspectives. Another general report from a body closely involved with Zimbabwe's struggle for independence is the Catholic Institute of International Relations' *1980 Rhodesian elections: a report* (London: Catholic Institute of International Relations, 1980). The political and military implications of ZANU (PF)'s victory are considered by Martyn Gregory in 'The Zimbabwe election: political and military implications', *Journal of Southern African Studies*, vol. 7, no. 1 (1980), p. 17-37, and he also provided a personal account of the election in '1980 Rhodesian elections – a first-hand account and analysis', *World Today*, vol. 36 (May 1980), p. 180-88. Another personal account is Stephen Chan's

The Commonwealth Observer Group in Zimbabwe: a personal memoir (Gweru: Mambo Press, 1985. [Socio-Economic Series no. 18]) which details his experiences as the co-ordinator of observations in Matabeleland North and South, and also contains letters and poems written during that time. The unusual administrative problems posed by holding elections in a country during a cease-fire, when stable administration had not been established over the whole territory are considered in C. Baker's 'Conducting the elections in Zimbabwe 1980', *Public Administration and Development*, vol. 2, no. 1 (1980), p. 45-58. The nature of nationalist politics and its influence on the election results are considered by Lionel Cliffe, Joshua Mpofu and Barry Munslow in 'Nationalist politics in Zimbabwe: the 1980 elections and beyond', *Review of African Political Economy*, vol. 18 (1980), p. 44-67.

216 **A peace in Southern Africa: the Lancaster House conference on Rhodesia, 1979.**
Jeffrey Davidow. Boulder, Colorado; London: Westview Press, under the auspices of the Centre for International Affairs, Harvard University, 1984. 143p. (Westview Special Studies on Africa).

Davidow was sent to Rhodesia by US President Carter as a diplomatic observer of the internal settlement of 1979. Although Carter did not wish to lift sanctions and opposed the settlement, pressure from Capitol Hill and increasing American support for Muzorewa resulted in Davidow's appointment to monitor the Muzorewa regime. Davidow had previously been in the US Embassy in South Africa from 1974-76, and then served as the Department of State's Rhodesian desk officer. He stayed in Rhodesia for three years and did not actually attend the Lancaster House conference, but on his return to the US he undertook research for a book on the conference whilst a fellow at Harvard's Centre for International Affairs. From his viewpoint as a pragmatic diplomat, he believes the conference was a success. His analysis focusses on the day-to-day business of the conference and the personalities of the various delegates, and from this narrow perspective the fact that an agreement was finally hammered out between such opposing forces certainly was remarkable. However the long-term ramifications of the conference terms for Zimbabwe's development are not addressed. The book also provides insights into American policies towards Rhodesia and Zimbabwe in this period.

217 **Documents on the Southern Rhodesian constitutional conference held at Lancaster House, London, September-December 1979.**
Journal of Southern African Affairs, vol. 4, no. 4 (1979), p. 401-512.

This is a useful reference for the serious scholar of the Lancaster House agreement, although probably too detailed for the more general reader. Another detailed source on this period which is useful for research purposes is 'Rhodesian settlement initiatives', *Southern African Record*, vol. 18 (Dec. 1979) p. 1-46. This article focusses on the role of American President Carter and the Secretary of State, Cyrus Vance, and the period from March 1979 to the Commonwealth Conference held in Lusaka.

218 **Sally Mugabe: Zimbabwe's first lady: a biography.**
Ministry of Information, Posts and Telecommunications. Harare: Government Printer, 1988. 16p.

This government publication provides a short biography on Sally Mugabe, the President's wife. Born in Ghana, her non-Zimbabwean origins were always an obstacle to her full acceptance in Zimbabwe. She suffered serious health problems throughout her years as First Lady, and died in 1992.

219 **Matabeleland since the amnesty.**
Terence O. Ranger. *African Affairs*, vol. 88, no. 351 (1989), p. 161-73.

In 1988 Ranger returned for a research visit to Matabeleland after the amnesty had been agreed between ZANU and ZAPU. He provides an account of the conditions he encountered, generally in positive terms. In an earlier essay, 'Bandits and guerillas: the case of Zimbabwe', in *Banditry, rebellion and social protest in Africa* (London: James Currey; Portsmouth, New Haven: Heinemann, 1986, p. 373-96) edited by Donald Crummey, Ranger considered the nature of the Matabeleland 'dissidents', in the context of a broader historical analysis which also included the participants in the 1896-97 uprisings, and the guerilla war during UDI. The African fighters in the latter two struggles are identified as guerillas, having both support from the peasantry and from a political movement. The 'dissidents' could not be so identified, he argues, although some could claim to be social bandits, with some legitimacy bestowed by the peasants.

220 **Legacies of the past? The results of the 1980 election in Midlands Province, Zimbabwe.**
Tony Rich. *Africa* (UK), vol. 52, no. 3 (1982), p. 42-55.

This analysis of the independence elections in 1980 focusses on Midlands Province. The author finds ethnicity was not such a significant factor as European commentators might have predicted. The article is reprinted in item 9.

221 **Peacemaking in civil war: international mediation in Zimbabwe 1974-80.**
Stephen John Stedman. Boulder, Colorado; London: Lynne Rienner, 1991. 254p.

The fact that Zimbabwe finally achieved independence through a negotiated ceasefire leading to elections means that the processes and conditions which facilitated a peaceful conclusion to the war have been subjected to close scrutiny. This study aims to discover what lessons may be learnt from the experience of Zimbabwe and applied to other civil war situations. The author tests Zartman's theory of 'ripeness' which contends that such negotiations are only likely to succeed if there is a mutual sense of 'hurting stalemate' for the parties directly involved. This theory adds a new dimension to the material covered here, since there is now a wide literature on the international, regional and local aspects of the final settlement. Stedman asserts that 'ripeness' could be achieved when key patrons of the warring sides perceive a stalemate, since it is argued that Mugabe's forces could have won the war if Mozambique had been prepared to continue its support. In addition, the paradoxical situation where Mugabe, Nkomo and Muzorewa all believed they could win the elections, was favourable for the negotiations. Stedman also stresses the significance of the role played by Josiah Tongogara, the military leader of ZANU's guerilla army, who was persuaded that Mozambiquan support would be withdrawn if the war continued, but also believed that Mugabe would win an election, and thus lent his support to a negotiated solution. Another political science study of the peace process in Zimbabwe is M. Tamarkin's *The making of Zimbabwe: decolonization in regional and international politics* (London; Savage MD: Frank Cass, 1990). In this book the application of political theory, relating to the goals and strategic options of the key players, to the study of the resolution of the conflict, is less illuminating than Stedman's study. The period covered runs from the Portuguese coup in 1974 to the Lancaster House agreement in 1979, and the handling of events is again competent. This study also emphasizes the key roles played by the regional patrons in the war: South Africa, Mozambique and Zambia.

222 **From Rhodesia to Zimbabwe: the politics of transition.**
Henry Wiseman, Alastair M. Taylor. New York: Pergamon Press for the International Peace Academy, 1981. 170p.

Wiseman and Taylor are both Canadian academics at the International Peace Academy which enjoyed observer status during the run-up to the elections after Lancaster House. This book deals with the final phase of the transfer of power in Rhodesia as part of the Academy's study of the development of the organization and modalities of peacekeeping and conflict resolution. It focusses on the implementation of the Lancaster House agreements for the transitional period to independence, the nature of the monitoring forces, and the international observers. Wiseman was Director of the Peacekeeping Programs in Rhodesia whilst he was an observer, and thus was in an excellent position to record events and the attitudes prevalent amongst the diverse groups involved in the election campaign, including that of the British governor, Lord Soames. The authors report that there was a degree of intimidation by all actors involved in the transfer of power, including the British, whom they additionally suspect gained undue influence over the outcome of the negotiations which led to eventual independence by holding the conference in London at Lancaster House. They also criticize Lord Soames for not being even-handed in his role, and tending to favour the white security forces. They are nevertheless generally positive about the management of transition and the elections. Of particular interest for the researcher are the appendices which contain an opinion survey of accredited observers, a list of observers, and details on the parties contesting the elections and the results, the deployment of the monitoring force, the election council, the common roll election, complaints by parties placed before the election council, reports from the Commonwealth Observer Group, the modus operandi of the Commonwealth sub-committees, intimidation recorded on the governor's intelligence map, and an attachment to the ceasefire agreement.

The politics of reconciliation: Zimbabwe's first decade.
See item no. 2.

Historical dictionary of Zimbabwe.
See item no. 3.

Zimbabwe: politics, economics and society.
See item no. 14.

The road to Zimbabwe: 1890-1980.
See item no. 108.

Serving secretly: an intelligence chief on record. Rhodesia into Zimbabwe 1964 to 1981.
See item no. 175.

Exit Rhodesia.
See item no. 209.

Population

General and demographic change

223 **Zimbabwe: 1982 population census. A preliminary assessment.**
Central Statistical Office.   Harare: Central Statistical Office, 1984.
39p.

This is a useful introduction to the basic demographic features of the Zimbabwean population. Concise information is presented on fertility, mortality, migration, urbanization and population distribution. The changes in the European population are briefly presented. Previous censuses differentiated more clearly between the races, with separate reports on the African population. The 1960s censuses were fairly comprehensive in their coverage and were reported by the Central Statistical Office in *Rhodesia: 1969 population census. Interim report: 1. The European, Asian and Coloured population. 2. The African population* (Salisbury: Central Statistical Office, 1971), *1961 census of the European, Asian and Coloured population* (Salisbury: Central Statistical Office, 1963), and *Final report of the April/May 1962 census of Africans in Southern Rhodesia* (Salisbury: Central Statistical Office, 1964). The 1992 census has not yet been published; projections of population based on the 1982 census are available in *Population Projections of Zimbabwe: 1982-2032* (Harare: Central Statistical Office, 1986).

224 **Zimbabwe 1982 population census: main demographic features of the population.**
Central Statistical Office.   Harare: Central Statistical Office, 1988.
8 vols.

The first post-independence census was held in 1982. The full demographic details were not published for years, and the preliminary report (see item 223) is a useful concise source on basic indices. This full report is published in separate volumes for each province. Further demographic details for each province have also been published by the CSO Population and Planning Unit as *Comparative Tables: district population indicators and information for development planning* (Harare: Central Statistical

Office, 1989). At the time of writing, the latest 1992 census had still not been published.

225 **Towards a population policy for Zimbabwe-Rhodesia.**
George R. Kay. *African Affairs*, vol. 314, no. 79 (1980), p. 95-114.

In this paper Kay makes a case for cutting the African population growth rate and encouraging rural-urban migration. His thesis is that environmental degradation in the communal lands could only worsen as population pressure increased even further, and that this could only be alleviated by diverting the surplus population into urban-based employment, and forcing the migrants to cut their ties with the land. Unfortunately such a policy would involve urban investment in jobs, and a social security system on a scale which Zimbabwe could not attain. Another paper on the need for a population policy in Zimbabwe at the time of independence is 'A population policy for Zimbabwe-Rhodesia', *Zimbabwe Journal of Economics*, vol. 1, no. 2 (1979), p. 63-71, by John Hanks. Kay makes similar arguments about the need to end circular migration, and the introduction of individual titles to land in 'Zimbabwe's independence: geographical problems and prospects', *Geographical Journal*, vol. 147, no. 2 (July 1981), p. 179-187, and 'Population redistribution in Zimbabwe', in *Redistribution of population in Africa* (London: Heinemann, 1982, p. 85-94), edited by John I. Clarke and Les A. Kozinski.

226 **Zimbabwe National Family Planning Council: Zimbabwe Reproductive Health survey 1984.**
Marvellous Mhloyi. *Journal of Social Development in Africa*, vol. 1, no. 2 (1986), p. 101-10.

Zimbabwe has the highest uptake of contraception amongst women in sub-Saharan Africa. The surge in contraceptive use was quite sudden, and the Reproductive Health Survey discussed in this paper was one of the main pieces of research which established the new development (see item 231). Nevertheless although fertility is falling it remains high. A study of pre-independence fertility in Salisbury is available in W. R. Castle and K. Hakutangwi's 'Patterns of fertility amongst Africans in Glen Norah township', *Central African Journal of Medicine*, vol. 25, no. 6 (1979), p. 126-30. Reviews of the continuing increase in the evidence for high contraceptive uptake for child-spacing purposes are E. S. Boohane and T. E. Dow's 'Contraceptive prevalence and family planning program effort in Zimbabwe', *International Family Planning Perspectives*, vol. 13, no. 1 (1987), p. 1-7, and T. Dow (et al.), 'Characteristics of new contraceptive acceptors in Zimbabwe', *Studies in Family Planning*, vol. 17, no. 2 (1986), p. 107-13.

227 **Strategic planning and management in the Zimbabwe programme.**
Nobert O. Mugwagwa. In: *Strategic management of population programmes*. Edited by Gayl Ness, Ellen Sattar. Kuala Lumpur: International Committee for the Management of Population Programmes, 1989. p. 122-51.

The focus of this article is the management of Zimbabwe's population policies. These are very successful in comparison to other African countries. Major increases in contraceptive uptake have occurred since independence, and the fertility rate is falling. Government commitment to the programme is shown to be high, and the use of village-based distribution for contraceptive information and products has improved access to contraception.

228 **Pregnancy, childbirth, mother and child care among the indigenous peoples of Zimbabwe.**
Jane Mutambirwa. *International Journal of Gynaecological Obstetrics*, vol. 23, no. 4 (1985), p. 275-85.

Traditional attitudes and practices concerning pregnancy and birth are explained in this paper. The role of traditional birth attendants was generally dismissed in the colonial era, but their skills are now more valued. Traditional Shona childbirth practices and fertility control are also discussed, along with some more technical material in I. M. Brown's 'Perspectives in obstetric care in Zimbabwe', *Central African Journal of Medicine*, vol. 27, no. 3 (1981), p. 37-41. An account of the development of maternity services for whites with brief mention of African facilities is Michael Gelfand, *Midwifery in tropical Africa: the growth of maternity services in Rhodesia* (Harare: Department of Medicine, University of Zimbabwe, 1978).

229 **Traditional Shona concepts on family life and how systems planned on the basis of these concepts effectively contained the population growth of Shona communities.**
Jane Mutambirwa. *Zimbabwean Journal of Economics*, vol. 1, no. 2 (1979), p. 96-103.

The preferred size of the traditional Shona family was about seven children, far fewer than would result if restrictions on fertility were not being exercised. In this paper, which focuses on socio-cultural practices and is therefore rather strangely located in an economics journal, the author first examines Shona conceptions of the role and major significance of the family unit. She goes on to examine the range of customs and practices which traditonally influenced fertility behaviour. Apart from various forms of contraception, she shows how families were encouraged not to exceed the numbers of children they could support.

230 **Population and development problems in Zimbabwe: a national population policy study.**
Whitsun Foundation. Harare: Whitsun Foundation, 1983. 191p. (Project 1.08).

In this report on demographic factors in Zimbabwe shortly after independence, strong concern is registered about the rate of population growth. This leads to criticism of the independent government, which is said to be neglecting this issue. In fact, the report overestimated the problem. The Zimbabwean government has pursued a population policy, and during the 1980s fertility fell, and the uptake of contraception increased.

231 **Zimbabwe Reproductive Health Survey 1984.**
Zimbabwe National Family Planning Council. Columbia, Maryland: Westinghouse Public Applied Systems, 1985. 209p.

The 1985 reproductive health survey produced comprehensive data on all aspects of fertility and reproduction in Zimbabwe. Of great significance were the findings that fertility decline was already under way, albeit from very high levels, and that contraceptive uptake amongst black Zimbabwean women had increased enormously, making Zimbabwe the country with the highest contraceptive uptake in Africa. The policy of using village health workers to encourage women to space their children appeared to be effective. These findings indicate that the prognostications of the

Whitsun Foundation's report on population (item 230) were overly gloomy. Other publications relevant to fertility behaviour include a report on family planning amongst Africans from 1948-72 by Duncan Clarke, 'Problems of family planning amongst Africans in Rhodesia', *Rhodesian Journal of Economics*, vol. 6, no. 2 (1972), p. 36-48, and a survey of urban women's attitudes to family planning by D. S. Macdonald, 'Factors influencing the acceptance of family planning by Blacks in Salisbury, Zimbabwe', *South African Medical Journal*, vol. 61, no. 12 (1982), p. 437-39. *Family planning pioneering in Rhodesia (Zimbabwe) 1957-70* (Harare: Paddy Spilhaus, 1981), by Paddy Spilhaus is a rather dull study of the development of family planning in Rhodesia which does however contain useful details on the types of contraceptives promoted. The trends towards lower fertility and increased uptake of modern contraception were confirmed by the Department of Census and Statistics in *Zimbabwe Demographic and Health Survey 1988: preliminary report* (Harare: Department of Census and Statistics, 1989).

232 **Changing patterns of population distribution in Zimbabwe.**
Lovemore Mondiwa Zinyama, Richard Whitlow. *Geojournal*, vol. 13, no. 4 (1986), p. 365-84.

This paper critically evaluates the causes and consequences of changes in population distribution from the end of the 19th century to 1982. One factor discussed is the impact of land tenure and alienation on the population. The distribution of the African population in 1982 is described in detail, and compared to the situation in the 1962 and 1969 censuses. Changing patterns of settlement and land-use in the communal areas and the impact of increasing population pressure, urbanization, and post-independence policies on population distribution including agricultural resettlement are also covered.

Zimbabwe: towards a new order – an economic and social survey. vol. 2.
See item no. 16.

Ecological dynamics and human welfare in Southern Zimbabwe.
See item no. 634.

Zimbabwe national household survey capability programme (ZNHSCP): reports on demographic socio-economic survey, 1983/4.
See item no. 706.

Peoples and culture

233 **Symbols of life: an analysis of the consciousness of the Karanga.**
Herbert Aschwanden, in collaboration with the Karanga nurses of the Musiso Hospital at Zaka, Zimbabwe, translated into English by Ursula Cooper. Gweru: Mambo Press, 1982. 332p. (Shona Heritage Series, no. 3).

Originally published in German as *Symbole des Lebens* (Zuerich and Freiburg: Atlantis Verlag, 1976.), this is the first in a trilogy of studies on the Karanga by Aschwanden. It provides detailed material on the symbols and rituals of the Karanga people of Ndenga communal area, south-east of Masvingo. Aschwanden was doctor in charge of the mission hospital from 1965-71; the information was collected by his nurses from elderly patients, partly because he realized his Western scientific approach to diagnosis and treatment sometimes hindered his treatment of patients who perceived their medical problems from a radically different cultural perspective. He includes material on beliefs concerning the beginning of life, the soul, the person, childhood and education, puberty, marriage, the sexes, sexual intercourse, pregnancy and birth.

234 **Symbols of death: an analysis of the consciousness of the Karanga.**
Herbert Aschwanden, in collaboration with the Karanga nurses of the Musiso Hospital at Zaka, Zimbabwe, translated into English by Ursula Cooper. Gweru: Mambo Press, 1987. 332p. (Shona Heritage Series, no. 4).

This is a complementary volume to Aschwanden's *Symbols of Life* (see item 233). It focusses on Karanga traditions and beliefs related to disease and death. For many medical problems a natural explanation is accepted, and these are known as 'diseases from God', but others are attributed to witchcraft or the displeasure of ancestors. The final part of the trilogy is *Karanga mythology: an analysis of the consciousness of the Karanga in Zimbabwe* (Gweru: Mambo Press, 1989. [Shona Heritage Series no. 5]), which includes discussion of myths surrounding important events such as birth and marriage, myths about God and the night, and consideration of the role of n'angas (spirit mediums).

235 **The Shona peoples: an ethnography of the contemporary Shona, with special reference to their religion.**
Michael F. C. Bourdillon. Gwelo: Mambo Press, 1987. 3rd rev. ed. 359p. bibliog. (Shona Heritage Series, no. 1).

This is one of the most important and comprehensive works on the Shona, by a leading anthropologist at the University of Zimbabwe who has an outstanding research record. The discussion of the Shona in this book is extremely wide ranging, making it a useful reference volume. As the title suggest, religion is particularly well covered. Other topics include history, economics, kinship, chiefs, superstitions, witchcraft, customary law, health issues, and the impact of urbanization. The original 1976 edition was revised in 1982 with substantial additions and alterations to the information on the economic and urban characteristics of the Shona. This was in response to the rapidly growing body of new research on the Shona, and Bourdillon makes special reference to studies by Angela Cheater. Further modifications were made for this 1987 edition, in particular on the position of women and on courts in rural and urban areas. The useful bibliography was also extended. Other general studies of the Shona are Kuper (see item 248) and the many works by Gelfand (see item 240).

236 **Ndebele religion and customs.**
Reverend W. Bozongwana. Gweru: Mambo Press in association with the Literature Bureau, 1983. 56p.

This short book provides a useful introduction to modern Ndebele culture and customs, and how these are related to and rooted in Ndebele history. A wide variety of topics are covered including clans, totem animals, beliefs and taboos for children, the roles of women and men, childbirth and initiation customs, relationships and marriage, death and burial, types of spirits, festivals, rain-making and Ndebele mythology. The author is a primary-school headmaster and an Anglican priest in the diocese of Matabeleland, but most significant is his direct descent from Lobengula's high priest, who was his grandfather.

237 The Mashona and the Matabele.
Charles Bullock.   Johannesburg: Juta, 1950. 310p.

Although wide-ranging in its treatment of the cultures of the Shona and Ndebele, this volume suffers from its colonial origins, which colour the author's perspective. The approach is paternalist at best, with more details on the Shona than the Ndebele. The author worked in native administration in Rhodesia for thirty-seven years, eventually becoming chief native commissioner, and this text was often used by his staff. He was also a poet and novelist, and edited NADA (see item 840) from 1944 to 1945. A similarly colonial perspective from a later era informed Harold Child's *The history of the amaNdebele* (Salisbury: Ministry of Internal Affairs, 1969), an official publication on the Ndebele's society and economy, also written by a native administrator, this time of thirty-eight years' experience.

238 The Indian community of Southern Rhodesia.
D. M. Desai.   Salisbury: Rhodesian Printing and Publishing Company, 1948. 39p.

This booklet provides excellent data on the characteristics of the Indian population of Southern Rhodesia shortly after the Second World War. The author, who was Secretary of the Hindu Society in Salisbury, provides a fairly straightforward account of the origins of Asian settlement, and their current roles and locations.

239 The Indian minority of Zambia, Rhodesia and Malawi.
Floyd Dotson, Lillan O. Dotson.   New Haven, Connecticut; London: Yale University Press, 1968. 444p.

This is the major study of the Asian population of Central Africa, which includes substantial sections on Zimbabwe. Although the work is now outdated, as the research was carried out between 1959 and 1966, it remains a useful reference. The analysis is directed mainly at cultural, social and political aspects of this minority, rather than their economic activities. On Asian economic history in Rhodesia, see B. A. Kosmin's ' "Freedom, justice and commerce": some factors affecting Asian trading patterns in Southern Rhodesia, 1897-1942', *Rhodesian History*, vol. 6 (1975), p. 15-32. On Asian politics see P. Stigger, 'Asians in Rhodesia and Kenya: a comparative political history', *Rhodesian History*, vol. 1 (1970), p. 1-18, and Hasu H. Patel, 'Asian political activity in Rhodesia from the Second World War to 1972', *Rhodesian History*, vol. 9 (1978), p. 63-82. For a local Asian perspective on the Asian community in the 1940s, see Desai (item 238).

240 The genuine Shona: survival values of an African culture.
Michael Gelfand.   Gwelo: Mambo Press, 1973. 205p.

Michael Gelfand was one of the leading European academic authorities on Shona culture and wrote very extensively about their beliefs, values and behaviour. He taught at the University of Rhodesia and then the University of Zimbabwe in the Department of Medicine. This is one of his many major works on Shona values and culture, which includes consideration of how urbanization was affecting traditional behaviour. Others include *The African background: the traditional culture of the Shona* (Cape Town: Juta,

1965); *African crucible: an ethnico-religious study with special reference to the Shona-speaking people* (Cape Town: Juta, 1968); *Shona religion* (Cape Town: Juta, 1962); and *Medicine and magic of the Shona* (Cape Town: Juta, 1956). *The African witch* (Edinburgh: Livingstone, 1967) deals in detail with the beliefs and practices associated with Shona witchcraft. Specific case studies on the different religions of the sub-groups within the Shona peoples were also published, dealing in particular with traditional religious attitudes, ancestral spirits, n'angas or spirit mediums, and marriage and death procedures. These are *Shona ritual with special reference to the Chaminuka cult* (Cape Town: Juta, 1959); *Shona religion with special reference to the Makorekore* (Mystic, Connecticut: Lawrence Verry, 1965; Cape Town: Juta, 1962); *Vakaranga: an African religion* (Juta: Cape Town, 1966); and *The spiritual beliefs of the Shona: a study based on field work amongst East-Central Shona* (Gwelo: Mambo Press, 1977). In marked contrast to most of his white contemporaries prior to independence, Gelfand's views on Shona culture were almost entirely positive, and his research output may be criticized for the lack of a critical perspective.

241 **Growing up in Shona society: from birth to marriage.**
Michael Gelfand. Gwelo: Mambo Press, 1979. 228p.
In this study of yet another aspect of Shona culture, Gelfand discusses the customary methods of bringing up children within Shona society, based on research in the communal areas over a period of twenty-five years. Gelfand is highly positive about these processes, and this is not a totally balanced account. The role of grandparents is stressed, and the use of games, songs and riddles in socializing children is discussed. The upbringing of urban children is also covered.

242 **The Shona woman.**
Michael Gelfand. *NADA*, vol. 10, no. 5 (1973), p. 41-50.
Gelfand's high opinion of the Shona is yet again reflected in this paper, which argues that the status of women in Shona society is generally higher than most outsiders believe. He discusses various aspects of women's status and roles including marriage and divorce, 'witchcraft', and economic position.

243 **Ukama: reflections on Shona and western cultures in Zimbabwe.**
Michael Gelfand. Gweru: Mambo Press, 1981. 133p.
In this study, Gelfand discusses Shona culture from a largely philosophical angle. Ukama is the term for the close family relationships which he states are the main characteristic of Shona life. In comparison with western culture, which he dismisses as materialistic and individualistic, he finds Shona culture to be more rewarding, with stronger spiritual and humanistic values. He states that for a Shona, the 'chief concern is about others'. This is a rather abstract work, and in common with other books on the Shona by Gelfand, tends to idealize Shona culture. Another item on African culture and European attitudes towards Africans is Michael Bourdillon's *Myths about Africans: myth-making in Rhodesia* (Gweru: Mambo Press, 1976.) which concentrates on the building of racial stereotypes.

244 **Afrikaners in Rhodesia: a partial portrait.**
Richard Hodder-Williams. *African Social Research* (Zambia), vol. 18 (1974), p. 611-42.
This article examines changes in the Rhodesian Afrikaner community between 1890 and 1970.

245 **Some 'Shona' tribes of Southern Rhodesia.**

J. F. Holleman. In: *Seven tribes of British Central Africa*. Edited by E. Colson, M. Gluckman. London: Oxford University Press, 1951. p. 354-95.

The Shona are not one ethnic group, but are made up of a number of different sub-groups with differing traditions and regional affiliations. One of these groups is the Zezuru of central Mashonaland, and this paper focuses on four sub-groups within the Zezuru: two of them Rozwi, one Mbiri and one Hera. These groups are to be found in the Buhera, Marondera and Charter areas. The author doubts whether the classification 'Shona' has any significance for these groups, and in this he concurs with a number of other authorities who have questioned the pre-colonial existence of a Shona identity (see for example items 252). Their differing economies, societies and political groupings are described and analysed, including discussion of typical habitats and means of subsistence, land tenure and land allocation, the nature of settlement patterns, and the influence of Rhodesian government legislation on traditional behaviour. The second section of the paper contains analysis of genealogical groupings and the importance of kinship ties.

246 **The coloured people of Southern Rhodesia.**

Percy Ibbotson. *Race Relations Journal*, vol. 9, no. 1 (1942), p. 47-51.

Little has been published on Zimbabwe's coloured population, which, unlike in South Africa, is a very small minority. This article, written by the regional representative of the South African Institute of Race Relations, is of use only as an historical reference for the social conditions and characteristics of the coloured population in the 1940s. It appeared in a special issue of Race Relations Journal on the coloured population of Southern Africa.

247 **Majuta: a history of the Jewish community of Zimbabwe.**

Barry A. Kosmin. Gweru, Zimbabwe: Mambo Press, 1980. 223p. (Zambeziana Series on Culture and Society in Central Africa, no. 10).

Kosmin was born in Britain, and educated at McMaster University, Hamilton, Ontario and the University of Rhodesia. He obtained his PhD in Rhodesia with a study of Asian, Hellenic and Jewish populations in Rhodesia, 1898-1945. This book chronicles the experiences of Rhodesia's Jewish community from the late 19th century to just before independence. It specifically documents the incidence of anti-semitism in Rhodesia. An earlier work by the same author is 'A note on Southern Rhodesian Jewry, 1890-1936', *Jewish Journal of Sociology*, vol. 15, no. 2 (Dec. 1973), p. 205-12. Another brief history was produced by Salisbury's Jewish community: *75 years, Salisbury Hebrew congregation, 1895-1970* (Salisbury: Sebri Printers, [ca.1970]).

248 **The Shona and the Ndebele of Southern Rhodesia.**

Hilda Kuper, Arthur John Brodie Hughes, J. van Velsen. London: International African Institute, 1954. 131p. map. bibliog.

This is an important and comprehensive study, which made a substantial contribution to research on the culture of the two main ethnic groups in Zimbabwe at the time of publication, and remains a standard ethnographic reference. It was published as part of the International African Institute's Ethnographic Survey of Africa. The section on the Shona is provided by Kuper, and the Ndebele section by the other two authors. Language, culture, history, demography, religion, politics and details of the traditional socio-economy and factors inducing change are covered. For a factual rather than analytical account of Ndebele habitat and subsistence, population, history, political and social organization, and genealogical ties see also Arthur J. B. Hughes' *Kin, caste and nation among the Rhodesian Ndebele* (Manchester, England: Manchester University Press for Rhodes-Livingstone Institute, 1956. [Rhodes-Livingstone Paper, no. 25]) which is based on fieldwork carried out in the early 1950s.

249 **The Goba of the Zambezi: sex roles, economics and change.**
Chet S. Lancaster. Norman, Oklahoma: University of Oklahoma Press, 1981. 350p.

This is a detailed and comprehensive account of the Goba's agricultural system and society. Their agriculture is based on slash-and-burn techniques, and population densities in the area are low. Both their culture and their economy are women-centred. The study uses a human ecology perspective, stressing the Goba's role in, and interaction with, the ecosystem within which they live.

250 **My friend Kumalo: sidelights on Matabele tradition.**
Mhlagazanhlansi (Neville Jones). Bulawayo, Rhodesia: Rhodesian Printing and Publishing Co., 1945. 54p. Reprinted, Bulawayo: Books of Rhodesia, 1972.

This curious volume considers various aspects of Ndebele history and traditions expressed in terms of an oral story. Apart from the historical and political material, there is commentary on a wide range of cultural themes, including material culture, domestic life, linguistic curiosities, proverbs and superstitions. The clan names (isibongo) and discussion of the Ndebele military structure are contained in appendices. The book was prepared by Neville Jones from discussions with Reverend Kumalo, whom he met in about 1913. Kumalo was a member of the royal Khumalo family, and his father had fought under Mzilikazi. Another book on a member of the Khumalo clan also emerged from an oral history project. This is 'The story of Ndansi Kumalo of the Matabele tribe, Southern Rhodesia', by J. W. Posselt and Margery Perham, p. 63-79 in *Ten Africans* (London: Faber & Faber, 1936. Reprinted, 1963. 2nd ed., Evanston, Illinois: Northwestern University Press, 1964), edited by Margery Perham. Ndansi Kumalo fought in the 1896 rebellion, and played Lobengula in the film *Rhodes of Africa*. His story includes rather artless comments on a visit he made to England. Archibald Campbell, a Southern Rhodesian district commissioner for eighteen years from 1896, also published an account of Ndebele history from 1820-1896 based, or so he claimed, on oral testimony from an Ndebele informant. See *'Mlimo': the rise and fall of the Matabele* (Pietermaritzburg, South Africa: Natal Witness, 1925. Reprinted, Bulawayo: Books of Rhodesia, 1972) by Mziki (pseudonym for Campbell).

251 **The Matabele at home.**
Peter Nielsen. Bulawayo: Davis, [n.d.]. 73p.

This brief volume is chiefly of interest as an example of the racism and bigotry typical of white settler attitudes towards the indigenous population. The author deals with the manners and customs of the Matabele, their religious ideas, and 'the man himself'. Some of the facts about customs are broadly correct, but most of the rest is illustrative of the uninformed prejudices of European colonialists.

252 **Missionaries, migrants and the Manyika: the invention of ethnicity in Zimbabwe.**
Terence O. Ranger. In: *The creation of tribalism in Southern Africa.* Edited by Leroy Vail. London: James Currey; Berkeley, Los Angeles, California; University of California Press; Claremont: David Phillip, 1989, p. 118-50.

This essay argues that whilst Shona-speaking peoples of the 19th century had similar cultural traits, they had no conscious ethnic identity beyond local chieftaincies. Terms used by the Europeans to sub-divide the Shona, such as Ndau and Korekore, did not depict any actual ethnic sub-groups, but as they came to be widely used by local administration and chiefs, gradually were adopted by individuals for self-identification. The processes are illustrated with a case study of Chief Makoni's area, Makoni District. The role of the missionaries and migration is emphasized. Ranger developed this theme originally in a paper entitled *The invention of tribalism in Zimbabwe* (Gweru: Mambo Press, 1985) in which he attacks the tendency to ascribe all conflict and political tensions to ethnicity which is perceived as natural and deep-rooted. He suggests that this type of tribalism did not exist in pre-colonial Zimbabwe.

253 **Dance, civet cat: the Tonga and child labour in Zimbabwe.**
Pam Reynolds. London: Zed Books; Athens, Ohio: Ohio University Press; Harare: Baobab Books, 1991. 176p. bibliog.

This is an important study of the Tonga people of Zimbabwe. Reynolds has worked extensively on children, and this interest is reflected here. A special focus of the study is the work that children do, especially in agriculture. She assesses not only the contribution they make to household economies, but also how their involvement in work affects the children's social development. Children's rights within Tonga society, and the value placed upon them are also discussed. The author is a Zimbabwean sociologist, who has taught at universities in Zimbabwe and South Africa.

254 **Oral history: the Zvimba people of Zimbabwe.**
Stanlake John William Samkange. Harare: Harare Publishing House, 1986. 91p.

Robert Mugabe comes from the Zvimba area, whose people are the subject of this book. Through the medium of a narrative expressed as oral history, the book traces the genealogy of this group of Zezuru people.

255 **The Tonga people on the southern shore of Lake Kariba.**
Anna Katherina Hildegard Weinrich. Gwelo: Mambo Press, 1977. 109p. (Mambo Occasional Papers, Socio-Economic Series, no. 8).

This is a fairly straightforward ethnographic study of the Tonga. Their culture, social and political structures, and religious beliefs are discussed, and the impact of resettlement caused by the flooding of their ancestral lands by Lake Kariba. In keeping with many of her studies the author also examines the impact and role of the Catholic church on this ethnic group.

256 **The tears of the dead: the social biography of an African family.**
Richard P. Werbner. Edinburgh: Edinburgh University Press for the
International African Library; Washington, DC: Smithsonian
Institution Press, 1991; Harare: Baobab Books, 1992. 211p.

This fascinating family history is the first account of its kind for Southern Africa, and
possibly for the whole continent. After extensive research with living members of the
family Lupondo of the Kalanga ethnic group, Werbner has constructed one hundred
years of family history. This gives us the story of several generations, and a strongly
personal viewpoint on the development of Rhodesia's political economy, with firsthand
experience of evictions from ancestral land, resettlement, the guerilla war, and the
unrest in Matabeleland in the 1980s. In addition the book details the concepts, value
systems, and family morality which shape individuals' behaviour, and how these
changed in reaction to events during the colonial and post-colonial era.

Pre-historic Rhodesia.
See item no. 93.

The Karanga empire.
See item no. 113.

Gold regions of Southeastern Africa.
See item no. 122. (vol. 10; Silver Series: vol. 19).

**Islands of white: settler society and culture in Kenya and Southern Rhodesia
1890-1939.**
See item no. 153.

**Southern Rhodesia: the effects of a conquest society on education, culture and
information.**
See item no. 720.

Migration

257 **Circulatory migration in Rhodesia: towards a decision model.**
G. Kingsley Garbett. In: *Town and country in Central and Eastern
Africa.* Edited by David Parkin. London: International African
Institute, 1975, p. 113-25.

Garbett did extensive field research in the Tribal Trust Lands (see item 305). Labour
migration was one of the aspects of village life which he studied and in this essay he
proposes a model of how migration decisions are made. He challenges analyses which
focus only on the factors influencing the migrant, since this presupposes an
individualism which he believes was not typical of rural culture. Instead he suggests
that the motivations of the migrant's kin group should be taken into account, since kin
could derive advantages and disadvantages from such migration, and would have a
major influence on any group member's decision-making. Such a model would not
satisfy structural analysts, who would stress the political and economic context of land
alienation and the underdevelopment of African agriculture in explaining migrant

labour (see items 481, 588 and 690). In this same volume also see J. Clyde Mitchell's article, 'Factors in rural male absenteeism in Rhodesia', p. 93-112. This applies statistical tests to a vast range of socio-economic variables on different districts in the Tribal Trust Lands, in an attempt to identify factors which cause high rates of male absenteeism. The results unfortunately are either obvious or not very illuminating.

258 **African unemployment and the rural areas of Rhodesia.**
   T. E. Mswaka. *Rural Africana*, vol. 24, (Spring 1974), p. 59-74.
This paper on rural unemployment and circular migration appeared in a special edition of *Rural Africana* on 'Rural labour in Southern Africa', edited by Robert Boeder. Mswaka examines the role of the Tribal Trust Lands in providing a cushion for African unemployment, and a subsidy to the wage economy. He discusses the various institutional and legal forces that cause circular migration, and provides figures on African employment and unemployment by district for the years 1961 and 1969.

259 **Rural-urban migration in contemporary Harare: why migrants need their land.**
   Deborah H. Potts, Christopher C. Mutambirwa. *Journal of Southern African Studies*, vol. 16, no. 4 (1991), p. 177-98.
This article reports the results of two major surveys conducted within the high density areas of Harare and Chitungwiza amongst post-independence migrant households. The authors were concerned with establishing the characteristics of rural-urban migration in the new Zimbabwe, where institutionalized restrictions on migration and urban residence had been lifted. In addition they address a number of theoretical issues about the desirability of circular migration and the maintenance of communal land tenure which facilitates circulation. It is reported that there have been significant shifts in migrant profiles, with longer-term or working-life migration becoming more common and many families no longer divided, and others having adopted complex visiting patterns. Nevertheless the lack of an urban welfare net, the uncertainties of urban employment, and the severe housing shortage are all factors which encourage many migrants to maintain rural links and plan to return to rural areas eventually. Patterns of land-use and agricultural labour for urban households with rural land are examined. These findings are discussed in the light of theories about agrarian reform in Southern Africa, and the policy implications of removing rights to land. Deborah Potts is a lecturer in geography at the School of Oriental and African Studies, University of London, and Chris Mutambirwa lectures in the Geography Department at the University of Zimbabwe. The impact of enforced circular migration on African society in the colonial era is addressed in G. L. Chavunduka, 'Rural and urban life', *Zambezia*, vol. 4, no. 2 (1976), p. 69-78. He presents information on how migration has affected population distribution, marriage and divorce, economic relationships between urban and rural family members, women's roles and agricultural practices. Also on labour circulation, see J. Clyde Mitchell's 'Structural plurality, urbanization and labour circulation in Rhodesia', in *Migration* (Cambridge: Cambridge University Press, 1969), edited by J. A. Jackson.

Missionaries, migrants and the Manyika: the invention of ethnicity in Zimbabwe.
See item no. 252.

Labour supplies in perspective: a study of the proletarianization of the African peasantry.
See item no. 481.

Agrarian policy in migrant labour societies: reform or transformation in Zimbabwe.
See item no. 599.

Race Relations

260 Crossroads.

Asian Association.   Salisbury: The Asian Association, 1960. 13p.

This short report on Asian feelings about discrimination in Rhodesia provides an interesting insight into the strength of Asian anger at petty apartheid, as well as broader political issues.

261 Racism and apartheid in Southern Africa: Rhodesia.

Reginald Austin.   Paris: UNESCO, 1975. 122p.

This is one of three volumes commissioned by UNESCO (see items 366, 539) to provide information on the nature of institutionalized racism in Rhodesia in the 1970s. Topics covered are land issues, labour, political parties, education, economics and the liberation struggle. The constitution is also discussed, and the state constitution as well as the constitutions of various organizations are reproduced as appendices. Another more substantive general survey of racism in the early 1970s was produced for the Centre for Inter-racial Studies at the University of Rhodesia by Dorothy Davies: *Race relations in Rhodesia: a survey 1972-73* (London: Rex Collings; Lotowa, New Jersey: Rowman & Littlefield, 1975). This publication also covers the additional topics of crime, urban areas, sport, religion, international relations, Tribal Trust Lands, and population. A fascinating report on racial discrimination was also commissioned by the State President (see item 268).

262 Cold Comfort confronted.

Guy Clutton-Brock, Molly Clutton-Brock.   London, Oxford: Mowbrays, 1972. 201p.

Cold Comfort Farm, which is now within Harare's borders, was more than an experiment in multi-racial economic and social co-operation; it was also a symbol of defiance against the racism of the white minority regime. The farm, and its sister establishment, St. Faith's at Rusape, were run as Christian communes, and were therefore also perceived by the UDI government as practicing dangerous agrarian ideologies as well. The courageous Clutton-Brocks were the moving force behind Cold

Comfort and St. Faith's and were outspoken in their opposition to the Rhodesian Front. This account does not only deals with the issue of Cold Comfort Farm, but provides many insights and details on the development of African nationalism and opposition to racism and UDI within Rhodesia generally. Guy Clutton-Brock also produced a pamphlet describing and explaining the commune, *Cold Comfort Farm Society* (Gweru: Mambo Press, 1970). See also Anna K. H. Weinrich, *Cold Comfort Farm Society: a Christian commune in Rhodesia* (Old Umtali: Methodist Mission Press, 1975). On the fate of St. Faith's which the Diocese took over in 1959 and reverted its operation back to the status of a 'proper Anglican mission', see Patricia Chater, *Grass roots: the story of St. Faith's farm* (London: Hodder & Stoughton, 1962). Further details about the extraordinary Clutton-Brocks can be found in *Guy and Molly Clutton-Brock: reminiscences from their family and friends on the occasion of Guy's 80th birthday* (Harare: Longman Zimbabwe,1987).

263 **The two nations: aspects of the development of race relations in the Rhodesias and Nyasaland.**

Richard Gray. London: Oxford University Press, 1960. 373p.

Reprinted, Westport, Connecticut: Greenwood Press, 1974.

The second volume in a trilogy for the Institute of Race Relations, which also includes two titles by Mason (see item 137, 166), this is an authoritative and scholarly analysis of the economic history of the two Rhodesias and Nyasaland from 1918 to 1953, and the relationship between economic change and racial discrimination. The author demonstrates how, despite many hopes and promises, African advancement did not go hand-in-hand with economic growth. Instead racial discrimination tended to increase. Gray was Professor of History at the School of Oriental and African Studies, University of London until his retirement in 1991.

264 **Zimbabwe: the facts about Rhodesia.**

International Defence and Aid Fund. London: International Defence and Aid Fund, 1977. 76p.

This is a straightforward report on racial discrimination in Rhodesia. There is useful coverage of the historical background and the economy, the constitution, the liberation movements, denial of rights and freedom, the armed struggle and the various attempts at settlement which had occurred up to 1977.

265 **Racial conflict in Rhodesia: a socio-historical study.**

Graham C. Kinloch. Washington DC: University Press of America, 1978. 321p.

This study of racial conflict covers each decade from 1890 to the 1970s, focussing on the changing attitudes and policies of the white elite towards the black majority, and, to a lesser extent, on African reaction to discriminatory policies. The author attempts to interpret Rhodesian race relations over time within a dynamic and integrated conceptual framework, and tries to correlate changes in attitudes with the demographic and economic characteristics of society. The attempt to quantify the complexities of race relations makes this a rather odd study, and some of the terminology is rather obscure. Another study of white attitudes by the same author is *Flame or lily?: Rhodesian values as defined by the press* (Durban: Alpha Graphic, 1970), in which he used a random sample of 2,639 editorials drawn from the *Rhodesia Herald, Bulawayo Chronicle* and *Umtali Post* as examples of the dominant values of the white élite over time. His interpretation of white society is largely positive, and Africans appear to be perceived as a minority. A similar methodology was used in his study of African attitudes towards the discrimination of the colonial period 'Changing black reaction to white domination', *Rhodesian History*, vol. 5 (1974), p. 67-78. In this article he analysed 2,500 letters to the *Bantu Mirror*, *African Weekly*, and *African Daily News* from the late 1930s to 1970. He believes that resistance to discrimination was correlated with increased urbanization The author was born in Umtali, Rhodesia, and educated in South Africa and the USA.

266 **Inequalities in Zimbabwe.**
Minority Rights Group. London: Minority Rights Group, 1979.
(Report, no. 8).

Published just before independence, this is a really useful guide to conditions in Zimbabwe at this time. The information is concisely expressed, but detailed, and the analysis is supported by well-chosen data. General background information on politics and the population is followed by a discussion of the land issue. The subsequent sections on employment, wages and poverty are particularly useful and stress the impact of the decline in Rhodesian economic performance in the mid-1970s. By 1979 black wage employment was estimated to be 25,000 less than in 1975. Urban living standards for Africans had fallen as families paid fifty per cent more for basics in 1979 compared to 1974, and had not received a corresponding wage increase. In addition refugees from the rural areas added to the economic burden of urban families. The study also considers discrimination and promotion, civil and political liberty, health, education and women's issues. A new edition of this report, written by Christopher Hitchen and David Stephens, was published in 1981. The Minority Rights Group produced a similar overview of racial discrimination in Rhodesia at the beginning of the 1970s, which included strong opposition to the 1971 UK White Paper on a Rhodesian settlement which envisaged keeping a qualified franchise for the African vote: see C. J. Grant, *The Africans' predicament in Rhodesia* (London: Minority Rights Group, 1972).

267 **The cross between Rhodesia and Zimbabwe: racial conflict in Zimbabwe 1962-79.**
Dickson A. Mungazi. New York; Washington, DC: Vantage Press, 1981. 338p.

This study of racial conflict in Zimbabwe focuses on the UDI period. The conflicts between black and white during this time are described and analysed chronologically. Unfortunately the style is rather dull and not very scholarly.

268 **Report of the commission of inquiry into racial discrimination.**
Under the chairmanship of Honourable Sir Vincent Quénet Q.C.
Salisbury: Government Printer, 1976.

This is a fascinating document which provides excellent detailed information on forms of institutionalized racial discrimination in Rhodesia at the height of UDI. The context of the report is most interesting, with the beleaguered government apparently clutching at straws by asking for information on racial discrimination in everyday life which promoted racial friction, and 'taking into account the practical, economic and cultural implications' asking for advice on ending discrimination which was 'no longer considered desirable or necessary'. Given that the basis of the Smith regime was fundamentally racist, this could only lead to a host of recommendations for change, few of which were actually implemented. The report drew on many sources, including memoranda submitted by the public, oral evidence, and information from the security forces. The detailed description of discriminatory legislation provides a useful research tool. Topics covered include land, electoral laws, education, opportunities for employment, the railways, public amenities, passes, and discrimination against African women.

269   **A native policy for Africa: an analysis of the native policy of Southern Rhodesia and an examination of those of the Union and the Colonial Office.**
David Stirling, N. H. Wilson.   Salisbury: Capricorn Africa Society, 1950. 52p.

Stirling founded the Capricorn Africa Society in 1949 and served as its president. The society's aims were theoretically to foster the basis for peaceful coexistence in multi-racial societies in British East and Central Africa, but the policies recommended in this publication were essentially discriminatory against Africans, and moreover were founded on a complete misunderstanding, possibly wilful, of the nature of the impact of colonialism on Rhodesian African socio-economic circumstances. Thus, for example, the authors believed that land alienation had not undermined the African economy and stated that 'the Southern Rhodesian native is in no danger of being compelled to enter the European economy and accept whatever conditions are offered him, as were the peasants driven off the land of England by the Enclosures Act; he has a real freedom of choice, as the South African native has not'. The authors were opposed to Colonial Office native policy because it did not recognize the colour bar and wanted black political representation. They were also against apartheid as practised in South Africa because it discouraged European immigration since whites could not do unskilled work under apartheid. They recommended a two-pyramid policy with two separate systems for the races, and virtually no contact between them, with Europeans protected from competition by strict rates of pay and other conditions based on 'civilized standards': extraordinarily this policy was presented as a liberal concept. The policy document was accompanied by forewords from Huggins, the Rhodesian Prime Minister at the time, Roy Welensky, the future Prime Minister of the Federation of Rhodesia and Nyasaland which the authors greatly supported, and Winterton, the Southern Rhodesian Minister of Native Affairs. Africans attracted to the Capricorn concept included Lawrence Vambe and Leopold Takawira. A later document on the Capricorn society is *The Capricorn declarations: a statement of principles and aims for East and Central Africa* (Salisbury: 1952). An easily accessible paper by David Stirling is 'The Capricorn contract', *African Affairs* (UK), vol. 56 (1957), p. 191-99.

Zimbabwe's inheritance.
See item no. 12.

Birth of a dilemma: the conquest and settlement of Rhodesia.
See item no. 137.

Huggins of Rhodesia: the man and his country.
See item no. 163.

Black and white élites in rural Rhodesia.
See item no. 329.

Race Relations

The premiership of Garfield Todd: racial partnership versus colonial interest, 1953-58.
See item no. 374.

Southern Rhodesia: the price of freedom; a series of nine essays by nine Rhodesians on the present political impasse.
See item no. 379.

Education, race and employment in Rhodesia.
See item no. 719.

Languages

270 **Duramanzi: a Shona-English dictionary.**
D. Dale. Gweru: Mambo Press, 1981. Reprinted 1983, 1989. 249p.
This is a very popular Shona-English dictionary, which is regularly reprinted. Dale has also compiled an English-Shona dictionary, which has also been reprinted many times: *A basic English-Shona dictionary* (Gweru: Mambo Press, 1990). Another useful source is M. Hannan, *Standard Shona dictionary* (Salisbury: Mardon Printers for Rhodesia Literature Bureau, 1972. 2nd ed.).

271 **The Shona companion: a practical guide.**
D. Dale. Gweru: Mambo Press, 1986. 337p. 7th ed.
This very popular guide to the Shona language was originally published in 1968, revised in 1972, and is now in its seventh edition. It provides a useful introduction to the spoken language. Apart from guidance on vocabulary and grammar, it also covers the complex topic of tone. Dale has also provided a shorter, more portable version, *The Shona mini-companion* (Gweru: Mambo Press, 1981), last reprinted in 1990. A very scholarly and detailed study of Shona which is much less accessible but of historical importance is Clement M. Doke's, *A comparative study in Shona phonetics* (Johannesburg: University of the Witwatersrand, 1931). Doke left an outstanding collection of language documents and materials, which are housed in the library of the University of Zimbabwe.

272 **Elements of Shona.**
George Fortune. Harare: Longman Zimbabwe, 1986. 2nd ed. 10th impression. 286p.
This guide to Shona aims to provide people with a gradual approach to obtaining an elementary grasp of the language. It contains forty-two linked lessons, and in this second edition has translations of all dialogues included, plus keys to the various exercises. No attempt is made to cover the subject of tones, and it is pointed out that

97

regular conversation with Shona speakers is necessary to achieve this aspect of the language. A more technical publication by the same author is *An analytical grammar of Shona* (London: Longmans & Green, 1955), which focusses on the grammar of the Zezuru dialect, and is also relevant to the Karanga and Manyika dialects.

273 **Tsumo-shumo: Shona proverbial lore and wisdom.**
Introduced, translated and explained by Mordikai Hamut-ijinei, Albert B. Plangger. Gweru: Mambo Press, 1987. 484p. (Shona Heritage Series, no. 2).

This is the second edition of this book which was first produced in 1971. It has now been revised and enlarged. The Shona language is rich with proverbs, and this book provides a guide to their use, and to their deeper idiomatic and metaphorical meanings.

274 **Figurative language in Shona discourse: a study of the analogical imagination.**
Alec J. C. Pongweni. Gweru: Mambo Press, 1989. 234p.

The author provides an analysis of the use of analogy, metaphors, proverbs and similes in the Shona novels written by Patrick Chakaipa, Charles Mungoshi and I. M. Zvareshe.

275 **What's in a name: a study of Shona nomenclature.**
Alec J. C. Pongweni. Gweru: Mambo Press, 1983. 98p.

The author is Chair of Linguistics at the University of Zimbabwe, and lectures in English and Linguistics there. This short study discusses the social significance and linguistic meaning of various Shona names.

276 **A new Ndebele grammar.**
J. R. Shenk. Bulawayo: Brethren in Christ Church, 1971. 229p.

Ndebele has received far less attention than Shona in terms of guides for people who wish to learn the language. Zulu guides have often been used, but this is not an ideal solution. Apart from this grammar, there are basic lessons designed for English speakers in *Lessons in Ndebele* (Salisbury: Longman Rhodesia, 1974) by James and Pamela Pelling, which has a companion exercise book *The Ndebele work book* (Bulawayo: The authors, 1975). James Pelling has also written *A practical Ndebele dictionary* (Bulawayo: Daystar Publications, 1966; Salisbury: Longman Rhodesia, in association with Rhodesian Literature Bureau, 1971. 2nd ed.), and *Ndebele proverbs and other sayings* (Gwelo: Mambo Press in associations with Rhodesian Literature Bureau, 1975).

Religion

General

277 **The Catholic Church and Zimbabwe 1879-1979.**
Anthony J. Dachs, W. F. Rea. Gweru: Mambo Press, 1979. 260p.
This book was produced to mark the centenary of Catholic endeavours in Southern
Zambezia, and the entry of Jesuits into the area. Nevertheless the book also discusses
the much earlier influence of Portuguese missionaries in the region, so that the period
under review is longer than suggested by the title. The perspective is very much a white
settler one. The 1893 war against the Ndebele is viewed as a positive and necessary
action, and the penultimate chapter on church-state relations, although generally anti-
racist, is rather mooted in its antipathy towards the UDI state. The treatment of the
main topic is chronological covering the establishment of new missions, the
development of schools, and the widening regional impact of Catholicism. See also
A. J. Chennells' 'The Catholic Church and Zimbabwe', *Zambezia*, vol. 8, no. 2
(1980), p. 195-212.

278 **Old and new in Southern Shona independent churches. Vol. 1:
Background and rise of the major movements. Vol. 2: Church growth:
causative factors and recruitment techniques. Vol. 3: Leadership and
fission dynamics.**
Martinus Louis Daneel. The Hague, Paris: Mouton Atlantic
Highlands, New Jersey: Humanities Press; Gweru: Mambo Press, 1971;
1974; 1988. 3 vols. (Monographs under the auspices of the Afrika-
Studiecentrum, Leiden).
Daneel's research into Shona independent churches has been intensive and exhaustive,
and he is the pre-eminent authority on this topic. These three vast volumes are based
on detailed field work. During the 1960s and 1970s Daneel, who was born in Rhodesia
and speaks Shona, was attached to Morgenster Dutch Reformed Mission near
Masvingo, and the research for the first two volumes was carried out during that

period. It was sponsored by the Afrika Studie Centrum Leiden, Holland. The third volume draws on fieldwork carried out from 1984 to 1986, as well as the earlier Dutch-sponsored research. The first volume deals with the beginnings of independent churches, in the context of influences from traditional religion, missionaries and government. Different movements emerged from different historical and socio-economic circumstances, and these are examined. The second volume explains the growth and popularity of these churches, and examines the various methods of recruiting new members adopted by them. It contains discussion of faith healing, prophetism and wizardry. The third volume evaluates the nature of leadership in these movements. The leaders are often called Messianic, but Daneel asserts that iconic leadership is a more apt term. These churches are prone to fission, and he traces this characteristic to the custom of kraal-splitting in traditional Shona society. A fourth volume is scheduled. Other publications by the same author on Shona independent churches are *Zionism and faith-healing in Rhodesia: aspects of African independent churches* (The Hague: Mouton, 1970), translated by V. A. February, 'Shona independent churches and ancestor worship', in *African initiatives in religion* (Nairobi: East African Publishing House; New York: International Publications Service, 1971), edited by David B. Barrett, and *Fambidzano: ecumenical movement of Zimbabwe's independent churches* (Gweru: Mambo Press, 1989). Daneel has been Professor of Missiology at the University of South Africa in Pretoria since 1981.

279 **Spirit and truth. Part 1: religious attitudes and life involvements of 2200 African students.**

Tord Harlin. Uppsala, Sweden: University of Uppsala, 1973.

Based on his PhD thesis for the University of Uppsala, this survey of 2,200 school students and their religious attitudes is rather over-numerical in its approach, but nevertheless contains interesting information. The influence of schools and churches on religious attitudes is evaluated, and the impact of educational level. The students were asked about their feelings about Christianity and traditional religion, but more interestingly they also discussed whether it was acceptable to combine the two, a subject pertinent to the development of some of the independent churches.

280 **The Mazowe Vapostori of Seke: utopianism and tradition in an African church.**

Clive Kileff, Margaret Kileff. In: *The new religions of Africa*. Edited by Jules-Rosette Benetta. Norwood, New Jersey: Ablex Publishers, 1979, p. 127-44.

The Apostolic church, or Va Postori as it is locally termed, has experienced rapid growth in Zimbabwe. This study examines the development of the sect in Seke, just outside of Harare. The authors discuss the important role of women in this church and their traditional ability to act as spirit mediums. Other writings on this religious group are *African apostles: ritual and conversion in the church of Jo-Anne Maranke* (Ithaca, New York: Cornell University Press, 1975), by Jules-Rosette Benetta; 'Religious interdependence among the Budjga Vapostori', in *African initiatives in religion* (Nairobi: East African Publishing House; New York: International Publications Service, 1971, p. 109-21) edited by David B. Barrett. 'The social organization of the Vapostori weMaranke', *Social Analysis*, vol. 7 (1981), p. 24-49, by Angela Cheater; and 'Against alienism: the response of the Zionist and Apostolic African independent "Christian" church movements to European capitalism in Zimbabwe', *Journal of Southern African Affairs*, vol. 1 (1979), p. 5-28, by Madziwanyika Tsomondo.

281 **Islam in Zimbabwe.**
E. C. Mandivenga. Gweru: Mambo Press, 1983. 81p.

This is the only book on Islam in Zimbabwe, where it is very much a minority religion. It is descriptive rather than analytical in approach, and covers the historical background of Islam in Zimbabwe, the major importance of Malawian Muslims who make up the majority of the Muslims in the country, Asian Muslims, and the indigenous Muslims (known as the Varemba) to whom Islam was reintroduced in 1961. Islamic organizations and various aspects of Muslim society and social aspirations are also examined.

282 **God gave growth: history of the Lutheran church in Zimbabwe 1903-80.**
Hugo Söderström. Gweru: Mambo Press; Uppsala, Sweden: Swedish Institute of Missionary Research, 1984. 237p. (Studia Missionalia, no. 40).

This study of one of the smaller mission churches was sponsored by the Swedish Institute of Missionary Research. It covers the growth and development of the Swedish Lutheran missionary influence and establishment of Lutheran churches from their inception to independence. This church was first established in Southern African in Zululand, and in Southern Rhodesia it first located at Mberengwa. Its sphere of influence has not greatly extended beyond that area.

The politics of reconciliation: Zimbabwe's first decade.
See item no. 2.

Gold regions of Southeastern Africa.
See item no. 122.

The Zambesian past: studies in Central African history.
See item no. 160.

A bishop in Smith's Rhodesia: notes from a turbulent octave 1962-70.
See item no. 184.

The Shona peoples: an ethnography of the contemporary Shona, with special reference to their region.
See item no. 235.

The theology of promise: the dynamics of self-reliance.
See item no. 415.

Missionaries and Christianity

283 **Christianity south of the Zambezi. Volume 2.**
Edited by Michael F. C. Bourdillon. Gweru: Mambo Press, 1977. 219p.

This volume is the second in a trilogy of the same title, each with a different editor, and contains the overflow of papers from Volume 1 edited by Anthony J. Dachs (see item 285). The collection of thirteen papers makes a further valuable contribution to the research work on the development and impact of Christianity in Southern Africa. The papers are 'The economics of the Zambezi missions 1580-1759', by W. F. Rea; 'The image of the Ndebele and the 19th century missionary tradition', by A. Chennells; 'African nationalists and the missionaries in Rhodesia' by C. M. Brand; 'Missionary influences in Shona literature', by G. P. Kahari; 'The hymnody of the mission churches among the Shona and Ndebele', by J. Lanherr; 'Kuvora Guva and Christianity', by J. Kumbirai; 'Traditional medicine and Christian beliefs', by G. L. Chavunduka; 'Functional aspects of religious conversion among the Sotho-Tswana', by A. J. Dachs; 'Religious attitudes and life involvements of African students', by Todd Harlin; 'Growth and significance of Shona independent churches', by Martinus L. Daneel; 'Traditional religion and an independent church', by Michael Bourdillon, T. Mashita and M. Glickmann; 'The Korsten basketmakers', by C. M. Dillon-Malone; and 'Trade and early missionaries in Southern Zambezia', by Hoyeni Bhila.

284 **Christianity south of the Zambezi. Volume 1.**
Edited by Anthony J. Dachs. Gwelo: Mambo Press, 1973. 214p.

This is the first in a three-volume series on Christianity south of the Zambezi. The other two volumes were edited respectively by Michael Bourdillon, and Carl Hallencreutz and Ambrose Moyo (see items 283, 299). This first volume contains fifteen papers which cover two general themes: the expansion and growth of missions and their influence on social change; and the role of missionaries and Africans and the growth of African independent churches. The papers are 'Traditional religions in Shona society', by Michael F. C. Bourdillon; 'The initial impact of Christianity on the Shona: the Protestants and the southern Shona', by David N. Beach; 'Missionary activity among the Ndebele and Kalanga' by N. M. B. Bhebe; 'Christian missionary enterprise and Sotho-Tswana societies in the 19th century', by Anthony J. Dachs; 'The influence of the Wesleyan-Methodist missionaries in southern Rhodesia 1891-1923' by C. J. M. Zvobgo; 'Nenguwo Training Institution and the first Shona teachers' by W. R. Peaden; 'Missionary contribution to early education in Rhodesia', by N. D. Atkinson; 'The contribution of the London Missionary Society to African education in Ndebeleland' by D. G. H. Flood; 'Medicine and the Christian missionaries in Rhdoesia 1857-1930' by Michael Gelfand; 'African religious practices and Christianity among the Shona people', by Rev. S. K. Madziyire; 'Shona marriage and the Christian churches', by Rev. R. P. Hatendi; 'African customs connected with the burial of the dead in Rhodesia' by Rev. E. B. Magava; 'Shona independent churches in a rural society', by Martinus Daneel; 'Teaching the laity: some problems of the Christian churches in Rhodesia' by T. McLoughlin; and 'The Catholic church and the race conflict in Rhodesia', by Dieter D. Scholz.

285 **The new crusaders: Christianity and the new right in Southern Africa.**
Paul Gifford. London; Concord, Massachusetts: Pluto Press, 1991. 131p.

Gifford, who lectured in the department of religious studies at the University of Zimbabwe, and is now a consultant with the All African Conference of Churches in Nairobi, provides a detailed analysis of the rise of fundamentalist right-wing churches in Southern Africa. The third of four chapters is devoted to sociological and historical analysis of the religious right in Zimbabwe, which has flourished since 1982. The links to the roots of this movement in the southern United States of America are emphasized. Theological contrasts are made with the liberation theology of some Latin American churches, and that of Zimbabwean individuals such as Canaan Banana. The organizations in Zimbabwe which Gifford discusses are Campus Crusade, Youth with a

Mission, Full Gospel Businessmen's Fellowship International (FGBFI), Jimmy Swaggart ministries, World Vision International, Christ for all Nations, Rheme Bible Church, and the Moonies.

286   Modumede Moleli: teacher, evangelist and martyr to charity: Mashonaland 1892-96.
Reverend Brandon Graaff.   Gweru: Mambo Press, 1988. 135p.

Moleli was a South African Sotho man who volunteered for missionary work in Mashonaland in 1892. He taught at the Methodist mission forty-five miles south-east of Salsbury, which later became the Waddilove Institution. This is the first published account of his mission and his murder during the Shona rebellion of 1896, when he attempted to aid a dying white man. A better-known African missionary who was also killed during the Shona revolt was Bernard Mizeki. The published account of his mission and subsequent death is more strongly Eurocentric in its perspective than Graaff's publication. See Jean Farrant, *Mashonaland martyr: Bernard Mizeki and the pioneer church* (Cape Town: Oxford University Press, 1966) which has been abridged by Margaret Snell as *Bernard Mizeki of Zimbabwe* (Gweru: Mambo Press, 1986).

287   The clash of cultures: Christian missionaries and the Shona of Rhodesia.
Geoffrey Z. Kapenzi.   Washington, DC: University Press of America, 1979. 104p. bibliog.

This study of tensions between Christian missionaries and Shona culture was written by the son of a Shona Methodist minister. Particular themes are the cultural clashes which emerged from specific missionary educational practices, and consideration of how Christianity might be promoted in a way which would fit better with Shona aspirations. See also Chengetai J. M. Zvobgo, 'Shona and Ndebele responses to Christianity in Southern Rhodesia 1897-1914', *Journal of Religion in Africa*, vol. 8 (1976), p. 41-51.

288   Missions in Southern Rhodesia.
Compiled by Paul S. King.   Cape Town: Inyati Centenary Trust, 1959. 80p.

This is a valuable, though rare, reference for checking details of the activities and locations of different missions in Zimbabwe before 1959. It is essentially a descriptive listing, with information contributed by many different authors. Missions and missionaries have an extensive literature (see items 282, 300, 304), and missionary writings are an important source of historical information (see for example item 138). Other relevant writings include Iris Clinton in *These vessels: the story of Inyati, 1859-1959* (Bulawayo: Stuart Manning, 1959) and *Hope Fountain story: a tale of one hundred years* (Gwelo: Mambo Press, 1969); Henry St John Evans, *The Church in Southern Rhodesia* (London: Society for the Promotion of Christian Knowledge, 1945); Clarence Thorpe, *Limpopo to Zambezi: sixty years of Methodism in Southern Rhodesia* (London: Cargate Press, 1951).

289   Christianity and the Shona.
Marshall W. Murphree.   London: Athlone Press; Atlantic Highlands, New Jersey: Humanities Press, 1969. 200p.

Based on fieldwork in Mutoko communal land in the early 1960s, this is the most extensive single study on the impact of Christianity on the Shona, and their responses to the new religion. Murphree argues that several aspects of Shona traditional religion enhanced their acceptance of the central themes of Christianity. The book draws on his 1965 doctoral thesis for the University of London.

290 The missionary factor in Southern Rhodesia.

William Francis Rea. Salisbury: Historical Association of Rhodesia and Nyasaland, 1962. 11p. bibliog. (Local Series, no. 7).

This is a short and straightforward account of Rhodesia's early missionaries, from the 16th century to 1900. It focusses on the missionaries' proselytizing role, rather than their medical impact. Rea has also written specifically on the role of Portuguese missionaries in the region, and his University of London doctorate was on this topic. On Silveira, a Portuguese missionary who visited Rhodesia in the 16th century and was martyred at the kingdom of Monomotapa, see Rea's *Gonçala da Silveira: a life*, (Salisbury: Rhodesiana Publications, 1961. [Publications, no. 6]). Also on the Portuguese missionary impact, see Hugh T. Tracey's, 'Antonio Fernandes: Rhodesia's first pioneer', *Rhodesiana*, vol. 19 (1968), p. 1-27.

291 Mainstream Christianity to 1980 in Malawi, Zambia and Zimbabwe.

J. Weller, Ian Linden. Gweru: Mambo Press, 1984. 224p. bibliog.

This is a general introductory text to the study of Christian religion in Central Africa, which was originally written as a text for theology students studying by correspondence. It was used for some years in Malawi before this published edition became available, which incorporated relevant events surrounding Zimbabwe's independence. The text discusses the Jesuit missions on the Zambezi from 1560-1700 and other pre-colonial missions, but its main focus is an examination of mainstream denominations in the three countries from the colonial period to 1980. For Zimbabwe the discussion centres on the Anglican, Roman Catholic and Methodist churches. Finally there is an evaluation of the role of the church in national affairs. Christian history in Zimbabwe is also treated in contributions to *Themes in the Christian history of Central Africa* (Berkeley: University of California Press, 1975), edited by Terence O. Ranger and John Waller.

292 The Wesleyan Methodist missions in Zimbabwe, 1891-1945.

Chengetai J. M. Zvobgo. Harare: University of Zimbabwe Publications, 1991. 169p. bibliog. (Supplement to *Zambezia*).

This is a scholarly account of the establishment and growth of Wesleyan Methodist missions up to the Second World War.

Gold regions of Southeastern Africa.
See item no. 122 (Silver Series: vol. 24).

The way of the white fields in Rhodesia: a survey of Christian enterprise in Northern and Southern Rhodesia.
See item no. 157.

Christianity and traditional religion in western Zimbabwe 1859-1923.
See item no. 293.

Godly medicine in Zimbabwe: a history of its medical missions.
See item no. 335.

Indigenous religious beliefs

293 Christianity and traditional religion in western Zimbabwe 1859-1923.
Ngwabi M. B. Bhebe. London: Longman, 1979. 190p.

Belying the title this book begins with an examination of the dynamics of traditional religion among the Ndebele in western Zimbabwe before 1859, and the impact of the first missionaries. Bhebe argues that previous views on traditional religions tended to view them as largely static, and he challenges this perspective, demonstrating how religion in this region adapted to changing environmental and socio-political circumstances. The mixing of groups such as the Shona, Ndebele and Sotho led to religious changes, and Bhebe enters into the debate about the Ndebele and the Mwari cult (see items no. 114, 139, 160, 295), arguing that the Ndebele did adopt parts of the cult into their religious practices. When Christian influences entered the region they were at first resisted, but by the early colonial period the Ndebele had begun to embrace Christianity, although it was usually coloured by local beliefs and practices, portending the later growth of independent churches.

294 Religion and authority in a Korekore community.
Michael F. C. Bourdillon. *Africa* (London), vol. 49, no. 2 (1979), p. 172-81.

This study, based on field research amongst the Korekore, examines the relationship between religion and leadership.

295 The God of the Matopo Hills: an essay on the Mwari cult in Rhodesia.
Marthinus Louis Daneel. The Hague: Mouton; Atlantic Highlands, New Jersey: Humanities Press, 1970. 95p.

Mwari, the God of the Matopo Hills in southern Zimbabwe, is of key significance to Shona religion, and also influential in Ndebele religion. Mwari, and the religious practices of the cult, have been extensively analysed by academics from various disciplines. In addition the role of the Mwari cult in promoting resistance to colonial oppression has been hotly debated (see for example items 114, 123, 139, 160). This was the first full-length analysis of the cult. Other studies since include David Beach, 'Great Zimbabwe as a Mwari-cult centre', *Rhodesian Prehistory*, vol. 11 (Dec. 1973); Terence Ranger, 'The meaning of Mwari', *Rhodesian History*, vol. 5 (1974), p. 5-17; and R. M. G. Mtetwa, 'The relationship between the Gutu dynasty and the Mwari cult in the nineteenth century', *Rhodesian History,* vol. 6 (1976), p. 89-95.

296 Spirits of protest: spirit-mediums and the articulation of consensus among the Zezuru of Southern Rhodesia (Zimbabwe).
Peter Fry. Cambridge, England; New York: Cambridge University Press, 1976. 145p. (Cambridge Studies in Social Anthropology, no. 14).

Spirit mediums, men or women possessed by important ancestral spirits, have always been, and remain central to traditional religious beliefs in Zimbabwe. When possessed by their spirit they enter a trance and become an oracle for the spirit to communicate to the living. The role of spirit mediums in articulating the needs and perceptions of their society in Zimbabwe has attracted much academic attention, particularly in regard to their role in political protest in the 19th and 20th centuries (see items 114 and 139). This study is an important example of this genre, although its focus is not specifically political. The spirit mediums under examination were from Chihota communal land, and the research was carried out in the early 1960s. Fry's analysis contends that the mediums played a very significant political role, and are important influences on local moral attitudes. The analysis includes discussion of the decline of Christianity in Chihota as more people turned to the spirit mediums as a form of resistance to European domination. The author was a lecturer in anthropology at the Universidade Estadual de Campinas, Sao Paulo, Brazil. Also on the social role of spirit mediums see G. Kingsley Garbett's 'Spirit mediums as mediators in Korekore society', in *Spirit mediumship and society in Africa*, edited by John H. Beattie and John Middleton (London: Routledge & Kegan Paul; New York: Africana Publishing House; Holmes & Meier, 1969).

297 **Confessions of a wizard: a critical examination of the belief system of a people based mainly on personal experience.**
Masotsha Hove. Gweru: Mambo Press, 1985. 191p.

This curious book is the verbatim account of a wizard named Masesesese, recorded and translated by Hove. Many bizarre and inexplicable incidents are related, and Hove claims that, with one exception, all are true.

298 **Guardians of the land: essays on Central African territorial cults.**
Edited by J. M. Schoffeleers, foreword by Terence O. Ranger. Gweru: Mambo Press, 1979. 315p. (Zambeziana Series on Culture and Society in Central Africa, no. 5).

A territorial cult is a cult whose constituency is territorial groups identified by common occupation of a particular land area, rather than membership deriving from ethnicity or kinship. This collection of essays on such cults in Central Africa originated in a conference in Lusaka in 1972, and was funded as one of a series on African religions supported by the Ford Foundation. The issues addressed by territorial cults are of more than just religious significance, since they also have an important bearing on environmental management. The various case studies presented examine such issues as the social interpretation of the environmental process, or African philosophies of the earth. Topics considered include the production and distribution of food, the protection of natural resources, and the control of migration. The African belief is that the management of nature depends on the correct management and control of human society, and thus that social problems can lead to environmental degradation. There are four papers on Zimbabwe: 'The cults of Dzivaguru and Karuva amongst the Northeastern Shona people' by Michael Bourdillon; 'Transformations of the Musika vanhu territorial cult in Rhodesia' by J. K. Rennie; 'The Ndebele and Mwari before 1893: a religious conquest of the conquerors by the vanquished', by N. M. B. Bhebe; and 'An organized model of the Mwari shrines' by J. M. Schoffeleers and R. Mwanza.

The genuine Shona: survival values of an African culture.
See item no. 240.

Church and state

299 **Church and state in Zimbabwe. Volume 3: Christianity south of the Zambezi.**
Edited by Carl F. Hallencreutz, Ambrose Moyo. Gweru: Mambo Press, 1988. 510p. maps. bibliog.

The genesis of this third volume on Christianity south of the Zambezi is different from that of the other two (see items 283, 284). It grew out of a research project of the Department of Religious Studies at the University of Zimbabwe, which held a series of research seminars and two special workshops on religious themes in 1986. The main focus of the thirteen contributions is the interaction between the church and the state in Zimbabwe during UDI and the independence era. Specific mention is made in the editorial preface of Terence Ranger's pioneering, but unpublished, work on this topic, and the first paper, 'The African franchise question: an aspect of church-state relations in colonial Zimbabwe, 1921-72' by C. J. M. Zvobgo, attempts to update that work and place it in a wider context. The papers are divided into three categories. The first, entitled 'Towards independence' focuses on church-state relationships during the UDI period. The contributions are: 'A council in crossfire, ZCC 1964-80' by Carl Hallencreutz; 'Anglican church and state from UDI in 1965 until the independence of Zimbabwe in 1980', by M. Lapsley; 'Refugees and religion in the camps in Mozambique and Zambia during Zimbabwe's liberation struggle', by J. Mclaughlin; 'Rural Christians and the Zimbabwe liberation war: a case study', by Michael Bourdillon and P. Gundani; and 'The evangelical Lutheran Church in Zimbabwe and the war of liberation 1975-80', by N. M. Bhebe. The second section, entitled 'Independent Zimbabwe', considers church-state relationships after 1980. The papers are: 'Religion and political thought in independent Zimbabwe', by A. M. Moyo; 'The Catholic church and national development in independent Zimbabwe', by P. Gundani; 'Ecumenical challenge in independent Zimbabwe', by Carl Hallencreutz; 'Church and state in Zimbabwe: an evangelical appraisal', by S. M. Bhebhe; 'Anglican integration', by J. Weller; 'Church-state relations in the Dutch Reformed Church (NGK) in Zimbabwe', by F. Maritz; and 'Some contemporary trends in independent churches in Zimbabwe: the cases of ZCC (Zimbabwe Christian Church) and AACJM (Joanne Maranke's Vapostori)', by D. Mackay and P. Motsi. The third section examines theological dimensions of the churches' response to the state. The paper are 'Theological perspectives on development in Zimbabwe', by A. M. Moyo; 'Mishpat: a basis for social justice', by T. M. Mafico; 'The role of the President: the theology of Canaan S. Banana', by Paul Gifford; 'Human rights: a motive for mission', by A. Plangger; 'The priorities of the Zimbabwe Catholic Bishops' Conference since independence', by P. Mutume; and 'Christianity and scientific socialism in Zimbabwe', by S. Bakere. Professor Carl Hallencreutz, from the University of Uppsala, Sweden, was on research leave based at the Department of Religious Studies at the University of Zimbabwe whilst the research project culminating in this book was being conducted. Ambrose Moyo is a lecturer in Traditional Religion in the same department.

300 **Neutrality or co-option: the Anglican church and the state from 1964 until the independence of Zimbabwe.**
Michael Lapsley. Gweru: Mambo Press, 1986. (Mambo Occasional Papers, Missio-pastoral Series, no. 16).

The majority of white settlers were affiliated to the Anglican church, and its attitudes to UDI and the serious issues of social and political justice which it raised were ambiguous. In this study, Lapsley, a member of the Society of Sacred Mission, examines the church's role in UDI, and the attempts of the state to co-opt Anglican support for the white settler position.

301 The Catholic church and the struggle for Zimbabwe.
Ian Linden. London: Longman, 1980. 310p.

This is an academic and critical study of the role of the Catholic church during the independence struggle. Originally published in Germany as *Church and state in Rhodesia 1959-79* (Munich: Kaiser; Mainz, Germany: Matthias-Grünewald-Verlag, 1979) its approach is rather different from the essentially factual studies on a similar theme by Father H. Randolph (see item 303). Linden argues that the international capitalist system wanted the church in Rhodesia to minister to the state, and sustain 'bourgeois Christian civilization'. However this met with resistance from the church, which did not perceive this as its role. He analyses Catholic attitudes to civil rights and African nationalism in Rhodesia over twenty years, and discusses its role in the liberation struggle, including its contacts with the guerillas and involvement in international diplomacy.

302 Church and politics: from theology to a case history of Zimbabwe.
Enda Mcdonagh. Notre Dame, Indiana: University of Notre Dame Press, 1980. 177p. bibliog. (Also published as *The demands of simple justice. A study of the church, politics and violence with special reference to Zimbabwe* [Dublin: Gill & Macmillan, 1980]).

Mcdonagh was asked by Catholics in Zimbabwe to advise theologically on how they should deal with the conflicting moral problems posed by the liberation struggle and the violence of the civil war. His study combines consideration of the church and the state during the UDI period, with theological considerations about the justice of the guerilla war, and the issue of violence.

303 Dawn in Zimbabwe: the Catholic church in the New Order.
R. H. Randolph. Gweru: Mambo Press, 1985. 235p. (Mambo Occasional Paper, Missio-pastoral Series, no. 13).

Primarily of interest to researchers on Catholicism in Zimbabwe, this volume is subtitled '*A report on the activities of the Catholic Church in Zimbabwe for the five years 1977-81*'. Every five years the Diocesan bishops visit Rome to report on the areas under their authority, and these reports are summarized here. The book also contains background material on politics and the struggle for independence, with three historical chapters on UDI, the war for liberation, and a brief overview of missionary endeavours in Zimbabwe from 1879-1981. This is a sequel to Randolph's *Report to Rome* (Gweru: Mambo Press, 1978) which covered the years 1972-76. He also produced a study of church-state relationships in the early UDI period, *Church and the state in Rhodesia 1969-71: a Catholic view* (Gweru, Mambo Press, 1971).

304 State and church in Southern Rhodesia, 1919-1939.
Terence O. Ranger. Salisbury: Historical Association of Rhodesia and Nyasaland, 1961. 28p. (Local Series, no. 4).

Ranger provides a critical and comparative analysis of three missionaries in early Southern Rhodesia: John White, Arthur Shearly Cripps and C. Kadabe. Another major biographical study of John White is *John White of Mashonaland* (London:

Hodder & Stoughton, 1935. Reprinted, Westport, Connecticut: Negro Universities Press), by Charles F. Andrews. The life of Cripps, a saintly man who was revered by his African congregation, is covered by Douglas V. Steere in *God's irregular: Arthur Shearly Cripps* (London: Society for the Propagation of Christian Knowledge, 1973). He was a genuine advocate of land segregation as a means of protecting the African population's land rights from the commercial power of Europeans, little suspecting the disastrous ends to which such a policy could be put. His views on this are found in his book *An Africa for Africans: a plea on behalf of territorial segregation areas and of their freedom in a South African colony* (London: Longmans, Green, 1927. Reprinted, Westport, Connecticut: Negro Universities Press).

Social Conditions

General

305 **Social change in a Shona ward.**
Gordon L. Chavunduka. Salisbury: Department of Sociology,
University of Rhodesia, 1970. 56p. (Occasional Paper, no. 4).

This study of rural social change is particularly valuable because it is part of a long-term study. Chavunduka studied six villages near the Roman Catholic mission of Musami about forty-eight miles from Harare, which had originally been surveyed in 1948 by Dr. B. Bernardi. This study was published as *The social structure of the kraal among the Zezuru* (Cape Town: School of African Studies, University of Cape Town, 1950). The villages were also studied by G. Kingsley Garbett in the late 1950s and described in his *Growth and change in a Shona ward* (Salisbury: University College of Rhodesia and Nyasaland, Department of African Studies, 1960. [Occasional paper, no. 1]). This final study by Chavunduka provides evidence of previously identified trends continuing, but also of some changes in social direction. The three studies covered a wide variety of topics including marriage, kinship, migration patterns, and leadership succession and provide a wealth of detailed socio-cultural and economic statistics on the villages' inhabitants. Amongst other changes, by 1970 marital instability had increased, polygny had decreased, and migration was becoming more crucial as married men were absent for longer periods.

306 **Rural housing programmes in Zimbabwe: a contribution to social development.**
M. Chenga. *Journal of Social Development in Africa*, vol. 1, no. 1 (1986), p. 43-47.

Urban housing is usually the main priority of housing programmes in developing countries and Zimbabwe is no exception. In this article the author considers government policy towards rural housing, and the programmes that exist. The positive effects of enhancing the quality of rural housing are stressed.

110

307 **Lobola: the pros and cons.**
Aeneas Chigwedere. Harare: Books for Africa, 1982. 59p.

Lobola, or brideprice, is a subject which is often subjected to public scrutiny in Zimbabwe, and it arouses fierce sentiments on both sides. This short treatise, despite its title, is basically a plea for its retention in a 'purified' form. Many of the arguments put forward are rather old-fashioned and the author holds a traditional view of the status of women, but his ideas are probably representative of the views of a large number of Zimbabwean men. The author maintains that lobola's role in keeping marriages together is an important advantage, and also believes that it provides women with respect from their husbands. Much useful information on how lobola operates is presented. The discussion of matrilineal marriages, as practised in Malawi where no brideprice is paid, is however confused in many details. A detailed critique of Chigwedere's views is found in Moses Chinyenze's 'A critique of Chigwedere's book "Lobola: the pros and cons" in relation to the emancipation of women in Zimbabwe', *Zimbabwe Law Review*, vol. 1 & 2 (1983-4), p. 229-50. Chinyenze puts a strong case for the abolition of lobola as a precondition for the real emancipation of women.

308 **The economics of African old age subsistence in Rhodesia.**
Duncan G. Clarke. Gwelo: Mambo Press, [1977]. 72p. (Mambo Occasional Papers, Socio-Economic Series, no. 10).

In this report, commissioned by the local School of Social Work, Clarke addresses the problems faced by elderly Africans with no or inadequate pensions. He provides a review of the arrangements which existed in the mid-1970s for the elderly, and identifies trends in provision. The traditional role of kinship in providing security is examined, as well as demographic change which means that there are more elderly people to care for. The nature and problems of pensions for Africans, and contemporary policies affecting social security for the elderly in different sectors of the rural and urban economy are identified, including the racist nature of pension schemes at the time. Also see Gordon L. Chavunduka, 'Changing life goals and life styles of African urban workers with special reference to pension schemes', *Rhodesian Journal of Economics*, vol. 10, no. 4 (1976), p. 177-83. The aged in the rural areas are discussed in J. Hampson, 'Marginalisation and the rural elderly: a Shona case study', *Journal of Social Development in Africa*, vol. 5, no. 2 (1990), p. 5-23.

309 **Old age: a study of aging in Zimbabwe.**
Joe Hampson. Gweru: Mambo Press, 1982. 96p. (Mambo Occasional Papers, Socio-Economic Series, no. 16).

This survey of ageing amongst Africans in Zimbabwe was published in recognition of the Year of the Aged in 1982. Demographic and cultural issues are examined, and the author emphasizes the problems which arise from a lack of welfare provision for this sector of the population in a society where the influence of modernization is strong, and the traditional roles of the elderly are undermined. The importance of maintaining access to rural land as a safeguard against old age for urban migrants is stressed. An evaluation is made of proposals for a 'pay-as-you-go' pension scheme which might address the needs of people forced to move in and out of the wage sector during their working lives.

310 **Community-supportive crisis management in Zimbabwe.**
R. Laing. *Refugee Participation Network*, vol. 8, (1990), p. 15-16.

There are thousands of Mozambican refugees in eastern Zimbabwe. The help given to the Zimbabwean liberation struggle by Mozambique means that some Zimbabweans feel that assisting these refugees is small recompense for that vital assistance, but unfortunately human rights abuses by the Zimbabwean army have occurred, in part as response to attacks in the area by Renamo, who are believed to have infiltrated the refugee camps. There is very little published on the refugees however, although there are many unpublished reports. A general study, by Naison Mutizwa-Mangiza and K. H. Wekwete is available in *An evaluation of the Mozambican refugee camp programme* (Harare: HelpAge, 1988), although this work may be difficult to obtain. The Refugee Studies Programme in Oxford, England has a useful library which contains much of the relevant unpublished material.

311 **African aged in town.**
Olivia N. Muchena.   Harare: School of Social Work, 1978.

This brief study examines from a sociological viewpoint the growing numbers of elderly Africans permanently living in urban areas, and the problems they face in maintaining themselves. See also item no. 7 by Nyanguru and Peil.

312 **Rural water supply and sanitation in Zimbabwe: recent policy developments.**
Naison Mutizwa-Mangiza.   Harare: Department of Rural and Urban Planning, University of Zimbabwe, 1988. 25p. (Department of Rural and Urban Planning Occasional Papers, no. 14).

Zimbabwe has developed some excellent appropriate technology for improving rural water and sanitation, and has had much success in implementing these improvements in rural areas. This short paper provides an overview of policies towards this sector since independence. The technologies used are described in Peter Morgan, *Rural water supplies and sanitation* (Harare: Blair Research Laboratory, Ministry of Health, 1990).

313 **Black and white: the 'perils of sex' in colonial Zimbabwe.**
John Pape.   *Journal of Southern African Studies*, vol. 16, no. 4 (1991), p. 699-720.

In this interesting historical study Pape examines sexual relations between the races during the colonial period, and discusses the myths and obsessions which influenced perceptions of sex between black men and white women.

314 **African marriage in Zimbabwe and the impact of Christianity.**
Anna Katherina Hildegard Weinrich.   Gweru: Mambo Press, 1982. 212p. (Zambeziana Series on Culture and Society in Central Africa, no. 13).

This study is based on a major survey conducted by the author on behalf of the major Christian churches in Zimbabwe which were concerned because few Africans tended to marry in church. The fieldwork was conducted from 1972-75, and consisted of a questionnaire completed by 5,662 couples, combined with participant observation. The sample was widely drawn, covering twenty-one communities from Tribal Trust Lands, urban areas, Native Purchase Areas, mining centres and comercial farms. Most ethnic groups were represented. The author's analysis relates marriage patterns to prevailing modes of production. She considers a range of issues including the nature of traditional marriages, changes in African marriage under capitalism, fertility, polygamy and divorce. Weinrich's study has been criticized for methodological shortcomings by Joan May, 'African marriage in Zimbabwe: essay review', *Zambezia*, vol. 11, no. 2 (1983), p. 139-42. A short paper on the dilemmas faced by Shona and Ndebele Christians over the issue of polygyny is discussed in Gordon Chavunduka, 'Polygny among urban Shona and Ndebele Christians', *NADA*, vol. 12, no. 1 (1979), p. 10-20. Weinrich, one of the most significant sociologists in pre-independence Zimbabwe, is a nun and is also known as Sister Mary Aquina. She was a senior lecturer in sociology at the University of Rhodesia and published extensively on social, religious, ethnographic and socio-economic issues. She left Rhodesia in protest in 1975 and went on to become Professor of Social Anthropology at the University of Dar es Salaam in Tanzania.

315 **Knowledge about AIDS and self-reported sexual behaviour among adults in Bulawayo.**
D. J. Wilson, (et al.). *Central African Journal of Medicine*, vol. 34, no. 5 (1988), p. 95-97.

AIDS is a serious problem in Zimbabwe, although until well into the 1980s the government tried to hide the scale of infection. Objective analysis and good data on the topic can be hard to find. Journalistic reports frequently exaggerate, or make spurious projections from data from non-representative samples. This article deals with a notoriously difficult topic to research. The major finding that more than fifty per cent of those surveyed did not know that condoms could reduce infection rates obviously suggests that public education on the topic needs to be more effective. A brief overview of available estimates and data is A. S. Latif, G. Sikipa and J. Emmanuel, 'Aids update: Zimbabwe', *Zimbabwe Science News*, vol. 21, no. 9/10 (1987), p. 129-30.

316 **Unwanted pregnancies and baby dumping: whose problem?**
Women's Action Group. Harare: Women's Action Group, [1985]. 23p.

In Zimbabwe the topics of unwanted pregnancies, usually amongst teenagers, and baby dumping in urban areas, are highly publicized, and cause great public concern. They are frequently addressed in newspaper editorials and magazine articles, but this is the only publication specifically on these issues. It contains the report on the proceedings of a workshop held by the Women's Action Group in October, 1985. The discussion was wide-ranging and addressed the causes of these problems, government policies which affect them, the legal position and the issue of abortion. The report shows that women were concerned about men evading their responsibilities for the children they had fathered. The low rate of adoption because of traditional beliefs about blood ties and the ancestral spirits is also addressed. Two other workshops by the Women's Action Group on topics of particular concern to women have also resulted in reports. These are *Women of Zimbabwe speak out*, held in May, 1984, which addressed a range of issues from marriage and lobola, to land rights, inheritance and opportunities in education, and *Women at work*, held in January 1985, which focussed on working conditions, sexual harrasssment, training opportunities and pay.

Zimbabwe since independence: a people's assessment.
See item no. 7.

Marriage, perversion and power: the construction of moral discourse in Southern Rhodesia 1894-1930.
See item no. 353.

Black industrial workers in Rhodesia: general problems of low pay.
See item no. 681.

Food and nutrition

317 **Diet and tradition in an African culture.**
Michael Gelfand. Edinburgh, London: E. & S. Livingstone; London: Longman, 1971. 248p.
Gelfand wrote on many aspects of Shona culture, and in this volume he turns to the subject of food and its cultural significance. He covers the preparation of food and its ritual value, and describes the diet which contains many wild foods, as well as cultivars, and includes products from trees, shrubs, roots and insects. The staple is maize, which combined with other basics such as sorghum, millet, rice, cassava and bread make up to eighty per cent of calorific intake.

318 **The socioeconomics of nutrition under stressful conditions: a study of resettlement and drought in Zimbabwe.**
Bill H. Kinsey. Harare: Centre for Applied Social Sciences, University of Zimbabwe, 1986. 55p.
Using case study material from three resettlement areas, Kinsey discusses the causes of nutritional problems amongst their populations. Drought is one of the contributing factors, and a number of other social and economic causes of malnutrition are assessed. The author contends that relocation itself has not caused malnutrition.

319 **Drought and drought relief in southern Zimbabwe.**
Roger Leys. In: *World recession and the food crisis in Africa.* Edited by Peter Lawrence. London: James Currey with Review of African Political Economy, 1986, p. 258-74.
This paper discusses the results of a research study in four villages in Masvingo province which attempted to assess the impact of the provision of drought relief in the early 1980s. The operation of the relief programme is explained, and it is shown to have been generally successful. Local ZANU (PF) party structures are shown to have played a major role. The drought is shown to have exacerbated existing social differentiation, between the rural 'salatariat' and others. There was never a shortage of food in local stores, so it is argued that the food entitlement approach is the most relevant for the study of food issues in Zimbabwe's communal areas during droughts.

320 **Socioeconomic factors associated with child health and nutrition in peri-urban Zimbabwe.**
Robert Mazur, David Sanders. *Ecology of Food and Nutrition*, vol. 22, no. 1 (1988), p. 19-34.

This analysis of child nutrition is based on research conducted in 1985 in Chitungwiza, Harare's dormitory town. The survey focussed on the under-fives, and their nutritional status is correlated with various indices of their families' social and economic status to assess which factors have most influence on their diet. Another survey of urban nutrition is S. Mathe (et al.), 'Nutritional status of an urban community in Zimbabwe', *Central African Journal of Medicine*, vol. 31, no. 3 (1985), p. 59-62.

321 **The development of food supplies to Salisbury (Harare).**
Paul Mosley. In: *Feeding African cities: studies in regional social history*. Edited by Jane Guyer. Manchester, England: Manchester University Press for the International African Institute, 1987, p. 203-224.

In this essay Mosley presents evidence to show how the interests of food producers have historically dominated those of urban food consumers, resulting in the urban population paying relatively high prices for its food. The food products surveyed are maize, groundnuts, beef, dairy products, fruit and vegetables. The policies pursued often meant that local prices exceeded the export price. This is in contrast to the normal African pattern, where farmers have been underpaid in order to keep urban food prices low. The situation is argued to have continued after independence, although it originated as a means of protecting inefficient white farmers. A more detailed study of post-independence food pricing is found in item 613. On food production and distribution systems within Harare see David Drakakis-Smith (item 526).

322 **The root causes of hunger in Zimbabwe: an overview of the nature, causes and effects of hunger and strategies to combat hunger.**
S. Moyo, N. Moyo, R. Lowenson. Harare: Zimbabwe Institute of Development Studies, 1985. 99p.

This paper provides an excellent overview of hunger issues, and contains sections on the role in combatting hunger played by women's organizations, churches and community-based strategies. The authors also show how co-operatives, which it was hoped would increase food security for their members, had failed to meet expectations. On malnutrition see David Sanders, 'The origins of malnutrition in Zimbabwe', *Central African Journal of Medicine*, vol. 28, no. 8 (1982). See also T. Takavarasha, 'The relationship between food, agriculture and nutritional policies in Zimbabwe', *Zimbabwe Science News*, vol. 21, no. 11/12 (1987), p. 139-40, in which it is argued that the main cause of malnutrition is the conflict between growing cash crops and food crops.

Social Conditions. Food and nutrition

323 **Food security for Southern Africa.**
Edited by Mandivamba Rukuni, Carl K. Eicher. Harare: University
of Zimbabwe and Michigan State University Food Security Project,
Department of Agriculture, Economics and Extension, University of
Zimbabwe, 1987. 406p.

In this volume the papers are mainly drawn from the second annual conference on
food security research in Southern Africa held at the University of Zimbabwe, which
was part of a major collaborative research venture between the Department of
Agriculture and Michigan State University. Part three of the volume consists of six
chapters on food security in Zimbabwe; there are also two papers on low rainfall areas
in Zimbabwe in part four, and a paper on the role of the Grain Marketing Board in
serving Zimbabwe's communal farmers. The annual proceedings of this conference
have been regularly published and contain many very useful papers on Zimbabwean
food security issues. The third annual conference proceedings, entitled *Southern
Africa: food security policy options* (Harare: Department of Agriculture, Economics
and Extension, University of Zimbabwe, 1988), edited by Mandivamba Rukuni and
Richard Bernstein, contain nine chapters on Zimbabwe which consider the effect on
food security of market liberation and the ending of subsidies, the growth of
smallholder maize production, food insecurity in low rainfall areas, smallholder maize
production 1979-85, sorghum research for commercial farmers, water use efficiency on
commercial wheat farms, the economics of increasing wheat production, wheat policy
options, and the external grain trade. The fourth conference produced *Household and
national food security in Southern Africa* (Harare: Department of Agriculture,
Economics and Extension, University of Zimbabwe, 1989), edited by Godfrey D.
Mudimu and Richard Bernstein. This includes six articles on Zimbabwe which cover
grain retention and consumption among rural households, pan-territorial and pan-
seasonal maize pricing, small grain markets, household strategies in low rainfall areas,
exchange rate overvaluation and agricultural performance, and increasing food access
and nutrition. The fifth conference proceedings are published as *Food security policies
in the SADCC region* (Harare: Department of Agriculture, Economics and Extension,
University of Zimbabwe, 1989), edited by Mandivamba Rukuni, Godfrey Mudimu and
Thomas S. Jayne. The four papers specifically on Zimbabwe are on food security issues
and challenges for the 1990s, grain market reliability and growth, household income
and food production and marketing in low-rainfall areas, and a case study of
horticultural marketing. All these volumes also contain regional papers which are of
relevance to Zimbabwe. The 1990 proceedings are *Food, security policies in the
SADCC region*, (Harare: Department of Agriculture, Economics and Extension,
University of Zimbabwe, 1990) edited by Mankdikamba Rukuni (et al.).

324 **The food problem.**
Vincent Tickner. Catholic Institute for International Relations, 1979.
76p. (From Rhodesia to Zimbabwe, no. 8).

This volume in the CIIR's *From Rhodesia to Zimbabwe* series, which provided
overviews and policy proposals for a wide variety of Zimbabwe's economic and social
sectors, focusses on food issues. Its comprehensive and detailed coverage makes it an
excellent source of information on the way in which food was produced and consumed
in the late 1970s, and much of the information is still very relevant. The book begins
with a section covering the context of food production including food sources, the
population and agricultural production structures. Food consumption patterns,
nutrition, food distribution and government involvement are then considered. Specific
products are then covered including livestock and meat, fish, poultry and eggs, dairy

produce, maize, wheat, other grains, oils, fruit, beans, pulses and vegetables. Finally proposals are made for future food policies. A short article by the author on food policy is 'Food policy in Zimbabwe', *Food Policy* (UK), vol. 5, no. 3 (1980), p. 166-67.

325 **Socio-economic factors in food production and consumption: a study of twelve households in Wedza communal land, Zimbabwe.**
     Kate Truscott. *Food and Nutrition*, vol. 12, no. 1 (1986), p. 27-37.
This survey is the result of detailed field research in Wedza communcal land, focussing on twelve households and the food eaten and produced by the various household members. Details are provided on eating habits and diet, and on the 'culture of food'. There is also discussion of food production, including the role of Agritext, the research and extension institution. The origins of all food consumed are carefully traced, and differentiation made between food purchased or grown. The article also contains a brief historical discussion of agricultural food production and consumption from around 1940 to the 1980s, and data are provided on the dietary and economic aspects of specific food crops.

Zimbabwe: towards a new order – an economic and social survey. vol. 2.
See item no. 16.

Zimbabwe: the political economy of transition 1980-86.
See item no. 417.

Urban food distribution and household consumption: a study of Harare.
See item no. 526.

Zimbabwe's agricultural 'success' and food security in Southern Africa.
See item no. 581.

The transport and marketing of horticultural crops by communal farmers into Harare.
See item no. 589.

A regional inventory of the agricultural resource base.
See item no. 591.

Group interests and the state: an explanation of Zimbabwe's agricultural policies.
See item no. 612.

Land and food in the Wedza communal area.
See item no. 624.

Ecological dynamics and human welfare in Southern Zimbabwe.
See item no. 634.

Social strata

326 **Contradictions in modelling 'consciousness': Zimbabwean proletarians in the making?**
Angela Cheater. *Journal of Southern African Studies*, vol. 14, no. 2 (1988), p. 291-303.

The academic debate over whether, or to what extent, a true proletariat has been created in Zimbabwe is of long standing. The emphasis of this paper is on the nature of the models used by different analysts discussing these questions, rather than the formation of the proletariat specifically. The author shows how perspectives on class consciousness differ between various models which she categorizes as 'home-made' or 'ideological', and that cultural factors influence the form of these models.

327 **Social differentiation in the communal lands of Zimbabwe.**
Ben Cousins, Dan Weiner, Nick Amin. *Review of African Political Economy*, vol. 53, (1992), p. 5-24.

In this paper the authors discuss the evidence for emerging class differentation within the communal lands. They conclude that differentation, begun under the colonial regime, has continued under the independent government. There is also strong differentiation within households along gender lines. The discussion is based on field research experience and literature published during the 1980s. Four primary classes are identified: petty commodity producers, worker-peasants, the lumpen semi-proletariat, and the rural petty bourgeoisie. The future of rural class formation is also considered. Ian Phimister has published on the early development of differentiation in the communal areas. See his 'Commodity relations and class formation in the Zimbabwean countryside 1893-1920', *Journal of Peasant Studies*, vol. 13, no. 4 (July, 1986), p. 240-57, and 'Peasant differentiation in Southern Rhodesia, 1898-1938', in *The state and the market: studies in the economic and social history of the Third World* (London: Sangam Books, 1988) edited by C. Dewey.

328 **Zimbabwe's emerging African bourgeoisie.**
Barry Munslow. *Review of African Political Economy*, vol. 19, (1980), p. 63-69.

In this paper Munslow, who lectures in politics at Liverpool University, examines the question of whether there is an embryonic African bourgeoisie in Zimbabwe which might be able to develop since the institutional discrimination practised by the colonial state had gone.

329 **Black and white élites in rural Rhodesia.**
Anna Katherina Hildegard Weinrich. Manchester, England: Manchester University Press; Lotowa, New Jersey: Rowman & Littlefield, 1973. 244p.

Weinrich conducted many social and anthropological surveys in Rhodesia, most of which yielded important insights into various aspects of African social, cultural and economic organization and development. This study, based on 1962-64 data, included a small sample of fifty whites who had close contacts with rural Africans, including missionaries, district commissioners and European farmers. A much larger sample of African 'élites' were also interviewed. The analysis focusses on the influence of class, or at least different socio-economic roles, on attitudes to the 'other' race, and on aspirations. Similar themes are treated for urban African populations in item 533. An overly quantified study of white attitudes in the late 1950s is Cyril A. Rogers and Charles Frantz, *Racial themes in Southern Rhodesia: the attitudes and behavior of the white population* (London; New Haven, Connecticut: Yale University Press, 1962. Reprinted, Port Washington, New York: Kennikat, 1973).

Zimbabwe: politics, economics and society.
See item no. 14.

Idioms of accumulation: rural development and class formation among freeholders in Zimbabwe.
See item no. 641.

Social Services, Health and Welfare

Health

330   **Issues of equity in and access to health care in Zimbabwe.**
Samuel Takarinda Agere.   *Journal of Social Development in Africa*,
vol. 5, no. 1 (1990), p. 31-38.

The author discusses the health care system in Zimbabwe, and identifies groups of
people who are being excluded from the system. The causes of this neglect are
discussed, and recommendations made on how to improve health care delivery to such
groups.

331   **Traditional healers and the Shona patient.**
Gordon L. Chavunduka.   Gwelo: Mambo Press, 1978. 139p.
(Zambeziana Series on Culture and Society in Central Africa, no. 3).

This scholarly study is based on research conducted from 1968-72 for the author's PhD
from the University of London. The study surveyed urban Shona patients in one ward
of Salisbury, with the aim of providing insights into Shona reaction to disease. Their
medical case histories were obtained, and if they consulted a n'anga (traditional
healer), he or she was interviewed. The processes of determining whether one is ill,
and how sickness is defined, is shown to be culturally influenced. Only a small
percentage of the patients studied sought professional help at first, with most trying
home remedies. The urban communities were found usually to turn next to 'scientific'
western-trained doctors. The fact that n'angas can be more expensive than 'scientific'
medicine is one factor in this choice. However fifty-three per cent of these people did
go on to consult n'angas. On the care of the sick, Chavunduka shows that a perceived
advantage of n'angas was their willingness to discuss and explain the patient's problem,
and that the help of kin remains an important security net for the ill. One conclusion of
the survey is that the Shona tend to take specific forms of 'African' sickness to n'angas,
and other types of disease to 'scientific' medicine. In this Chavunduka differs from the
conclusions of Gelfand and his research team (see 337).

332 **The Zimbabwean traditional healers' association (ZINATHA).**
Gordon L. Chavunduka.   Harare: ZINATHA, 1984. 44p.

ZINATHA is the national organization which coordinates and regulates the traditional health sector. It was formed shortly after independence on July 12, 1980, with Professor Chavunduka as its first President. A number of organizations for n'angas or traditional healers existed previously but their potential contribution to health delivery was dismissed by the colonial regimes. The new organization has government support and its first meeting was organized by the Ministry of Health. This short book discusses traditional medicine and its persistence in the face of western 'conventional' medicine. The relationship between traditional religion and healers is examined, and the relationship with government and the debate about the potential formal role of traditional healers is discussed. The strong code of conduct set up by the organization for healers is explained. More available sources on ZINATHA and traditional medicine in the post-independence era are Tony Cavender, 'The professionalization of traditional medicine in Zimbabwe', *Human Organization*, vol. 47, no. 3 (1988), p. 251-54, and Chavunduka's 'The organisation of traditional medicine in Zimbabwe', in *The professionalisation of African medicine* (Manchester, England: Manchester University Press in association with the International African Institute, 1986 [International African Seminars New Series, no. 1]), edited by Murray Last and Gordon L. Chavunduka, p. 29-49. On the relationship between traditional medicine and Christianity see Chavunduka's paper 'Traditional medicine and Christian beliefs' in Bourdillon, item 283.

333 **Liberated health in Zimbabwe? The experience of women 1981-83.**
F. Chinemana. In: *Women's health and apartheid: the health of women and children and the future of progressive primary health care in Southern Africa.* Edited by Marcia Wright, Zena Stein, Jean Scandlyn.   New York: Columbia University, 1988, p. 90-113.

Independence in Zimbabwe saw a shift towards a greater emphasis on primary health care, which should in theory improve access for women and children. In this paper which was presented at a workshop at Columbia University on 'Poverty, health and the state in Southern Africa', the author considers the new policies in the context of a wider discussion of women's health. She presents results from a major survey into the health and health needs of women in post-independence rural and urban Zimbabwe. The relationship between women's socio-economic roles and their health is highlighted, and she also provides a useful overview of colonial health policies, and the use of health issues to control women.

334 **Stabilisation policies and the health and welfare of children: Zimbabwe 1980-85.**
Rob Davies, David Sanders. In: *Adjustment with a human face: country case studies.* Edited by G. A. Cornia, Richard Jolly, Frances Stewart. New York: UNICEF; Oxford, England: Clarendon Press, 1987, p. 272-300.

Economic stabilisation policies, which usually include cutbacks in government expenditure, often have very undesirable effects on the poor, unless they are tempered with special policies aimed at vulnerable groups. Shortly after independence Zimbabwe adopted its own 'stabilisation' strategies in an attempt to address the size of the budget deficit and debt burden. In this article which appears in a UNICEF collection of case studies on the problems of economic adjustment, Davies and Sanders analyse the impact of Zimbabwe's policies on children, with a special focus on health. The country has experienced laudable reductions in infant mortality and morbidity since independence, but the early adjustment programme affected the availability of resources for health. Nevertheless the authors found this had made little impact on children's nutritional status, which various government policies had helped to maintain. The article also contains very useful data on trends in real wages, prices, and subsidies 1980-84. A similar study by the same authors appeared in the *Review of African Political Economy*, vol. 38 (1987), p. 3-23. Also see David Sanders and Rob Davies, 'Economic adjustment and current trends in child survival: the case of Zimbabwe', *Health Policy and Planning*, vol. 3, no. 3 (1988), p. 195-204, which compares the local situation with international trends.

335 **Godly medicine in Zimbabwe: a history of its medical missions.**
Michael Gelfand. Gweru: Mambo Press, 1988. 302p.

This account of Zimbabwe's medical missions reached Mambo Press just before Gelfand's death, and is the last of his many publications on culture, health and religion in Zimbabwe. The origin of the title is attributed to Terence Ranger, who had worked on godly medicine in Tanzania. The study covers the entire missionary period from the early days to the 1980s. The introduction discusses medical missions in general, and more specifically those in Zimbabwe, and the rest of the text is basically a chronological history. Every aspect of missionary medicine is covered, including the development of the services, the funding of this aspect of missionaries' work, the type and number of patients treated, technical aspects of the missionaries' practices, the missions' involvement in nurse training, and the establishment of the Association of Church-related hospitals.

336 **A service to the sick: a history of the health services for Africans in Southern Rhodesia (1890-1953).**
Michael Gelfand. Gwelo: Mambo Press, 1976. 187p. (Zambieziana Series on Culture and Society in Central Africa, no. 1).

This is a straightforward descriptive account of the positive contributions made by European technology and knowledge to African health. As a source on institutions, individuals, diseases and policies it is valuable, but it makes no attempt at objective critical analysis, or consideration of health problems created by the European impact. It updates Gelfand's earlier work, *Tropical victory: an account of the influence of medicine on the history of Southern Rhodesia, 1890-1923* (Cape Town: Juta, 1953).

337 **The traditional medical practitioner in Zimbabwe: his principles of practice and pharmacopoeia.**
Michael Gelfand, S. Mavi, R. B. Drummond, B. Ndamara. Gweru: Mambo Press, 1985. 411p. (Zambeziana Series on Culture and Society in Central Africa, no. 17).

This major study of n'angas or traditional healers in Zimbabwe is the result of ten years of research and observation by Dr. Gelfand and his assistants. After a general survey of the principles and practice of n'angas, and consideration of the special complaints they treat and some of the best known medicines used, the authors provide a detailed discussion of the plants used in n'anga remedies. The plants, animals and birds mentioned in the book are listed at the end along with their scientific names. The authors contend that many people do visit n'angas for objectively recognizable ailments, rather than for 'special' African complaints only. In this they differ from the view of Dr. Chavunduka, the President of the traditional healers' association, ZINATHA (see item 331). They also feel that since specific plants tend to be used habitually to treat specific diseases, it is probable that many of them are worthy of pharmaceutical study. This is widely accepted in Zimbabwe; the fear is that without careful regulation by ZINATHA, drug companies will obtain invaluable knowledge without paying. An earlier study by the author on the same topic is *Witch doctor: traditional medicine man of Rhodesia* (New York: Praeger, 1965). For biographical notes on Dr. Gelfand, see item 240. He died in 1985 just before the publication of this book which is seen as a memorial to his work.

338 **The struggle for health.**
John Gilmurray, Roger Riddell, David Sanders. London: Catholic Institute of International Relations; Gweru: Mambo Press in association with Catholic Institute of International Relations and Joint Peace Commission of the Roman Catholic Conference of Bishops in Zimbabwe, 1979. 59p. (From Rhodesia to Zimbabwe Series).

This short study was one of a number commissioned by the CIIR during the 1970s. It focusses on health issues, with a brief overview of the inequalities in health provision which existed at the time. The survey provides details on African health, and proposals for restructuring health delivery to improve access.

339 **AIDS: action now. Information, prevention and support in Zimbabwe.**
Helen Jackson. Harare: AIDS Counselling Trust, 1988. 153p.

This publication is basically aimed at the general public in Zimbabwe, and focusses on general factual information about the disease. Of interest to a wider audience, however, is the examination of the public reaction to AIDS in Zimbabwe, the very short section on the AIDS situation in Zimbabwe, and the analysis of the policies which have been adopted by the government and future policy options. The author is a lecturer at the School of Social Work in Harare, and a founder member of the AIDS Counselling Trust, a non-governmental organization established in 1988. A regional study of AIDS which includes information on the situation in Zimbabwe is Sholto Cross and Alan Whiteside, *Facing up to AIDS: the socio-economic impact in Southern Africa* (Basingstoke, England: Macmillan, 1993).

340 **Equity in health: Zimbabwe nine years on.**
David Sanders. *Journal of Social Development in Africa*, vol. 5, no. 1 (1990), p. 5-22.

This is a very useful reference for an overview of changes in the health delivery service in Zimbabwe since independence, and an examination of the progress in health which has been achieved. The Village Health Worker (VHW) programme is discussed, and the need to encourage community participation in this aspect of health delivery. The lessons for the Southern African region to be derived from Zimbabwe's health care experience are discussed in Sanders' 'Reorganisation of the health sector: the way forward in the light of Zimbabwe's experience', in *Women's health and apartheid: the health of women and children and the future of progressive primary health care in Southern Africa* (New York: Columbia University Press, 1988), edited by Marcia Wright, Zena Stein, and Jean Scandlyn, p. 253-73. This also provides an overview of the development of primary health care in Zimbabwe, and various other health-related policies including those on family planning, nutrition, diarrheal disease, immunization, health infrastructure and buildings, decentralization, rehabilitation of the disabled, village health workers, and medical education. A short paper in the same volume which puts a pro-government case is R. G. Choto, 'Zimbabwe: health infrastructure and directions', p. 249-52.

341   **Zimbabwe National Traditional Healers' Association: the first six years 1980-85.**
       ZINATHA. Harare: ZINATHA, 1986. 10p.
ZINATHA is the organization which coordinates and represents the traditional healers of Zimbabwe. Prior to independence traditional healers had no legal status, but in 1981 a bill was passed finally giving them recognition. By 1985 there were 340 branches of ZINATHA, and about 22,000 registered practitioners, which indicates the significance of this sector for the country's health. This book gives a brief history of ZINATHA, explains its aims and objects and reports on its first congress.

A decade of development Zimbabwe 1980-90.
See item no. 1.

Zimbabwe since independence: a people's assessment.
See item no. 7.

Zimbabwe: a land divided.
See item no. 8.

Zimbabwe: a country study.
See item no. 11.

Zimbabwe: politics, economics and society.
See item no. 14.

Zimbabwe: towards a new order – an economic and social survey. Vol. 2.
See item no. 16.

Zimbabwe: the political economy of transition 1980-86.
See item no. 417.

Law and medicine in Zimbabwe.
See item no. 424.

Social services and welfare

342   **NASCOH: a historical survey of facilities for handicapped people in Zimbabwe.**
       Joan Addison.   Harare: Bardwell, 1986. 36p.
In 1981 there were estimated to be 276,000 disabled people in Zimbabwe: 12.5 per cent were disabled during the war, and nearly half were disabled by disease. This report was prepared for NASCOH, the National Association of Societies for the Care of the Handicapped, an umbrella organization for groups involved in caring for the disabled

in Zimbabwe. After a historical survey of the development of special care for the disabled, there is an account of the current facilities available. The role of the government is also considered. Two journals have also devoted special issues to the latest developments in care for the handicapped in Southern Africa: the *African Rehabilitation Journal* (Zimbabwe), 1984, and the *Bulletin for Eastern and Southern Africa* (UNESCO) from Kenya.

343 Zimbabwe steps ahead: community rehabilitation of people with disabilities.

Mary McAllister (et al.). London: Catholic Institute for International Relations, 1990. 96p.

Zimbabwe's enlightened policy on disabled people is the theme of this book, written by a group of authors who have all worked as therapists. The aim of the policy is to try to rehabilitate disabled people within their families and communities. The authors discuss the policy, and the radical re-examination of the roles and abilities of disabled people associated with it. The community-based approach is assessed with reference to interviews with disabled people and their families, and rehabilitation workers. Policies towards the disabled are also discussed in Livion Nyathi, 'The disabled and social development in rural Zimbabwe', *Journal of Social Development in Africa*, vol. 1, no. 1 (1986), p. 61-65.

344 Support for the dying and bereaved in Zimbabwe: traditional and new approaches.

Patricia Swift. *Journal of Social Development in Africa*, vol. 4, no. 1 (1989), p. 25-45.

Comparisons are made in this paper between the traditional African systems for the dying and bereaved, and the newer voluntary organizations providing such services. Whilst the latter used to cater for the white population, they are increasingly being used by urban blacks as well.

345 VOICE directory of social services in Zimbabwe 1983.

Voluntary Organizations in Community Enterprise. Harare: Aloe Press, 1983. 140p.

A compilation of information submitted by both government and non-governmental organizations involved in the provision of social services in Zimbabwe. For each organization the directory provides information on the service provided, (including services for the aged, children, disabled, and legal services), the area served, and the organization's address.

346 Social security study.

Whitsun Foundation. Salisbury: Whitsun Foundation, 1979. 59p. (Project 1.03).

This study is one of the many undertaken by the Whitsun Foundation around the time of independence on different sectors of Zimbabwean economy and society. It is a very useful source on the social security situation in Rhodesia, and contains excellent data displayed in many tables and graphs. It also contains the results of a questionnaire on the subject of pensions and urbanization, of great relevance in a society where many people retain access to land in the communal areas. Another general survey is Rashid

Faruqee, *Social infrastructure and services in Zimbabwe* (Washington, DC: International Bank of Reconstruction and Development, Economics Department, 1981). For an account of the inequalities in social welfare provision at independence and the need to improve access for Africans see Grace Gono in item 16.

347 **Zimbabwe's good samaritans: Jairos Jiri and the Jairos Jiri Association 1921-82.**
Chengetai Jones Zvobgo.   Harare: History Department, University of Zimbabwe, April 1988. 365p.

This is the major work on the well-known Jairos Jiri Association, an important association working for the rehabilitation of the blind and physically handicapped in Zimbabwe. The association is named after the founder, a Shona man born in 1921. It draws on archival material from the Jairos Jiri national headquarters in Bulawayo, the Bulawayo city archives and the national archives in Harare. The study grew from an original BA Honours dissertation. Zvobgo focusses on the association's work rather than the founder; for a biography of Jairos Jiri see June Farquhar, *Jairos Jiri: the man and his work, 1921-82* (Gweru: Mambo Press, 1987).

Zimbabwe since independence: a people's assessment.
See item no. 7.

Zimbabwe: towards a new order – an economic and social survey. vol. 2.
See item no. 16.

Zimbabwe: at 5 years of independence: achievement, problems and prospects.
See item no. 17.

AIDS: action now. Information, prevention and support in Zimbabwe.
See item no. 339.

Rural development and planning in Zimbabwe.
See item no. 608.

Women

348 Women in Zimbabwe.
Elinor Batezat, Margaret Mwalo. Harare: SAPES Trust, 1989. 73p.
(Southern African Political Economy Series).

The gap between the rhetoric of a government theoretically committed to improving women's status, and the reality of women's experience since independence is one of the themes of this study, which highlights the changes which have occurred for women since 1980. It is stressed that legislative change has not proved to be sufficient in many cases to enhance women's social and economic circumstances. Changes in general attitudes towards women must also occur. The study combines historical research with interviews with contemporary rural and urban women. There is an excellent bibliography. The authors both have a long history of involvement and dedication to the struggle to improve the position of Zimbabwe's women. Elinor Batezat works for the International Labour Organization, and Margaret Mwalo for Zimbabwe's Ministry of Labour, Manpower Planning and Social Welfare. Similar themes about policies towards women are treated in Susie Jacobs and Tracy Howard, 'Women in Zimbabwe: stated policy and state action', in *Women, state and ideology* (Basingstoke: Macmillan, 1987), p. 28-47, edited by H. Afshar, and by Joyce Kazembe (see item 417). Gay Seidman argues that part of the cause of the conflict over women evident in state actions is that there are three different views of women's roles in society extant within the government. See her 'Women in Zimbabwe: post-independence struggles', *Feminist Studies*, vol. 10, no. 3 (1984) p. 419-40. Three other general surveys of women in post-independent Zimbabwe are *Report on the situation of women in Zimbabwe* (Harare: UNICEF, 1982), *Zimbabwe report on UN decade for women* (Harare: UNICEF, 1985) and *Women in construction and reconstruction in post-independent Zimbabwe* (Harare: UNESCO, 1985) all prepared by the Zimbabwe Government, Ministry of Community Development and Women's Affairs. On women and children see *Situation analysis of women and children in Zimbabwe* (Harare: UNICEF, 1985).

349 **The changing economic role of women in the urban process: a preliminary report from Zimbabwe.**
David Drakakis-Smith. *International Migration Review*, vol. 18, no. 4 (1984), p. 1278-92.

This survey of women and urbanization in post-independent Zimbabwe also considers aspects of migration. Constraints on women's economic participation are considered, and their role in the informal sector. The weakness of the rural ties of specific groups of urban women in Harare has been studied by Ann Schlyter. See her 'Women in Harare: gender aspects of urban-rural interaction', in *Small town Africa: studies in rural-urban interaction* (Uppsala, Sweden: Scandinavian Institute of African Studies, 1990. [Seminar Proceedings, no. 23]), edited by Jonathan Baker, p. 182-96. Women's links to the communal areas are also considered in item 259. On women and urban housing see Schlyter's *Women households and housing strategies – the case of Harare* (Uppsala: The National Swedish Institute for Building Research, 1989).

350 **The role and position of women in colonial and pre-colonial Zimbabwe.**
Angela Cheater. *Zambezia*, vol. 13, no. 2 (1986), p. 65-79.

Cheater discusses how women's economic status deteriorated in the colonial period. She shows how although women were excluded from access to land in their own right in pre-colonial times, they could accumulate wealth through investing in livestock. She examines women's many cultural and social roles prior to colonialism. One way of gaining access to cattle was through their daughter's bridewealth payments, which included a head of cattle for the mother. The economic and social changes led to women becoming more economically dependent upon men.

351 **Operation clean up.**
Rudo Gaidzanwa. *Connexions: an international women's quarterly*, vol. 12 (1984), p. 16-18.

The occurrence of Operation Clean Up in Harare in 1982 was a terrible pointer to the fact that attitudes towards women, despite much lip service and some legislative change, had not fundamentally altered. Using the Emergency Clause of the notorious colonial Vagrancy Act of 1960, single women were suddenly taken from the streets of Harare one night, and removed to camps outside town. The official explanation, which was not justifiable, was that they were prostitutes. In fact many were not. This short paper describes the events and the context of the operation. It also examines the role of prostitution in urban Rhodesia, arguing that African prostitution was integral to the form of capitalism that developed since it was dependent on single, migrant males.

352 **Down memory lane with some early Rhodesian women.**
Compiled by Madeleine Heald. Bulawayo: Books of Rhodesia, 1979. 323p.

Drawing on interviews, letters and published works, this book documents the lives of sixty white women who lived in Rhodesia during the early colonial period 1897-1923. The general approach is to highlight their bravery in the face of much hardship and suffering. A wide spectrum of lifestyles are detailed, including both wealthy and relatively poor, and married and single women. The author spent her early years in mining camps, and subsequently lived in Bulawayo. She worked as a teacher and as a nurse in South Africa and Rhodesia. This book was compiled on behalf of the Matabeleland Branch of the National Historical Association of Rhodesia.

353 **Marriage, perversion and power: the construction of moral discourse in Southern Rhodesia 1894-1930.**
Diana Jeater. Oxford: Clarendon Press, 1993. 281p.

Whilst much has been written on marriage in Zimbabwe, and on the impact of colonialism on women, this study of African marriage relationships provides a fresh perspective by giving serious consideration to the subject of sexuality in colonial Rhodesia. Based on her Oxford PhD, Jeater's argument focusses on the 'moral realm' introduced by the whites which conceptualized issues of gender and sexuality in terms of specific acts, and strong ideas about what was 'perverse' . She contrasts this to African sexuality which was constructed in terms of lineage identity and obligation and was much concerned with choice of partner. The social changes introduced by colonialism meant that African men and women had to respond to each other in new circumstances, particularly in urban centres where customary social rules and considerations of kinship were not established. She demonstrates how white and black men in positions of power colluded to control black women's sexuality and restrict their independence. She concludes that the Europeans introduced the idea of individual sexual sin to societies which previously did not have this concept. The research included fieldwork undertaken in Gweru. The book is also a useful source for theories about bridewealth, and how it affected gender relations.

354 **Women and the rural energy economy in Zimbabwe: research findings and policy issues.**
Kristen Johnson. In: *Energy for rural development in Zimbabwe.* Edited by R. H. Hosier. Stockholm: Beijer Institute and Scandinavian Institute of African Studies, 1988, p. 110-41. (Energy, Environment and Development in Africa Series, no. 11).

Women play the major part in the delivery and consumption of energy in the rural sector, with woodfuel usually being the most important source. As woodfuel is in increasingly short supply and overuse has many environmental implications, this has become a topic of considerable research interest. Shortage of fuel means that women have to expend considerable amounts of their time searching for wood, and this article provides a detailed analysis of data on women's labour budgets and the gender division of labour in rural areas.

355 **Women's programmes in Zimbabwe.**
Edited by Kirsten Jørgensen. Copenhagen: KULU, Women and Development, 1982. 107p.

This volume provides a wealth of information on women in Zimbabwe, in the context of discussions of a wide range of institutions and programmes dealing with or affecting women. There are strong links between Nordic women's organizations and women in Zimbabwe, and the editor is a Danish woman who provides a chapter on the topic of co-operation between women in these areas. Olivia Muchena provides an assessment of Zimbabwean women's organizations, and Vivian Ncube discusses women's programmes operating in Bulawayo, and women and development issues in rural Matabeleland and the Midlands. There are also papers by J. van't Hoff on training ex-combatant women for employment, and by R. Mhonda on female health. A discussion of white women's organizations is found in a monotonous study by Winifred J. Needham, *A history of the Federation of Women's Institutes of Southern Rhodesia* (Salisbury: Art Printing Works, [ca. 1959]).

356 **Zimbabwe women: a neglected factor in social development.**
S. K. Kachingwe. *Journal of Social Development in Africa*, vol. 1, no. 1 (1986), p. 27-33.

The author contends that, despite their central role in agricultural production, women are still neglected in this vital area of the economy. A number of aspects of their disadvantaged position in this sector are reviewed, including marketing and the problems which they experience in making their voices heard in local decision-making bodies which remain dominated by men. This latter issue is covered in greater detail in Rumidzo Chivemba, 'Women and decision-making: the case of district councils in Zimbabwe' in *Women in Southern Africa* (London: Alison & Busby, 1987) edited by Christine Qunta. This study considers the causes of under-representation in the district councils which control rural areas, and the consequences for women's development of their political weakness.

357 **Settler wives in Southern Rhodesia: a case study.**
Deborah Kirkwood. In: *The incorporated wife*. Edited by H. Callan, S. Ardenes. London: Croom Helm, 1984, p. 143-64.

In this study it is suggested that the experiences and roles of European wives in colonial Southern Rhodesia were more differentiated and complex than the conventional stereotype allows. An examination and comparison is made of the different lifestyles of wives living on mines, farms and African rural areas. The thorny topic of the relationship between white wives and their domestic servants is also discussed, and the development of women's clubs for whites.

358 **Rhodesia's pioneer women (1859-1896).**
Jessie M. Lloyd, Constance Parry. Bulawayo: Rhodesia Pioneers' and Early Settlers' Society, 1974. 105p.

This publication is basically a listing of some 1,000 European women who settled in, or visited Rhodesia between 1859 and 1896. Available biographical details, which are generally fairly limited, are given for each woman. These usually include at least maiden names and husbands' names and occupations. Jessie Lloyd was born of a missionary family at Hope Fountain Mission, and worked in Rhodesia at the *Bulawayo Chronicle* and for the railways. Another study of pioneer women is J. M. Boggie, *Experiences of Rhodesia's pioneer women* (Bulawayo: Philpott and Collins, [n.d.]).

359 **Zimbabwean women in industry.**
Patricia Made, Birgitta Lagerström. Harare: Zimbabwe Publishing House, 1985. 60p.

This glossy publication contains demands for equality by women working in industry, and profiles of some activists. It is based on interviews with women workers in factories in Harare and Bulawayo. Also on women in industry see Elinor Batezat, *The working conditions of female workers in the food processing industry in Zimbabwe* (Harare: Zimbabwe Institute of Development Studies, 1986 [ZIDS Working Papers no. 10]), UNIDO, *Human resources in Zimbabwe's industrial development: the current and prospective contribution of women* (Vienna: United Nation's Industrial Development Organization, 1989. [UNIDO-PPD, 138]) and Donald P. Chimanikire, 'Women in industry: legal and social attitudes (with special reference to Zimbabwe)', *Africa Development* (Senegal), vol. 12, no. 4 (1987) p. 27-39.

360 **Women and revolution: the women's movement in Zimbabwe.**
Nyaradzo Makamure. *Journal of African Marxists*, vol. 6, (1984), p. 74-86.
This article examines the proliferation of women's organizations in Zimbabwe, and notes that women have failed to use their numbers to obtain their full rights in society. The relationships between gender and class struggles are analysed and the role of the liberation struggle in fostering the women's movement in Zimbabwe is explained. Another study of the impact of the liberation struggle on women's status and their roles in the war is found in chapter seven of R. E. Lapchick and S. Urdang, *Oppression and resistance: the struggle of women in Southern Africa* (Westport, Connecticut: Greenwood, 1982, p. 101-09).

361 **Changing people, changing laws.**
Joan May. Gweru: Mambo Press, 1987. 105p. (Mambo Occasional Papers, Socio-Economic Series, no. 22).
The subject of this study is Zimbabwean family law. Women have received short shrift under both legal systems in the past, never being regarded as adults capable of representing themselves. The author deals with the need to create a new and culturally sensitive body of law for the future. She covers comprehensively a range of family law matters including customary law and the law courts, lobola, the traditional family, legal changes since independence, the Legal Age of Majority Act, marriage and property, custody and maintenance of children, and widows and inheritance. An earlier study by the same author which examines the experience of women under the law is *Zimbabwean women in colonial and customary law* (Gweru: Mambo Press, 1983 [*Zambeziana* Series vol. 14]). See also Doris P. Galen, 'Internal conflicts between customary and general law in Zimbabwe: family law as a case study', *Zimbabwe Law Review*, vol. 1 & 2 (1983/4), p. 3-42, which examines four types of marriage and the question of which body of law is appropriate for courts to implement when dealing with each type.

362 **African women in urban employment: factors influencing their employment in Zimbabwe.**
Olivia N. Muchena. Gwelo: Mambo Press, 1979. 83p. (Mambo Occasional papers, Socio-Economic Series, no. 12).
This useful empirically based study of women employees in towns covers not only the obvious topics of wages and occupations, with much relevant illustrative data, but also more general issues. The differences between married and single women are addressed, the issue of fertility in the context of employment, and the opportunities and problems faced by housewife-farmers who are based in both rural and urban areas. The role of the informal sector for income generation for women is discussed. Another study on urban women by the same author is *Women in town. A socio-economic survey of African women in Highfield township, Salisbury* (Salisbury: Centre for Applied Social Studies, University of Zimbabwe, 1980). This again provides much empirical material on 370 women interviewed for the study, with details on their incomes, role in the family and involvement with women's organizations.

363 **The dynamics of the social relations of production and reproduction in Zimbabwean communal areas.**

Donna Pankhurst.   PhD thesis, University of Liverpool, Liverpool, England, 1988. 458p.

This research study provides useful insights into the ways in which gender relations and the gendered nature of production patterns have changed over time in the communal areas of Zimbabwe. These changes are traced through discussion of the themes of marriage, chiefs and their authority, land tenure and farming systems. The research material and analysis are limited to the Shona areas of Zimbabwe. An important aspect of the study is the uncovering of 'the finer workings of the social mosaic in a contemporary village case study'. Pankhurst demonstrates how relationships between the genders vary with economic circumstances, but stresses that women share a common material insecurity within marriage. A more accessible article based on part of her thesis is 'Constraints and incentives in "successful" Zimbabwean peasant agriculture: the interaction between gender and class', *Journal of Southern African Studies*, vol. 17, no. 4 (1991), p. 611-632. The themes of gender and agriculture in the communal areas are also considered in 'Gender, age and the ownership of agricultural resources in the Mhondoro and Save North communal areas of Zimbabwe', *Geographical Journal of Zimbabwe*, vol. 18 (1987), by Lovemore Zinyama.

364 **Peasants, traders and wives: Shona women in the history of Zimbabwe, 1870-1939.**

Elizabeth S. Schmidt.   Portsmouth, New Haven: Heinemann (Social History of Africa Series); Harare: Baobab Books; London: James Currey, 1992. 289p.

This book is based on the author's 1987 doctoral thesis *Ideology, economics and the role of Shona women in Southern Rhodesia 1850-1939* for the University of Wisconsin. Her study focusses on Shona women and their role in shaping Zimbabwean history. She reviews women's response to the European occupation and mission education, their role in the emergence of the African peasantry in the early years of colonial rule, and the implications for their social and economic status when the peasantry declined. Schmidt argues that the overall effect of these factors was to decrease the status of women, and make them more vulnerable. The views and interests of colonial administrators, missionaries and African male elders about how women should be treated could differ, but on the whole they assisted one another in keeping control over African women's labour, sexuality and mobility. A short article based on her doctoral reseach is 'Negotiated spaces and contested terrain: men, women and the law in colonial Zimbabwe 1890-1939', *Journal of Southern African Studies*, vol. 16, no. 4 (1990), p. 622-48.

365 **Mothers of the revolution: the war experiences of thirty Zimbabwean women.**

Compiled and edited by Irene Staunton.   Harare: Baobab Books, 1990; London: James Currey; Bloomington, Indiana: Indiana University Press, 1991. 306p.

Whilst much attention has been paid to the experiences of those women who joined the guerilla armies, this book focusses on the fate of those who remained behind and their experiences with the UDI forces, as well as the guerillas. The text is made up of first-hand accounts from thirty women from different regions throughout the country.

366 **Women and racial discrimination in Zimbabwe.**
Anna Katherina Hildegard Weinrich. Paris: UNESCO, 1979. 143p.
This study presents selected results of empirical research conducted from 1972-75 by
the author. The original survey was on the topic of African marriage (see item 314),
and here the information on women's socio-economic position and role in traditional
life has been selected for discussion. The research covered all ethnic African groups
and all major settlement types, but does not cover non-African women. Secondary
sources are also used to build up a picture of how economic change affected black
Rhodesian women, and how their families were structured. The function of
bridewealth and legal issues affecting women are also discussed. The study was
prepared as a result of a resolution passed at the World Conference of International
Women's Year, and was published by UNESCO as a contribution to the World
Conference to Combat Racism and Racial Discrimination. It forms part of a series of
UNESCO studies on Rhodesia during the 1970s (see items 261, 539). Weinrich also
published a short study on how independence had affected women which is generally
positive in tone: 'Changes in the political and economic role of women in Zimbabwe
since independence', *Culture*, vol. 8, no. 4 (1982).

367 **The women of Zimbabwe.**
Ruth Weiss. Harare: Nehanda Publishers, 1986. 151p.
The author of this survey of women in Zimbabwe is a journalist who was deported
from Rhodesia during UDI. She went on to work in London and Zambia, then
returned to Zimbabwe as a freelance writer and broadcaster. This book describes the
dynamic role of women in the war and their commitment to independence, often using
the words of the large number of women interviewed for the study. It provides some
insights into the lives of women during and after the war. There is very little on non-
African women however, even those who were opposed to UDI, and this tends to be
simplistic. White Rhodesian women's lives during the war are described in *Profiles of
Rhodesia's women* (Salisbury: National Federation of Business and Professional
Women of Rhodesia, 1976) which heralds the role of gun-toting white women standing
by their men.

368 **Women's guide to law through life.**
Women in Development Research Unit, Centre for Inter-Racial
Studies, University of Rhodesia. Salisbury: University of Rhodesia,
1979. 43p.
This is a simple handbook for Zimbabwean women on the laws and regulations that
affected their lives prior to independence, which brought some changes. The laws
discussed relate to marriage, birth, children, death and widowhood, and the general
position of women. Both customary law and the law of Rhodesia based on Roman
Dutch law are covered.

369 **'We carry a heavy load'. Rural women in Zimbabwe speak out.**
Zimbabwean Women's Bureau. Salisbury: Zimbabwean Women's
Bureau, 1981. 51p.
The Zimbabwean Women's Bureau has produced a fascinating document in this short
book, which is easily accessible to the general reader interested in women's lives in
Zimbabwe, but also provides excellent case-study material for the scholar. The text
draws on 3,000 interviews conducted with women alone, and in groups, to provide
compelling insights into the problems women face in a society where colonial

discrimination embraced and generally reinforced the discrimination already practised by a strongly patriarchal system. Their economic struggles to maintain their children and families in the face of land shortages, and a migrant labour system are illustrated in rich detail, often in the women's own words. The economic circumstances of Shona women in rural Zimbabwe just prior to independence are discussed in Olivia N. Muchena, 'Changing position of African women in rural Zimbabwe-Rhodesia', *Zimbabwe Journal of Economics*, vol. 1, no. 1 (1979), p. 44-61.

A decade of development Zimbabwe 1980-90.
See item no. 1.

Zimbabwe's prospects: issues of race, class, state and capital in Southern Africa.
See item no. 13.

Gold regions of Southeastern Africa.
See item no. 122. (vol. 11).

Thy Beginning.
See item no. 136.

Women and the armed struggle for independence in Zimbabwe (1964-1979).
See item no. 211.

Pregnancy, childbirth, mother and child care among the indigenous peoples of Zimbabwe.
See item no. 228.

Traditional Shona concepts on family life and how systems planned on the basis of these concepts effectively contained the population growth of Shona communities.
See item no. 229.

The Shona woman.
See item no. 242.

Lobola: the pros and cons.
See item no. 307.

Unwanted pregnancies and baby dumping: whose problem?
See item no. 316.

Zimbabwe: the political economy of transition 1980-86.
See item no. 417.

Family law in Zimbabwe.
See item no. 429.

The legal situation of women in Zimbabwe.
See item no. 431.

Evaluating the impact of NGOs in rural poverty alleviation: Zimbabwe country study.
See item no. 507.

Zimbabwean women in co-operatives: participation and sexual equality in four producer co-operatives.
See item no. 517.

Women's access to and control over land: the case of Zimbabwe.
See item no. 564.

Women's land rights in Zimbabwe: an overview.
See item no. 566.

Zimbabwe: state, class and gendered models of land resettlement.
See item no. 571.

Land tenure, gender relations, and agricultural production: the case of Zimbabwe's peasantry.
See item no. 630.

Women: the silent farm managers in the small-scale commercial areas in Zimbabwe.
See item no. 643.

Industrial development in Zimbabwe: the case of women in manufacturing industry.
See item no. 650.

The rural labour market in Zimbabwe.
See item no. 674.

Income-generating projects: a report on forty-seven project groups of the Association of Women's Clubs.
See item no. 684.

Images of women in Zimbabwean literature.
See item no. 743.

Young women in the liberation struggle: stories and poems from Zimbabwe.
See item no. 750.

Women's organizations in Zimbabwe.
See item no. 852.

Women in Zimbabwe: an annotated bibliography.
See item no. 868.

Women and development in Zimbabwe: an annotated bibliography.
See item no. 870.

Politics

Pre-independence

370 **From spears to ploughshares: changes in the political structure of the AmaNdebele.**
H. Ashton. In: *Politics in leadership: a comparative perspective*. Edited by William A. Shack, Percy J. Cohen. Oxford: Clarendon Press, 1979, p. 66-92.
This essay on the nature of politics among the Ndebele examines how political structures changed over the period 1822-1974. It includes consideration of the development of African nationalism and leadership amongst the Ndebele, and the impact of community development on the role of Ndebele chiefs in the 1960s. Also on the political history of the Ndebele nation see David Chanaiwa, 'The army and politics in pre-industrial Africa: the Ndebele nation 1822-93', *African Studies Review*, vol. 19, no. 2 (1976) p. 49-67.

371 **The struggle for independence: documents on the recent development of Zimbabwe (1975-80).**
Goswin Baumhögger, with the assistance of Ulf Engel, Telse Diedeerichsen. Hamburg: Institute of African Studies, African Documentation Centre, 1984. 7 vols.
These seven volumes reproduce political documents from the last years of the colonial period, covering December 1974 to April 1980, and are therefore a most convenient aid to research on that period. 1185 documents are reproduced within volumes 2-7 which contain nearly 1500 pages: about sixty per cent of the text is taken up with 1060 original published documents such as manifestos, and the rest comprises newspaper clippings, transcriptions of radio broadcasts and commentaries, and newspaper and journal editorials. The newspaper entries are mainly drawn from African and British newspapers, and the radio entries are usually from African sources. Volume I provides a comprehensive guide to the documents, with a table of contents and an index. The

material is subdivided into chapters of periods of time, with documents in strict chronological order. Documents are dated according to time of speech or statement, for example, rather than the date of report. Volume 1 also contains footnotes to the individual document entries, and these are an invaluable aid to the researcher.

372 **Politics in Rhodesia: white power in an African state.**
Larry Wells Bowman. Cambridge, Massachusetts: Harvard University Press, 1973. 206p.

A major study of white politics and the Rhodesian Front party in the 1960s, this book is based on two years' field research for the author's doctoral thesis for Brandeis University. Bowman stresses the authoritarian nature of the state and the unity of the whites, factors which were thought to increase the likelihood of the UDI state's survival. Also on white politics during the early years of UDI see Ian Henderson, 'White populism in Southern Rhodesia', *Comparative Studies in Society and History*, vol. 14 (Sept. 1972), p. 387-99, which traces the roots of the Rhodesian Front back to 1906, and Richard Hodder-Williams' case study of Marondera, 'White attitudes and the Unilateral Declaration of Independence: a case study', *Journal of Commonwealth Political Studies*, vol. 8 (Nov. 1970), p. 241-64. Lewis Gann provided an admiring analysis of the UDI regime and white politics in 'Rhodesia and the prophets', *African Affairs*, vol. 71 (1972), p. 125-43.

373 **The African National Council and the Rhodesian situation: Rhodesia, mid-1974.**
Ariston Chambati. Braamfontein, South Africa: South African Institute of Race Relations, 1974.

The African National Council (ANC) was established in 1971, and led by Bishop Abel Muzorewa. It was a response to the proposed Anglo-Rhodesian settlement of 1971, which led to the Pearce Commission. This work on the party was written by an ANC official, who was a lecturer in political science at the University of Rhodesia. A balanced analysis of the ANC and its leadership during its heyday is 'The African National Council: past performance and present prospects in Rhodesia', *Africa Today* (USA), vol. 22, no. 1 (1975), p. 5-29, by A. K. H. Weinrich.

374 **The premiership of Garfield Todd: racial partnership versus colonial interest, 1953-58.**
David Chanaiwa. *Journal of Southern African Affairs*, vol. 1, (Oct. 1976), p. 83-94.

Todd, a New Zealander, was Prime Minister of Southern Rhodesia during the Federation of Rhodesia and Nyasaland, 1953-58. He is generally regarded as a liberal, a view which is challenged here by Chanaiwa who argues that he was really no more liberal than other white leaders, including Welensky. For an alternative view see item 380 by Todd's daughter, Judith Todd.

375 **White liberals, moderates and radicals in Rhodesia 1953-80.**
Ian Hancock. London: Croom Helm; New York: St. Martin's Press, 1984. 230p.

Whilst many whites were opposed to the draconian racism of the Rhodesian state during UDI, and to the blatant discrimination of earlier colonial periods, such

137

opposition took many forms and was founded on widely differing attitudes and theoretical perspectives. In this book Hancock successfully guides the reader through the complexities of this aspect of white politics, and explains how it changed from the federal period of 1953-63 when there appeared to be a gradual liberalization of the political economy encouraged by changing economic circumstances. He shows how the hopes of the liberals were dashed by the events of 1965, and inevitably some whites began to take up more radical political positions. Hancock provides general theoretical discussion of white politics in the early chapters, and then analyses the trends in white opposition by chronological period.

376 **White farmers in Rhodesia, 1890-1965: a history of the Marandellas District.**
Richard Hodder-Williams.   London: Macmillan, 1983. 256p.
This fluently written book is the major scholarly work on European farmers and their politics, which draws on research conducted in Rhodesia from 1965 to 1967. The author focussed on one area, Marondellas (now called Marondera), some eighty kilometres south-east of Harare. His methodology included archival research, interviews, and the use of various local sources such as diaries and letters. He admirably fulfils his purpose of presenting a detailed illustration of white farming life and social and economic institutions in order to throw some light on Rhodesian European politics in the 20th century. The analysis only extends to the African community where this impinged on the European farmers under study. The work also contains insights into European social life, and the changing nature of large-scale commercial farming over this period.

377 **Electoral machinery and voting patterns in Rhodesia 1962-77.**
Anthony Lemon. *African Affairs*, vol. 77, no. 309 (1978), p. 511-30.
This article discusses the nature of elections from the end of the Federation and for much of the UDI period.

378 **European politics in Southern Rhodesia.**
Colin Leys.   London; New York: Oxford University Press, 1959. 323p.
This is the major study of white politics during the 1950s, when Garfield Todd was Prime Minister, and Southern Rhodesia was part of the Federation of Rhodesia and Nyasaland. Leys deals in detail with political processes, including the franchise, elections, parties and the self-interested dealings of white politicians. This was Leys' first research study on Africa, and he went on to become an important Africanist scholar, teaching at the Kivukeni College in Dar es Salaam, Tanzania, Makerere College in Uganda, and the University of Nairobi in Kenya. He also taught at the universities of Oxford, Sussex and Sheffield in Britain, and is currently Professor of Politics at Queen's University, Ontario, Canada. This study ends before Todd's defeat in 1958; for an analysis of white politics from that time to UDI see Stephen Hintz, 'The political transformation of Rhodesia, 1958-65', *African Studies Review*, vol. 15, no. 2 (1972), p. 173-83.

379 **Southern Rhodesia: the price of freedom; a series of nine essays by nine Rhodesians on the present political impasse.**
Fred B. Rea.   Salisbury: Stuart Manning; Que Que, Rhodesia: Midrho Press, 1964. 141p.

This collection of nine essays from a Capricorn Africa society meeting held in 1963 provide a good representation of liberal white and black political views at the end of the federal period.

380 **The right to say no.**
Judith Todd.   London: Sidgwick and Jackson, 1972; New York: Third Press, 1973; Harare: Longman Zimbabwe, 1987. 204p.

Judith Todd is the daughter of the former liberal Rhodesian prime minister, Garfield Todd. Their sympathy for the African nationalists' cause made her a target for the UDI security forces, and she was kept in solitary confinement in 1971 for five weeks, during the negotiations for the failed Anglo-Rhodesian settlement. In this book, republished in Zimbabwe since independence, she strongly criticized the proposed 1971 settlement which led to the Pearce Commission when African attitudes to the proposal were solicited. The outcome was the abandonment of the proposal. She also wrote a survey of the background to the illegal declaration of independence in 1965 entitled *An act of treason: Rhodesia 1965* (Harare: Longman Zimbabwe, 1982), and *Rhodesia* (London: MacGibbon and Kee, 1966; New York: International Publications Service, 1966), an account of Rhodesia based on the life of her father, who at one point was 'regarded by white Rhodesians as something very like Public Enemy Number One'. Other publications on the events surrounding the Pearce Commission are *The Africans' predicament in Rhodesia* (London: Minority Rights Group, 1972. [Report no. 8]) by G. C. Grant, a local missionary, 'African response to the Pearce Commission' by Tony Rich, in *Conference on Zimbabwe* (Leeds: University of Leeds, 1980), edited by Department of Politics, University of Leeds, and the Pearce Commission Report, *Rhodesia: report of the commission on Rhodesian opinion under the chairmanship of the Right Honourable Lord Pearce* (London: HMSO. 1972. Cmnd. 4964).

381 **Transforming settler societies: communal conflict and internal security in Northern Ireland and Zimbabwe.**
Ronald Weitzer.   Berkeley, California: University of California Press, 1990. 278p.

This comparative analysis of two settler states first analyses the development and eventual collapse of the settler regimes. The study concentrates on the development of repressive state apparatuses for internal security, and how elements of these have been retained by the new post-settler states. With respect to Zimbabwe the author contends that there was little prospect that the worst aspects of the internal security system would be lifted. Similar themes are treated in his 'In search of regime security: Zimbabwe since independence', *Journal of Modern African Studies*, vol. 22, no. 4 (1984), p. 529-57.

382 **Source book of parliamentary elections and referenda in Southern Rhodesia 1898-1962.**
Edited by F. M. G. Willson, compiled by Gloria C. Passmore, Margaret T. Mitchell.   Salisbury: University College of Rhodesia and Nyasaland, Department of Government, 1963. 255p. maps.

This is a useful reference for checking on the details of specific elections and parliamentary sessions held from the end of the 19th century to the year before the end of the Federation. Information is provided on all candidates and the districts contested for all elections, and the results are detailed. By-elections and referenda are also covered. Information is provided on the electoral legislation affecting each election and the nature of the electorate. The introduction sets the context, dealing with the franchise, constituency boundaries, the electoral system and methods of voting. For details of individuals in various governments before 1964 see *Southern Rhodesia: holders of administrative and ministerial office, 1894-1964, and members of the Legislative Council, 1899-1923, and the Legislative Asembly, 1924-64* (Salisbury: University College of Rhodesia and Nyasaland, Department of Government, 1966) which was produced by the same editorial team.

383 **The Rhodesian problem: a documentary record 1923-73.**
Elaine Windrich.   London; Boston, Massachusetts: Routledge & Kegan Paul, 1975. 312p.

This volume, combined with Nyandoro and Nyangoni (item 392), provides an excellent reference collection of reprinted political documents illustrating Zimbabwean political history from 1923 to independence. Windrich, who was involved with the Labour Party in Britain, has here collected sixty-two documents, including speeches, excerpts from official inquiries and reports, and press reports, which illustrate a range of views from all sides of the political spectrum including the colonial power. Brief contextual discussion is provided as a guide to the documents.

From Rhodesia to Zimbabwe: behind and beyond Lancaster House.
See item no. 5.

Zimbabwe: a country study.
See item no. 6.

Zimbabwe's inheritance.
See item no. 12.

Zimbabwe's prospects: issues of race, class, state and capital in Southern Africa.
See item no. 13.

Zimbabwe: politics, economics and society.
See item no. 14.

Gold regions of Southeastern Africa.
See item no. 122 (vols. 19, 22).

Turmoil and tenacity: Zimbabwe 1890-1990.
See item no. 398.

Catalogue of the parliamentary papers of Southern Rhodesia and Rhodesia, 1954-70.
See item no. 857.

African nationalism and liberation movements

384 **The creation of political myths: African nationalism in Southern Rhodesia.**
John Day. *Journal of Southern African Studies*, vol. 2, (1975), p. 52-65.

Day analyses various views about the nature of African nationalism from the 1950s. Many of these ideas had come to assume common currency, although they had little basis in reality. Examples are the African belief that majority rule was imminent, and that Africans were unified politically, and the European myth that only a negligible proportion of Africans were interested in politics.

385 **The insignificance of tribe in the African politics of Zimbabwe, Rhodesia.**
John Day. In: *From Rhodesia to Zimbabwe*. Edited by W. H. Morris-Jones. London: Frank Cass, 1980, p. 85-109.

In this important article Day challenges the common assumptions which lead many academics and the media to believe that Zimbabwean politics can most usefully be understood by reference to ethnic factors. This sort of analysis states that since the Shona are the most numerous 'tribe' and the Shona support ZANU, it is inevitable that ZANU will govern, and that because of historical enmities between the Shona and the Ndebele, who support ZAPU, political friction and violence are almost inevitable. Day argues that ethnicity has not commonly been a major explanatory factor in African political behaviour in Zimbabwe, and that when it has been influential there is no simple explanation of its cause or effect. His view is that other factors, including dissatisfaction with leaders, rivalries for power, and differences of strategy have been more important in influencing political developments in the African nationalist movement. Day's paper is reprinted in *Journal of Commonwealth and Comparative Politics*, vol. 18 (1980), p. 85-109. Other analyses of ethnicity and black politics are W. J. Breytenbach 'Ethnic factors in the Rhodesian power struggle', *Bulletin of the Africa Institute* (South Africa), vol. 15, no. 2/4 (1977), p. 70-75, and Kenneth Kirkwood, 'Zimbabwe: the politics of ethnicity', *Ethnic and Racial Studies*, vol. 7, no. 3 (1984), p. 435-38, which discusses these issues within the context of a review of Joshua Nkomo's autobiography. Day has also considered similar themes in 'The divisions of the Rhodesian African nationalist movement', *World Today*, vol. 33, no. 10 (1977), p. 385-94. Elaine Burgess argues that ethnic cleavages have diminished in Zimbabwe in 'Ethnic scale and intensity: the Zimbabwean experience', *Social Forces*, vol. 59, no. 3 (March 1981), p. 601-26.

386 **The Chitepo assassination.**
David Martin, Phyllis Johnson. Harare: Zimbabwe Publishing House,
1985. 134p.

Herbert Chitepo was National Chairman of ZANU and the leader of its war council in
1975, when he was assassinated by a car bomb in Lusaka on 18th March. The
controversy surrounding his death, which led to many allegations about intra-party
duplicity and rivalry, including ethnic tensions, is laid to rest by this well-documented
book. Johnson and Martin's main evidence is a first-hand admission from an ex-
Rhodesian Central Intelligence Organization officer that his friend, Chuck Hind, was
the assassin. The Rhodesians thereby hoped to weaken ZANU with rumours that the
death was caused by party members, and they did achieve a split in the party, and the
detention in Zambia of a thousand ZANLA guerillas by Kenneth Kaunda. The
interview on which the book's conclusion is based is printed as an appendix. For
information on the authors see item 204.

387 **Our war of liberation: speeches, articles, interviews 1976-79.**
Robert Mugabe. Gweru: Mambo Press, 1983. 214p.

This publication contains a variety of material generated by Mugabe in the four years
leading up to independence. The material acts as an indicator of his ideas, thoughts,
principles and ideology as he expressed them at the time. It is divided into five parts
dealing with items on the armed struggle; the party, army and ideology and the
objectives of the struggle; constitutional and political development in Zimbabwe from
1975-79; the heroes of the struggle, including a speech on Herbert Chitepo; and
international solidarity and external relations. An introduction is provided by Nathan
Shamuyarira and C. M. B. Utete which includes an account of the split in ZANU
which led to Sithole's fall and Mugabe's rise to power.

388 **Black behind bars: Rhodesia 1959-74.**
Didymus Mutasa, foreword by Maurice Nyagumbo. Harare:
Longman Zimbabwe, 1983. 150p.

Mutasa, who became the first Speaker of the House of Assembly after independence,
was imprisoned by the Rhodesian Front regime from 1970-72. Prior to this he had been
active in nationalist politics, and was chairman of the Cold Comfort Farm Society. This
is his account of contemporary political affairs, and his experiences of confinement by
the Rhodesian security forces, which has been widely read. The book was banned in
Rhodesia until independence. The work was also published under the title *Rhodesian
black behind bars* (London: Mowbrays, 1974).

389 **Rise up and walk: an autobiography.**
Abel Tendakai Muzorewa, edited by Norman E. Thomas. London:
Evan Brothers, 1978. 289p.

This is the often emotive autobiography of Bishop Abel Muzorewa who, at the time of
its publication, was set to become the first black Prime Minister of Rhodesia.
Muzorewa was born in 1925, and was active in the liberation movement, becoming the
President of the African National Council. He was widely regarded as having betrayed
his principles by the forces of the Patriotic Front, since he agreed to take part in the
internally negotiated settlement of the late 1970s. He was duly elected as Prime
Minister at the head of a transitional government, but since the settlement which led to

his election was not recognized by the international community, his position was short-lived. In the British-supervised elections of 1980 he was defeated by Robert Mugabe who became the first leader of independent Zimbabwe.

390 Nkomo: the story of my life.

Joshua Nkomo. London: Methuen, 1984. 269p.

As one of the founders of African nationalism in Rhodesia, and the leader of the Zimbabwe African People's Union, Joshua Nkomo is one of the most significant political figures of the liberation war and post-independence politics. This autobiography covers his life from his birth in 1917 up to 1983. The account ends with the upsurge of anti-government action in Matabeleland in the early 1980s, which was attributed to ZAPU dissidents, when relations between Nkomo and ZAPU, and the ruling party, were at their lowest and most bitter. The book is an excellent reference source for the development of African nationalism in Rhodesia.

391 With the people: an autobiography from the Zimbabwean struggle.

Maurice Nyagumbo, foreword by Terence O. Ranger. London: Manchester University Press; Salisbury: Graham Publishers, 1980. 248p.

Maurice Nyagumbo was one of the senior members of Mugabe's government. During UDI he spent much of his time in jail, hence the sub-title of the book: *Some of us must remain with the people – even if it means to be in jail with them.* The first half of the book covers Nyagumbo's childhood, his years in South Africa and subsequent deportation from that country, and the second half focusses on his association and involvement with African nationalism in Rhodesia. The manuscript of this book was smuggled out of prison after two earlier drafts were confiscated. Nyagumbo also contributed to the debate about socialism in Zimbabwe in 'The role of the party in Zimbabwe's transition to socialism', in *The transition to socialism in Zimbabwe* (Harare: Zimbabwe Institute of Development Studies, 1984). He went on to hold various ministerial posts in the post-independence government, and committed suicide in 1989 when his name was linked with the Willowgate car scandal.

392 Zimbabwe independence movements: select documents.

Edited by Christopher Nyangoni, Gideon Nyandoro. New York: Harpers and Row, 1979. 456p.

A useful reference source for the development of the nationalist and independence movements up to the end of 1976, this wide-ranging collection of documents presents African viewpoints and attitudes towards the Rhodesian constitutional problem. The seventy-three documents include speeches, memoranda, resolutions, press releases, letters, proposed constitutions, policy statements and submissions made by nationalist leaders, political parties, international organizations and leaders of independent African nations. The documents are organized chronologically into four periods: protest 1957-64; direct confrontation 1964-71; armed struggle 1971-74; and detente 1974-76. Short notes on key political figures and movements are included.

393 **The colonial heritage of strife: sources of cleavage in the Zimbabwean liberation movement.**
Barry M. Schutz. *Africa Today* (USA), vol. 25, no. 1 (1978), p. 7-27.
In this article Schutz traces the historical roots of divisions between and among the various parties involved in the struggle for independence in the 1970s. Other publications on a similar theme are *Zimbabwean struggles within the struggle* (Salisbury: Rujeko Publishers, 1979), 'Ethnicity and factionalism: Zimbabwe nationalist politics 1957-79', *Ethnic and Racial Studies*, vol. 3, no. 1 (1980), p. 17-39, both by Masipula Sithole, and 'The struggles of the Zimbabwes: conflicts between the nationalists and with the Rhodesian regime', *African Affairs*, vol. 305, no. 76 (1977), p. 495-518, by Julian Henriques.

394 **Crisis in Rhodesia.**
Nathan Shamuyarira. London: Andre Deutsch; Levittown, New York: Transatlantic, 1965. 240p.
This is one of a number of publications on Rhodesia by African political activists written during the UDI period. These accounts usually contain discussions of African nationalism, and are useful sources for first-hand material on contemporary political figures. This work contains specific political perspectives on political events of the time, including insights into conflicts inside the liberation movements. Shamuyarira has held a number of ministerial posts since 1980 in the ZANU (PF) government, including Foreign Affairs. He was a journalist in the 1950s and 1960s and active in African politics. This book provides contemporary historical details, including information on the ZANU split in which the author was involved. Other analyses which include autobiographical details are Enoch Dumbutshena, *Zimbabwe tragedy* (Nairobi: East African Publishing House, 1975). Also see Sithole (item 768), and Wellington W. Nyangoni, *African nationalism in Zimbabwe (Rhodesia)* (Washington, DC: University Press of America, 1977), which makes good use of party literature and speeches to trace changing political positions and attitudes in the liberation movements.

395 **African nationalism.**
Ndabaningi Sithole. London; New York: Oxford University Press, 1968. 2nd ed. 174p.
Sithole was one of the most important figures in African nationalist politics during the 1960s and 1970s. An ordained minister, who had studied divinity in New Hampshire in the United States from 1955 to 1958, he entered nationalist politics in 1960, and soon joined ZAPU. When the organization was banned in 1962, he disagreed with Nkomo about strategy and founded ZANU in 1963. When this was in turn banned, he spent several periods in prison, and in 1969 was jailed for six years. At this stage he disavowed violence, and this later led to problems in ZANU with its commitment to armed struggle. Mugabe replaced him as leader of the party in 1974 whilst they were in prison, although he remained President. He was soon rejected by the party membership after his release from prison, and became increasingly identified with the collabarationist position of Abel Muzorewa in the late 1970s, taking part in the internal settlement elections of 1979 as leader of ZANU (Sithole). His new party failed to win any seats at the independence elections, and he left for the United States in 1984, where he has been a vocal critic of socialism and the Mugabe government. This important discussion of the origins and nature of African nationalism was originally published in 1959 and has been widely read. The author's included the belief that

adherence to Christian beliefs would eliminate racism. Sithole also published *Letters from Salisbury prison* (Nairobi: Transafrica, 1976).

396 From Rhodesia to Zimbabwe.
Lawrence C. Vambe. London: Heinemann; Pittsburgh, Pennsylvania: University of Pittsburgh Press, 1986. 289p.

This autobiographical account is a continuation of the author's previous book, *An ill-fated people* (item 159), and covers the period from 1930 to 1960. In both works, he records discrimination from Europeans with some passion, and he is dismissive of the 'racial partnership' promises of the federal period. Vambe was a journalist and his story includes interesting information on a number of African nationalists, including Joshua Nkomo.

Historical dictionary of Zimbabwe.
See item no. 3.

Mao Tse-Tung and Chimurenga: an investigation into ZANU's strategies.
See item no. 208.

The struggle for independence: documents on the recent development of Zimbabwe (1975-80).
See item no. 371.

Turmoil and tenacity: Zimbabwe 1890-1990.
See item no. 398.

Makers of history. Who's Who 1981-82. Nationalist leaders of Zimbabwe.
See item no. 403.

Soviet strategy towards Southern Africa: the national liberation movement connection.
See item no. 470.

Post-independence

397 Zimbabwe: a break with the past? Human rights and political unity.
Africa Watch. New York; Washington, DC; London: Africa Watch Committee, 1989. 109p.

The Africa Watch Committee was set up in the 1980s to monitor human rights in African countries. This report is the most comprehensive on the subject of human rights in the post-independence era. The research on which it is based included a visit to Zimbabwe in April 1989. Human rights abuses which had occurred in Matabeleland are covered, and the report notes the improvements which had followed the December

Politics. Post-independence

1987 Unity Accord between ZANU and ZAPU, and the Committee's relatively free access to information during its research. However it also records a number of continuing abuses. These include the detention of opposition politicians and banning of meetings of opposition political parties, evidence of torture by the Central Intelligence Organization (CIO), and government interference with the press. The latter abuse particularly pertains to the 'promotion' of Geoff Nyarota, who was removed from his editorship of the *Bulawayo Chronicle* which had exposed the Willowgate car scandals (see Sandura, item 409) which led to ministerial resignations and the suicide of Maurice Nyagumbo. The abuses perpetrated by the Mozambique National Resistance on Zimbabweans in the Eastern Highlands are also covered, and the army's response involving the expulsion and ill-treatment of Mozambiquan refugees. The important role of the Catholic Commission for Justice and Peace in Zimbabwe as a local human rights organization is also discussed. Human rights issues in post-independence Zimbabwe are also considered in William Spring's *The long fields: Zimbabwe since independence* (Basingstoke, England: Pickering and Inglis, 1986). Apart from the Fifth Brigade's activities in Matabeland he also discusses the case of six white airforce officers who had been held on charges of sabotage, and were re-detained after being acquitted by the Zimbabwean courts. See also Bill Berkeley, *Zimbabwe: wages of war* (New York: Lawyers' Committee for Human Rights, 1986).

398 **Turmoil and tenacity: Zimbabwe 1890-1990.**
Edited by Canaan Sodindo Banana. Harare: College Press, 1989. 376p.

This volume, edited by Zimbabwe's first President, Canaan Banana, contains seventeen papers which deal with various issues concerning the country's political development over the previous one hundred years. The interesting feature of this book is that the papers are contributed not only by academics, but also by many leading political figures, including Mugabe and Nkomo. Thus whilst the analyses are not always scholarly or objective, they do serve as an insight into the experience and attitudes of Zimbabwean politicians, and the topics covered include many key episodes during the war and struggle for a settlement in the 1970s, told by those directly involved. The signing of the Unity Accord is also covered in detail, as is the expulsion of ZAPU ministers in the early years of independence, the dissident problem in Matabeleland, the establishment of the opposition party, the Zimbabwe Unity Movement (ZUM), and the closure of the University. Banana contributes an introduction, and the papers are as follows: Nathan Shamuyarira, 'Overview of the struggle for unity and independence'; Misheck Sibanda, 'Early foundations of African nationalism'; Ngwabi Bhebe, 'The national struggle 1957-62'; Judith Todd, 'White policy and politics 1890-1980'; Anthony Chenells, 'White Rhodesian nationalism – the mistaken years'; Emmerson Mnangagwa, 'The formation of the Front for the Liberation of Zimbabwe: FROLIZI' and 'The formation of the Zimbabwe People's Army: ZIPA'; Ariston Chambati, 'National unity – African National Congress: ANC'; Shepherd Nzombe, 'Negotiations with the British'; Canaan Banana, 'The role of the church in the struggle for liberation in Zimbabwe'; Fay Chung, 'Education with production before and after independence'; Emmerson Mnangagwa, 'Post-independence Zimbabwe (1981-87); Willard Chiwewe, 'Unity negotiations'; Didymus Mutasa, 'The signing of the Unity Accord'; Joshua Nkomo, 'The significance of national unity and the future'; Welshman Ncube, 'The post-unity period: development, benefits and problems'; and Robert Mugabe, 'The Unity Accord: its problems for the future'.

399 **State politics in Zimbabwe.**
Jeffrey Herbst. Harare: University of Zimbabwe Publications;
Berkeley, California: University of California Press, 1990. 283p. map.

Based on the author's 1987 doctoral dissertation for Yale University, this is a well-researched and comprehensive account of politics in the post-independence period. After a theoretical introduction on choice and African politics, Herbst provides seven case studies which illustrate the government's handling of political pressures and allocation processes. These are the land issue and the competing claims of white farmers, communal farmers and squatters; agricultural product pricing policy; policies towards foreign investment, multinational companies and mineral marketing; ethnic and class claims on the health service; and the national minimum wage policy. Education is unfortunately absent from the analysis. Herbst concludes with discussion of the evolution of politics since 1980, the development of the politics of reconciliation, and the interplay between ideology and pragmatism, focussing on understanding the nature of the state and the nature of decision-making. The book also contains useful statistical data on the land issue and mineral production. Two shorter papers by the author on two of the themes he develops in the book are 'Political impediments to economic rationality: explaining Zimbabwe's failure to reform its public sector', *Journal of Modern African Studies*, vol. 27, no. 1 (1989), p. 67-84, which highlights the problems the state has faced in the parastatal sector, and 'Societal pressures and government choices: agricultural price policy in Zimbabwe', *Comparative Politics*, vol. 20, no. 3 (1988), p. 265-88.

400 **Conflict in Zimbabwe: the Matabeleland problem.**
Richard Hodder-Williams. *Conflict Studies*, vol. 151 (1983), 20p.

This issue of *Conflict Studies* was devoted to the Matabeleland problem. In the early 1980s Matabeleland was in turmoil with much bloodshed and violence resulting from anti-government activities. The belief amongst ZAPU dissidents that the ZANU government was betraying the ideals for which the war had been fought was one reason for the conflict. South African-trained and supported freelance bandits were also involved, as South Africa attempted to destabilize Zimbabwe. Many arms which should have been handed in before independence were still available to the dissidents. The government reacted with great harshness, sending in the Korean-trained Fifth Brigade which rapidly became notorious, and it later transpired that there were a number of massacres which included innocent villagers. Hodder-Williams discusses the roots of dissent, and criticizes the government for its strong-arm methods, but explains that its reaction can only be understood in the wider context of Zimbabwean politics.

401 **The Zimbabwe general election of 1985.**
Anthony Lemon. *Journal of Commonwealth and Comparative Politics,* vol. 26, no. 1 (1988), p. 3–21.

ZANU increased its majority at the 1985 elections, and in this paper Lemon examines the ruling party's success. This is also a useful source on the procedures used in the 1985 elections, which are compared to the 1980 elections. For brief factual details on spatial patterns of voting in these two elections, see Daniel S. Tevera, 'Voting patterns in Zimbabwe's elections of 1980 and 1985', *Geography*, vol. 74, no. 2 (1989), p. 162-65. Both elections have also been analysed by Christine Sylvester in 'Zimbabwe's 1985 elections: a search for national mythology', *Journal of Modern African Studies*, vol. 24, no. 2 (1989), p. 229-55, and 'Unities and disunities in Zimbabwe's 1990 election', *Journal of Modern African Studies*, vol. 28, no. 3 (1990), p. 375–400.

402 **The one-party state and democracy: the Zimbabwean debate.**
Edited by Ibbo Mandaza, Lloyd Sachikonye. Harare: Southern
African Political Economy Series (SAPES) Trust, 1991. 202p. (State
and Democracy Series, no. 1).

There was much academic and public debate about the pros and cons of a one-party
state throughout the 1980s in Zimbabwe. This reached a peak in 1990 with the expiry
of the Lancaster House constitution which had prevented the government from
introducing this form of government. Mugabe has always professed a commitment to a
one-party state, and the contributions to this book were written in the context of this
still being a live political issue. However, by the time of publication it was clear that
Mugabe had lost this particular political battle, with the opposition from within his own
party mounting. The papers in this edited volume provide an excellent reflection of the
debate amongst the local intelligentsia, with contributions from civil servants,
intellectuals, public figures, journalists, trade unionists and students, almost all of
whom strongly opposed the one-party system. Wider issues of public accountability
and government tolerance of opposition are also addressed. Most of the contributions
also express a strong desire for socialist development, and theoretical discussion of
Marxism and its relationship to the form of the state is found in several papers. The
contributors are lecturer and poet Musaemura Zimunya; Masipula Sithole; Jonathan
Moyo; Kempton Makamure; Andries Matenda Rukobo; Fay Chung, the former
Minister of Education; Arthur Mutambara, the President of the University of
Zimbabwe's Student Representative Council 1989–90; Albert Musarurwa, a lawyer,
and legal adviser to the Zimbabwe Congress of Trade Unionists until 1990; law lecturer
Welshman Ncube; John Makumbe; and the editors, Mandaza and Sachikonye. Lloyd
Sachikonye is a Senior Research Fellow and Head of Labour Studies at the
Zimbabwean Institute of Development Studies. For biographical notes on Mandaza,
see item 417. The one-party state debate and its relation to Marxist theory is also
discussed in William H. Shaw, 'Towards the one-party state in Zimbabwe: a study in
African political thought'. *Journal of Modern African Studies*, vol. 24, no. 3 (1986),
p. 373–94.

403 **Makers of history. Who's Who 1981–82. Nationalist leaders of
Zimbabwe.**
Diana Mitchell. Salisbury: Diana Mitchell, 1982. 170p.

This is a useful source for brief biographical details on nationalist leaders in
Zimbabwe, including most of those in the government at the time of publication. A
1982–83 supplement to this volume includes details of an early cabinet reshuffle, and
eighty new entries. Mitchell also wrote *Who's Who 1980: African nationalist leaders in
Zimbabwe* (Salisbury: Cannon Press, 1980) and, with Robert Cary, *African nationalist
leaders in Rhodesia: Who's Who* (Bulawayo: Books of Rhodesia; Johannesburg;
Africana Book Society, 1977). The books also contain lists of some of the military
leaders of the liberation war, and of members of the senate and parliament. The 1977
volume has a complete list of African members of parliament from 1954–1977, but its
main focus is on African nationalist political parties and groups. The author is a white
liberal whose sympathies were with the liberation movements during the war. Another
very different publication giving biographical details on Rhodesian Africans is
Prominent African personalities of Rhodesia (Salisbury: Cover Publicity Servies, 1977)
which provides short biographical details on a very diverse selection of people. Much
of the information was garnered from biographies posted to the publishers, often by
business people and professionals. The purpose of the book was apparently to inspire
the young by providing accounts of outstanding achievements by local people.

Remarkably, although individuals such as Mugabe and Nkomo are included, there is virtually no mention of their political significance or of their imprisonments and exile. This publication was updated to include some whites and Asians as *Prominent Rhodesian personalities* (Salisbury: Cover Publicity Services, 1978).

404   **The ideological formation of the Zimbabwean ruling class.**
David B. Moore.   *Journal of Southern African Studies.* vol. 17, no. 3 (1991), p. 472-95.

Moore questions the relevance of the debate about whether the Zimbabwean revolution failed (see item 414). He believes that the rise to power of a new group of intellectuals and their construction of a new form of hegemony was, in itself, a successful revolution. He does not agree that it was inevitable that this ruling class would fail to push through a transformation of the political economy, believing that there were times when there was the potential for a more dynamic class to emerge as rulers. However he does believe that the present ruling class is 'passive', and has opted for capitalism and élitism rather than Marxism and populism, and that the young Marxist intellectuals have been sidelined. This view on Zimbabwean politics can be compared to Christine Sylvester's (item 412).

405   **Voting for democracy: electoral politics in Zimbabwe.**
Jonathan S. Moyo.   Harare: University of Zimbabwe Publications, 1992. 145p.

This book analyses the 1990 general elction, in which ZANU (PF) maintained its huge majority. At the time of that election the one-party state was still a live issue, yet a major questionnaire survey of voters reported in this book found that most voters were against the idea. The book is also an indictment of the government's electoral campaign, and its efforts to prevent the opposition from competing on an equal basis. The Electoral Commission which declared the elections free and fair is heavily criticized. For a critical analysis of politics in the 1990s see his 'State politics and social domination in Zimbabwe', *Journal of Modern African Studies*, vol. 30, no. 2 (1992), p. 305-30.

406   **The February 1980 Zimbabwe elections: the Matabeleland North and South provinces.**
Joshua Mpofu.   In *Conference on Zimbabwe, June 21-22, 1980*. Edited by the Department of Politics, University of Leeds in collaboration with the *Review of African Political Economy*. Leeds, England: University of Leeds, 1980. [n.p.]

This analysis of the independence elections in 1980 focusses on the results in Matabeleland where ZAPU dominated the voting. Another analysis of specific regional results is found in the same edited volume: Lionel Cliffe and Barry Munslow. 'The 1980 elections in Victoria Province, Zimbabwe: an interim report'. The volume is available from the University of York library.

407   **The 1990 Zimbabwe elections: a post-mortem.**
Lloyd Sachikonye.   *Review of African Political Economy*, vol. 48 (1990), p. 92-99.

The 1990 elections saw a complete change in the nature of Zimbabwe's internal politics. The Unity Accord between ZANU (PF) and ZAPU had removed the latter from its previous position as the primary opposition party. This role had been taken over by ZUM, the Zimbabwe Unity Movement, which had no clear agenda, a notorious leader, and traded mainly on the ruling party's mistakes. This party appeared to have considerable backing in the urban areas, but ZANU (PF) still won by a huge majority. This article examines the election, including the procedures involved and allegations of unfair practices, in the context of the development of class and ethnic relations since 1980. A specific issue addressed is whether Zimbabwe should be considered a *de facto* one-party state after the outcome of this election.

408 **Hunhuism or Ubuntuism: a Zimbabwean indigenous political philosophy.**
Stanlake John William Samkange, Marie Samkange. Salisbury: Graham Publishing, 1980. 106p.

The Samkanges' thesis is that Zimbabwean culture contains an indigenous political philosophy in which people are the central focus, and that this should inspire and guide the future leadership and governments. There are parallels between this philosophy and that of the humanism espoused by Kenneth Kaunda, the President of Zambia until 1991.

409 **Report of the Commission of Inquiry into the distribution of motor vehicles.**
Under the chairmanship of Mr Justice W. R. Sandura. Harare: Zimbabwe Government, 1989. 121p.

The 'Willowgate' scandal which led to the commissioning of this report was a notorious example of corrupt behaviour by government officials, including Ministers. The scandal involved the illicit use of official influence to obtain cars at controlled prices from a local car assembly plant. This fascinating report is a symbol of the rapid shift of many members of the Zimbabwean government away from socialist principles. Its particular interest lies in its detailed and uncompromising coverage of defendants' and witnesses' statements, and its hard-hitting recommendations for action. The ambivalence of party leaders towards the issue is reflected in the fact that the government did not interfere in the inquiry, and made the report freely available, but generally ignored the recommendations for punishment it contained. Nevertheless, Maurice Nyagumbo, one of the heroes of national liberation, committed suicide as a result of this inquiry. This report is also a useful source of information on the vehicle industry in the 1980s.

410 **Zimbabwe: in search of a stable democracy.**
Masipula Sithole. In *Democracy in developing countries: Africa*, vol. 2. Edited by Larry Diamond, Juan J. Linz, Seymour M. Lipset. Boulder, Colorado: Lynne Rienner; London: Adamantine, 1988, p. 217-57.

This paper was written before the Unity Accord between ZANU (PF) and ZAPU, and the author contends that the then extremely antagonistic relationship between the two main political parties boded ill for the future of democracy in Zimbabwe. The paper also provides a brief examination of white democracy in colonial times, and debates the one-party issue.

411 **Mugabe.**
David Smith, Colin Simpson, Ian Davies.   London: Spere Books;
Salisbury: Pioneer Head, 1981. 217p.

This is a very sympathetic biography of Robert Mugabe, stressing how he had been typified and vilified as an extremist for decades and caused great surprise by his moderate and pragmatic approach once he was elected Prime Minister. Written just after independence by two journalists, this account covers Mugabe's early life and career as a teacher, his entry into political activities in 1960 in the National Democratic Party and ZAPU, and his escape after several arrests to Tanzania in 1963. He then joined Sithole's new ZANU, becoming its secretary general, but on his return to Zimbabwe was re-arrested, and spent ten years in prison. In 1974, whilst still imprisoned, he replaced Sithole as leader of the party, and after his release later that year he went to Mozambique where he organized ZANU's armed struggle. The work stresses Magabe's reconciliatory approach to his opponents at independence, but was written too early to assess his independence record.

412 **Zimbabwe: the terrain of contradictory development.**
Christine Sylvester.   Boulder, Colorado: Westview Press; Aldershot,
UK: Dartmouth Publishing, 1991. 212p. (Westview Profiles: Nations of
Contemporary Africa.)

This is a general overview of the political economy of Zimbabwe at the end of the first decade of independence. The focus is on the contradictions inherent in Zimbabwe's development strategy, with remarkable survivals from its racist past such as the continued dependence of the agricultural export sector on white farmers. Sylvester's work on Zimbabwe has stressed the existence of societal and political tendencies that are pulling the country in different directions, but she also identifies prospects for a less contradictory future. Papers based on her research into the conflicts in Zimbabwean political and development processes are 'Continuity and discontinuity in Zimbabwe's development history', *African Studies Review*, vol. 28, no. 1 (1985), p. 19-44, and 'Simultaneous revolutions: the Zimbabwean case', *Journal of Southern African Studies*, vol. 16, no. 3 (1990), p. 452-75. The author is Associate Professor of Political Science at Northern Arizona University.

413 **Election handbook: a guide to the general election of July 1985.**
Prepared and compiled by Zimbabwe Inter-African News Agency,
foreword by Professor W. J. Kamba, Chair of the Electoral Supervisory
Committee.   Harare: Zimbabwe Inter-African News Agency, 1985.

This handbook contains a wealth of electoral information on both the 1985 and 1980 national elections. It was published prior to the election, and therefore does not contain the results, but it is a primary resource for those interested in the electoral process. After discussion of the government of the day, it details the constituencies and provides a map of their boundaries including the urban constituencies. Estimates of the number of eligible voters are provided, with lists of candidates and the manifestos of both ZANU (PF) and ZAPU; unfortunately other party manifestos are omitted. The white roll is discussed, and the fate of the various white members of parliament elected in 1980 is detailed. Finally the candidates for the 1980 elections are listed, and the names of the elected members of parliament. Further details on the first independence parliament are found in *A concise guide to the first Parliament of Zimbabwe* (Harare: Government Printer, 1984) by the Ministry of Information, Posts and Telecommunications, which contains profiles of the national leadership, with an introduction on political development up to independence. Detailed biographical notes are also provided on the President, Ministers and Deputy Ministers, the President of the Senate and the Speaker of the House of Assembly.

Socialism

414 Zimbabwe: a revolution that list its way?
André Astrow.   London: Zed Press, 1983. 254p.

Astrow was one of the earliest critics of the Zimbabwean government's socialist demeanour, which he dismisses in this book as mere pretension. He notes in this book that little had really changed with independence, and that tensions had already arisen between Mugabe's government and the masses. His major thesis is that the state at independence came under the control of the petty bourgeoisie, who had always been the class best represented in the leadership of the liberation movements. Moreover he argues that this was inevitable since the independence struggle was a nationalist, rather than class, struggle. This argument has often been applied to explain the nature of the state in African countries after independence – the difference in Zimbabwe's case being that UDI and the war might have pushed through a more radical outcome. Astrow also denies the possibility, accepted at the time by some other analysts, of an eventual transition through democracy and the mobilization of the working class to real socialism. He was criticized by Stoneman and Cliffe (see item 14) for thus categorizing the new state as neo-colonial by definition, rather than as a result of particular experiences. The Zimbabwean government is also criticized for its lack of commitment to socialist transformation in *Southern Africa after Zimbabwe* (London: Pluto Press, 1981) by Alex Callinicos, who analyses the ZANU victory and asserts that Mugabe opted for legislative rather than social reform. He also considers the future of black-white relations in Southern Africa in the wake of Zimbabwe's independence.

415 The theology of promise: the dynamics of self-reliance.
Canaan Sodindo Banana.   Harare: College Press, 1982. Reprinted 1989. 160p.

In this treatise, the first President of independent Zimbabwe analyses the past and present circumstances which have led to suffering in Zimbabwe, and attempts to reconcile the socialist revolution with Christian faith. He believes the socialist goals of the state and the teachings of the church are compatible, and that the church should clearly identify itself with social justice. See also, by the same author, *Towards a socialist ethos* (Harare: College Press, 1987). Banana is an ordained Methodist minister, who was educated in Zimbabwe, Japan, the United States of America, and South Africa. He was the first vice-president of the African National Council in 1971, and played a key role in opposing the Anglo-Rhodesian settlement initiative in 1972. He joined ZANU in 1976 whilst in Geneva as a member of an ANC delegation, and was imprisoned twice by the UDI state.

416 **Editorial: the prospects for Zimbabwe.**
Lionel Cliffe, Barry Munslow. *Review of African Political Economy*, vol. 18 (May-Aug. 1980), p. 1-6.
Cliffe and Munslow edited a special volume of this leading radical journal on African politics on Zimbabwe. The theme of this editorial introduction is the importance of labour rather than land as the key issue for the prospects of socialism. Two debating papers at the end of the volume consider the nature of the settler mode of production, and the relationship between imperialism and settler capitalism.

417 **Zimbabwe: the political economy of transition 1980-86.**
Edited by Ibbo Mandaza. Dakar: CODESRIA, 1986. 430p. bibliog.
This key collection of papers on Zimbabwe's political economy contains thirteen papers written 'by Zimbabweans for Zimbabweans'. The editor, Mandaza, studied at the University of Rhodesia and was expelled for his political activity in 1973. He remained involved with the liberation movement whilst obtaining his PhD in political economy at York University, England, and then lecturing at the Universities of Botswana and Dar es Salaam from 1977 to 1980. After independence Mandaza held a number of positions in the Ministry of Manpower Planning and Development and was also active in the establishment of ZIDS (Zimbabwe Institute of Development Studies). He is currently Executive Director of the Southern African Political Economic Series (SAPES) Trust, and editor of *Southern African Political and Economic Monthly*. Mandaza is a radical critic of both the continued inequalities in Zimbabwean society, and what he perceives as a largely Euro-American tendency to analyse the transition to an independent Zimbabwe in terms of a 'failed revolution', and a betrayal of the heroes of the guerilla war. In his opinion there was no logical reason to expect an armed struggle to lead to socialism in the short term. The post-colonial state is viewed as essentially dependent on international capital, and the new class alliances which have emerged as antithetical to the demands of the masses. Nevertheless this does not exclude the possibility of worker and peasant resistance. In this he differed from the analysis suggested by Astrow (see item 414), who felt the revolution had totally failed. The papers cover five main topics: politics, economics, the agrarian question, the labour movement, and social development. For politics, Mandaza provides an overview of the post-independence situation, and Masipula Sithole analyses the first three general elections of 1979, 1980 and 1985. Xavier Kadhani provides an overview of the economy, Theresa Chimiombe discusses foreign capital, and Daniel Ndlela industrialization. The agrarian question contributions are from Sam Moyo on land, Clever Mumbengegwi on agricultural policy, and Thomas Shop on hunger. Contributions on the labour movement come from Lloyd Sachikonye on trade unions, and Brian Raftopoulos on human resources and labour utilization. The social development contributions are from Rungano Zvobgo on education, Samuel Agere on health, and Joyce Kazembe on women.

418 **An agenda for Zimbabwe.**
Herbert Sylvester Masiyiwa Ushewokunze. Harare: College Press; Trowbridge, England: Redwood Burn, 1984. 198p.
Ushewokunze served in several ministerial posts in Mugabe's governments, but blotted his copy book many times and was finally ousted from any key position. It is paradoxical that he should have been one of ZANU's most published analysts of the prospects for socialism in the newly independent state, since he has also been one of the party leaders subject to allegations of taking undue advantage of their position, and accumulating wealth and land. This collection of essays contains the texts of various

speeches he delivered after independence on the theme of where 'socialist' Zimbabwe was heading. The topics covered are socialist theory and reality, including analysis of the state of emergency in Matabeleland, agriculture, the politics of health, and the relationship between Zimbabwe and South Africa, and destabilization. Another paper on Zimbabwean socialism, originally delivered by Ushewokunze at a rally to university students, is 'Zimbabwe: problems and prospects of socialist development', *Race and Class*, vol. 23, no. 4 (1982), p. 275-83. Amongst the issues it deals with are elitism, and the possibility that opting for economic and political policies of short-term pragmatism might lead to the eventual neglect of long-term transformation. In these his analysis was remarkably, if ironicially, percipient.

419 Prospects for socialist transition in Zimbabwe.

Peter Yates pseud. *Review of African Political Economy*, vol. 18 (1980), p. 68-80.

This early article on Zimbabwean socialism highlighted many of the problems which socialist transformation would face, and identified some of the debates which later contributions to the issue of transformation all addressed. It is a useful start for those interested in the debate about socialism in Zimbabwe, which is considered in greater detail in Astrow, Mandaza, and Stoneman and Cliffe (items 14, 414, 417). The author believed that the Lancaster House settlement had come too early, and by preventing a complete victory by the liberation forces, had faced the new government with a set of restrictive factors which were bound to slow the pace of fundamental change. In any case ZANU was not a workers' party, and was therefore unlikely to be wholehearted about radical restructuring of the political economy. In the discussion of changes which had occurred, some positive aspects are identified such as free medical treatment for those earning less than Z$150 per month. One of the most important hindrances to any form of socialist transformation is shown to be the extremely high levels of foreign control of productive capital, which is estimated at ninety per cent of production and trade. This control is often channelled through the South African headquarters of multinational companies.

The politics of reconciliation: Zimbabwe's first decade.

See item no. 2.

Zimbabwe's prospects: issues of race, class, state and capital in Southern Africa.

See item no. 13.

Zimbabwe: politics, economics and society.

See item no. 14.

With the people: an autobiography from the Zimbabwean struggle.

See item no. 391.

Constitution, Legal System and Human Rights

Common law

420 **Women and law in Southern Africa.**
Edited by Alice Armstrong, Welshman Ncube. Harare: Zimbabwe Publishing House, 1987. 281p.

This collection of papers examines aspects of law which affect women in Southern Africa. It is primarily aimed at university students, and contains sober, empirical analysis of the problems generated for women under a dual system of laws. A number of papers specifically address women's legal issues in Zimbabwe. Two of these are concerned with property rights: Julie Stewart, 'Playing the game: women's inheritance of property in Zimbabwe' and Welshman Ncube, 'Underprivilege and inequality: matrimonial property rights of women in Zimbabwe'. Ncube also discusses women's new status as legal 'adults' in 'Released from legal minority: the legal age of majority Act in Zimbabwe'. Traditionally African women have few rights over their children in the patrilineal societies common in Zimbabwe. The legal aspects of this are considered in M. Maboreke, 'The love of a mother: problems of custody in Zimbabwe'. On abortion, which is illegal in Zimbabwe, see Ian Chikanza and Webster Chinamora, 'Abortion in Zimbabwe: a medico-legal problem', which provides some data on the incidence of illegal abortion in Harare, and makes a strong case for reform of the law.

421 **Legal aspects of doing business in Zimbabwe.**
J. H. P. Back. *Zimbabwe Law Journal*, vol. 22, no. 2 (1982), p. 162-68.

An overview of the legal system in Zimbabwe is provided, with special reference to aspects which affect businesses. Other relevant titles for business people are *Zimbabwe company law* (Harare: Zimbabwe Law Journal, Department of Law, University of Zimbabwe, 1981. 2nd. ed.) by Nanette Chadwick and Peter L. Volpe, respectively a barrister, and an advocate of the High Court as well as a Senior Lecturer in Law at the University of Zimbabwe. This updates the 1974 work, *Rhodesian Company Law*, and contains an additional section on the new topic of co-operative law. It is aimed primarily at students. Business law is also tackled by I. Bampton and D. Drury, *An introduction to Zimbabwe business law* (Harare: Legal Resources Foundation, [n.d.]) which covers issues such as the laws of contract and sale, and is aimed at the intelligent layperson.

422 **Witches, witchcraft and the law in Zimbabwe.**
Gordon L. Chavunduka. Harare: ZINATHA, 1982. 27p.
(ZINATHA Occasional Paper, no. 1).

The subject of witches is controversial, but the colonial authorities took the problem seriously enough to legislate against witchcraft in 1899, and the Witchcraft Suppression Act remains on the books. Chavunduka attempts to define witchcraft within the local context, describes the different types that are recognized, and goes on to discuss the implications of the Act. His interest in the topic derives from his position as President of the Traditional Healers' Association, some of whom might be affected by the Act. In an earlier paper the author discussed the different treatment of witchcraft by the western and customary legal systems. See 'Witchcraft and the law in Zimbabwe', *Zambezia*, vol. 8, no. 2 (1980), p. 129-47. A substantial earlier study which focusses mainly on witchcraft amongst the Shona, and details 103 recorded cases from 1956-62 is J. R. Crawford, *Witchcraft and sorcery in Rhodesia* (London, New York: Oxford University Press, 1967).

423 **A guide to Zimbabwean criminal law.**
Geoff Feltoe. Harare: Legal Resources Foundation, 1989. 143p.

This guide is aimed primarily at legal practitioners, including those who are foreign-trained and unfamiliar with local case law, and as an introduction for law students. Topics covered include the criminal law system in Zimbabwe, the courts, general principles, defences, specific crimes, and the vicarious liability of companies. It does not aim to provide comprehensive coverage of criminal law, but will facilitate the locating of relevant cases on a particular subject.

424 **Law and medicine in Zimbabwe.**
Geoffrey Feltoe, T. J. Nyapadi. Harare: Baobab Books in association with Legal Resources Foundation, 1989. 141p.

This is another publication on local legal issues from the excellent Zimbabwean Legal Resources Foundation. The book provides a guide to those aspects of the law which affect the practice of medicine in Zimbabwe.

425 **Consolidated index to the Zimbabwean law reports, 1964-83.**
Edited by M. J. Gillespie. Harare: Legal Resources Foundation, [1984]. 609p.

This was the first publication of the Foundation, which has produced a steady stream of useful guides and analyses of various aspects of Zimbabwean law. It covers the twenty year period since the last published index in 1963. All the cases tried since then are listed, plus all the cases and statutes referred to in the trials, indexed by subject.

426 **Some famous Rhodesian trials.**
Alan Hardy. Bulawayo: Books of Zimbabwe, 1981. 151p.
This is a journalistic account of nine famous legal cases which were tried in colonial Rhodesia. These are written up in a fashion reminiscent of a thriller, with details on the crime, evidence, court case, verdict and sentence, illustrated by numerous photographs. All pertain to crimes committed by whites, with the exception of a brief account of a witchcraft case.

427 **A comparative study of Comrade's Courts under socialist legal systems and Zimbabwe's village courts.**
Kempton Makamure. *Zimbabwe Law Review*, vol. 3, no. 1/2 (1985), p. 34-61.
During the liberation war some areas of the country developed revolutionary tribunals to deal with local legal issues and conflicts. These evolved into village courts after 1980, and this paper discusses the nature of these courts and compares them to local courts in a number of socialist countries.

428 **African custom and western law: the development of the Rhodesian criminal law for Africans.**
Emmet V. Mittlebeeler. New York, London: Africana Publishing Company, 1976. 248p.
The imposition on black Rhodesians of a criminal law system developed under an alien culture caused many problems since conceptions of criminality vary with culture. This book discusses the interplay between western law and African custom from a European viewpoint. Rhodesian legal history is reviewed, and conflicts arising from the new laws are discussed in a number of areas including marriage, sexual offences, witchcraft, homicide, administration orders and compensation. The tension arising from the usurpation of traditional authority is also reviewed. Many examples of actual legal cases from 1900 to 1970 are provided as illustration.

429 **Family law in Zimbabwe.**
Welshman Ncube. Harare: Legal Resources Foundation, 1989. 227p.
This discussion of family law is one in a series of useful guides to various aspects of Zimbabwean law produced by the Legal Resources Foundation.

430 **Introduction to the legal system of Zimbabwe.**
J. Redgment. Harare: Belmont Printers, 1981. 81p.
This is a concise general introduction to Zimbabwe's legal system designed for students and the general public. It is now rather dated as there have been some important legal changes since 1981. A short introductory article on the legal system is available by J. A. Bennett, 'The legal system of Zimbabwe', *Zimbabwe Law Journal*, vol. 22, no. 2 (1982), p. 147-61.

431 **The legal situation of women in Zimbabwe.**
Julie Stewart, Alice Armstrong, Welshman Ncube, M. Maboreke. In: *The legal situation of women in Southern Africa.* Edited by Julie Stewart, Alice Armstrong. Harare: University of Zimbabwe Publications, 1990.

This paper appeared in a companion volume to *Women and Law in Southern Africa* (see item 420), which contains papers from a workshop held at the University in 1988 resulting directly from the first book. All the contributions have an activist orientation. For a brief review of changes in laws affecting women, which deals with marriage, proprietary rights, legal reforms, maintenance, the Legal Age of Majority Act, and seduction damages, see Joyce Kazembe and Marjon Mol, 'The changing legal status of women in Zimbabwe since independence', *Canadian Women's Studies*, vol. 7, nos. 1 & 2 (1986), p. 53-59. Similar themes are covered in their 'Zimbabwe, state, law and women', in *Empowerment and the law: strategies of Third World women* (Washington, DC: OEF International, 1986, p. 299-305), edited by Margaret Schuller.

Zimbabwe: at 5 years of independence: achievement, problems and prospects.
See item no. 17.

Changing people, changing laws.
See item no. 361.

Women's guide to law through life.
See item no. 368.

Conflict of laws: the application of customary law and the common law in Zimbabwe.
See item no. 432.

The United Nations, international law, and the Rhodesian independence crisis.
See item no. 475.

Statute Law of Zimbabwe.
See item no. 842.

Customary law

432 **Conflict of laws: the application of customary law and the common law in Zimbabwe.**
T. W. Bennett. *International and Comparative Law Quarterly*, vol. 30, no. 1 (1981), p. 59-103.

There are inevitable conflicts caused by the different interpretation of legality and illegality according to customary or common law. The rules determining which system be used were substantially modified in 1969. In this article the author examines six types of conflict which often arise in Zimbabwe because of the existence of two legal systems. Women in particular can face difficulties: this topic is tackled specifically by Angela Cheater, 'Fighting over property: the articulation of dominant and subordinate legal systems governing the inheritance of immovable property among blacks in Zimbabwe', *Africa* (UK), vol. 57, no. 2 (1987) p. 173-95. Under customary law women's rights to property were weak, especially for widows who could find themselves left destitute by their husband's death when his relatives stripped the home. Although they now have new legal rights, these are not always honoured, and the articulation of the customary law and western law is often resolved against women's interests. This can lead to precedents which discriminate against women's rights, of particular economic significance when they lose their access to land and other means of agricultural production.

433   **A Shona urban court.**

Gordon L. Chavunduka.   Gweru: Mambo Press, 1979. 72p.

(Occasional Papers, Socio-economic Series, no. 14).

In order to write this book Chavunduka, then a lecturer in sociology at the University of Zimbabwe, attended Makoni Tribal Court in St. Mary's, Seke from September 1977 to January 1978 with further visits in 1978 and 1979. He also studied case summaries from October 1970 to May 1974. The aim of his study is to describe the operation of a traditional urban court and its application of Shona customary law. Previous studies of this law drew on rural village practice and this was the first to focus on practices in an urban area. Chavunduka shows how the law has adapted as the standards and values of society in an urban context have changed. He also discusses some of the stresses engendered by this social change, such as the inability of urban families to deal with the needs of their kin in the same way that their rural counterparts do, and the problems encountered as women's roles change.

434   **The history and extent of recognition of tribal law in Rhodesia.**

Harold Child.   Salisbury: Ministry of Internal Affairs, 1976. 2nd ed. 255p.

This second edition updated an earlier 1965 version, since the passing of the African Law and Tribal Courts Act of 1969 had made some significant changes. These included provisions whereby Africans could choose to be tried under the common law, and non-Africans could be tried under customary law if the case also involved an African.

435   **Customary law and family predicaments.**

Siphikekelo Chizengeni.   Salisbury: Centre for Applied Social Science, University of Zimbabwe, 1979. 78p.

This study is sub-titled 'a report on the application of customary law in a changing society and its effects on the family, with special reference to the women and children in Zimbabwe'. The focus of the study is the 1960 Marriage Act.

436   **African law and custom in Rhodesia.**

Bennie Goldin, Michael Gelfand.   Cape Town: Juta, 1975. 325p.

This book provides a general overview of customary law and relevant legislation, and also discusses differences between Shona and Ndebele practices. Topics covered include family law, tribal courts, contracts, criminal law, and succession. The major study on Shona customary law is Johan Holleman's *Shona customary law: with reference to kinship, marriage, the family and the estate* (Cape Town: Oxford University Press, 1952; Manchester, England: Manchester University Press, 1969).

437 Customary law in practice.

J. G. Storry. Cape Town: Juta, 1979. 144p.

This handbook to customary law in Zimbabwe is written by an advocate and aims to explain the practice of customary law, as it has developed and manifested itself through judicial interpretation and the application of relevant statutes. The establishment of precedents is thus an important theme, and the growth during the 20th century of a common code of practice. The book is not therefore concerned with substantive law, and caters primarily for the requirements of legal practitioners. The book makes much use of Holleman, and Goldin and Gelfand (see item 436).

Past and present in Zimbabwe.
See item no. 9.

Constitution and human rights

438 Individual freedoms and state security in the African context: the case of Zimbabwe.

John Hatchard. Harare: Baobab Books; London: James Currey; Athens, Ohio: Ohio University Press, 1993. 209p.

Hatchard, a former senior lecturer in the Law Department at the University of Zimbabwe, uses Zimbabwe as a case study in this examination of the relationship between the use of emergency powers during a state of emergency and the fate of individual freedoms in Africa. Zimbabwe was under a state of emergency from 1965 to 1990, and retains wide-ranging security legislation including the Law and Order (Maintenance) Act which has been compared to South Africa's Internal Security Act. This book examines the justifications for the original declaration of a state of emergency in Zimbabwe and its subsequent maintenance after independence, plus the scope of the regulations and their impact on civil rights. The author attempts to define what safeguards could be implemented in these circumstances to prevent abuses of power. Appendices on the constitution, the Emergency Power Act, and the emergency regulations are included.

439 Racial discrimination and repression in Southern Rhodesia.

International Commission of Jurists. London, Geneva: Catholic Institute for International Relations and International Commission of Jurists, 1976. 119p.

This is the most extensive study of human rights abuses by the UDI state. The research on which it is based was conducted by four University of California students who examined allegations of torture, detention and illegal killings and other civil liberties issues. Various legal cases arising from the liberation struggle from 1973 to 1975 are listed. Laws which contravened human rights are discussed in Christopher Zimmerli, 'Human rights and the rule of law in Southern Rhodesia', *International and Comparative Law Quarterly*, vol. 20, no. 2 (1970), p. 239-300.

440   **Zimbabwe. Wages of war: a report on human rights.**
Lawyers' Committee for Human Rights.   New York: Lawyers'
Committee for Human Rights, 1986. 171p.

This is a report on the violence which led to many violations of human rights in
Matabeleland during the first few years of independence. The LCHR sent
representatives to Zimbabwe in 1983-84, 1985 and 1986. They met with numerous
victims of human rights violations and their relatives, primarily in Southwest
Matabeleland. They also talked to religious leaders, attorneys, party leaders,
journalists, academics and human rights workers, and actively sought the views of the
government. The role of the dissidents and the Fifth Brigade in the violence is
discussed. The significant involvement of young people in intimidation is highlighted,
and there is brief mention of South African support for some of the dissidents.

441   **Rhodesian constitutions and politics: in a dispute for national
independence.**
Mudimuranwa A. B. Mutiti.   Nairobi: Kenya Literature Bureau,
1979. 218p.

The author is a Zimbabwean lawyer, who was lecturing at the University of Dar es
Salaam when he published this book. His main theme is the racially discriminatory
nature of Rhodesia's constitutions over the decades, but he also provides a general
overview of the constitutions from a lawyer's perspective. The constitutions discussed
are the Southern Rhodesian constitution of 1923, the constitution of the Federation of
Rhodesia and Nyasaland in 1953, the UDI constitution and the 1969 constitution. The
Pearce Commission is also analysed.

442   **The constitutional history and law of Southern Rhodesia, 1888-1965:
with special reference to imperial control.**
Claire Palley.   London; New York: Oxford University Press, 1966.
872p.

This is the major source on Zimbabwe's constitutions and legal system prior to UDI. It
is a monumental reference work, and covers these topics in great detail. Divided into
two parts, the first deals with constitutional matters, which are further considered in
nineteen appendices, and the second with governing institutions. The ways in which
race affects most aspects of government and the law are stressed. The study is based on
Palley's University of London doctorate.

443   **Law and an unequal society: discriminatory legislation in Rhodesia
under the Rhodesian Front from 1963 to 1969.**
Claire Palley.   *Race* (UK), vol. 12, no. 1 (1970), p. 15-47; vol. 12,
no. 2, p. 139-67.

New forms of racial discrimination were introduced by the Rhodesian Front in the
UDI era, in some cases reversing some of the improvements in African rights which
had occurred in the 1950s. Palley provides a description and analysis of these new laws.
On earlier legislated forms of discrimination see her 'A note on the development of
legal inequality in Rhodesia: 1890-1962', *Race* (UK), vol. 12, no. 1 (1970), p. 87-93, or
see her substantive study (item 442).

Constitution, Legal System and Human Rights. Constitution and human rights

The politics of reconciliation: Zimbabwe's first decade.
See item no. 2.

Zimbabwe: a land divided.
See item no. 8.

Zimbabwe's prospects: issues of race, class, state and capital in Southern Africa.
See item no. 13.

Zimbabwe: politics, economics and society.
See item no. 14.

Zimbabwe: a break with the past? Human rights and political unity.
See item no. 397.

Zimbabwean co-ops and class struggle.
See item no. 512.

The politics of the mass media: a personal experience.
See item no. 819.

Military and Police

444 **Blue and old gold: a selection of stories from The Outpost – the regimental magazine of the British South African Police.**
Cape Town: Howard B. Timmins, [1953]. 199p.
This rather odd publication has a large number of short stories which were written for the police magazine, *Outpost* (see item 826). Whilst few are of any literary merit, they are evocative of perceptions and attitudes towards the country and its people amongst a group of whites who were generally right-wing. Racist sentiments are common. The stories are accompanied by rather bizarre photographs, such as one of a crocodile with a human arm protruding from its mouth.

445 **The Fifth Brigade and Zimbabwean soldiery.**
Africa (UK), vol. 140, (April 1983), p. 15-17.
This is a useful, if short, article on the Fifth Brigade which gained such notoriety during the anti-dissident campaign in Matabeleland. The special nature of the brigade's training and arms are discussed, and its relationship to the rest of the army.

446 **The history of the British South Africa Police.**
Peter Gibbs. Salisbury: Mardon Printers, 1972, 1974. 2 vols.
These two volumes comprise an extensive historical study of this police force from 1889 to 1939. The tone is laudatory, and the study concentrates on the Europeans in the force, and their courageous exploits. Volume one, sub-titled *The first line of defence*, covers the period 1899-1903, and volume two, sub-titled *The right of the line*, covers 1903-39. Similar themes are treated in Colin Harding, *Frontier patrol: a history of the British South African Police and other Rhodesian forces* (London: G. Bell, 1937).

447 **Gukurahundi: the development of the Zimbabwe defence forces 1980-87.**
     Strategic Review for Southern Africa, vol. 10, no. 1 (1988), p. 1-37.

This paper describes the way in which the post-independence national army was formed from the previous Rhodesian army and the guerila armies of the liberation movements. It critically reviews the developments which occurred in the defence forces up to 1987. The article contends that military politicization is a major drawback since it undermines the professional capacity of the defence forces.

448 **Rhodesia patrol.**
     F. E. Lloyd.   Ilfracombe, England: Arthur H. Stockwell, 1965. 268p.

This is an account of the Rhodesian police force from 1931 up to the beginning of the 1960s by a former serving police officer. The author is sympathetic to Smith's position, and the account is of interest in illustrating the attitudes and views which were probably almost universal amongst the police force at the time. The book contains a foreword by Welensky.

449 **The guardians: the story of Rhodesia's outposts and of the men and women who served in them.**
     Joy Maclean.   Bulawayo: Books of Rhodesia, 1974. 305p.

This is a popular history of the Southern Rhodesian Native Affairs Department which was responsible for 'native administration' during the colonial period. Its members had the closest contact with Africans living in the Tribal Trust Lands, although this did not always give them much insight into their way of life, or the problems created by colonial rule. Of particular interest in this account is the inclusion of details concerning the lives of the wives of the members of the department. For a personal and very extensive account of the experience of 'native administration' from the colonial perspective in one particular district see also *Valley of the Ironwoods: a personal record of ten years served as District Commissioner in Rhodesia's largest administrative area, Nuanatsi, in the southwestern lowveld* (Cape Town: Bulpin, 1972) by Allan Wright. This covers the period 1958-68, and includes much information on local wildlife and the setting up of Gona re Zhou game reserve.

450 **Evolution of the Southern Rhodesian military system 1903-27.**
     Peter Mclaughlin.   PhD thesis, University of Zimbabwe, Harare, 1982. 307p.

This is a major academic study of the colonial military forces in the early 20th century. Mclaughlin argues that the nature of the military system during the period under study was shaped by perceptions and attitudes developed during the 1896-97 Shona and Ndebele uprisings which prevented a rational appraisal of the country's real defence needs. The study includes analysis of the British South Africa police, and the Southern Rhodesian volunteers.

451 **Ragtime soldiers: the Rhodesian experience in the First World War.**
     Peter Mclaughlin.   Bulawayo: Books of Rhodesia, 1980. 159p.

This book mainly focusses on the white Rhodesian experience of the Great War, although one chapter is devoted to the role of African Rhodesians, drawing on material in the author's doctoral thesis (item 450). A first-hand account of the campaign in East Africa is A. E. Capell, *The Second Rhodesian regiment in East Africa* (London: Simson, 1923). On Rhodesian forces in the Boer War see Colonel A. S.

Hickman's two-volume *Rhodesia served the Queen: Rhodesian forces in the Boer War, 1899-1902* (Salisbury: Government Printer, 1970). The major study of Rhodesia and the Second World War is by J. F. Macdonald (see item 122).

452 Towards a history of Rhodesia's armed forces.
R. S. Roberts. *Rhodesian History*, vol. 5, (1974), p. 103-110.

This article provides a concise review of the history of Rhodesia's armed forces, including the police, from the 1890s up to UDI. Relevant literature is also reviewed.

453 A pride of men: the story of Rhodesia's army.
Beverley White. Salisbury: supplement to *Illustrated Life Rhodesia*, 1975. 145p.

This publication provided illustrated popular format coverage of different sections of the Rhodesian army, from fighting regiments to the role of women and chaplains. Its perspective is pro-settler and UDI. Insights into army life and attitudes can also be gained from the army's magazine which was published in Salisbury from 1964-79: *Assegai: the magazine of the Rhodesian army*. This was first published as *Assegai: the magazine of the Rhodesian and Nyasaland army* (Salisbury: 1961-64).

Counter-insurgency in Rhodesia.
See item no. 196.

The elite: the story of the Rhodesian Special Air Service.
See item no. 197.

War in the air: Rhodesian air force 1935-80.
See item no. 198.

Exit Rhodesia.
See item no. 209.

Selous Scouts: a pictorial account.
See item no. 210.

Administration and Local Government

454 **The promotion of self-reliance and self-help organizations in community development in Zimbabwe: a conceptual framework.**
Samuel T. Agere. *Community Development Journal* (UK), vol. 17, no. 3 (1982), p. 208-15.

This paper focusses on the need to promote the participation of the Zimbabwean people at the grass-roots level in local policy development and implementation.

455 **Beyond community development: the political economy of rural administration in Zimbabwe.**
M. Bratton. London: Catholic Institute of International Relations; Gweru: Mambo Press in association with Catholic Institute of International Relations and the Justice and Peace Commission of the Roman Catholic Bishops' Conference, 1978. 62p. (From Rhodesia to Zimbabwe Series).

This discussion of rural administration in the African areas draws heavily on the work of Holleman and Passmore (see item 463), since the research was conducted from outside Rhodesia. Although the community development approach to administration was theoretically adopted by the government in 1962, this analysis contends that there was never sufficient decentralization of authority. Based on a basic needs approach, the author makes recommendations for the future which include the unification of administration, thereby ending the division between white and black rural areas, the Africanization of the administration, the redrawing of administrative boundaries ending the recognition of chiefs' areas, and the designation of growth points.

456 **The romance of the posts of Rhodesia, British Central Africa and Nyasaland, incorporating the cancellations of the Rhodesias and Nyasaland.**
H. C. Dann. Bulawayo: Books of Zimbabwe, 1981. 311p.
This extensive book is a newly set reprint of the 1940 and 1950 editions of this study of postal services in the region, including Zimbabwe. It is anecdotal in style, and covers the establishment of postal services and the development of a post office system up to 1949. The most exciting aspect is the description of the conditions which faced the early postmen, runners who often had close encounters with wildlife.

457 **Development administration and management.**
Edited by Josef Deckers. German Foundation for International Development, [1983]. 414p.
This volume contains papers reporting on a training workshop, run by the German Foundation on International Development, on various aspects of public administration. The workshop was held in Harare between 20th September 1982 and 18th March 1983. The participants were Assistant Secretaries and Chief Executive Officers from the Zimbabwean government, and the topics covered included the constitution, constitutional law, ministerial responsibility, ombudsmen, development and economic planning, policy formulation, banking systems, the concept of the civil service and its role, decentralization of decision-making, and public ethics. For an analysis of the civil service from colonial times to independence see Michael Bratton, 'The public service in Zimbabwe', *Political Science Quarterly* (USA), vol. 95, no. 3 (1980), p. 441-66.

458 **Limits to decentralization in Zimbabwe.**
Edited by A. H. J. Helmsing, Naison Mutizwa-Mangiza, Des Gasper, C. M. Brand, K. H. Wekwete. Harare: University of Zimbabwe Publications, 1990. 223p.
This edited volume contains papers which consider various aspects of Zimbabwe's experience in local government change, regional planning and administrative decentralization.

459 **Local government in Zimbabwe: an overview.**
J. D. Jordan. Gweru: Mambo Press, 1984. 92p. (Mambo Occasional Papers, Socio-Economic Series, no. 17).
This brief volume provides a useful overview of local government in Zimbabwe, focussing particularly on the larger urban areas. The changes that arose at independence are a major concern, and the author refers to these as the 'one-city concept', since the former white and black areas were amalgamated under one administration. Topics covered include local elections, services, finances, planning, development and relations with central government. The author lectures on local government at the University of Zimbabwe. On local government legislation in the pre-UDI period see Gloria Passmore, *Local government legislation in Southern Rhodesia up to 30th September, 1963* (Salisbury: Department of Government, University College of Rhodesia and Nyasaland, 1963), which provides a straightforward description and explanation of the legislation.

460   **The government system in Southern Rhodesia.**

David J. Murray.   London; New York: Oxford University Press, 1970.
393p.

Murray endeavours to show how government attitudes towards Africans from 1923-62
alternated between harshly racist and mildly liberal. His interpretation differs
somewhat from that of Leys (see item 378). The author sees 1962 as a watershed, with
white politics taking a radical new direction. The book is a basic reference for details
on electoral and constitutional history, the nature of the administration, and
methodical analysis of shifts in government economic policy.

461   **Community development in pre-independent Zimbabwe.**

Naison Mutizwa-Mangiza.   Harare: University of Zimbabwe, 1985.

79p. (Supplement to *Zambezia*, Journal of the University of
Zimbabwe).

This is an excellent account of the development and eventual failure of the Rhodesian
government's attempt to impose 'community development' as the form of local
government in the African rural areas. The author discusses the conceptual
framework, and then details the origins and aims of the policy, its implementation and
its achievements and failures. He highlights how the form of development established
increased the subordination of the community to the authority of the chiefs, who did
not necessarily command the allegiance of local people. The hostility between the
chiefs and progressive forces is examined, with opposition coming from ordinary
villagers, missionary teachers, educated Africans and African nationalists. The latter
tended to see the policy as a racist tool designed to check the growth of nationalism.
Critical analyses of this policy written whilst it was being implemented are Graham C.
Kinloch, 'Problems of community development in Rhodesia', *Community Development
Journal* (UK), vol. 7, no. 3 (1972), p. 189-93, and D. A. Kotzé, 'Community
development in Rhodesia', *Bulletin of African Institute* (Pretoria, South Africa), vol. 8,
no. 10 (1970), p. 397-402. The official government version of the community
development policy is described by Passmore in item 463.

462   **Local government and planning in Zimbabwe: an examination of recent
changes, with special reference to provincial-regional level.**

Naison Mutizwa-Mangiza.   *Third World Planning Review*, vol. 8,
no. 2 (1986), p. 153-75.

In this review of planning at local government level, the author focusses on the changes
which have occurred at the middle-tier level of the province and region. District level
planning issues are discussed in his *Decentralization in Zimbabwe: problems of
planning at the district level* (Harare: Rural and Urban Planning Department,
University of Zimbabwe, 1989. [Occasional Paper no. 16]). Another reference on local
government is Kadmiel H. Wekwete, 'The local government system in Zimbabwe –
some perspectives on change', *Planning and Administration*, vol. 15, no. 1 (1988). See
also the relevant section in item 608.

463 **The national policy of community development in Rhodesia: with special reference to local government in the African rural areas.**
Gloria C. Passmore.   Salisbury: University of Rhodesia, Department of Political Science, 1972. 360p.

Community development became the policy for local government in the reserves in 1962. The theory, as expounded by the government and described in this officially sponsored study, was that this approach would end the paternalism and authoritarianism of the district commissioner system, and improve African conditions by increasing local autonomy with more power vested in traditional leaders. This was not, however, how the policy was viewed or experienced by most Africans (see item 461). This study provides useful historical material on the local government background to community development, including discussion of the much-hated Native Land Husbandry Act. A well-received study of the problems created by the previous system of local government in the reserves, which focusses on a case study of Mangwende reserve and the conflicts between local leaders and the district commission is Johan Holleman, *Chief, councillor and commissioner: some problems of government in Rhodesia* (Assen, Netherlands: Afrika-Studiecentrum, 1968; London: Oxford University Press; Atlantic Highlands, New Jersey: Humanities Press, 1969). Holleman, a social anthropologist and ex-administrator in Rhodesia, had high hopes for the new community development system.

464 **Tradition and travesty: chiefs and the administration in Makoni district, Zimbabwe 1960-80.**
Terence Ranger.   *Africa (UK)*, vol. 52, no. 3 (1982), p. 20-41.

In this article Ranger discusses how the European government attempted to use 'traditional' methods of local government to channel colonial administrative requirements. He argues that this attempt at indirect rule largely failed because the adminstrators' views of tradition in this context tended to be at odds with reality. This essay was reprinted in *Past and Present in Zimbabwe* (Manchester, England: Manchester University Press, 1983) edited by J. D. Y. Peel and T. O. Ranger (see item 9).

465 **Rhodesia, a postal history: its stamps, posts and telegraphs.**
R. C. Smith.   Salisbury: Mardon, 1967. 454p.

A major descriptive account of the post office and associated services from 1890 to the beginning of the UDI period. The author, who was controller of stores and transport in the postal services during the Federation, issued a sixty-two page supplement to this publication in 1970 when the post office was passed over to a Statutory Board.

466 **Chiefs and councils in Rhodesia: transition from patriarchal to bureaucratic power.**
Anna Katherina Hildegard Weinrich.   London: Heinemann Educational; Columbia, South Carolina: University of South Carolina Press, 1971. 252p.

This study approaches the issue of local government in the reserves and the changing role of the chiefs through the medium of a major case study of a succession dispute in a Karanga area. Based on her extensive research in this area, Weinrich demonstrates how the chiefs' traditional methods of exercising power, based on patriarchy and consensus, were radically altered as the central government intervened to appoint co-operative leaders through which to channel its policies.

The political economy of Zimbabwe.
See item no. 10.

Gold regions of Southeastern Africa.
See item no. 122 (vol. 15).

The guardians: the story of Rhodesia's outposts.
See item no. 449.

Rural development and planning in Zimbabwe.
See item no. 608.

International Relations

467 **Supping with the devil: Zimbabwe-South Africa relations.**
James Barber. *International Affairs Bulletin* (Johannesburg), vol. 6,
no. 1 (1982), p. 4-16.

Zimbabwe inherited a set of close links with South Africa, the result of historical and
personal ties, culminating in South Africa's attempts to support the white minority
regime in the early years of UDI. Some of the links are formalized in bilateral
agreements. This article discusses such agreements, and the dilemmas they pose for an
independent Zimbabwe which is also committed to the regional grouping, SADCC.
The latter excludes South Africa and has amongst its aims the lessening of dependence
on that country. A fuller discussion of the relationships between Rhodesia and South
Africa is found in Sprack (item 478).

468 **Unconsummated union: Britain, Rhodesia and South Africa 1900-45.**
Martin Chanock. Manchester, England: Manchester University Press,
1977. 289p. maps.

The 'unconsummated' union of the title refers to the potential incorporation of the
territory of Southern Rhodesia into South Africa. This possibility was often mooted,
and the white settlers were offered this as one option in a referendum when the British
South Africa Company rule came to an end. However they opted for 'responsible self-
rule'. Chanock demonstrates how South African interests and perceptions were
weighted towards union, whilst the British still believed that their imperial interests
would be best served by a separate Rhodesia. The reasons for the settlers' rejection of
the South African option are also examined in *Incorporation in the Union of South
Africa or self-government: Southern Rhodesia's choice, 1922* (Pretoria: Communications of the University of South Africa, 1965) by Murray A. G. Davies, and are also
well covered in the more accessible general history by Robert Blake (item 148). Also
see Philip Warhurst, 'Rhodesian-South African relations, 1900-23', *South African
Historical Journal*, vol. 3 (Nov. 1971), p. 92-108.

469 **Beggar your neighbours: apartheid power in Southern Africa.**
Joseph Hanlon. London: Catholic Institute for International
Relations in collaboration with James Currey, 1986. 352p.

In this book Hanlon details the policies and actions pursued by South Africa in its
efforts to destabilize the surrounding region as part of the strategy to maintain white
minority political power. Three chapters address these issues specifically for
Zimbabwe. Apart from direct and indirect military actions, such as supporting anti-
government forces both within Zimbabwe and its transit route state, Mozambique,
South Africa's actual and potential economic interventions are detailed. A chapter on
the role of the most important South African-controlled companies in Zimbabwe is co-
authored by Colin Stoneman. Similar themes are addressed in the sections on
Zimbabwe in Hanlon's *Apartheid's second front: South Africa's war against its
neighbours* (London: Penguin, 1986). South Africa's destabilization tactics and their
impact on Zimbabwe are also detailed in Hasu H. Patel, 'Regional security in Southern
Africa – Zimbabwe', *Survival*, vol. 30, no. 1 (1988), p. 38-58.

470 **Soviet strategy towards Southern Africa: the national liberation
movement connection.**
Daniel R. Kempton. New York, London; Westport, Connecticut:
Praeger, 1989. 261p. bibliog.

One of the four chapters in this study is a very detailed and well-researched analysis of
Soviet policy towards ZAPU, which the USSR supported during the liberation war.
An important question is why the Soviets did not shift their support when ZANU was
established, since in the long run they were left backing the wrong, and a less radical,
horse. The author's explanation includes the longstanding relationship between the
Soviets and ZAPU (which began before the armed struggle), Soviet reluctance to
adopt what it at first perceived as a mere splinter group, and ZANU's later Maoist
tendencies. Kempton contends that the Soviet influence on ZAPU was very limited – it
did not develop as a vanguard party and Soviet advice not to negotiate an internal
settlement was superfluous since Nkomo would not have agreed to this anyway. The
significant improvements in Soviet-ZANU relations post-independence are also
discussed. The study was written before the break up of the Soviet Union. Soviet
policy towards Zimbabwe up to the mid-1980s is covered in James Mayall, 'The Soviet
Union, Zimbabwe and Southern Africa', in *Southern Africa in the 1980s* (London:
George Allen & Unwin, 1985), edited by Olajide Aluko and Timothy M. Shaw, p. 89-
119.

471 **The 'Tar Baby' option: American policy towards Southern Rhodesia.**
Anthony Lake. New York: Columbia University Press, 1976. 316p.

The weakness of America's public commitment to political rights in Southern Africa,
including Rhodesia, which was largely proclaimed for domestic consumption, is
exposed in this authoritative study. The 'Tar Baby' option was America's chosen policy
towards the region, which attempted to combine a belief that the white minority
regimes would remain and that this largely served American business interests with the
need to pursue at least a cosmetic liberal approach to the cause of African liberation.
The author worked in the United States' State Department from the early 1960s to
1970, when he resigned over the issue of the bombing of Cambodia. He rejoined in
1976 when Carter came to power. This study was sponsored by the Carnegie
Endowment for International Peace. The cosmetic nature of the United States' stance
on Rhodesia was particularly illustrated by its infamous action over Rhodesian chrome,

which it perceived to be of strategic significance and therefore passed legislation, the Byrd Amendment, to allow the contravention of internationally agreed sanctions. This issue is also dealt with in great detail in *Rhodesian chrome* (Washington, DC: United Nations Association, 1973. Also published as a 'Special Wraparound Supplement', 30 April 1974), by the Washington Intern Program of the Student and Young Adult Division, an activist association. The pragmatic, self-interested nature of America's policy towards Rhodesia is also discussed in Edgar Lockwood, 'The case of Zimbabwe', in *American policy in Southern Africa: the stakes and the stance* (Washington, DC: University Press of America, 1981. 2nd ed. p. 167-90), edited by René Lemarchand. America also broke the sanctions against arming Rhodesia. See 'Evading the embargo: how the United States arms South Africa and Rhodesia', *Issue: a quarterly journal of Africanist opinion*, vol. 9, no. 1/2, (1979), p. 42-46, by Michael Klare and Eric Prokosch.

472 **Political and economic implications of sanctions against South Africa: the case of Zimbabwe.**
Margaret C. Lee. *Journal of African Studies*, vol. 15, no. 3/4 (1988), p. 52-60.

This paper discusses the difficulties faced by Zimbabwe in imposing sanctions against South Africa. Zimbabwe has been a major actor in the international arena in calling for tougher sanctions against the apartheid regime, but its close ties to the Republic, its landlocked status and its smaller economy make it very vulnerable to retaliatory economic and military action if it were to adopt such sanctions itself. Lee considers the various strategies which South Africa might adopt in these circumstances, highlighting Zimbabwe's vulnerability.

473 **Zimbabwe: apartheid's dilemma.**
David Martin, Phyllis Johnson. In: *Destructive engagement: Southern Africa at war*. Edited by Phyllis Johnson, David Martin. Harare: Zimbabwe Publishing House for the Southern African Research and Documentation Centre, 1986, p. 43-72.

This is a review, written in a rather journalistic style, of South African destabilization of Zimbabwe, including details on direct military action, clandestine support for banditry, assassination, espionage, economic sabotage, propaganda and disinformation.

474 **The Rhodesian border blockade of 1973 and the African liberation struggle**
Simbi V. Mubako. *Journal of Commonwealth and Comparative Politics*, vol. 12, no. 3 (1974), p. 297-312.

In 1973 the Rhodesians closed their border with Zambia on the grounds that the Zambians were providing territorial bases for ZAPU guerillas. The intention was that the closure would be temporary. Zambia had been attempting, with limited success, to avoid using the Rhodesian railway system because of sanctions since 1965 and tensions were running high. The Zambian president, Kenneth Kaunda decided to make the blockade permanent. This paper details the events surrounding the decision to blockade, using a variety of sources including contemporary newspapers. The significance of Zambian freight as a source of foreign exchange for the sanctioned economy is highlighted. The Zambian perspective on these events is given in R. Hall,

The high price of principles: *Kenneth Kaunda* (New York: Africa Publishing Corporation, 1973). The expense of alternative routes eventually forced Zambia to reopen the border in 1978.

475 **The United Nations, international law, and the Rhodesian independence crisis.**
Jericho Nkala. Oxford: Clarendon Press, 1985. 288p.

This examination and analysis of various legal issues raised by UDI considers in particular the issues raised by the imposition of UN enforcement action under Chapter VII of the UN Charter. The study is detailed and fairly technical in parts, dealing for example with the legal basis of the UN's intervention in the Rhodesian crisis, and the legal effect of abstention on key proposals by some members of the UN Security Council. The final chapter discusses the future of UN non-military enforcement of its resolutions in the light of the Rhodesian experience.

476 **No master, no mortgage, no sale: the foreign policy of Zimbabwe.**
Hasu H. Patel. In: *Regional development at the national level. Volume II*. Edited by Timothy M. Shaw, Yash Tandon. Lanham, Maryland: University Press of America, 1985, p. 219-64.

This essay details the nature of Zimbabwe's foreign policy stance in the post-independence era, from a generally sympathetic perspective. Coverage includes Zimbabwe's non-alignment, its membership of various international agencies, its support for a number of liberation movements throughout the world, foreign capital policy and attitudes towards external capital, and relationships with Britain and the United States of America. The nature of dependence upon South Africa is covered, and the problems Zimbabwe faces because of deliberate South African destabilization which discouraged the government from allowing territorial bases for the South African liberation movements. Patel is professor of politics and administration studies at the University of Zimbabwe.

477 **The Soviet Union and Zimbabwe: the liberation struggle and after.**
Keith Somerville. In: *The Soviet impact in Africa*. Edited by R. Craig Nation, Mark V. Kauppi. Lexington, Massachusetts: Lexington Books, 1984, p. 195-200.

This article provides a useful introduction and discussion of Zimbabwe's relationship with the Soviet Union during the liberation struggle and the immediate post-independence period. During the latter period the influence of the Soviet Union is shown to have been very limited.

478 **Rhodesia, South Africa's sixth province: an analysis of the links between South Africa and Rhodesia.**
J. Sprack. London: International Defence and Aid Fund, 1974. 287p. maps.

The subject of this book is evident from the title, and this is the most comprehensive study available on relations between South Africa and Rhodesia. The author considers not only the economic and political links, but the cultural ties created by the nature of white settlement, with many early settlers coming from white South African stock. Useful statistics illustrate the strength of trade, investment, and military links, and the extent of blood ties. In addition the author examines the way in which Rhodesia gradually adopted legislation and institutions imposing racial discrimination which mirrored segregation and apartheid practices in South Africa, and he provides a useful comparative chronology as illustration. An alternative perspective on the South Africa-Zimbabwe relationship which concentrates on the history of tensions between the two countries is Colin Vale, 'South African and Zimbabwe: too close for comfort', *South African International*, vol. 12, no. 2 (1981), p. 357-74.

479 **Challenge to imperialism: the Front Line States in the liberation of Zimbabwe.**

Carol B. Thompson.   Harare: Zimbabwe Publishing House, 1985. 322p.

In this book the author provides a comprehensive analysis of the role of Angola, Botswana, Mozambique, Tanzania and Zambia in supporting and influencing the liberation movements in Zimbabwe. The author is clearly sympathetic to the liberation cause, but the account is well-documented and academic, being based on extensive research and interviews with many former exiles from ZANU and ZAPU. She indicates the way in which the Front Line States suffered economically on behalf of Zimbabwe, yet could also cause problems for the liberation movements, and outlines the pressures put on the Front Line States to push the Patriotic Front into the Lancaster House negotiations. An important element of the study is analysis of the tensions caused by helping Zimbabwe both between the countries of the Front Line States, and within the individual states. The formation of SADCC is also discussed. The author is a research associate of the University of Zimbabwe, and Associate Professor of Political Science at the University of Southern California, and has published extensively on Zimbabwe's role in SADCC.

480 **Britain and the politics of Rhodesian independence.**

Elaine Windrich.   London: Croom Helm, 1978. 273p.

This is a balanced and clear account of British policy towards Rhodesia from 1962 to 1977. The author attempts to account for the failure of both Labour and Conservative British governments to find a satisfactory solution to the decolonization of Rhodesia. Her thesis is that whilst Britain had responsibility in Rhodesia, it actually had very little power, especially since force was ruled out almost immediately. In her opinion sanctions were ineffective, leaving diplomacy as the only means to try and obtain a solution. She covers in detail the complexities and frequent hypocrisy of British government attitudes. There is also discussion of the international repercussions and the reaction of the United Nations to UDI. At the time of publication, Windrich was a visiting scholar at Stanford University in America. A short article by the same author on the 1977 Anglo-American initiative to impose a settlement on Rhodesia is 'The Anglo-American initiative on Rhodesia', *World Today*, vol. 35, no. 7 (1979), p. 294-305. On the attitudes of the British Labour party to the Rhodesian situation from 1961-74 see Maxey Kees, 'Labour and the Rhodesia situation', *African Affairs*, vol. 299, no. 75 (1976), p. 152-62.

From Rhodesia to Zimbabwe: behind and beyond Lancaster House.
See item no. 5.

The political economy of Zimbabwe.
See item no. 10.

Zimbabwe's prospects: issues of race, class, state and capital in Southern Africa.
See item no. 13.

Zimbabwe: politics, economics and society.
See item no. 14.

The road to Zimbabwe: 1890-1980.
See item no. 108.

UDI: the international politics of the Rhodesian rebellion.
See item no. 176.

Rhodesia: white racism and imperial response.
See item no. 177.

The United Nations and economic sanctions against Rhodesia.
See item no. 191.

The United Nations and Rhodesia: a study in international law.
See item no. 195.

From Rhodesia to Zimbabwe.
See item no. 214.

A peace in Southern Africa: the Lancaster House conference on Rhodesia, 1979.
See item no. 216.

Peacemaking in civil war: international mediation in Zimbabwe 1974-80.
See item no. 221.

Economy, Trade and Investment

General

481 **Labour supplies in historical perspective: a study of the proletarianization of the African peasantry.**

Giovanni Arrighi. *Journal of Development Studies* (UK), vol. 6, no. 3 (1970), p. 197-234.

This important paper is required reading for those interested in the development of debates about the migrant labour system, African agriculture and land issues in colonial Zimbabwe. Arrighi's main thesis is that the African farming population suffered from the active, state-sponsored development of underdevelopment. This was mainly in response to the articulated needs of the vociferous white farming sector, who desperately wanted their labour at rates which were insufficient to generate a natural flow of labour out of the reserves. In addition white farmers were not prepared to compete with African farmers who frequently had a comparative advantage in supplying agricultural products. Restrictions on African access to land, and the neglect of, or active attacks on, commercial activity in the reserves are therefore set in a specific political context. This perspective on the problems faced by African agriculture is in direct opposition to that taken by most colonial planners and authorities who viewed them as being due to poor techniques, cultural obstacles and ignorance. Arrighi's seminal work informed a number of subsequent writers on associated topics including Clarke, Harris, Kosmin, Phimister and van Onselen. This paper is also published in *Essays on the political economy of Africa* (London, New York: Monthly Review Press, 1973), edited by Giovanni Arrighi and John Saul.

482 **The political economy of Rhodesia.**

Giovanni Arrighi. The Hague: Mouton; Atlantic Highlands, New Jersey: Humanities Press, 1967. 60p.

Adopting a fairly standard Marxist structuralist approach to the analysis of Rhodesian society, Arrighi examines the class interests and conflicts which have determined the nature of racial discrimination and the distribution of resources, including land. He emphasizes the importance of the white agrarian bourgeoisie's fight against economic competition from Africans in creating the institutionalized racial inequality of colonial Rhodesia. A similar essay has been published in various other publications which may be more accessible: *New Left Review* (UK), vol. 31 (Sept. 1966), p. 35-65; *Essays on the political economy of Africa* (New York: Monthly Review Press, 1973) edited by Giovanni Arrighi and John Saul; and *African politics and society* (New York: Free Press, 1970), edited by I. L. Markowitz. For a critique of Arrighi's work see Arnold Sibanda, 'Theoretical problems on the development of capitalism in Zimbabwe: towards a critique of Giovanni Arrighi', *Zimbabwe Journal of Economics*, vol. 1, no. 2 (1985), p. 11-20.

483 **Spectrum guide to Zimbabwe.**
Compiled and edited by Camerapix.   Harare: Books for Africa Publishing House, 1991. 375p.

This is a guide aimed mainly at potential investors, but it also contains some material for the tourist. It has a glossy format, with more than 200 colour plates. Topics covered include history, art, culture, travel and tourism, and urban centres, as well as detailed discussion of the economy, business and investment opportunities. Another general publication which contains much useful information, in an easily accessible format, on the private and public sector is *Zimbabwe: the first decade 1980-1990* (Harare: Roblaw Publications, 1990). This describes and assesses the role and form of each government ministry, parastatal and non-governmental organization, and the nature of each major company in the private sector.

484 **Commission of inquiry into taxation.**
Under the chairmanship of Raja J. Chelliah.   Harare: Government Printer, 1986. 419p.

This comprehensive report on the taxation system in Zimbabwe was commissioned for the President, and is one of a number of major reports on various aspects of the economy drawn up after independence. It is the definitive source for information on all types of taxes, expenditure and borrowing, and local government finances. Various recommendations for future taxation policy are made.

485 **Distribution of income and wealth in Rhodesia.**
Duncan G. Clarke.   Gwelo: Mambo Press, 1977. 125p. (Mambo Occasional Papers, Socio-economic Series, no. 7).

This is one of a series of studies on various aspects of the Rhodesian economy commissioned by the Catholic Bishops' Conference on Justice and Peace Commission (CBCJPC). Together the series provided an extremely detailed and comprehensive description of Rhodesian socio-economic conditions, and a damning indictment of the inequalities and injustices that the racist state had fostered. This volume analyses the income distribution pattern, stressing the huge gap between black poverty and white wealth. The many excellent tables provide a clear statistical picture of this inequality. Discussion of income distribution at the beginning of the 1960s is found in Michael L. O. Faber, 'The distribution of income between racial groups in Rhodesia', *Race* (UK), vol. 2, no. 2 (May 1961), p. 41-52, when the average ratio of white:black wages was 12:1.

486   **Foreign companies and international investment in Zimbabwe.**
Duncan G. Clarke.   London: Catholic Institute of International
Relations; Gweru: Mambo Press, 1980. 275p.

This book provides a very useful and highly detailed overview of the nature and extent
of foreign involvement in the Zimbabwean economy at independence. The information
provided includes details on the origins of international investment from 1870, the
sectoral disposition of foreign companies, and analysis of foreign involvement in
specific sectors including agriculture, mining, manufacturing, and finance and banking.
Approximately two-thirds of the 300 principal foreign companies were British,
although South African influence was also very high and often difficult to distinguish
from British ownership. Three useful appendices are included showing the major
foreign companies by country of origin; the major economic areas in which such
companies are involved; and operational details such as share ownership, profits and
directors for the very largest mining and industrial companies. Clarke lectured in
economics at the University of Rhodesia 1970-75, and then went to the International
Labour Organization in Geneva.

487   **Economic survey of the Federation of Rhodesia and Nyasaland, with
special reference to the possibility of expanding its economy.**
H. R. Fraser.   Johannesburg: Anglo-American Corporation of South
Africa, [1958]. 2 vols. maps.

This major survey of the Federation by Anglo-American contains a wealth of material
on Southern Rhodesia's economy at the end of the 1950s, which would be of interest to
those researching economic issues. The first volume covers the resources of the
federation, and is illustrated with some really excellent maps. Topics covered include
population, minerals, transport, land, power and water which are all analysed in
relation to their potential contribution to economic growth. Volume II surveys the
economy including the mining sector, agriculture, industrial production, trade and the
federal nature of the economy. Discussion of industries in the federation is found in
Industries of the Federation: a study in progress (Salisbury: Industrial Press, [1954]),
which discusses manufacturing in the region in general, and lists all the companies
operating and their products.

488   **The Meikle Story.**
Graham Publishing Company.   Salisbury: Graham Publishing
Company, 1975. 97p.

This is an anecdotal account of the development of a major series of capitalist
enterprises by the three Meikle brothers who first came to Rhodesia in 1892. Their
range of investments included hotels, ranching, property, insurance, department
stores, textiles and tea estates. The text is illustrated with contemporary photographs.

489   **Foreign trade with particular reference to co-operation between South
Africa and Rhodesia.**
D. C. Krogh.   *Rhodesian Journal of Economics*, vol. 4, no. 2 (1970),
p. 10-17.

The share of South Africa in Rhodesia's external trade increased significantly after
UDI, as other partners imposed sanctions. A special trade agreement also exists
between the two countries. This article reviews Rhodesia's external trade, focussing on
the South African component.

490 **South Africa: the sanctions report: documents and statistics.**
Edited by Joseph Hanlon. London: James Currey; Portsmouth, New
Haven: Heinemann, in association with the Commonwealth Secretariat,
1989. 352p.

The threat of international sanctions on South Africa was often met by a counter-
threat from the apartheid regime to impose sanctions on its neighbours. Zimbabwe,
being landlocked, was vulnerable, especially since its natural transit route state,
Mozambique, was totally destabilized by the South African-sponsored Mozambique
National Resistance. Analyses of sanctions against South Africa therefore frequently
included discussion of this counter-threat. This major study was prepared for the
Commonwealth Committee of Foreign Ministers on Southern Africa, and includes an
examination of the impact of South African sanctions on Zimbabwe and other SADCC
states. A more gloomy study is R. A. Gibbs' 'Effects on the Front Line States of
economic sanctions against South Africa', *Transactions of the Institute of British
Geographers*, vol. 12, no. 4 (1987).

491 **Zimbabwe agricultural and economic review.**
Modern Farming Publications, foreword by Robert Mugabe. Harare:
Modern Farming Publications, 1982. 188p.

This is a general, introductory reference to the Zimbabwean economy shortly after
independence, in a glossy format. The coverage includes commerce, manufacturing,
mining, urban centres, tourism, transport, and energy, but the most detailed sections
by far are on the agricultural sector including information on land issues, crops and
livestock, irrigation, finance and marketing, and research. A similarly general overview
is provided by *Zimbabwe: industry and commerce 1982/3* (Harare: Argosy Press,
[1983]), by Argosy Press, which has sections on land and people, industrial sectors,
transport, agriculture, finance, education, health, urbanization, and SADCC.

492 **Zimbabwe at work, 1989.**
Modus Publications, in conjunction with Samuel Gozo Ltd. Harare:
Modus Publications, 1989. 2nd ed. 272p.

This is basically a propaganda exercise to encourage investment in Zimbabwe, in a
glossy format. Nevertheless, it contains useful information and data on all the major
private companies, and parastatals. It was first published in 1986, and is irregularly
updated. Also of historical interest, as it provides a listing of companies as well as
general economic information and details on the economies of the main towns is
Industrial Rhodesia: a record of industrial development in Southern Rhodesia
(Salisbury: Rhodesian Publications, 1945).

493 **The settler economies. Studies in the economic history of Kenya and
Southern Rhodesia 1900-63.**
Paul Mosley. London, New York: Cambridge University Press, 1983.
289p. bibliog. maps. (African Studies Series, no. 35).

This is a serious academic study of two settler economies, in which Mosley examines
the forces which shaped the nature of white economic patterns, and the consequences
for the African economies and African livelihoods. An excellent bibliography is
provided on pages 271-85, and there are fifty-three tables of data to illustrate the
analysis. Another comparative study of settler colonialism which compares Kenya,
Rhodesia, Algeria and South Africa is Kenneth Good's 'Settler colonialism: economic

development and class formation', *Journal of Modern African Studies*, vol. 14, no. 4 (1976), p. 597-620. Also by Good, see 'Settler colonialism in Rhodesia', *African Affairs*, vol. 290, no. 73 (1974), p. 10-36, which covers the period 1896-1973. Analysis of settler economics is also found in W. Biermann and R. Kossler's 'Settler mode of production: the Rhodesian case', *Review of African Political Economy*, vol. 18 (1980), p. 106-16.

494 **Dualism in the Rhodesian colonial economy.**
Daniel B. Ndlela.   Lund, Sweden: Department of Economics,
University of Lund, 1981. 241p. (Lund Economic Studies, no. 2).
This is a major economic study which focusses on the colonial period, but also contains consideration of the pre-colonial economy. The analysis is developed within the context of the theory of dualism, and the development of two contrasting sectors – the modern, state-supported European economy, and an exploited African rural sector – is examined. The most detailed material and discussion is of the agricultural sector, including analysis of land tenure, the agricultural labour market, agricultural credit, and agricultural produce markets.

495 **Doing business in Zimbabwe.**
Price Waterhouse.   London: Price Waterhouse, 1984. 143p.
This is a useful general guide for business people, although the serious investor would need more detailed information on subjects such as business regulations and taxes, and there have been important changes in government policy in the later 1980s with the introduction of the structural adjustment programme. The first chapter describes the general investment climate covering topics such as the population, education, resources, industries, energy, transport, government policies and working conditions and labour attitudes. There is then an examination of exchange controls and restrictions on foreign investment, which includes details on local banking and finance, and labour relations and social security. Auditing and accounting practices are described, and the final section explains the taxation system.

496 **From Rhodesia to Zimbabwe: alternatives to poverty.**
Roger Riddell.   London: Catholic Institute of International Relations,
1977. 22p.
This short study was one of a number commissioned by the CIIR in the 1970s. Riddell outlines the problems of economic inequality which an independent Zimbabwe would inherit, and makes various recommendations for policies to improve the situation. His proposals involve restructuring the economy towards a more socialist system.

497 **Report of the commission of inquiry into income, prices and conditions of service.**
Under the chairmanship of Roger C. Riddell.   Harare: Government
Printer, 1981. 330p.
This is one of the key reports commissioned at independence which provided overviews and analyses of vital sectors of the economy, and recommended policy action. This report, frequently referred to as the Riddell Commission, is extremely comprehensive, and a most useful source of data and indication of egalitarian concerns in the early years of independence. Apart from the topics indicated by the title, the report also covers industrial relations, pension and social security issues, taxation,

foreign trade and foreign exchange and unemployment. The analysis is supported by twenty-eight tables of economic data, and various appendices. The report was critically reviewed by Gavin Williams in 'Equity, growth and the state: the Riddell report', *Africa*, vol. 52, no.3 (1982), p. 114-20, reprinted in *Past and Present in Zimbabwe* (Manchester, England: Manchester University Press, 1983), edited by J. D. Y. Peel and T. O. Ranger.

498 **Zimbabwe: an introduction to the economics of transformation.**
Peter Roussos. Harare: Baobab Books, 1988. 184p.

The author of this work teaches economics at Harare Polytechnic where he is head of the Economics Department. This is a text book on Zimbabwe's economy designed essentially for students, but it is also useful to the layperson as a simple, factual introduction to the subject. Much of the text had previously been published as weekly articles in local financial newspapers. General themes include the generation and distribution of wealth, ownership in the economy, dependencies and weaknesses, and possible growth strategies. There is also sectoral coverage of agriculture, manufacturing, mining, money and banking, and foreign investment.

499 **Debt and the development options in Central Africa: the case of Zambia and Zimbabwe.**
Ann Seidman. In: *Recession in Africa: background paper to the seminar: Africa – which way out of the recession?* Edited by Jerker Carlsson. Uppsala, Sweden: Scandinavian Institute of African Studies, 1983, p. 80-107.

This paper was originally presented at a seminar on African debt held in Uppsala in September, 1982. Ann Seidman explains the causes of Zimbabwe's large national debt, which she believes derived largely from the government's hesitation in altering the inherited stuructures of the productive sector, and particularly the role of the multi-national companies. The dilemmas facing African countries dealing with the IMF are stressed.

500 **Outposts of monopoly capitalism: Southern Africa in the changing global economy.**
Neva Makgetla Seidman, Ann Seidman. Westport, Connecticut: Lawrence Hill; London: Zed Press, 1980. 370p.

The Seidmans have been important contributors to the literature on foreign investment and industrial development in the region. Their view is that multi-national companies are generally exploitative, and that the surpluses they divert from the region could have transformed many of the local economies, had they been productively invested locally. In this study there are several sections of direct relevance to Zimbabwe, or which use Zimbabwean illustrations. Chapter eleven, 'The seeming paradox of Southern Rhodesia', addresses specifically the colonial roots of Rhodesia's migrant labour system and the profitability of this system for capital, the role of South African and transnational companies in economic growth in the UDI period, and the increasing military confrontation of the mid-1970s. Neva Makgetla Seidman has also written 'Transnational corporations in Southern Rhodesia', *Journal of Southern African Affairs* (USA), vol. 5, no. 1 (Jan. 1980), p. 57-88. On the question of multinational disinvestment see Lovemore Zinyama, 'Multinational disinvestment: localisation or socialist transformation in Zimbabwe's manufacturing sector', *Area*, vol. 21, no. 3 (1989), p. 229-35.

501 **The World Bank and the IMF in Zimbabwe.**
Colin Stoneman. In: *Structural adjustment in Africa*. Edited by Bonnie Campbell, John Loxley. London: James Currey; Toronto: University of Toronto Press; Basingstoke, England: Macmillan, 1989, p. 37-66. (Macmillan International Political Economic Series).

This is a vital reference for the student of economic policy in Zimbabwe, which affords crucial insights into the context within which industrial and general economic decisions have been made in the 1980s. Stoneman argues that Zimbabwe's early management of the economy involving controls on currency and imports, although not without problems, was basically sound as a strategy for long-term development. He shows that the first structural adjustment period (1982-84) did not result in complete capitulation to the formulae of the World Bank and IMF, but demonstrates that the government was operating in an extremely difficult international climate. The latter point is illustrated by a deeply critical and technical analysis of two World Bank reports on Zimbabwean industry. These found that Zimbabwean industry was very efficient by African standards, yet through the use of deeply flawed methodology and procedures, combined with ideological biasses against any non-market solutions to development, still recommended the dismantling of the policy framework which Stoneman argues enhanced the industrial sector's long-term prospects. He also demonstrates that Zimbabwe's policy choices have not been made freely, with aid being made conditional on restructuring away from policies designed to assist self-reliance. This study of the industrial sector and appropriate policies is usefully complemented by Riddell (item 655). See also Stoneman's 'Forced economic choices in Zimbabwe', in *Witness from the front line: agression and resistance in Southern Africa* (London: Institute for African Alternatives, 1990, p. 29-33), edited by Ben Turok, and 'Policy reform or industrialization? The choice in Zimbabwe', in *Industrial and trade policy reform in developing countries* (Manchester, England: Manchester University Press, 1992, p. 97-110), edited by R. Adhikari.

502 **Trade and investment in Zimbabwe.**
Whitsun Foundation. Harare: Whitsun Foundation, [n.d.]. 2 vols. (Project 1.07).

These two volumes contain much detailed analysis and statistical data on trade and investment in Zimbabwe in the early 1980s. They are particularly useful for their tables.

Socio-economic review of Zimbabwe 1980-85.
See item no. 4.

From Rhodesia to Zimbabwe: behind and beyond Lancaster House.
See item no. 5.

Zimbabwe: a country study.
See item no. 6.

Zimbabwe since independence: a people's assessment.
See item no. 7.

The political economy of Zimbabwe.
See item no. 10.

Zimbabwe: a country study.
See item no. 11.

Zimbabwe's inheritance.
See item no. 12.

Zimbabwe's prospects: issues of race, class, state and capital in Southern Africa.
See item no. 13.

Zimbabwe: politics, economics and society.
See item no. 14.

Zimbabwe: towards a new order – an economic and social survey. vol. 1.
See item no. 15.

Zimbabwe: towards a new order – an economic and social survey. vol. 2.
See item no. 16.

Zimbabwe: at 5 years of independence: achievement, problems and prospects.
See item no. 17.

An economic and social history of Zimbabwe 1890-1948: capital accumulation and class struggle.
See item no. 155.

Zimbabwe: the political economy of transition 1980-86.
See item no. 417.

Political and economic implications of sanctions against South Africa: the case of Zimbabwe.
See item no. 472.

Economic policy and development planning

503 **Zimbabwe: a framework for economic reform (1991-95).**
Government of Zimbabwe. Harare: Government Printer, 1991. 27p.

This government policy document marked the end of any attempt to bring about a socialist restructuring of the economy. It introduces the policies associated with ESAP, the Economic Structural Adjustment Programme, which have moved Zimbabwe in the direction of trade liberalization, currency devaluation and general deregulation; the economic formulae of the World Bank and IMF. The text is supplemented by important annexes and a matrix detailing policy reforms in public enterprises, the monetary and financial sectors, and the need to alleviate the negative social effects of adjustment.

504   **Growth with equity: an economic policy statement.**
Government of the Republic of Zimbabwe.   Harare: Government
Printer, 1981. 19p.

The newly independent government's first published policy statement deals with each
sector by turn and stresses the need to redress the gross inequalities of the past,
decrease foreign ownership, and establish a society founded on socialist, democratic
and egalitarian principles.

505   **ZIMCORD – Let's build Zimbabwe together: conference
documentation.**
Ministry of Economic Planning and Development.   Salisbury:
Government Printer, 1981. 111p.

This government publication presents documentation from the Zimbabwe Conference
on Reconstruction and Development, held in March 1981, which appealed to the
international community for funds for reconstruction and development of the
economy. Part I contains a policy overview and description of sectoral strategies, and
Part II descriptions of projects for which the government hoped to raise funds.
Verbatim reports of the discussions are contained in *Zimcord, Report on Conference
Proceedings* (Salisbury, Ministry of Economic Planning and Development, 1981).

506   **'Home grown' austerity measures: the case of Zimbabwe.**
Thandika Mkandawire.   *Africa Development*, vol. 10, no. 1/2 (1985),
p. 236-63.

An analysis of the economic adjustment programme adopted by the government in the
early 1980s, and to what extent this was an internal decision or imposed by the
International Monetary Fund. The general economic trends are assessed rather
negatively.

507   **Evaluating the impact of NGOs in rural poverty alleviation: Zimbabwe
country study.**
Ann Muir, with additional material by Roger C. Riddell.   London:
Overseas Development Institute, 1992. 126p.

The work and influence of non-governmental organizations (NGOs) in Zimbabwe has
grown rapidly since independence, and they provide services in almost every sector of
the economy. This book undertakes a very useful task, by asking some searching
questions about the aims and achievements of NGOs in general, and detailing the
activities of four projects in particular. These projects are the Silveira House farmer
credit project, Christian Care's Mzarabani farmer credit project, the Simukai collective
farming co-operative, and the Zimbabwe Trust and the Campfire project on wildlife
utilization in Dande communal area. These projects are then evaluated on six criteria:
reaching the poor; the group approach; gender; credit, economic impact and cost-
effectiveness; promoting local institutions; and sustainability. The author is a freelance
consultant based in Harare, and this study is part of an Overseas Development
Institute project on the impact of NGOs in poverty alleviating projects in different
regions and institutional settings. Also on Simukai, see Nyathi, item 514, and on
Campfire see item 83.

508 **Second five year development plan 1991-95.**
Republic of Zimbabwe. Harare: Government Printer, 1992. 2 vols.
Despite the title, this is the third national development plan for independent
Zimbabwe. The first was the *Transitional national development plan 1982/3 – 1984/5*
(Harare: Government Printer, 1983), and the second was entitled *First five-year
national development plan 1986-90* (Harare: Government Printer, 1988. 2 vols.) They
are all key references for research on government policy and intentions, although
planned expenditure under many headings has often not materialized.

509 **Zimbabwe's experience of foreign investment policy.**
Roger C. Riddell. In: *Developing with foreign investment.* Edited by
Vincent Cable, Bishnodat Persand. London, New York, Sydney:
Croom Helm and the Commonwealth Secretariat, 1987, p. 280-300.
This is a useful reference on foreign investment in Zimbabwe, and the policies pursued
in the early years of independence, by the prolific Riddell. It contains helpful data on
the stock of foreign capital, although the author warns of the difficulties of making
accurate estimates for this economic factor. He goes on to make a detailed and fairly
technical economic analysis of the relationship between foreign capital and the balance
of payments, and reviews government policy and action towards foreign investment,
including its purchase of holdings in many key companies including those in the
pharmaceutical, coal, newspapers and banking sectors. The perceptions of potential
investors both already involved in Zimbabwe, and those outside are evaluated, and
particularly significant issues are detailed. This paper was also published in *Papers and
proceedings of the seminar on foreign investment: policies and prospects* (London:
Commonwealth Secretariat, 1985).

510 **Trade and financing strategies for the new NICs: the Zimbabwe case
study.**
Peter B. Robinson. London: Overseas Development Institute, 1987.
141p. (Working paper, no. 23).
The ODI made assessments of a number of intermediate-level developing countries in
the 1980s in order to make recommendations on an appropriate choice of external
strategies which would assist economic development. For Zimbabwe the recommendations were broadly in line with socialist change, including land redistribution, the
development of the production of mass consumption goods rather than luxury goods,
and further strengthening of import substitution measures. Such recommendations
were in opposition to the usual strategies proposed by the IMF, inter alia, during the
1980s, which would tend towards a free market in land purchase, and the ending of
protection of industry. The author develops similar points in 'Autarchy or
incorporation: trade strategy and development in independent Zimbabwe', *Zimbabwe
Journal of Economics*, vol. 1, no. 1 (1984), p. 5-15. Zimbabwean government policy
towards trade and industry has tended to move away from the strategies favoured by
Robinson, and he provides a critical analysis of the 1986-90 First Five Year National
Development Plan in 'Zimbabwe', *Trade, finance and developing countries: strategies
and constraints in the 1990s* (New York: Harvester Wheatsheaf, 1990. p. 165-211),
edited by Sheila Page.

The political economy of Zimbabwe.
See item no. 10.

Zimbabwe's prospects: issues of race, class, state and capital in Southern Africa.
See item no. 13.

Zimbabwe: politics, economics and society.
See item no. 14.

Zimbabwe: towards a new order – an economic and social survey. vol. 2.
See item no. 16.

Zimbabwe: at 5 years of independence: achievement, problems and prospects.
See item no. 17.

Stabilisation policies and the health and welfare of children: Zimbabwe 1980-85.
See item no. 334.

The mining industry in Zimbabwe: labour, capital and the state.
See item no. 647.

Zimbabwe.
See item no. 655.

Industrialisation and self-reliance in Zimbabwe.
See item no. 658.

Co-operatives

511 **Agricultural co-operative development in Zimbabwe.**
Langford Chitsike. Harare: Zimbabwe Foundation for Education with Production, 1988. 162p. maps.

A comprehensive survey of the agricultural co-operative movement in Zimbabwe, including its historical background, the ideologies and concepts involved, the origins and development of different types of co-operatives, master farmers' clubs, savings clubs and credit unions, and a description of the situation in 1988, including maps. Case studies of five co-operatives are presented, as well as the results of a survey of various types of clubs. The experience of the co-operative movement has attracted much interest, as it is viewed as a matter of great ideological significance, which signals the success or failure of socialist development in the rural areas. In fact there has been relatively limited development of co-operatives in agriculture, or any other sector, partly because support from the government has rarely been on the scale expected. Those that have succeeded, therefore, have often done so in spite of the government. Chitiske analyses the co-operative movement in the context of Zimbabwean history and culture, as well as in economic terms. The author is with Silveira House, a significant agent in the co-operative movement, and Chair of the Association of Appropriate Technology. See also *Agricultural co-operatives and the development of peasant agriculture in Zimbabwe with special reference to the provinces of Mashonaland East, Mashonaland West and Masvingo* (London: School of Oriental and African

Studies, University of London, 1983), by Charles Mukora, a doctoral thesis which found that co-operatives could yield many benefits for peasant farmers.

512 **Zimbabwean co-ops and class struggle.**
Roger England. *South African Labour Bulletin*, vol. 12, no. 6/7 (1987), p. 122-48.

In this article the author evaluates the role that the co-operative movement in Zimbabwe has in improving the conditions for social transformation. The development of collective co-operatives in agriculture, industry, mining and the retail sector is discussed. The conclusion is that collective co-operatives can have an important influence on the class struggle in Zimbabwe.

513 **Zimbabwean cooperatives, five years after.**
N. C. G. Mathema. *Social Change and Development*, vol. 10, (1985), p.17-20.

A review of, and data on, the co-operative movement five years after independence is presented, and a discussion of the racially separate co-operatives established in the colonial era.

514 **Tomorrow is built today: experiences of war, colonialism and the struggle for collective co-operatives in Zimbabwe.**
Andrew Nyathi, John Hoffman. Harare: Anvil Press, 1990. 137p.

This is Nyathi's autobiography which covers his experiences as a rural youth who became a wage worker, then a trade union organizer, a student and, during the war, a guerilla commander. The book also details the establishment and progress of one of the better known collective co-operatives in Zimbabwe, the Simukai co-operative which is run by ex-combatants.

515 **The development of co-operatives in post-independence Zimbabwe: with additional reference to the experiences in Swaziland and Mozambique.**
Mokoto Sato. PhD thesis, University of Leeds, Leeds, England, 1987.

An analysis of co-operative development in Zimbabwe in the post-independence era, which pays particular attention to the theoretical role co-operatives could play in a transition to socialism. The author describes how states tend to ascribe two different roles to co-operatives. The first role is primarily as a tool for modernizing agricultural production. The second is as an institution with the potential for transforming the social relations of production. The different roles involve fundamentally different perceptions about co-operatives and therefore lead to conflict within state policy-making institutions. It is asserted that the general tendency in Zimbabwe is for the modernizing role to dominate, and thus marketing co-operatives are favoured with resources, thereby alienating collective co-operatives and leaving them with insufficient capital.

516 **An evaluation of the structures, goals and planning procedures and practices of the organisation of collective co-operatives in Zimbabwe.**
Sipho R. Shabalala, Sam Moyo.   Harare: Zimbabwe Institute of Development Studies, 1986. 58p.

This paper reviews the administration, management and planning processes of collective co-operatives in Zimbabwe, and assesses their effectiveness.

517 **Zimbabwean women in co-operatives: participation and sexual equality in four producer co-operatives.**
S. M. Smith.   *Journal of Social Development in Africa*, vol. 2, no. 1 (1987), p. 29-48.

This article aims to identify the major constraints which prevent full participation by women in co-operatives in Zimbabwe. One problem is sexual discrimination. Current policy on women and co-operatives is evaluated, and a comparison made with the experiences of co-operative movements in other socialist countries.

518 **Directory of co-operative products and services: Zimbabwe.**
Prepared by Zimconsult, on behalf of Central Association of Co-operative Unions and Organization of Collective Co-operatives in Zimbabwe.   Harare: Memorial Co-operative Society, 1985. 106p.

This is a basic reference on the co-operative authorities and movement in Zimbabwe. It also includes the results of a survey on the approximately 1,500 co-operatives registered by mid-1985. For the third of these that replied provincial listings are provided, together with a products and services index.

Cold Comfort confronted.
See item no. 262.

Evaluating the impact of NGOs in rural poverty alleviation: Zimbabwe country study.
See item no. 507.

Agricultural producer co-operatives and agrarian transformation in Zimbabwe: policy, strategy and implementation.
See item no. 607.

Settlement Patterns

Urbanization and urban growth

519 Poor, harrassed but very much alive: an account of street people and their organizations.
Michael F. C. Bourdillon. Gweru: Mambo Press, 1991. 107p.

Housing shortages combined with poverty, and the goverment's policy on squatting, mean that a large number of people live and sleep on the streets in Harare. They are regularly harrassed by the police, and any attempt to construct permanent shelters is usually swiftly brought to an end. In this rather moving research study, conducted through interviews with homeless people and observation of their attempts to organize themselves, Bourdillon highlights the dreadful vulnerability of these powerless people, and shows that the government's tendency to portray them as shiftless criminals is far from the truth. The study demonstrates the need to reconsider the notion that all black Zimbabweans have recourse to rural kin in times of need: a tradition that no longer always holds true in a society as altered by capitalist forces as Zimbabwe. The study also provides a chronology of removals of a group of homeless people who originally resided at the railway station and were evicted in 1979. They set up home on wasteland in Eastlea, but a year later their shelters were burnt and they were moved to a farm in Mazowe, only to be evicted again three months later. Bourdillon's recommendations for more sensitive and fair handling of homeless people is made in the context of criticisms of current housing policy, which operate building standards which exclude the poorest.

520 From Avondale to Zimbabwe: a collection of cameos of Rhodesian towns and villages.
R. Cherer-Smith, illustrated by M. M. Carlisle. Salisbury, Borrowdale, Rhodesia: R. Cherer Smith, [1978]. 314p.

This is a non-academic account of 130 towns and villages in Zimbabwe, including major 'white' suburbs of the main towns. For each centre there is a concise history with information on the settlement's origins, on local personalities, and the flora and fauna.

190

521 **Towards self-reliance: urban social development in Zimbabwe.**
I. R. N. Cormack.   Gweru: Mambo Press, 1983. 280p. (Zambeziana: Series on Culture and Society in Central Africa, no. 15).

The main theme of this book is social planning in urban areas, and the need for new approaches such as community participation. The data and information tend to be from before independence, and thus some of the newer aspects of urbanization are not addressed. The book is divided into five sections with the first two addressing social development theory and principles of value systems. The third part gives a historical overview and social analysis of African urban areas, covering topics such as urban growth, administration, social structure and social problems, and the role and changing status of African women in towns. The fourth part is oriented towards policy development and focusses on training needs in urban planning. Finally the author comments on the relationships between social science research and urban planning.

522 **The urban poverty datum line in Rhodesia: a study of the minimum consumption needs of families.**
Verity S. Cubitt, Roger C. Riddell.   Salisbury: Faculty of Social Studies, University of Rhodesia, 1974. 139p.

Studies on the urban poverty datum line in Rhodesia usually found that many, if not most, African families had incomes below that necessary to cover their basic needs such as food and shelter. The data in this book were collected amongst African urban households in Salisbury, Bulawayo and Fort Victoria. The study provides a very useful data base on subjects such as incomes, rents, food bills, tenancy and lodging, and consumption for urban dwellers in the 1970s. This was subsequently updated and re-costed for the same urban centres in 1979 by Cubitt in *1979 supplement to the urban poverty datum line in Rhodesia* (Salisbury: Faculty of Social Studies, University of Rhodesia, 1979). The practical use of the poverty datum line is discussed in *The poverty datum line as a wage-fixing standard: an application to Rhodesia* (Gweru: Mambo Press, 1975, Socio-Economic Series no. 4) by Roger Riddell and Peter S. Harris. It is argued that supply and demand should not be used to define wages, especially in a sanctioned economy where markets were distorted. Information on existing urban employment practices is also presented. Also see Duncan Clarke, 'The determination of subsistence wages: some aspects of the 1974 urban poverty datum line in Rhodesia', *South African Labour Bulletin*, vol. 2, no. 7 (1976), p. 30-44. An earlier work on African incomes and poverty is *The poverty line in Salisbury* (Cape Town: School of Social Science, University of Cape Town, 1945), by Edward Batson.

523 **Post-colonial urban residential change in Zimbabwe: a case study.**
Sioux D. Cummings. In: *Cities and development in the Third World.* Edited by R. B. Potter, A. T. Salau.   London, New York: Mansell in association with the Commonwealth Foundation, 1991, p. 32-50.

Research by Sioux Cummings on the movement of African residents into the former white suburbs in Harare is the most detailed and specific available. Using data from the accounts departments of urban utilities, she demonstrates in this paper how African residential mobility was very rapid during the early years of independence when house prices were exceedingly low. Certain suburbs were also more favoured than others. The study is illustrated with useful maps showing the chronology of residential changes. An earlier paper by the same author under her maiden name is, 'Black residential mobility in a post-independence Zimbabwean city', by Sioux Harvey in

Settlement Patterns. Urbanization and urban growth

Geographical perspectives on development in Southern Africa (Australia: Commonwealth Geographical Bureau at James Cook University of North Queensland, [1986]) edited by Geoff Williams and Adrian Wood. Also see Robin Heath (item 530), and Claire Pickard-Cambridge, *Sharing the cities: residential desegregation in Harare, Windhoek and Mafikeng* (Braamfontein, South Africa: South African Institute for Race Relations, 1988).

524 **Towards an urbanization strategy for Zimbabwe.**
D. Hywel Davies. *Geojournal Supplementary Issue*, vol. 2 (1981), p. 73-84.

Davies provides an overview of rural-urban migration and urban growth, and the rapid increase in migration once legislative controls were lifted. He goes on to review the literature on regional planning and urbanization in Zimbabwe, and associated policies, including writings by Kay and Heath (see items 225, 550). He recommends the development of a hierarchy of growth centres in the country to improve the geographical spread of developmental influences. The larger centres, chosen on economic criteria, should be based in the former white-controlled 'core', and Davies recommends Gweru, KweKwe and Redcliff, and Mutare as secondary centres. In addition a limited number of rural service centres chosen on social equity criteria should be located in the 'periphery', the former Tribal Trust Lands. The proposals are based on the theory that the rural service centres would intercept step migration to the 'core', and act as links in a chain carrying innovations to the African farming areas. Unfortunately there is little evidence from other countries that these somewhat pious hopes can be achieved by policies such as these. An alternative policy view is found in S. G. Mishi, *Towards an urbanization strategy for Zimbabwe: an alternative case to growth pole/growth centre strategy* (Harare: Zimbabwe Institute of Development Studies, Discussion Paper, 1986).

525 **From Salisbury to Harare: citizen participation in public decision-making under changing ideological circumstances in Zimbabwe.**
Neil Dewar. *African Urban Quarterly*, vol. 2, no. 1 (1987), p. 37-48.

This paper is based on the author's extensive thesis on how local government changed in Harare after independence. After a discussion of the history of urban local government and the exclusion of Africans from participation during the colonial era, he outlines the development of a hierarchical system of ZANU (PF) urban structures which are claimed to have improved communication between the administration and urban residents. On Harare's finances he has written 'Procedural and interpretational problems concerning the geography of public finance in Southern Africa: the case of Harare, Zimbabwe', *South African Geographical Journal*, vol. 67, no. 2 (1985), p. 212-21.

526 **Urban food distribution and household consumption: a study of Harare.**
David Drakakis-Smith. In: *Retailing environments in developing countries*. Edited by Allan Findlay, R. Paddison, J. A. Dawson. London: Routledge, 1990, p. 156-80.

This paper discusses the nature of food retailing in Harare and policies which afffect it, and then presents the results of a questionnaire survey conducted in three Harare suburbs of Mabelreign, Glen View, and Epworth on expenditure on food items, types of food purchased, retailing source for different products, the utilization of peri-urban land for food production, and the contribution of food from rural landholdings.

527 **Urbanisation in the socialist Third World: the case of Zimbabwe.**
David Drakakis-Smith. In: *Urbanisation in the developing world.*
Edited by David Drakakis-Smith. London: Croom Helm, 1986,
p. 141-57.

In this paper Drakakis-Smith evaluates the nature of urbanization in Zimbabwe and
the urban policies being pursued by the government in relation to the expectations of
socialist urban theory. He concludes that there has been very little policy change which
would challenge the 'monopoly capitalism of the cities'. The author is Professor of
Geography at the University of Keele. This department has a special British aid-
funded link with the Geography Department at the University of Zimbabwe, and has
been involved in a number of local research projects. Other publications on this
research include items 526 and 349. For other analyses of urban Zimbabwe which focus
on housing and socialist theories, see item 547.

528 **The administration of transition: African urban settlement in Rhodesia.**
Eric Gargett. Gwelo: Mambo Press, 1977. 104p. (Socio-Economic
Series, no. 5).

This volume in Mambo Press's useful Socio-Economic Series is a really excellent
source for information on legislative measures affecting the nature of African
urbanization in Rhodesia, and on the changing attitudes of white urban administrators
and planners to the process of this urbanization. The book is well written and
documented, and the information easily accessible to the non-specialist. It takes the
reader from the Municipal and Town Management ordinances of 1894 when local
authorities were first given powers to set aside urban land for African residence, to the
1969 Land Tenure Act which reduced the civic status of Africans which had very
gradually improved in the post-war period. The origins and nature of segregation are
discussed, and the restrictive legal framework through which migration to town was
controlled. The author condemns the injustice of the system which meant that most
urban Africans lived within a climate of permanent insecurity.

529 **African life in an urban area: a study of the African population of
Bulawayo.**
Boris W. Gussman. Bulawayo: Federation of African Welfare
Societies, 1952-53. 2 vols.

This huge survey covers a wide range of social and economic characteristics of Africans
living in Bulawayo at the beginning of the 1950s, and as such is a key historical
reference on urbanization.

530 **The socio-economic characteristics of selected Harare suburbs three
years after independence.**
Robin Heath. *Proceedings of Geographical Association of Zimbabwe,*
vol. 17, (1986), p. 34-67.

In this article the results of a survey into the economic and social conditions of urban
households in three different Harare suburbs are reported. See also an earlier survey in
one township, 'A social survey of Dzivaresekwa township, Salisbury', *Zambezia,*
vol. 2, no. 2 (1972), p. 67-72 by G. L. Chavunduka, which covers age and sex
characteristics, household composition, education, occupation and earnings.

531 **Salisbury's changing skyline 1890-1980.**
Alex Jack, with text by D. G. Cobban. Bulawayo: Books of
Zimbabwe, 1981.

This study of Zimbabwe's capital city consists mainly of illustrations by an architect in watercolour, and pen and ink, of the city's changing building styles. The accompanying text which draws on contemporary records is mainly anecdotal and somewhat nostalgic. There is apparently also a companion record by the same author which has not been seen entitled *Bulawayo's changing skyline: 1893-1980* (Bulawayo: Books of Zimbabwe, 1979). Another book which would be of interest to the student of Harare's history, and to those interested in colonial architecture is *Historic buildings of Harare 1890-1940* (Harare: Quest Publications, 1986) by Peter Jackson, with photographs by Neil Lassen. Apart from these two topics, Jackson, an architect who has lived in Harare since 1980, also provides a guide to all Harare's historical buildings (including those now destroyed), and discusses government policy towards them and a strategy for conservation. Jackson is a member of the Historic Buildings Advisory Committee to the National Museums and Monuments Board.

532 **Salisbury: a geographical survey of the capital of Rhodesia.**
Edited by George Kay, Michael Smout. Sevenoaks, England: Hodder
and Stoughton, 1977. 119p.

This still remains the most comprehensive study of Zimbabwe's capital city, although much of the information is now out of date, and there have been enormous changes in the physical expanse of the city and its institutional characteristics. However some of the material is still relevant, including articles on the physical geography of the city's site and situation, and discussion of the early settlement development and the cadastral framework. Articles on the suburban shopping centres in the former white areas, on the industrial areas, and on the city centre still contain useful information, although the papers on the city population, transport system and urban problems and prospects have little modern currency. The book did recognize that Salisbury's major problems stemmed from racial division, inequality and discrimination. A new edited volume on Harare from the University of Zimbabwe's geography department will shortly be published entitled *Harare: the problems and growth of the city* (Harare: University of Zimbabwe Press, [1993]), edited by Lovemore Zinyama, Daniel Tevera and Sioux Cumming. For a study of Salisbury's earliest days see A. J. Christopher, 'Salisbury, 1900: the study of a pioneer town', *South African Geographical Journal*, vol. 3 (1970), p. 757-66. Details on the population of Salisbury in the 19th century, drawn from the first census, are found in Barry A. Kosmin, 'On the imperial frontier: the pioneer community of Salisbury in November 1897', *Rhodesian History*, vol. 2 (1971), p. 25-37. Two popular historical studies of white settler Salisbury by a former mayor are *A scantling of time: the story of Salisbury, Rhodesia* (1890-1900) (Salisbury: Stuart Manning, 1965), and *A sequence of time: the story of Salisbury, Rhodesia, 1900 to 1914* (Salisbury: Pioneer Head, 1974), by George H. Tanser.

533 **Black suburbanites: an African élite in Salisbury, Rhodesia.**
Clive Kileff. In: *Urban man in Southern Africa*. Edited by Clive Kileff,
W. C. Pendleton. Gweru: Mambo Press, 1975, p. 81-98.

A study of the socio-economic characteristics, lifestyles and attitudes of black urban
dwellers who have attained a degree of permanency in town, this study falls in the
genre of urban sociological studies made popular by Mitchell, amongst others (see item
536). On African élites in the 1960s see M. B. Lukhero, 'The social characteristics of
an emergent élite in Harare', in *The new élites in tropical Africa* (London; New York:
Oxford University Press for the 6th International African Seminar [Ibadan, 1964],
1966), edited by Peter C. Lloyd, p. 126-38.

534 **Peri-urban agriculture 1955-80.**
David Mazambani. MPhil thesis, University of Zimbabwe, 1982.
(Available from Department of Rural and Urban Planning, University
of Zimbabwe).

This is a much cited and very useful MPhil thesis on peri-urban agriculture in Harare, a
topic which has generated much interest. More easily accessible, but less detailed, is
the author's 'Aspects of peri-urban agriculture and deforestation around Harare,
Zimbabwe' in *Geographical perspectives on development in Southern Africa* (Australia:
Commonwealth Geographical Bureau at James Cook University of North Queensland,
[1986]), edited by Geoff Williams and Adrian Wood, p. 189-97.

535 **Urban development in the main centres.**
Prepared by Ministry of Finance. Salisbury: Ministry of Finance,
1979. 29p.

Sub-titled 'A report on the population influx problem as part of the five year rural
development plan', this document was commissioned with a view to investigating
Rhodesia's urban centres which were expected to have to absorb large numbers of
rural-urban migrants after a majority government came to power. It therefore
represented an acceptance of the ending of influx controls, and is of some historical
significance. Various estimates are made of the expected growth rates of urban centres
in the future, and of the then current urban populations which had been suddenly
increased by war refugees. Recommendations for future housing policy based on aided
self-help housing are made. The report is also useful as a source of information on then
current urban populations, urban conditions and incomes.

536 **Cities, society and social perception: a Central African perspective.**
James Clyde Mitchell. Oxford: Clarendon Press, 1987. 336p.

Mitchell had been a prolific writer on social aspects of urbanization in colonial
Zimbabwe, and central African in general, for forty years by the time this work was
published. The book conveniently brings together the analysis and results of three sets
of survey material from Southern and Northern Rhodesia collected between 1954 and
1965, much of which had been published before as articles. Mitchell's research had
focussed on cognition and perception of urban life, exploring the ways in which social
relationships develop in urban centres, and the nature of African attitudes towards
urban life, usually in the context of comparison with rural life. Mitchell's theoretical
perspective in this book, not previously explicit in his published articles, is
Gluckmann's situational analysis. The empirical material reveals the strength of
commitment to extended family obligations and to rural societal norms, and also

discusses urban inter-ethnic relations, which are far more complex than often supposed. Later research on similar topics which identified certain changes in urban dwellers' social relationships and attitudes compared to Mitchell's findings include Peter Stopforth's *Survey of Highfield African township* (Salisbury: Department of Sociology, University of Rhodesia, 1971. [Occasional paper no. 6]) and *Two aspects of social change: Highfield African township, Salisbury* (Salisbury: Department of Sociology, University of Rhodesia, 1971. [Occasional paper no. 7]). See also Moller, item 537.

537 **Urban commitment and involvement amonst black Rhodesians.**
Valerie Moller. Durban: Centre for Applied Social Sciences, University of Natal, 1978. 473p.

This major research study reports the results of three sample surveys of African urban dwellers conducted between 1973 and 1975. The information solicited related to their attitudes towards urban life, their involvement in urban society, and their commitment to long-term urban living. These themes have been of great interest to urban researchers in the context of migrant labour societies such as Zimbabwe, where various forms of influx control combined with land alienation forced many workers to keep 'a foot in both worlds', and maintain their rural farms whilst needing an urban wage. The surveys were conducted amongst three different groups in Salisbury: hostel dwellers, male respondents and their wives in the townships of Mufakose and Kambuzuma, and Rhodesian-born single people or household heads in the same townships and some hostels. Many people are shown to keep their rural links, even when they have had long urban careers. This book is based on the author's PhD research at the University of Zürich, and she is now based at the University of Natal. An article on the impact of circular migration and social change on hostel dwellers by Moller is 'Migrant labour in Harare hostels, Salisbury', *Zambezia*, vol. 5, no. 2 (1977), p. 141-59.

538 **Changing patterns of African rural-urban migration and urbanization in Zimbabwe.**
Chris C. Mutambirwa, Deborah H. Potts. *Eastern and Southern African Geographical Journal*, vol. 1, no. 1 (1990), p. 26-39.

The restrictive context within which African urbanization occurred in colonial Rhodesia strongly affected the rate of urbanization, and the age and sex characteristics of the African population. This paper discusses the nature of the restrictions, and also compiles and presents data drawn from various sources on the African urban population from the early part of this century up until 1982. Early censuses only enumerated African workers in town, but it is shown that by the end of the 1950s the African populations in Salisbury and Bulawayo were extremely skewed towards 'single' male migrants residing in hostels, domestic quarters, employers' premises, and as lodgers in township family accommodation. The success of influx controls is stressed, and the measures continued to influence urban processess profoundly in the 1960s, when it is shown that the level of African urbanization was held constant. However the impact of the war led to the system largely collapsing in the late 1970s as refugees flowed in from the rural areas. Brief consideration is also made of the post-independence situation, which is considered in greater detail by the same authors in item 259. A brief factual paper on urban growth from 1962-82 is Naison Mutizwa-Mangiza, 'Urban centres in Zimbabwe: inter-censal changes 1962-82', *Geography*, vol. 71, no. 2 (1986), p. 148-50.

539 **Mucheke: race, status and politics in a Rhodesian community.**
Anna Katharina Hildegard Weinrich. New York: UNESCO; Paris:
Holmes & Meier, 1976. 278p.

Mucheke township was the segregated African residential area for Fort Victoria, now
Masvingo. In this major sociological study Weinrich paints a comprehensive picture of
African urban society, including aspirations, perceptions of status, leisure activities,
kinship and families, politics, culture and membership of urban voluntary associations.
The changes wrought by urbanization on 'traditional' African attitudes were a subject
of some fascination to academics, particularly from the 1950s. Most of these studies in
Zimbabwe focussed on Salisbury townships (see for example, items 536, 533).
Weinrich's study, which was commissioned by UNESCO, thus provides valuable
comparative material from a smaller urban centre. Also see William B. Schwab, 'Social
stratification in Gwelo', in *Social change in modern Africa*, edited by Aidan W.
Southall (London; New York: Oxford University Press, 1961, p. 126-44).

540 **Development of urban planning in Zimbabwe: an overview.**
Kadmiel H. Wekwete. *Cities*, vol. 5, no. 1 (1988), p. 57-71.

Apart from housing issues, the post-independence planning of large urban areas in
Zimbabwe has received relatively little attention from academics, in comparison to the
development of settlements at the lower end of the urban hierarchy. This paper is
unusual therefore in addressing general town planning issues, and providing a critical
analysis of the limited changes which have taken place in the municipal planning bodies
and the shortage of personnel. A problem identified by the author is the lack of a
general urbanization policy. The nature of planning decisions in Harare municipality
and the issue of participation is addressed in Neil Dewar's doctoral thesis, *From
Salisbury to Harare: the geography of public authority finance and practice under
changing ideological circumstances* (Cape Town: University of Cape Town, 1988).
These matters are also considered more briefly in the context of a general discussion of
development in Harare in Dewar's 'Harare: a window on the future for the South
African city?', in *Homes Apart: South Africa's segregated cities* (Bloomington;
Indianapolis: Indiana University Press; Cape Town: David Philip, 1991, p. 191-204),
edited by Anthony Lemon.

541 **Data bank no. 3: the urban sector.**
Whitsun Foundation. Salisbury: Whitsun Foundation, 1980. (Project
no. 1.05[b]).

This report was prepared to assist planners in the immediate post-independence
period. It contains detailed information on thirty-one urban centres including
population estimates and a breakdown by race and age, the urban structure, the
history of local government, employment by industry, economic output by main
centres by industry, housing and social infrastructure, and local government finance. It
is a useful reference for those working on any aspect of urbanization. For details on the
Whitsun Foundation see item 614.

Historical dictionary of Zimbabwe.
See item no. 3.

Zimbabwe: politics, economics and society.
See item no. 14.

'Good boys', footballers, and strikers: African social change in Bulawayo, 1933-53.
See item no. 158.

Changing patterns of population distribution in Zimbabwe.
See item no. 232.

African aged in town.
See item no. 311.

Socioeconomic factors associated with child health and nutrition in peri-urban Zimbabwe.
See item no. 320.

The development of food supplies to Salisbury (Harare).
See item no. 321.

The changing economic role of women in the urban process: a preliminary report from Zimbabwe.
See item no. 349.

A Shona urban court.
See item no. 433.

Urban housing

542 **The building societies and the housing market.**
R. L. Cole. *Rhodesian Journal of Economics*, vol. 7, no. 3 (1973), p. 139-48.
This article discusses the development of building societies in Zimbabwe from 1924-72.

543 **Urban low income housing in Zimbabwe.**
Christopher J. C. Mafico. Aldershot, England; Brookfield, Vermont: Avebury, 1991. 166p.
The stated aim of this book is to identify the failures of low income housing policy in Zimbabwe and provide a foundation for a viable strategy based on local experience, although the author is more successful in pinpointing the problems than in detailing how to solve them. It is disappointing that Zimbabwe appears to have learnt little from the mistakes of other African countries in the sphere of urban housing. Obvious pitfalls such as maintaining overly high building standards in low-income schemes, and blanket opposition to squatter settlements are characteristic of the Zimbabwean approach. Both the root causes of these policies and how they have manifested themselves in the immediate post-independence era are well documented here. The first part of the study provides useful local background and theoretical material on urban low-income housing. This is followed by an analysis of theories of the function of housing and interesting surveys of building traditions and housing functions for the Shona and Ndebele peoples. Government policy, urban planning

standards and housing finance are covered in detail, and the major issues identified, which are the 'hiding' of the housing shortage by overcrowding in existing legal dwellings, the unaffordability of the government's cheapest aided self-help house for the majority of the population, and the seemingly implacable maintenance of inappropriate standards in low-income schemes. On the planning of housing schemes see *Principles of planning and layout design for low-income housing developments in Zimbabwe* (Salisbury: Brian Colquhoun, Hugh O'Donnell & Partners, 1981), by the Housing Development Services Branch, Ministry of Local Government and Housing.

544 **Chirambahuyo: a case study in low income housing.**
Diana Patel, R. Adams. Gwelo: Mambo Press, 1981. 99p.

Towards the end of the 1970s influx controls on migration to the cities broke down, particularly as refugees from the war moved to the security of the towns. A number of squatter settlements grew up, and this book describes the fate of the residents of Derbyshire, a squatter settlement on quarry land in Salisbury. They were initially resettled on a plot of land adjacent to Chitungwiza, a large township in Seke communal land outside Salisbury, and allowed to rebuild. This new area was called Chirambahuyo. They were later moved again into various parts of Chitungwiza. The authors criticize the government for their treatment of the squatters, and argue that Chirambahuyo should have been allowed to remain, and been upgraded. This book is also a useful reference for information on restrictions on African urbanization, and Salisbury's development in the 1970s. For a general reference by Patel on the urban housing shortage see her paper in item 10.

545 **High-density housing in Harare: commodification and overcrowding.**
Deborah H. Potts, Christopher C. Mutambirwa. *Third World Planning Review*, vol. 13, no. 1 (1991), p. 1-25.

The Zimbabwe government's early planning documents included a stated commitment to the rapid eradication of the country's urban housing shortage, and this was accorded a high priority in the planned allocation of resources. The huge gap between the promises and the reality are described and explained in detail in this paper, which goes on to provide an overview of the existing low-income housing stock in the townships in 1980, and to examine the various housing schemes developed in Harare since then. A critical analysis of the type of site-and-service approach adopted by the government is provided. It is demonstrated that the vast majority of poor households in Harare do not have sufficient income to participate legally in these schemes, which operate inappropriately high building standards. Downward raiding by middle-income groups, who should theoretically be excluded from the schemes by income criteria, is one result. Another is the rapid commodification of the housing stock, as many houses are devoted entirely or largely to lodgers. High rents lead to overcrowding, and the available evidence on the incidence and degree of overcrowding is reviewed, including data from surveys in 1985 and 1988. A case study of a World Bank scheme is given, illustrating many of the problems with site-and-services in Zimbabwe, and the beginnings of building society involvement in this sector. The analysis of housing affordability in this paper updates the data provided in Naison Mutizwa-Mangiza's, 'Post-independence urban low-income shelter policies in Zimbabwe: a preliminary appraisal of affordability', in *Shelter, services and the urban poor* (Cardiff, University of Wales Institute of Science and Technology, 1986, p. 81-96), edited by S. Romaya and G. Franklin. Another useful source on urban housing policy is G. C. Underwood's 'Zimbabwe's low-cost housing areas: a planner's perspective', *African Urban Quarterly*, vol. 2, no. 1 (1987), p. 24-36.

546 **Housing policy, production and consumption in Harare.**
Carol Rakodi, Naison Mutizwa-Mangiza. *Zambezia*, vol. 17, no. 1
(1990), p. 1-30; vol. 17, no. 2, p. 111-32.
Most of the research on urban housing in Zimbabwe has focussed on the low-income
sector. In this study published in two parts in concurrent issues of *Zambezia* the
authors provide an overview of the entire housing sector in Harare, including medium
and high-income provision, and it is therefore a very useful addition to the housing
literature. The first part of the study concentrates on the production of housing, and
the second on housing consumption. The authors also provided an excellent review of
relevant housing literature during the 1980s.

547 **Urbanization and socialism in Zimbabwe: the case of low-cost housing.**
Paul Teedon, David Drakakis-Smith. *Geoforum*, vol. 17, no. 2
(1986), p. 309-24.
In this paper the authors analyse post-independence policy towards urban housing for
the poor in relation to Zimbabwe's claims to socialism. The article provides a useful
detailed review of various changes in housing policy in the immediate pre- and post-
independence period, including the Rhodesian adoption of ultra low-cost cores for the
development of Chitungwiza, and the new state's cost-cutting on its initial site-and-
service approach until only sites were provided, and the promotion of the use of
building brigades on new housing schemes. There is particular emphasis on Glen View,
a Rhodesian site-and-service scheme in Salisbury, which although apparently
successful, ended up with a mainly middle-income black population rather than the
poorer households for whom it was intended. The authors conclude that the nature of
Zimbabwean urban housing policies bear little relation to its early socialist ideals.
Similar themes are addressed in Teedon's 'Contradictions and dilemmas in the
provision of low-income housing: the case of Harare', in *Housing Africa's Urban Poor*
(London: International African Institute, 1990, p. 227-38), edited by Philip Amis and
Peter Lloyd and R. J. Davies and N. Dewar's 'Adaptive or structural transformation?
the case of the Harare, Zimbabwe, housing system', *Social Dynamics*, vol. 15, no. 1
(1989), p. 46-60.

548 **Finance for low-income housing.**
Whitsun Foundation. Harare: Whitsun Foundation, 1979. 113p.
(Project 4.02).
Funding the huge demand for low-income housing is one of the major problems facing
the Zimbabwe government. This report which came out just before independence
contains a wealth of useful information on the country's urban centres, and the
contemporary housing situation. It also tries to identify the problems in this sector, and
give guidelines for future development. The Foundation also produced *A credit system
for financing low-income housing in Zimbabwe* (Harare: Whitsun Foundation, 1981.
[Project 4.06]), which strongly recommended that existing building societies should be
encouraged to become involved in this sector.

The political economy of Zimbabwe.
See item no. 10.

Regional planning

549 Rural growth points and rural industries in Zimbabwe: ideologies and policies.
Des Gasper. *Development and Change*, vol. 19, no. 3 (1988), p. 425-66.

The growth point strategy which aims to strengthen the role of selected settlements in the rural areas of Zimbabwe is part of regional planning policy. This article discusses the nature of the strategy, and reviews various analyses of the programme. The specific focus of the paper is the development of infrastructure in these settlements in order to encourage the establishment of rural industry. On rural industry also see Rasmussen (item 654).

550 Rhodesian service centres and service regions.
Robin Heath. Harare: University of Zimbabwe, 1990. 217p. (Supplement to Zambezia).

This study fulfils the classic regional planning task of enumerating a country's rural service centres, providing an itinerary of their functions, and delineating their service areas and spheres of influence. Originally completed for the author's 1978 MPhil thesis at the University of Rhodesia, it formed the basis of the National Rural Development Plan's policies on rural settlements and selection of centres for upgrading and investment.

551 Rural industries and growth points' issues in an ongoing policy debate in Zimbabwe.
A. H. J. Helmsing. Harare: University of Zimbabwe, Department of Rural and Urban Planning, May 1986. 28p. (Occasional paper, no. 2).

This paper emphasizes the problems of low population thresholds in many rural settlements in Zimbabwe, which may make the provision of many services on a permanent basis inefficient. The author favours provision of mobile services.

552 Utility of a combined periodic service and regulated market system in the development of economic hinterlands: the case of Zimbabwe's Tribal Trust Lands.
Norman Reynolds. In: *The design of rural development: proposals for the evolution of a social contract suited to conditions in Southern Africa*. Edited by Norman Reynolds. Cape Town: Southern African Labour Development Research Unit, 1981.

The delivery of services to rural communities is an important aspect of rural development planning. Most policies proposed for pre- and post-independence Zimbabwe have focussed on the development of so-called growth centres or growth points. In this essay a review of such proposals is presented, with data on the existing pattern of settlements in the communal areas. Reynolds asserts that the central place theory on which growth centre strategies usually rest provides little insight into the processes of spatial economic development, and the assumptions of the central place model are not met in the communal areas. He therefore makes a counter-proposal which involves investing in centres serving between ten and twenty local periodic markets. This study can usefully be compared with Heath (item 550), and Davies (item 524).

553 **Physical planning in Zimbabwe: a review of the legislative, administrative and operational framework.**
Kadmiel H. Wekwete. *Third World Planning Review*, vol. 11, no. 1 (1989), p. 49-69.

A useful reference for an overview of physical planning during the colonial era, this paper goes on to examine the independent government's institutional changes and priorities in this area. The legislation and government bodies involved in planning at the local level are described. The main thrust of physical planning after 1980 became the development of the communal areas, and part of the Department of Physical Planning's policy in this area was the development of the growth centre strategy. Wekwete specifically addresses the growth centre policy in 'Growth centre policy in Zimbabwe', *Journal of Economic and Social Geography*, vol. 80, no. 3 (1989), p. 131-46, and 'Rural urbanisation in Zimbabwe: prospects for the future', in *Small town Africa: studies in rural-urban interaction* (Uppsala, Sweden: Scandinavian Institute of African Studies, 1990, p. 130-42. [Seminar Proceedings no. 23]), edited by Jonathan Baker. A critical review of the physical planning apparatus by the same author is 'Decentralised planning in Zimbabwe: a review of provincial, urban and district development planning in post-independence Zimbabwe (post-1980)', *Journal of International Development*, vol. 2, no. 1 (1990), p. 110-39. Wekwete is a lecturer in the Department of Rural and Urban Planning at the University of Zimbabwe.

Land

The land issue

554 Land apportionment in Southern Rhodesia.
Barry N. Floyd. *Geographical Review* (USA), vol. 52, (Oct. 1962), p. 566-88.

This paper is based on Floyd's 1960 doctoral thesis 'Changing patterns of African land use in Southern Rhodesia' from Syracuse University. He discusses the nature of the racial division of land and goes on to recommend the development of new employment opportunities for the African population of the reserves, to alleviate the overuse of land. The paper is of interest as an example of a fairly typical planner's approach of the period, since Floyd had worked as a land development officer in the reserves from 1957-58. Although he does not entirely neglect the political background, the focus is on 'the vicious cycle of land and human degradation'. He contributed to the debate about the pre-colonial use of red soils in the region (see item 560). Floyd's thesis also appeared in mimeograph (Lusaka: Rhodes-Livingstone Institute, 1959. 3 vols.), and this article also appears in *People and land in African south of the Sahara* (New York: Oxford University Press, 1972), edited by R. M. Prothero. Floyd taught at Michigan State University and also did research in West Africa.

555 The political economy of land in Zimbabwe.
H. Moyana. Gweru: Mambo Press, 1984. 194p.

Although there are better sources on the history of land segregation and its impact on agriculture, this text makes a worthwhile contribution to the land issue literature by also providing a detailed case study of Gazaland in the Eastern Highlands. This focusses on the notorious eviction of Chief Tangwena's people from their ancestral lands during UDI, and their heroic resistance through the courts and other means, in the face of violent retribution by the security forces. The author is principal of Morgan Zintec College, Harare.

556 **Africans and land policies: British colonial policy in Zimbabwe
1890-1965.**
Jon Geoffrey Mutambara.   PhD thesis, University of Cincinatti,
Cincinatti, Ohio, 1981.

This massive scholarly study of British colonial land policies in Rhodesia is the most comprehensive and detailed available, and will be of value to the serious academic researcher.

557 **Land and racial domination in Rhodesia.**
Robin Palmer.   Berkeley, California: University of California Press;
London: Heinemann, 1977. 307p. bibliog.

This scholarly study is the basic text on the unequal division of land in colonial Rhodesia. It is based on Palmer's PhD thesis for the University of London in 1968. The processes involved in the alienation of African land by Europeans from the 1890s to the late 1930s are described in detail, and rigorously analysed. The injustices suffered by the African population as more and more of their land was taken from them, particularly the areas with high agro-ecological potential or with good access to transport and markets, are sensitively documented here. The inadequacy of the reserves set aside for African occupation is shown to have combined with a host of policies designed to undermine African commercial competitiveness. Palmer was an undergraduate at the University College of Rhodesia and Nyasaland, and was deported for opposition to the UDI regime in 1966. He went on to become a senior lecturer at the University of Zambia, before coming to Britain, where he now works for Oxfam.

558 **White farmers, black tenants and landlord legislation: Southern
Rhodesia 1890-1930.**
J. K. Rennie.   *Journal of Southern African Studies*, vol. 5, no. 1
(1978), p. 86-98.

This article focuses on the ending of labour tenancy on white-owned farms in Southern Rhodesia. The legislation controlling African tenancy is discussed, particularly the application of the Southern Rhodesian Private Locations Ordinance of 1908. A case study of the impact in Melsetter (Chipinge) district is presented.

559 **The land problem in Zimbabwe: alternatives for the future.**
Roger Riddell.   Gweru: Mambo Press, in association with Catholic
Institute for International Relations, 1978. 135p. (Mambo Occasional
Papers, Socio-Economic Series, no. 11).

Riddell was one of the most influential academics involved in policy formulation for an independent Zimbabwe. He wrote and advised on many different sectors of the economy, but this is probably one of his best known studies. In it he recommends that land reform should take place once Zimbabwe became independent, and suggests that the most socially and economically advantageous form of farmer organization would be a communes system, in which farmers would work together and share the output. Thus he rejected the idea of individual family plots, which in fact remain the usual and preferred form of land tenure for African farmers in the communal and resettlement areas. Riddell accepted that multi-national companies would have to remain involved in Zimbabwean agriculture, but also recommended that the land should be nationalized – again this recommendation was never translated into policy. The study also provides an excellent review of the history and ramifications of land alienation in colonial Rhodesia. Other writings by Riddell on the land issue at this time include *The land question* (London: Catholic Institute for International Relations, [1977]. [From Rhodesia to Zimbabwe Series, no. 2]), and 'Zimbabwe's land problem: the central issue', *Journal of Commonwealth and Comparative Politics*, vol. 18, no. 1 (1980), p. 1-12, which is also reprinted in item 5. Riddell also chaired one of the key commissions on policy directions for independent Zimbabwe which included consideration of the land issue (see item 497).

560 **Division of land resources in Southern Rhodesia.**
Wolf Roder. *Annals of the Association of American Geographers*, vol. 54, (1964), p. 41-52.

This contribution to the land division debate by a geographer focussed on general ecological factors involved in land apportionment. European settlers would commonly justify their occupation of half the country's land by arguing that the land they had taken was empty, because it typically had heavy red clay soils which the African population found hard to work with their pre-colonial technology. Not only was this a gross over-simplification of land division by soil type, but according to Roder, there were no unoccupied areas and hoes could be used to till the heavier soils. The debate about this continues to this day in academic circles. Articles on the subject include 'Comments on "The division of land resources in Southern Rhodesia" by Wolf Roder', by Robert W. Oliver, Philip Mason and Barry Floyd on p. 53-58 in the same issue as Roder's article; Robin Palmer, 'Red soils in Rhodesia', *African Social Research* (Zambia), vol. 10 (Dec. 1970), p. 747-58; John M. Mackenzie, 'Red soils in Mashonaland: a reassessment', *Rhodesian History*, vol. 5 (1974), p. 81-88; and R. M. G. Mtetwa and A. J. Chennells, 'Notes, documents and revisions: "Red soils in Mashonaland: a reassessment": contrary evidence', *Rhodesian History*, vol. 6 (1975), p. 77-82. Current evidence that African farmers use both types of land, and have a sophisticated understanding of the advantages and disadvantages associated with each for agricultural production is provided by Ken Wilson (see item 634).

561 **The Tribal Trust Lands of Rhodesia – problems of development.**
Concern Sibanda. Norwich, England: Geo Abstracts for the Centre for Development Studies, University College of Swansea, 1979. Reprinted 1981. 60p. (Centre for Development Studies Monograph Series, no. 6).

This is a concise, well-written introduction to what were the Tribal Trust Lands, and are now known as the communal areas. These areas are those which were 'reserved' for African occupation during the colonial period, and remained under communal tenure. Sibanda explains the history of these areas, and the legislation which affected them. He emphasizes the unfairness of the distribution of land between blacks and whites, with the former possessing only about half the land area despite being the vast majority of population, and their land tending to be in the less productive agro-ecological regions. Very useful tables showing the areas and proportions of land allocated to each race under different land apportionment acts are included.

Land. The land issue

562 **Land use and agricultural productivity in Zimbabwe.**
Daniel Weiner, Sam Moyo, Philip O'Keefe, Barry Munslow. *Journal of Modern African Studies*, vol. 23, no. 2 (1985), p. 251-85.
The debate about land reform is highly politicized. White farmers held the best land and have fought a fairly successful battle to prevent loss of this asset, arguing that the country needs their production and that peasant farmers are inherently inefficient or liable to cause land degradation (see item 50). The grounds for the latter argument include claims about peasant land tenure, technology and ignorance which have all been challenged by research, conducted particularly in the post-independence era, in the communal lands. In addition there is the issue of underutilization of land in the former white agricultural areas, which has important implications for the debate over land redistribution. This extensive article analyses land-use in the various farming sectors in Zimbabwe, which are categorized according to tenure and scale. Convincing evidence is presented of significant underutilization of land in this sector, even at the most conservative estimates. The wide-ranging discussion also includes consideration of land resettlement issues and schemes, land division and agro-ecological regions, and crop yields. With respect to the latter, it is argued that the difference between yields achieved by African and European farmers are not as vast as usually contended, if other factors are held equal. Other writings on the land issue by Weiner are 'Agricultural restructuring in Zimbabwe and South Africa', *Development and Change*, (1989), vol. 20, p. 401-428; and his paper in item 13.

From Rhodesia to Zimbabwe: behind and beyond Lancaster House.
See item no. 5.

Past and present in Zimbabwe.
See item no. 9.

Zimbabwe: politics, economics and society.
See item no. 14.

Zimbabwe: towards a new order – an economic and social survey. vol. 2.
See item no. 16.

Whose heritage? The case of the Matobo National Park.
See item no. 45.

The relationship of agricultural history and settlement to severe soil erosion in Rhodesia.
See item no. 46.

The impact of international economic sanctions on the internal viability of Rhodesia.
See item no. 193.

Zimbabwe: the political economy of transition 1980-86.
See item no. 417.

Labour supplies in perspective: a study of the proletarianization of the African peasantry.
See item no. 481.

Report of the commission of inquiry into the agricultural industry.
See item no. 580.

Land tenure

563 **Formal and informal rights to land in Zimbabwe's black freehold areas: a case study from Msengezi.**
Angela Cheater. *Africa*, vol. 52, no. 3 (1982), p. 77-91.
In this article Cheater addresses the complexities of access to land in one of Zimbabwe's small-scale commercial farming areas, formerly known as the Native Purchase Areas. Here the basic land tenure system is one of freehold, but within each farm different family members have different rights and obligations with respect to access to land. She shows how changes occurred in the usufructuary allocation of land in Msengezi over the period 1973-80, when the war intensified pressures which were already in evidence. The influence of class interests on land allocation became more clearly defined. This article also appears in Peel and Ranger, item 9, p. 77-91. Cheater has worked extensively on Msengezi, the area which provides the case study material for this article (see also item 641). Another article by her on this area which tackles the topic of rights to land as well as other issues is 'Cattle and class? Rights to grazing land, family organization and class formation in Msengezi', *Africa* (UK) vol. 53, no. 4, (1983), p. 59-74. Land rights in another community are considered in 'Land rights and land use among the Valley Tongas of the Rhodesian Federation', by E. Colson, in *African agrarian systems* (London: Oxford University Press, 1963), edited by D. Biebuyck.

564 **Women's access to and control over land: the case of Zimbabwe.**
Ruvimbo Chimedza. Harare: Agricultural Economics and Extension Department, University of Zimbabwe, 1988. 65p. (Working Paper, no. AE 10/88).
The issue of women's access to land has very important economic and social implications since women are the backbone of the smallholder agricultural labour force. In addition, many rural households are female-headed, often because of absentee migrant husbands. Yet women are severely disadvantaged in terms of their rights to land in comparison to men in the patriarchal societies which are the norm in Zimbabwe. This paper gives an extensive overview of how women gain access to land in the rural areas, and what degree of control they have over that land.

565 **Contesting the land: communal tenure in Zimbabwe.**
Ben Cousins. *New Ground*, vol. 6, (Summer 1991/2), p. 19-21; vol. 7 (Autumn 1991/2), p. 35-36.
The issue of land tenure remains one of intense debate. The usual arguments focus on whether the communal tenure which remains the norm in the communal areas is a hindrance to raising agricultural productivity and maintaining sustainable usage of the land and other natural resources. There is also debate on what exactly communal tenure is, as it is not necessarily the same in all areas and changes over time, and even

to what extent it is or was the norm. In this two-part paper Ben Cousins focusses on the discussion about what form of land tenure is appropriate for development in the peasant sector. Although the paper is aimed at a general audience, it provides a valuable introduction and overview of this contentious topic. Topics covered include the history of changing tenure and land control in the communal lands, the vested interests which would prefer a move to freehold tenure, livestock stocking rates, and various national and local 'power plays' over tenure issues. He contends that the flexibility of communal tenure makes it the best option for most people in these areas.

566   **Women's land rights in Zimbabwe: an overview.**
Rudo Gaidzanwa.   Harare: Department of Rural and Urban Planning, University of Zimbabwe, 1988. 21p.

This short but useful paper outlines the way in which women's land rights are gradually being eroded. The author surveys the situation in the communal areas, the small-scale commercial farming areas and resettlement areas, and also discusses the impact of the Native Land Husbandry Act in the 1950s.

567   **Tribal land tenure – an obstacle to progress?**
Arthur John Brodie Hughes. *South African Journal of African Affairs*, vol. 1, no. 1 (1970), p. 56-73.

The system of communal land tenure has frequently been blamed for hindering agricultural progress. The problems usually cited as associated with this type or land holding include the point that land cannot be used as collateral for loans, and long-term land improvements are discouraged. This position is no longer uncritically accepted, as it reflects a vastly oversimplistic and rigid view of this type of tenure, which has and is adapting to changing circumstances. This paper is useful for its overview of why communal tenure is perceived to be a problem for the development of successful commercial agriculture in the communal lands, and its discussion of the government's policy in the 1960s of relinquishing control over land to the chiefs. The author's view is that agricultural advance could occur under 'tribal' tenure, providing essential adjustments were made to customary land law.

Development in rural Tribal Trust Lands: an overview.
See item no. 604.

Land reform and resettlement

568   **The political economy of agricultural resettlement and rural development in Zimbabwe: the performance of family farms and producer co-operatives.**
K. Akwabi-Ameyaw.   *Human Organization*, vol. 49, no. 4 (1990), p. 320-38.

The type of organization of labour in the resettlement areas is an issue of some significance, since it is argued that the prospects for socialist transformation would be enhanced by co-operative, or preferably collective, production. However family farms have remained the most common model on the schemes. This article looks at the performance of such farms and co-operatives. On social development in the resettlement areas see Sam Geza, 'The role of resettlement in social development in Zimbabwe', *Journal of Social Development in Africa*, vol. 1, no. 1 (1986), p. 35-42.

569   **The unsettled land: the politics of land redistribution in Matabeleland 1980-90.**
Jocelyn Alexander.   *Journal of Southern African Studies*, vol. 17, no. 4 (1991), p. 581-610.

The land resettlement programme progressed particularly slowly in Matabeleland in the 1980s because of the conflict there, and this useful paper, based on the author's doctoral research at Oxford University, examines the peculiarities of the land issue and resettlement process in western Matabeleland Province. These include the prevalence of 'poach-grazing' on commercial land by peasant livestock owners as a response to grazing land shortages, and the government's negative reaction to this form of land use; the impact of drought; the exodus of white ranchers in response to the conflict and the drought; and the government's attempts to prevent people gaining access to the land thus made available. The land that was acquired for resettlement in the mid-1980s was frequently used by ranchers, civil servants and parastatals. The relationship between dissident activity and the land issue is also analysed. Some improvements occurred after the Unity Accord, which allowed local political processes to lobby for changes. For another critical analysis of the resettlement process in a specific region see Ken Mufuka, 'The weak link in Zimbabwe's agricultural miracle 1980-90: a case study of Masvingo Province resettlement projects', *Development Southern Africa*, vol. 8, no. 3 (1991), p. 293-304.

570   **Land resettlement in Zimbabwe: a preliminary evaluation.**
John Cusworth, Judy Walker.   London: Overseas Development Association, 1988. (Overseas Development Association Evaluation Report, no. EV 434).

This report critically evaluating the progress of land resettlement in Zimbabwe is of great significance. Commissioned by the British Overseas Development Association, the major donor for land reform, it found that the land resettlement programme was on the whole very successful, in both social and economic terms. The economic returns on the investment in the programme were approximately twenty-one per cent, which, according to *The Economist*, makes it one of the most successful aid schemes in Africa. Some problems are highlighted, including a lack of infrastructure on the schemes, and the position of women. For a discussion of the importance of this report, and of other evaluations of land resettlement, see Palmer (item 575).

571   **Zimbabwe: state, class and gendered models of land resettlement.**
Susie Jacobs. In: *Women and the state in Africa*. Edited by Jane L. Parpart, Kathleen A. Staudt.   Boulder, Colorado: Lynne Rienner, 1989,

The selection process for land resettlement in Zimbabwe has tended to disadvantage women, and this issue is considered in this article. Also by Jacobs on women and land resettlement, see 'Changing gender relations in Zimbabwe: the case of individual family resettlement areas', in *Male bias in the development process*, edited by Diane Elson (Manchester: Manchester University Press, 1991).

572 **Forever gained: resettlement and land policy in the context of national development in Zimbabwe.**
Bill H. Kinsey. *Africa* (UK), vol. 52, no. 3 (1982), p. 92-113.

This is an early and often cited contribution to the debate on agrarian issues and land resettlement in Zimbabwe, which was also published in item 9. The policy of land resettlement, which would transfer land from European ownership to African use, was understood to be fundamental to the independent government's policies, and the phrase 'forever gained' refers to a quotation from Charles Mungoshi's *Year of the uprising* about returning to Zimbabwe when the land is regained. In this paper Kinsey describes the various elements of the government's early resettlement policy, including land acquisition, settler selection, and the various models of resettlement possible. He also identifies issues needing consideration and resolution, particularly the question of land tenure and the government's emphasis on technical aspects of the programme, rather than its wider socio-political implications. See also his 'Emerging policy issues in Zimbabwe's land resettlement programme', *Development Policy Review*, vol. 1, no. 2 (1983), p. 163-96.

573 **Intensive resettlement: policies and procedures.**
Ministry of Lands, Resettlement and Rural Development.   Harare: Government of Zimbabwe, [1984]. 42p.

This is the first main policy document from the government on the land resettlement programme, which contains straightforward descriptions of the programme, its objectives, settler relocation planning and implementation, financial control, land tenure on resettlement farms, and monitoring. Eight appendices describe the different models of resettlement and include the application forms for prospective settlers. Irregular government publications reviewing the progress of the schemes are produced. For example, Ministry of Lands, Agriculture and Rural Resettlement, Monitoring and Evaluation Section, *First annual survey of settler households in normal intensive Model A resettlement schemes: main report* (Harare: Ministry of Lands, Agriculture and Rural Resettlement, 1986) which provides interesting general data, and observations on the size, gender and age composition of households and the allocation of land to women; and Ministry of Local Government, Rural and Urban Development, Department of Rural Development, *Resettlement progress report as of August 31st, 1987* (Harare: Ministry of Local Government, Rural and Urban Development, Department of Rural Development, 1987).

574 **Prospects for the socialist transformation of agriculture in Zimbabwe.**
Barry Munslow. *World Development*, vol. 13, no. 1 (Jan. 1985), p. 41-58.

This paper examines critically the various internal and external obstacles to transforming the Zimbabwean agricultural sector through land reform. Such obstacles include the nature of the Lancaster House Agreement and the strength of vested class interests. Other analyses of these issues are found in items 13, 14, 417 and 575.

575 **Land reform in Zimbabwe: 1980-90.**
Robin Palmer. *African Affairs*, vol. 89, no. 355 (1990), p. 163-81.

This is the most comprehensive review so far of the land reform process in Zimbabwe, and the burgeoning literature on land reform and resettlement. Palmer's research on land issues in Rhodesia and Zimbabwe has been outstanding, and he here provides a balanced assessment of Zimbabwe's achievements in land reform during the first decade of independence. He highlights how the government's freedom of manoeuvre was severely restricted by the Lancaster House Agreement, with the willing-seller willing-buyer and payment in hard currency conditions particularly onerous. Early plans for resettlement soon had to be curtailed, and were clearly over-ambitious. The relative success and stability of the Zimbabwean economy also ensured rapid increases in land prices, and concomitant reductions in the amount of land the government could afford. Despite the problems the resettlement process has been largely successful, both economically and socially, although as Palmer indicates the internal and external anti-resettlement lobbies, which include the Zimbabwean commercial farming sector and the British government, rarely acknowledge this. He ends the article with a discussion of the future of land reform in the 1990s and the ending of the Lancaster House restrictions, forecasting (correctly) that the pace of reform would be slow as the issue became increasingly depoliticized. A major new publication on the land issue in Zimbabwe, edited by Ken Wilson and Michael Drinkwater (London: James Currey), is currently under preparation.

576 **Land reform in Zimbabwe.**
Whitsun Foundation. Harare: Whitsun Foundation, 1983. 169p.

This report by the conservative Whitsun Foundation takes a very cautious approach to land reform, and argues strongly against rapid resettlement. It contains very useful data, including twenty-six tables of relevant statistics.

577 *Post-independence land resettlement in Zimbabwe.*
Lovemore Mondiwa Zinyama. *Geography*, vol. 67, no. 2 (1982), p. 149-52.

A useful early paper on the government's land resettlement policy, which considers the various models put forward for those chosen for resettlement, and what has been achieved in the first few years. Also see his 'Land policy and access to land in Zimbabwe: the Dewure resettlement scheme', *Geoforum*, vol. 21 (1990), p. 359-70.

A decade of development Zimbabwe 1980-90.
See item no. 1.

Zimbabwe: a land divided.
See item no. 8.

Zimbabwe's prospects: issues of race, class, state and capital in Southern Africa.
See item no. 13.

Zimbabwe: politics, economics and society.
See item no. 14.

The conservation issue in Zimbabwe.
See item no. 37.

Land degradation in Zimbabwe: a geographical study.
See item no. 49.

Soil erosion and conservation policy in Zimbabwe: past, present and future.
See item no. 50.

Land. Land reform and resettlement

Changing patterns of population distribution in Zimbabwe.
See item no. 232.

The socioeconomics of nutrition under stressful conditions: a study of resettlement and drought in Zimbabwe.
See item no. 318.

Rural development and planning in Zimbabwe.
See item no. 608.

Agriculture

General

578 **African regional symposium on small holder irrigation.**
Edited by Malcolm J. Blackie. Wallingford, England: Overseas
Development Unit of Hydraulics Research, 1984. 437p.

The lack of surface water and high rates of evapotranspiration in Zimbabwe make
irrigation a very important topic for agricultural development. The vast majority of
development expenditure and research has concentrated on the large-scale sector,
although the returns to capital would probably be better for small holder irrigation.
The nine papers on small holder irrigation in Zimbabwe contained in this volume are
therefore an important contribution to the literature on agricultural development. The
symposium was held at the University of Zimbabwe, 5-7 September, 1984.

579 **Case study: the Zimbabwean Cotton Marketing Board.**
Malcolm J. Blackie. Harare: Department of Land Management,
University of Zimbabwe, 1983. 12p. (Working papers, no. 2/83).

This paper analyses the development and successful operation of Zimbabwe's cotton
marketing board, and the role of cotton in the national economy. It has also been
published in *Agricultural marketing success stories in the developing world* (London:
Wiley, 1984), edited by S. C. Abbott.

580 **Report of the commission of inquiry into the agricultural industry.**
Under the chairmanship of Gordon L. Chavunduka. Harare:
Zimbabwe Government, 1982. 199p. maps.

This important government report is a highly valuable source on Zimbabwean
agriculture shortly after independence, and contained important recommendations on
agricultural policy and land resettlement. Its coverage is very wide, including land
utilization, profit and indebtedness, agricultural labour, pricing policies, agricultural

inputs, credit, taxation policy, irrigation, agricultural extension and research services, and transport facilities. Useful illustrative statistics are presented in ninety-five tables.

581 **Zimbabwe's agricultural 'success' and food security in Southern Africa.**
Lionel Cliffe. *Review of African Political Economy*, vol. 43, (1988), p. 4-25.

For most of the 1980s Zimbabwe succeeded in producing food surpluses, particularly in maize. The majority of this marketed maize was coming from the peasant sector by the end of the 1980s, in complete contrast to patterns before independence when the large-scale white farming sector dominated the domestic food market. Cliffe examines the nature of this success story, and how far it can be used as a model for Southern Africa as a whole. In addition he discusses the need for much swifter agrarian reform in Zimbabwe, without which the peasant sector's potential cannot be fully realized. Very similar themes are discussed in Clever Mumbengegwi, 'The political economy of a small-farmer agricultural strategy in SADCC', in *Poverty, policy and food security in Southern Africa* (Boulder, Colorado: Lynne Rienner, 1988, p. 158-77), edited by Coralie Bryant.

582 **Grain handbook.**
Commercial Grain Producers' Association. Harare: Commercial Grain Producers' Association, 1980. Rev. ed.

The private sector produces a range of handbooks on various agricultural products, covering topics such as production techniques, pests, and government regulations. They are aimed at the formerly exclusively white, large-scale commercial farming sector. They are usually useful sources on the nature of the specific sector addressed. Other such publications are the *Dairy farmers' handbook* (Harare: National Association of Dairy Farmers of Zimbabwe, 1987) by the National Association of Dairy Farmers of Zimbabwe, and the *Coffee Handbook* (Harare: Cannon Press, 1987. 3rd ed.) by the Coffee Growers' Association. Research and Special Services of the Ministry of Agriculture are a vital resource for agriculture in Zimbabwe, and also produce handbooks for commercial farmers, as well as research journals. Publications by them include *Animal Foods of Central Africa, technical handbook no. 2* (Harare: Research and Special Services, 1978), and *Handbook of registered pesticides (excluding herbicides) in Zimbabwe* (Harare: Research and Special Services, [n.d.]).

583 **Department of Agricultural, Technical and Extension Services: Farm Management Handbook.**
Edited by J. de Tong. Harare: Farm Management and Workstudy Section, Planning Branch, Agricultural, Technical and Extension Services, 1982. 3rd ed.

This is a technical handbook aimed at local extension workers and farmers, which gives some insights into the operations of the extension services. The first edition was produced in 1968 and it has been updated twice since. The first part of this edition includes information and planning data on a wide variety of crops and vegetables commonly grown in Zimbabwe, plus advice and information on sources of agricultural finance, fertilizers, conservation techniques, irrigation and legal requirements such as permits. The second part is devoted to information on livestock. Agritex, as the government department responsible for this publication is usually known, also produces handbooks on specific local crops including oilseeds, sugarcane and cotton.

584 **Cropping in the semi-arid areas of Zimbabwe.**
Department of Agriculture and Extension Services. Harare:
Department of Agriculture and Extension Services, 1988. 2 vols.
(Proceedings of a workshop held in Harare, 24th-28th August 1987.)

This collection of nineteen papers was presented at a workshop organized to assess the available knowledge on cropping in semi-arid areas, to set research priorities and to provide advice to farmers. Topics covered include agroclimatology, agroforestry, maize yields, livestock, diseases, tillage systems, grain storage, intercropping, soil problems, and vlei cultivation. A handbook for agricultural extension workers, and agricultural research staff was produced as a result.

585 **Development of European agriculture in Rhodesia 1945-65.**
Harry Dunlop. Salisbury: University of Rhodesia, Department of Economics, 1971. 73p. (Occasional paper, no. 5).

This study focusses on economic aspects of European agriculture in the period between the Second World War and UDI.

586 **Commercial agriculture in Zimbabwe: 10th independence anniversary edition.**
Modern Farming Publications. Harare: Modern Farming Publications, 1990. 227p.

This is a well-produced basic guide to the commercial agriculture sector in Zimbabwe, which despite its appearance as a glossy format volume, is not merely an advertisement for the Commercial Farmers' Union but contains much useful and serious information on the commodities produced, and the support services available to this sector.

587 **Institutional responsibility for social forestry in Africa: lessons from Zimbabwe.**
Kay A. Muir, John Casey. *Journal of Social Development in Africa*, vol. 4, no. 2 (1989), p. 27-37.

Social forestry as a means of improving agricultural productivity and simultaneously protecting the environment has attracted much attention in Africa from academics and agricultural extension services. However, as this article demonstrates with reference to Zimbabwe, projects often fail because commercial forestry institutions, with no knowledge of local farming systems, are used to implement programmes. The authors discuss the inappropriateness of such institutions since social forestry must be incorporated into the peasant farm system, and assert that existing extension services should be expanded to embrace these new techniques. The article also considers some technical aspects and needs of this sort of forestry development.

588 **The agricultural history of Rhodesia.**
Robin Palmer. In: *The roots of rural poverty in Central and Southern Africa*. Edited by Robin Palmer, Neil Parsons. Berkeley, California: University of California Press; London: Heinemann Educational, 1977, 430p.

Robin Palmer was an undergraduate at the University College of Rhodesia and Nyasaland, and was deported from Rhodesia in 1966, later becoming a senior lecturer at the University of Zambia. He has been a major contributor of academic studies on the land question in Zimbabwe. This is probably the best introduction to African agriculture in colonial and pre-colonial Rhodesia, which falls within the genre of studies on the deliberate underdevelopment of successful peasantries. Palmer describes the traditional agricultural systems of the Shona and Ndebele, which were far more complex than most European accounts allow, with the Ndebele being involved in arable as well as pastoral production. He shows how both systems were able to produce marketable surpluses and competed successfully with European farmers, who were frequently ill-prepared for local conditions. The Ndebele were devastated economically by the loss of their highveld land and cattle in 1893, but the Shona began to develop into a successful peasantry involved in the market economy. The demand for labour at very low wages from mines, farms and other European enterprises is shown to be at the root of the subsequent destruction of African agricultural competitiveness. Twenty-five thousand workers were needed in 1905, and this had already grown to 62,000 by 1910. A welter of legislative and restrictive measures are detailed which, although the timing of their impact varied geographically, led to black peasants being squeezed out of the market place and into the migrant labour force. These measures were not accepted without resistance, and the Shona are shown to have avoided dependence on migrant labour by paying taxes with crop earnings for some time, although the Ndebele were rapidly incorporated into the system. The impact of land alienation, creation of reserves and eviction of black farmers from 'European' lands were the most fundamental measures which destroyed the African agricultural base, culminating in the Land Apportionment Act of 1930. Two other Rhodesian case studies of peasant response to commercial opportunities and underdevelopment are found in this same edited volume which is one of the key texts on African agriculture under colonialism in Southern Africa. These are Ian R. Phimister, 'Peasant production and underdevelopment in Southern Rhodesia, 1890-1914', previously published in *African Affairs* (UK), vol. 73 (1974), p. 217-28, and B. A. Kosmin, 'The Inyoka tobacco industry of the Shangwe people: a case study of the displacement of a pre-colonial economy in Southern Rhodesia, 1898-1938', previously published in *African Social Research* (Zambia), vol. 17 (June 1974), p. 554-77. The variability of African farmers' responses to commercialization are considered in Wolfgang Dopcke, 'Magamo's maize: state and peasants during the depression in colonial Zimbabwe', in *Economies of Asia and Africa in the inter-war depression* (London: Routledge, 1989), edited by Ian Brown.

589 **The transport and marketing of horticultural crops by communal farmers into Harare.**
José Smith. *Geographical Journal of Zimbabwe*, vol. 20, (1989), p. 1-13.

This paper presents the results of the author's research on the nature of vegetable marketing from peasant farmers in post-independence Harare. Vegetables, being highly perishable, present particular problems in terms of transport and sale, but can be important cash crops. This sector was also considered by Angela Cheater just prior to independence in *The production and marketing of fresh produce amongst blacks in Zimbabwe*, (Salisbury: University of Zimbabwe, 1979 [Supplement to *Zambezia*]).

590 **The story of maize and the Farmers' Co-op Ltd.**
Compiled by R. C. Smith. Salisbury: Farmers' Co-op, 1979. 190p.

The Farmers' Co-op Ltd. has been an important establishment for the white commercial farming sector from colonial days, providing a wide range of agricultural inputs. This is a straightforward history and chronology of its development and growth, and its role in the white commercial maize sector.

591 **A regional inventory of the agricultural resource base.**
Southern African Development Coordination Conference (SADCC),
Food Security Feasibility Study. Harare: Ministry of Agriculture,
Zimbabwe, 1982. 3 vols.

Zimbabwe has been assigned responsibility for food security for the region by SADCC. These volumes assess the feasibility of inventorizing the regional resource base for food production, and each country's potential for achieving food self-sufficiency. Volume one contains the summary and main report, volume two the assessment of food self-sufficiency potential, and volume three country reports. Information on Zimbabwe is contained in each volume, and the country report is especially useful with details on food production, marketing, aid, consumption, policy and planning and the physical factors affecting food production. Another SADCC, Food Security Feasibility Study publication, *A regional resources information system* (Harare: Ministry of Agriculture, 1982. 2 vols.) contains an examination of data availability on food production with regard to providing support for food security planning, and many tables with data on Zimbabwe. On an early warning system for food shortage in Zimbabwe see SADCC, Food Security Feasibility Study, *An early warning system for regional food security* (Rome: FAO, 1983). On the impact of the drought of the early 1990s on food security see Lloyd M. Sachikonye, 'Zimbabwe: drought, food and adjustment', *Review of African Political Economy*, vol. 53 (1992), p. 88-94.

592 **Tobacco and its economic contribution to Zimbabwe.**
Prepared by Tobacco Industry Council. Zimbabwe: Tobacco Industry
Council, [1986]. 2nd ed.

Tobacco is an extremely important agricultural product in Zimbabwe, being the principal foreign exchange earner. Its production is dominated by white-owned, large-scale commercial farms. This publication by the Tobacco Industry Council is largely a self-advertisement, but it contains much useful information on the tobacco sector.

593 **Transnational corporations in the sugar industry in Zimbabwe.**
United Nations, Economic Commission for Africa. New York:
United Nations, 1982.

Sugar production in Zimbabwe is dominated by transnational company production on large-scale irrigated plantations in the low veld. This report discusses the role of such companies.

A decade of development Zimbabwe 1980-90.
See item no. 1.

Socio-economic review of Zimbabwe 1980-85.
See item no. 4.

Zimbabwe: a country study.
See item no. 6.

Zimbabwe: a land divided.
See item no. 8.

The political economy of Zimbabwe.
See item no. 10.

Zimbabwe's inheritance.
See item no. 12.

Zimbabwe's prospects: issues of race, class, state and capital in Southern Africa.
See item no. 13.

Zimbabwe: politics, economics and society.
See item no. 14.

Zimbabwe: towards a new order – an economic and social survey.
See item no. 15.

Zimbabwe: towards a new order – an economic and social survey.
See item no. 16.

Zimbabwe: at 5 years of independence: achievement, problems and prospects.
See item no. 17.

The Save study: relationships between the environment and basic needs satisfaction in the Save catchment, Zimbabwe.
See item no. 35.

The relationship of agricultural history and settlement to severe soil erosion in Rhodesia.
See item no. 46.

Lake McIlwaine: the eutrophication and recovery of a tropical African man-made lake.
See item no. 47.

Cold Comfort confronted.
See item no. 49.

Land degradation in Zimbabwe: a geographical study.
See item no. 262.

The development of food supplies to Salisbury (Harare).
See item no. 321.

Food security for Southern Africa.
See item no. 323.

Zimbabwe: the political economy of transition 1980-86.
See item no. 417.

Labour supplies in perspective: a study of the proletarianization of the African peasantry.
See item no. 481.

Zimbabwe agricultural and economic review.
See item no. 491.

Agricultural co-operative development in Zimbabwe.
See item no. 511.

Zimbabwe and the CGIAR centres: a study of their collaboration in agricultural research.
See item no. 735.

Pasture research in Zimbabwe 1964-84.
See item no. 736.

Development and policy

594 **Agroforestry for Shurugwi, Zimbabwe: report of an appraisal exercise for agroforestry research and extension.**
N. O. J. Abel.   London: Commonwealth Science Council, 1989.
229p. (CSC [89], no. AGR-14 TP 277).
This is a major interdisciplinary study on the potential for agroforestry in one specific communal area, Shurugwi. It contains contributions from eighteen researchers and provides an extremely detailed and comprehensive survey of this production system, which is seen as well suited to combining the diverse demands of environmental conservation, food production for humans and livestock, and fuel production.

595 **Restructuring marketing systems for smallholders: cases in Zimbabwe.**
Malcolm J. Blackie. In: *Accelerating food production in sub-Saharan Africa*. Edited by John W. Mellor.   Baltimore, Maryland: Johns Hopkins University Press, 1987, p. 187-209.
Zimbabwe inherited a marketing system for agricultural produce based on parastatal marketing boards. This was an efficient system, but it was geared almost exclusively to the needs of large-scale white commercial farmers. The author discusses the need to restructure marketing arrangements to cater for the small-scale peasant sector. One obstacle he identifies is the lack of senior officials who have any experience or knowledge of this sector and its needs. See also 'An improved maize marketing strategy for Zimbabwe', *Food Policy*, vol. 10, no. 4 (1985), p. 365-73, by Blackie, with B. Child and K. Muir.

596 **The comrades and the countryside: the politics of agricultural policy in Zimbabwe.**
Michael Bratton.   *World Politics*, vol. 39, no. 2 (1987), p. 174-202.
This article examines the political context of agricultural policy decisions in the first five years of independence, and is an excellent reference for information on the nature of such policies. The author illustrates how political factors tempered the nature of agricultural development policies, and challenges the view typical of the World Bank

and IMF that political intervention in this sector is always disadvantageous. Four major factors in agricultural policy are analysed in detail: prices, land reform, agricultural service provision and bureaucratic growth. He contends that policies from 1980 to 1985 were very responsive to the needs of farmers, including the peasant sector, and that some components which could be construed as inefficient in the short-term would nevertheless yield important long-term benefits. The article is also a useful source for information on the removal of price subsidies for food.

597 **Financing smallholder production: a comparison of individual and group credit schemes in Zimbabwe.**
Michael Bratton. *Public Administration and Development*, vol. 6, no. 2 (1986), p. 115-32.

In this paper the author argues that lending to groups in the rural areas is generally more efficient in raising agricultural production than lending to individuals. Credit programmes for individual farmers have had many problems in Africa, and the evidence of post-independent lending schemes to smallholders in Zimbabwe is assessed to see how they compare with experience elsewhere. Joint liability schemes are shown to be preferable on a number of grounds, including higher repayment rates by the farmers involved. However the author stresses that the organization of the farmer group and its approach to encouraging repayment are also significant factors affecting the efficacy of credit schemes.

598 **Optimal grain pricing and storage policy in controlled agricultural economies: application to Zimbabwe.**
Steven T. Buccola, Chrispen Sukume. *World Development*, vol. 16, no. 3 (1988), p. 361-72.

Zimbabwe was greatly blamed for having sold off the maize surpluses it had accumulated in the 1980s, when drought struck in the 1990s. Yet it had previously been criticized for holding overly large food security stocks, which were expensive to maintain, and had sold the surpluses partly in response. This article is therefore of particular interest since it contends, on technical economic grounds, that the large maize stocks held were still less than the optimal amount.

599 **Agrarian policy in migrant labour societies: reform or tranformation in Zimbabwe.**
R. Bush, Lionel Cliffe. *Review of African Political Economy*, vol. 29, (1984), p. 77-94.

The worker-peasant and housewife-farmer syndrome of migrant labour societies is common in Zimbabwe, as migrant workers had to leave their families behind in the former Tribal Trust Lands because of the plethora of restrictions on permanent urban residence and unavailability of family housing. This syndrome is argued to have subsidised the capitalist sector in the urban areas, by keeping wages low (see item 481 by Giovanni Arrighi for the best-known discussion of this theory for Rhodesia). The question posed by this paper is whether the syndrome should be allowed to continue, given that the institutionalized migrant labour system is no longer extant. The impact of policies which refuse resettlement land to migrants' families is discussed, and the importance of land holdings for urban migrants. After making comparisons with Nicaragua, where circular migration continued after the revolution, Bush and Cliffe conclude that circular migration should not be prevented. Further discussion on this issue is found in two papers by David Simon, 'Agrarian policy in Zimbabwe and Southern Africa: reform or transformation', *Review of African Political Economy*, vol. 34 (1985), p. 82-89 and 'Regional inequality, migration and development: the case of Zimbabwe', *Journal for Economic and Social Geography*, vol. 77, no. 1 (1986), p. 7-17. The migrant peasant society is also considered in Diana Callear's 'Who wants to be a peasant? Food production in a labour-exporting area of Zimbabwe', in *Food systems in Central and Southern Africa*, edited by Johan Pottier (London: School of Oriental and African Studies, 1985). See also the paper on migration to Harare by Deborah Potts and Chris Mutambirwa (item 259).

600 **Zimbabwe's experience in rural development.**
D. Hywel Davies. *Development Southern Africa*, vol. 7, (1990), p. 166-82.

This paper reviews rural development policies for three eras: 1890-1977; 1977-80; and 1980-90. A major focus is environmental degradation in the communal lands. Like Whitlow (see item 50) the author questions the wisdom of land reform because he feels this would spread environmental problems into resettlement areas, a view which neglects the political and historical context of population pressure in the former Tribal Trust Lands.

601 **The Native Land Husbandry Act of 1951 and the rural African middle class of Southern Rhodesia.**
William B. Duggan. *African Affairs*, vol. 315, no. 79 (1980), p. 227-239.

The Native Land Husbandry Act was a very significant piece of legislation with enormous implications for agriculture in the communal areas. However its implementation and aims were riddled with ambiguities. This article is a very useful reference on the Act, providing many factual details about its stated purposes and planned costs, and reviewing the various interpretations of its real aims, its impact, and why it was abandoned. In addition a major theme of the analysis is to what extent the Act hoped to create an African middle class, and how far it succeeded. The author concludes that it failed in the reserves, and goes on to examine the role of the Native Purchase Areas in fostering this class of farmer, the later attacks on it by the Smith regime, and the possibilities of post-independence land reform similar to the Swynnerton Plan in Kenya.

602 **The implications of Zimbabwe's agricultural policies on women's access to agricultural resources and services.**
Ntombi R. Gata, Thokozile Ruzvidzo. In: *Women and agriculture in the SADCC region. Volume II: background documentation*. Edited by Susan Hurlich. Harare: Rural Science and Technology Institute for Canadian International Development Agency, 1986.

Agricultural pricing policies clearly influence the types of food produced by rural people, and therefore their nutrition. In this essay the authors assess women's access to agricultural resources, and their role as the primary food producers. Pricing policies are evaluated in terms of their impact on food and nutrition. They conclude that the drive for food self-sufficiency has led to an overproduction of cereals by rural households at the expense of certain more nutritious food crops. Also on women and extension services, see *An evaluation of agricultural extension services support to women farmers in Zimbabwe with special reference to Makonde district* (Harare: Zimbabwe Institute of Development Studies, 1987. [Consultancy Report Series, no. 12]) by P. M. Mutuma, Sam Moyo, and Sipho Magonya.

603 The Tribal Trust Land Development Corporation: rural development in Rhodesia.
P. Hawkins.   *Zimbabwe Journal of Economics*, vol. 1, no. 2 (1979), p. 104-108.

The Tribal Trust Land Development Corporation, TILCOR, was assigned the responsibility for developing the African farming areas by the UDI government, in an effort to distance itself from this sector. This article discusses a model for irrigated agricultural development then being imposed for cotton production in Gokwe TTL. Another paper on the corporation in this same issue of the *Zimbabwe Journal of Economics* is B. F. Hanratty, 'The Tribal Trust Land Development Corporation: planning and development in Victoria Province', p. 109-115. They are of interest as examples of the technocratic approach to agricultural planning typical of this organization. Also see *Agricultural production in Tribal Trust Land irrigation schemes and Tilcor estates* (Salisbury: Central Statistical Office, 1981).

604 Development in rural Tribal Trust Lands: an overview.
Arthur J. B. Hughes.   Salisbury: Tribal Areas of Rhodesia Research Foundation, 1974. 323p.

This major survey of the Tribal Trust Lands (TTL), undertaken six years before independence for the trustees of the Tribal Areas of Rhodesia Research Foundation, provides a comprehensive picture of development problems and policies and the institutions involved in TTL development. It also provides a useful guide to the paradigms within which TTL problems were usually considered in the colonial era, although Hughes' attitudes and views were not typical in every respect. The study was based largely on secondary sources and interviews with TTL-based organizations, supplemented by some field work. It is divided into four parts: the first provides a general picture of the situation then current in the TTLs, the second describes the various development agencies involved including government and non-government organizations, and the missions, whilst the third analyses some of the development policies which had been implemented. In the fourth section Hughes presents his own conclusions about the type of development and new research then needed, followed by the recommendations of the Research Advisory Committee of the Foundation. In Hughes' opinion the problems of TTL households were not primarily due to land shortage but to the use of poor agricultural techniques, a view which conveniently shifts any blame for TTL poverty from the process of land alienation. He also adhered to the view that one problem of communal tenure was that it allows people, such as migrant labourers, to maintain a stake in the land even though their primary economic support was not derived from agriculture, and that they therefore do not use the land efficiently. This view has been criticized for tackling the problem from the wrong end – since people have been driven into the migration process by the need to earn a cash income because they could not support themselves from the land. However Hughes does not simply dismiss communal tenure as a useless concept as many colonial analysts were prone to do. His analysis shows an appreciation of the complexities of the system, and an awareness that the failure of the Native Land Husbandry Act, which included attempts to introduce freehold tenure, might indicate that individual ownership of land may not function well in the TTLs.

605 **Maize control in Southern Rhodesia 1931-41: the African contribution to white survival.**
C. F. Keyter. Salisbury: Central African Historical Association, [n.d.]. 30p. (Local Series, no. 34).
This study analyses the causes and effects of state policy on maize marketing in Rhodesia in the 1930s. In essence the state's intervention in this market meant that African-grown maize was classed as the lowest quality, and the small European farmer was helped at the expense of his African competitor.

606 **Crop prices and wage policy in the light of Zimbabwe's development goals.**
Kay A. Muir-Leresche. PhD thesis, University of Zimbabwe, Harare, 1984.
This major study of government policy towards crop prices and wages focusses on the tensions between raising minimum wages for agricultural labourers and controlling crop prices. The large-scale commercial sector has reacted to this by reducing the numbers in agricultural employment, thereby heightening the unemployment problem. Published papers based on her thesis under the author's original name of Muir include 'Minimum wages in Zimbabwe: case study of family earnings on a flue-cured tobacco farm', *Zimbabwe Agricultural Journal*, vol. 79, no. 4 (1982), p. 115-17, and with Malcolm J. Blackie, B. H. Kinsey and M. L. A. de Swardt, 'The employment effects of 1980 price and wage policy in the Zimbabwe maize and tobacco industries', *African Affairs*, vol. 81, no. 322 (1982), p. 71-85.

607 **Agricultural producer co-operatives and agrarian transformation in Zimbabwe: policy, strategy and implementation.**
Clever Mumbengegwi. *Zimbabwe Journal of Economics*, vol. 1, no. 1 (1984), p. 47-59.
Co-operatives theoretically have a key role to play in agrarian reform. This article examines critically government policy towards agriculture producer co-operatives in Zimbabwe, and how these policies are being implemented. Also on the issue of agrarian reform see his 'Some observations on the problems and prospects of socialist agricultural transformation in Zimbabwe', *Economic Quarterly*, vol. 18, no. 4 (1983), p. 23-31.

608 **Rural development and planning in Zimbabwe.**
Edited by Naison Mutizwa-Mangiza, A. H. J. Helmsing. Aldershot, England: Avebury; Brookfield, Vermont: Gower, 1991. 481p. maps.
This is a very useful collection of papers reviewing the country's rural, local government and regional planning development experience and prospects some ten years after independence. The collection was put together by Mutizwa-Mangiza, who has also written on the urban sector, has held the Chair of the Department of Rural and Urban Planning at the University of Zimbabwe and has also worked in Kenya, and Helmsing, who was a visiting researcher from the Institute of Social Studies in the Hague. Many of the contributions had previously been published elsewhere, usually in journals, and their collection in one volume is very convenient. Some of these are covered as separate items in this bibliography. The collection is divided into five sections. The first contains two papers on the rural economy: J. Jackson and P. Collier,

Agriculture. Development and policy

'Incomes, poverty and food security in the communal lands of Zimbabwe', and H. Coudere and S. Marijsse, 'Rich and poor in Mutoko communal area'; the second covers agriculture and resettlement: K. H. Wekwete, 'The rural resettlement programme in post-independence Zimbabwe', and papers by Weiner, Moyo, Munslow and O'Keefe, and Zinyama.; the third focusses on growth points and rural industries: K. H. Wekwete, 'Growth centre policy in Zimbabwe: with special reference to district service centres', and three papers by A. J. H. Helmsing, 'Non-agricultural enterprises in the communal lands of Zimbabwe', 'A survey of district council income-generating projects' and a paper on rural industries and growth points; the fourth focuses on infrastructure and social services: F. Cleaver, 'Maintenance of rural water supplies: a case study from Makoni district', R. Loewonson, 'Health and health care in post-independence Zimbabwe', and a paper by Naison Mutizwa-Mangiza on rural water. The final section is on rural local government, and the papers are A. J. H. Helmsing, 'Transforming rural local government: Zimbabwe's post-independence experience'; and two papers by Mutizwa-Mangiza on local level planning.

609   **The Native Land Husbandry Act of Southern Rhodesia.**
Arthur Pendered, W. von Memerty.   *Journal of African Administration*, vol. 7, no. 3 (1975), p. 99-109.

This is an important reference on this very significant piece of legislation, which had the potential to transform utterly the nature of African agriculture in the reserves, by enforcing individual freehold tenure, and a host of other changes including many conservation measures. It was fundamentally misconceived both politically and technically, and its patchy implementation eventually had to end. The Act has been the subject of much academic and general published criticism; this reference however provides the official version of the reasons for the Act, and its aims, and was written by the undersecretary of native economic development, and an administrative officer of the Act. See also a government pamphlet on the Act, *What the Native Land Husbandry Act means to the rural African and Southern Rhodesia: a five year plan that will revolutionalize African agriculture* (Salisbury: Government Printer, 1955).

610   **The Sabi Valley irrigation projects.**
Wolf Roder.   Chicago, Illinois: University of Chicago, Department of Geography, 1965. 213p. (Research Paper, no. 99).

Most irrigation projects in colonial Zimbabwe were geared to the needs of white commercial farmers. However the Sabi Valley irrigation projects included small-scale peasant farmers. In common with many large irrigation schemes in Africa, the implementation of the scheme was not successful. This extensive survey discusses the origins of the projects, and the problems encountered as they developed. Both technical and institutional errors are identified, as is the lack of communication between decision-makers and the farmers. The scheme is also critically analysed in part of Weinrich's study of African farmers (see item 633). For comparative purposes it is interesting to contrast this survey with a glowing description of the plan by the chief economist of the project, P. J. Stanbridge, in 'Long range planning in under-developed countries: a case history', *Long Range Planning*, vol. 2 (Dec. 1969), p. 38-45.

611 **A participatory model of agricultural extension: the case of vleis, trees and grazing schemes in the dry South of Zimbabwe.**
Ian Scoones, Ben Cousins. *Zambezia*, vol. 26, no. 1 (1989), p. 45-66.
In this paper the authors discuss various methods of agricultural extension and demonstrate how it has frequently misunderstood the way in which peasants use, and need to use natural resources. They then illustrate their arguments through case studies of policies towards, and peasant use of three different types of agricultural resources: vleis, or dambos; trees; and grazing resources. They contend that extension services developed from farmer participatory research would result in more appropriate and successful policies.

612 **Group interests and the state: an explanation of Zimbabwe's agricultural policies.**
Tor Skålnes. *Journal of Modern African Studies*, vol. 27, no. 1 (1989), p. 85-107.
In this paper Zimbabwe's agricultural policies and development since independence are analysed with reference to the influential theories on African agriculture of Robert Bates. Bates' argument is that African governments have discoured farmers from producing by over-control of the markets, usually via inefficient parastatals, and underpricing of crops to assist in keeping urban food prices down. In Skålnes' view, Zimbabwe's agricultural policies have not followed these tendencies for a number of reasons. These include the country's efficient import-substitution industries, the relative efficiency of the marketing boards and the occasional raising of crop prices, the virtual elimination of taxing farmers to help agricultural-processing industries, and good support services. The subsidization of urban food is shown to be a complex matter, and whilst some indirect subsidies occur, in general urban consumers are bearing more of the real price of their food.

613 **Zimbabwe.**
Anne M. Thomson. In: *Agricultural pricing policy in Africa: four country case studies*. Edited by Charles Harvey. Basingstoke, England: Macmillan, 1988, p. 186-219.
The author of this paper provides an extensive critical analysis of agricultural pricing policy in Zimbabwe since independence. A rigorous analysis of the real profitability of various crops is carried out, and it is argued that pricing policies have generally been reasonably beneficial to the farmer. Some instances where problems have arisen in particular commodities are detailed. The gradual removal of subsidies for industry are described. Thomson also contends that the marketing boards have been efficient, and argues against deregulation of prices and a move towards a free market system on the grounds that it is not clear that this would enhance agricultural production or profitability, and would also be manifestly unjust to the communal farming sector since pricing policies had long been used to benefit white commercial farmers.

614 **A strategy for rural development: data bank no. 2: the peasant sector.**
Whitsun Foundation. Salisbury: Whitsun Foundation, 1978. (Project 1.05 [a]).
The Whitsun Foundation was inaugurated in August 1975 as a private, non-profit making development agency. Its aim was to serve Zimbabwe and advance education and development of skills, and promote the growth and development of the economy.

As part of the Foundations's programme, it produced a large number of special reports on many aspects of the country's economy and development. These are extremely useful for descriptions of the situation in the late 1970s or early 1980s. They tend to be written from a rather conservative viewpoint, and are often somewhat pessimistic in their prognoses; for example the authors generally hold to the view that rural development problems are largely due to the ignorance and bad practices of the peasantry. Rural-urban migration and the process of African urbanization are also generally negatively viewed, as they were throughout the colonial era. Most of the policy recommendations contained in these studies were ignored by the government in the early years of independence, although its later move to a more open, market economy has seen it shift closer to the approaches approved by the Whitsun Foundation. This volume contains very detailed data on both the physical and human aspects of rural development and is illustrated with many maps and tables. Other Whitsun Foundation reports of relevance to the rural sector are *Rural afforestation study* (Salisbury: Whitsun Foundation, 1981), *Rural service centres development study* (Salisbury: Whitsun Foundation, 1980), *Rural workshop and machinery centre: report and recommendations of the director on the proposed rural workshop and machinery centre, Sanyati tribal trust land* (Salisbury: Whitsun Foundation, 1977) and *Peasant sector credit plan for Zimbabwe* (Salisbury: Whitsun Foundation, 1980, 3 vols.).

A decade of development Zimbabwe 1980-90.
See item no. 1.

Zimbabwe: politics, economics and society.
See item no. 14.

African farmers in Rhodesia: old and new peasant communities in Karangaland.
See item no. 633.

Ecological dynamics and human welfare in Southern Zimbabwe.
See item no. 634.

Commercialisation of small-scale agriculture in Zimbabwe: some emerging patterns of spatial differentiation.
See item no. 637.

Livestock

615   **Zimbabwe livestock in large-scale commercial agricultural units 1981.**
Central Statistical Office.   Salisbury: Central Statistical Office, 1981.
20p.
Basic data on commercial livestock on European land just after independence is provided in this government report.

616 **People, land and livestock: proceedings of a workshop on the socio-economic dimensions of livestock production in the communal lands of Zimbabwe.**
Edited by Ben Cousins. Harare: Centre of Applied Social Science, University of Zimbabwe, 1989. 461p.

This is a most important collection of papers which reflects the very significant work on livestock production and grazing in the communal lands produced since independence by both local and foreign researchers. A number of new research directions have been developed, which have often challenged or overturned the preconceptions which dominated colonial research into this issue. The new approach tends to be more attuned to the needs and knowledge of local black farmers, and far less ready to criticize their grazing techniques, which have had to adapt to increasingly difficult conditions in the communal lands. In addition, the parameters of the new research include much more study of the local economic and socio-cultural aspects of livestock for black families engaged in small-scale farming. The twelve contributions in this book include surveys of social research, economic study, and ecological analysis. The importance of cattle for draught power and manure, as well as for cash income and social status are stressed. A short report and recommendations from the workshop were published separately as *Socio-economic dimensions of livestock production in the communal lands of Zimbabwe* (Harare: Centre of Applied Social Science, University of Zimbabwe, [1989]), edited by Ben Cousins, Cecilia Jackson and Ian Scoones. Specifically on the importance of cattle as draught power, see Michael Bratton, *Draft power, draft exchange and farmer organizations* (Harare: Department of Land Management, University of Zimbabwe, 1984. [Department of Land Management Working Paper no. 9]).

617 **A survey of current grazing schemes in the communal lands of Zimbabwe.**
Ben Cousins. Harare: Centre for Applied Social Sciences, University of Zimbabwe, 1987. 96p.

Grazing schemes involve major alterations in the management of livestock, particularly cattle, in the communal areas. They often involve rotating pasture areas, and fencing. The purpose of the schemes is theoretically to improve the efficiency with which livestock use grazing, and to limit environmental degradation, and they have official backing in Zimbabwe. This study is part of a major project by the Centre for Applied Social Sciences at the University of Zimbabwe on livestock management. It examines critically the concept of grazing schemes. These often do not benefit the poorer households in the communal areas because they have little power in the decision-making about how grazing schemes work in their rural communities.

618 **Pastoralism and Zimbabwe.**
Peter S. Garlake. *Journal of African History*, vol. 19, no. 4 (1978), p. 479-93.

Drawing in particular on archaeological evidence about cattle from a stone zimbabwe in Mozambique, this article provides a historian's perspective on the past role and significance of cattle for the cultures that occupied the zimbabwes of Zimbabwe. The wide-ranging discussion includes consideration of the impact of tsetse infestations on settlement location, of vegetation and water resource evidence, and the possibility that transhumance was an important feature of pre-colonial cattle husbandry.

619   **Meat and monopolies: beef cattle in Southern Rhodesia 1890-1938.**
       Ian R. Phimister.   *Journal of African History*, vol. 19, no. 3 (1978),
       p. 391-414.
This account of the beef industry from the beginning of the settler period to 1938
analyses its implications for later economic development.

620   **Livestock in the communal areas of Zimbabwe.**
       Stephen Sandford.   London: Overseas Development Institute, 1982.
       169p.
This major report on the size of livestock herds, and the role of livestock in the
communal land economies was produced for the Ministry of Lands, Resettlement and
Rural Development. A more recent, but shorter report from the ODI is John C.
Barrett, *The economic role of cattle in communal farming systems in Zimbabwe*
(London: ODI, 1992. [Pastoral Development Network Series, Paper no. 326]).

621   **Livestock populations and household economics: a case study from
       Southern Zimbabwe.**
       Ian Scoones.   PhD thesis, Imperial College, London, 1990.
This major research study on the role of cattle in the communal areas of Zimbabwe
combines field research in Masvihwa, Southern Zimbabwe, with archival material on
cattle policies and the historical relationships between cattle sales and various factors
including price and climatic variations. The study challenges many of the preconceptions about the role of cattle which tended to inform previous studies and policies
during the colonial era. These preconceptions included the idea that communal farmers
were uninterested in the economic value of their cattle which primarily played a social
role, would not sell them, and kept far too many livestock in relation to 'scientifically'
determined sustainable stocking rates. The whole concept of stocking rates is shown to
be based on misunderstandings about the way in which communal cattle are grazed,
and the significance of key resource areas, such as dambos (seasonally waterlogged
areas) for grazing is emphasized. African farmers' resistance to colonial cattle policies,
including destocking, is explained. Scoones also discusses the importance of cattle for
draught power and manure, factors rarely properly considered in such policies; neither
were the extreme inequalities in cattle holdings which typify cattle ownership. Data on
cattle sales and cattle numbers from 1923-86 are also analysed. This study, which was
in part prompted by Ken Wilson's work (see item 634), with other works by Scoones,
and research by Ben Cousins (e.g. items 565, 616, 617) amongst others have helped to
provide a re-interpretation of communal cattle, which has important policy implications. See also Nick Abel and Piers Blaikie's 'Land degradation, stocking rates and
conservation policies in the communal rangelands of Botswana and Zimbabwe', *Land
Degradation and Rehabilitation*, vol. 1, no. 1 (1989), which is also published by the
Overseas Development Institute in their ODI Pastoral Development Network Series,
Paper 291, March 1990.

**Formal and informal rights to land in Zimbabwe's black freehold areas: a case
study from Msengezi.**
See item no. 563.

A participatory model of agricultural extension: the case of vleis, trees and grazing schemes in the dry South of Zimbabwe.
See item no. 611.

Agriculture and livestock survey: communal lands 1985/86.
See item no. 625.

Overpopulation and overstocking in the native areas of Matabeleland.
See item no. 631.

Communal areas

622 **The use of dambos in rural development, with reference to Zimbabwe.**
Morag Bell, Richard Faulkner, Patricia Hotchkiss, Robert Lambert, Neil Roberts, Alan Windram.   Loughborough, England: Loughborough University, 1987. 236p. (Final Report of ODA project R3869).

This major study of the use of a specific ecological habitat for agriculture in the communal lands will be of value not only to those interested in agricultural and environmental issues, but also for material on the politics and history of conservation policy in Rhodesia. Dambos are a type of vlei, seasonally flooded wetlands which are key resources for dry season grazing and irrigated vegetables and crops in the communal areas. Under current legislation inherited from the colonial period it is illegal for communal farmers to cultivate dambos. Ostensibly this prohibition relates to environmental concerns, although, as this study indicates, European desires to stop African agricultural competition appear to be the true source of the ban. This study, funded by the British Overseas Development Administration, combines technical and socio-economic research to show that dambos can be, and indeed are being, safely and sustainably used for arable agriculture by African farmers, and that the income and other benefits derived from their use are often very significant for rural households. The study areas were in Chihota, Zwimba and Gutu communal areas. The research team consisted of social scientists and engineers from the Water, Engineering and Development Centre of Loughborough University, and an engineer from the Department of Civil Engineering in Zimbabwe. They recommend that the present legislation should be modified to incorporate safe levels of cultivation. Published papers on selected aspects of this research, which will be more easily accessible, include two papers by Morag Bell and Patricia Hotchkiss, 'Political interventions in environmental resource use: dambos in Zimbabwe', *Land Use Policy*, vol. 6, no. 4 (1989), p. 313-23, and 'Garden cultivation and household strategies in Zimbabwe', *Africa* (UK), vol. 61, no. 2 (1991) p. 202-21.

623 **Farmer organizations and food production in Zimbabwe.**
Michael Bratton.   *World Development*, vol. 14, no. 3 (1986), p. 367-84.

There are a wide variety of farmer organizations in Zimbabwe, dating from both before and after independence, and representing very different and sometimes conflicting needs. Many have an impact on how food is produced. The author evaluates the relationship between production and farmer organizations from 1980 to 1985, based on a survey of 464 farmer households and fifty farmer groups in Wedza, Gutu, Dande and Chipuriro communal areas. He found that membership of farmer groups was quite widespread. Four types of groups are considered: information, labour, marketing and multipurpose. He concludes that the impact of such groups is generally positive: they helped members to gain access to agricultural services and the dramatic increase in smallholder maize production was in part due to them.

624 **Land and food in the Wedza communal area.**
     Diana Callear. *Zimbabwe Agricultural Journal*, vol. 81, no. 4 (1984), p. 163-68.

The author's empirical research in the communal areas has focussed on agriculture and women, and in this paper she examines the incidence of female headed households, their role in agriculture, and the effects of labour constraints due to male migrancy on agricultural production. Similar themes are considered for Save North and Mhondoro communal areas in Lovemore Zinyama, 'Rural household structure, absenteeism and agricultural labour: a case-study of two subsistence farming areas in Zimbabwe', *Singapore Journal of Tropical Geography*, vol. 7, no. 2 (1986), p. 163-73.

625 **Agriculture and livestock survey: communal lands 1985/86.**
     Central Statistical Office. Harare: Central Statistical Office, [1986].

Useful data on communal livestock and agriculture are produced in this government report.

626 **The state and agrarian change in Zimbabwe's communal areas.**
     Michael Drinkwater. London: Macmillan, 1991. 348p.

This important study on the role of the colonial and post-colonial state in trying to effect change in the communal farming areas is based on the author's 1988 doctoral thesis from the University of East Anglia. A detailed examination is made of the changes which have occurred in agricultural production in the communal areas since independence, with particular reference to Midlands Province. A wide range of agricultural issues are considered including alternative strategies for managing livestock, maize production and household survival. Despite the major improvements in marketed agricultural production from the communal areas, there are many areas of debate about the nature of communal agricultural development since independence, the role of the state and its interaction with the peasantry. One of Drinkwater's major theses is that the state's intervention in the peasant sector is frequently still negative; in particular there is a continued reliance on technical approaches and 'scientific' solutions, which are quite often ill-conceived. Not only does the practice, common during the colonial era, of foisting these solutions on farmers with little or no consultation often persist, but also the techniques themselves sometimes make problems such as erosion worse. The result is political resistance or apathy from the farmers. There is now quite a range of published material on this and related aspects of Zimbabwean agricultural development. A shorter paper by Drinkwater is 'Technical development and peasant impoverishment: land use policy in Zimbabwe's Midlands Province', *Journal of Southern African Studies*, vol. 10, no. 2 (Jan. 1989), p. 287-305, in which he is critical of the post-independence land reform policies. See also items 39, 621, 634.

627 **Agricultural production and farmer co-operation in Mutoko communal land.**
M. Govaerts. Harare: Department of Rural and Urban Planning, University of Zimbabwe, 1986. 118p.

In this detailed case study of Mutoko communal land, a range of factors influencing agricultural production are considered. These include various types of co-operation and organization amongst farmers, and the impact of informal co-operation on problem solving in agriculture. The author also considers gender issues related to these topics, and co-operation between male and female household heads is analysed.

628 **An economic survey of Chiweshe reserve.**
R. W. M. Johnson. *Rhodes-Livingstone Journal*, vol. 36, (Dec. 1964), p. 82-108.

Four papers on agriculture in the reserves were included in this issue of the Rhodes-Livingstone Journal. This survey of Chiweshe by Johnson, an agricultural economist, includes analysis of farm work by gender and age in 1960-61. Women and children are shown to account for seventy per cent of farm work. The impact of government policy to centralize rural settlements, and various aspects of agricultural techniques are also discussed. The other three papers are Sister Mary Aquina (A. K. H. Weinrich), 'The social background of agriculture in Chilimanzi reserve'; P. Hamilton, 'Population pressure and land use in Chiweshe reserve'; and J. D. Jordan, 'Zimutu reserve: a land-use appreciation'. The collection provides many useful insights and data on agricultural systems and problems in the early 1960s. Another survey of agriculture in Chiweshe is 'Coercive development: land shortage, forced labour, and colonial development in the Chiweshe reserve, colonial Zimbabwe', *Journal of African Historical Studies*, vol. 25, no. 1 (1992), p. 29-65, by Leonard Bessant.

629 **Adaptation to marginal land amongst the peasant farmers of Zimbabwe.**
Kingston W. Nyamapfene. *Journal of Southern African Studies*, vol. 15, no. 2 (1989), p. 384-89.

This paper was one of the contributions on Zimbabwean farming issues which appeared in a special issue of the Journal of Southern African Studies on the Politics of Conservation. Nyamapfene describes various farming systems which have evolved in response to difficult agro-ecological conditions in different parts of Zimbabwe, primarily poor soils and inadequate and unreliable rainfall. He contends that these techniques demonstrate the considerable wisdom of peasant farmers, and that local research on farming systems has still not fully come to terms with this. In the same issue of this journal the theme of peasant knowledge is again addressed, along with analysis of the mistakes technical interventions have made with regard to trees, by Ken Wilson in 'Trees in fields in Southern Zimbabwe', p. 369-83. A paper containing useful discussion of physical constraints on successful agriculture in the communal areas, which shows that about eighty per cent of these areas lie outside the limits for dryland cropping and that extensive areas are covered with granite outcrops is R. J. Whitlow's 'Environmental constraints and population pressures on the tribal areas of Zimbabwe', *Zimbabwe Agricultural Journal*, vol. 77, no. 4 (1980), p. 173-81.

630   **Land tenure, gender relations, and agricultural production: the case of Zimbabwe's peasantry.**
Donna Pankhurst, Susie Jacobs. In: *Agriculture, women and land: the African experience*. Edited by Jean Davison.   Boulder, Colorado: Westview Press, 1988, p. 611-32.

Women are often disadvantaged in terms of gaining access to land, and Pankhurst and Jacobs provide an analysis of the gendered nature of land tenure, and its impact on women and agricultural production in the communal lands.

631   **Overpopulation and overstocking in the native areas of Matabeleland.**
J. R. V. Prescott. In: *Population and land in Africa south of the Sahara*. Edited by R. M. Prothero.   Oxford: Oxford University Press, 1972, p. 239-52.

Based on field work in 1958 and 1959, this paper examines the problems of overcrowding in the reserves of Matabeleland in the light of agro-ecological conditions and agricultural methods in those areas. The aridity of the reserves is stressed, and the difficulties of assured production. The paper is a good example of the focus on overstocking that typified the colonial approach to agricultural problems in the reserves, and makes the rather curious point that population pressure in the reserves had previously been alleviated, in 1930, 1950 and 1954, by increasing the area allocated to sole African occupation. Typical of its period, the paper completely ignores the historical context of land alienation in the country, given that all the land was originally African; the citation of 1930 in the context of increasing land availability is particularly indicative of the perceptual gap between many white commentators of this period and the black majority, since it refers to the enactment of the notoriously unjust Land Apportionment Act. Nevertheless Prescott goes on to recommend a transfer of white land to Africans, and points out that much white-owned land is underutilized.

632   **Agricultural extension in Zimbabwe's communal areas.**
Report of the workshop.   Harare: Zimbabwe Institute of Development Studies, 1990. 8p. (Zimbabwe Institute of Development Studies Special Paper Series, no. 6).

This report discusses the results of research carried out at the end of the 1980s in the communal areas. A variety of rural household parameters are examined, including gender and class, in relation to agricultural extension services.

633   **African farmers in Rhodesia: old and new peasant communities in Karangaland.**
Anna Katherina Hildegard Weinrich.   London, New York: Oxford University Press for the International African Institute, 1975. 342p. bibliog.

This much-cited study provides a wealth of detail on African farming systems and responses to change in Tribal Trust Lands, Native Purchase Areas, and irrigation schemes. Case studies of individual farmers are provided, based on research undertaken between 1962 and 1969. The author criticizes the Rhodesian government for its agricultural policies towards African farmers, which, she argues, largely fail because the difficult context within which farmers operate, with land shortages and insufficient access to resources and inputs, is of the government's own making. The author recommends an end to racial discrimination, and more community participation in policy decisions.

634 **Ecological dynamics and human welfare in Southern Zimbabwe.**
Ken Wilson. PhD thesis, University College London, London, 1990.

This extraordinary thesis is ostensibly a study of the interrelationships between child morbidity and mortality, and the ecology of the areas they inhabit, comparing two communal areas in Mazvihwa. Wilson is an exceptionally versatile researcher, and the thesis is also a wonderful resource for information on agricultural systems and the ways in which farmers cope with adverse conditions; farmers' attitudes to past and present government policies towards African agriculture, especially the often ill-conceived environmental measures; food production and consumption, particularly the use of wild animal and plant products in the diet; the importance of cattle; women's fertility; and health improvements since independence. The second volume of the thesis consists of an extensive bibliography, and several appendices dealing with some of the topics mentioned above in great detail. Wilson's contribution to new directions in research on the communal areas in the 1980s was significant, and some of the issues raised in this thesis have either led to, or been incorporated in, other major research studies (see for example items 41, 621, 622).

635 **Africans on the land: economic problems of African agricultural development in Southern, Central and East Africa, with special reference to Southern Rhodesia.**
Montague Yudelman. Cambridge, Massachusetts: Harvard University Press; London: Oxford University Press, 1964. 288p.

A useful source on the type of agriculture practised by farmers in the Tribal Trust Lands in the 1950s and 1960s, which draws on research carried out between 1956-60 sponsored by the Ford and Rockefeller Foundations. Most of the study focusses on Southern Rhodesia. It surveys the many problems preventing successsful commercial farming by Africans, including land shortages. Chapters on land tenure, labour, migration, rural capital, prices and marketing are included, and the Native Land Husbandry Act is discussed. This study is still a standard source on these topics. The author was born in South Africa and obtained a doctorate in agricultural economics at the University of California, Berkeley.

636 **Changes in settlement and land use patterns in a subsistence agricultural economy: a Zimbabwe case study 1956-84.**
Lovemore Mondiwa Zinyama. *Erdkunde*, vol. 42, no. 1 (1988), p. 365-84.

This study examines the historical impact of various government agricultural policies on patterns of land use in one area within Save North communal land, through the use of aerial photographs. The policies include land apportionment, settlement re-organization inspired by Alvord, and the Native Land Husbandry Act. The trend towards increases in cultivated land, and decreases in densely wooded land is illustrated along with changes in settlement patterns.

637 **Commercialisation of small-scale agriculture in Zimbabwe: some emerging patterns of spatial differentiation.**
Lovemore Mondiwa Zinyama. *Singapore Journal of Tropical Geography*, vol. 9, no. 2 (1988), p. 151-62.
This paper considers the success of Zimbabwe's small-scale black farming sector after independence in dramatically increasing its share of certain marketed crops, notably maize and cotton. In part this reflected the improved access to support services, such as credit and physical inputs, which had previously been very largely confined to the white commercial sector. The redistribution of land had little impact. However the source of this new productivity is unevenly distributed. Zinyama demonstrates that the communal areas in Mashonaland have been most able to benefit from the new opportunities – but the drier, and more remote areas are frequently hardly involved. Although the 'success' story has been criticized on the basis that it has not involved the whole peasantry, in fact this uneven distribution is an inevitable consequence of the geography of natural resources and markets, and could point to the need for the resettlement of peasants on good, accessible land, rather than the remoter, poorer areas which have tended to become available for redistribution. Zinyama is a lecturer in the Geography Department of the University of Zimbabwe, and also Dean of Social Sciences. Other publications by him on the agricultural sector in the communal lands are 'Agricultural development policies in the African farming areas of Zimbabwe', *Geography*, vol. 311, no. 71, pt. 2 (1986) p. 105-15, 'Farmers' perceptions of the constraints against increased crop production in the subsistence communal farming sector of Zimbabwe', *Agriculture, Administration and Extension*, vol. 29 (1988), p. 97-109, and 'Technology adoption and post independence transformation of the small scale farming sector in Zimbabwe', in *Urban and regional change in Southern Africa*, edited by David Drakakis-Smith (London: Routledge, 1992, p. 180-202). See also item 638.

638 **Rural household structure, absenteeism and agricultural labour: a case study of the subsistence farming areas in Zimbabwe.**
Lovemore Mondiwa Zinyama. *Singapore Journal of Tropical Geography*, vol. 7, no. 2 (1986), p. 163-73.
This study is based on the result of household surveys in the communal areas, which assessed the impact of males frequently being absent because they are working in the wage sector. A significant proportion of the households in the areas where the research was conducted were headed by women, and Zinyama suggests that shortages of labour prevent such households from being fully productive in the agricultural sector. He concludes that men who migrate should lose their rights to communal land, a very controversial topic in Zimbabwe. In this he is in agreement with George Kay (see item 225), although Zinyama stresses that the stabilizing of families in the rural and urban areas should occur in the context of providing them with acceptable standards of living, which would require new social welfare provisions. The worker-peasant household has also been attacked by the left, since it is a symbol of the exploitative nature of the migrant labour system. For a discussion of this debate, and the case for migrants retaining their land rights, see Potts and Mutambirwa (item 259).

A decade of development Zimbabwe 1980-90.
See item no. 1.

Zimbabwe's prospects: issues of race, class, state and capital in Southern Africa.
See item no. 13.

Zimbabwe: politics, economics and society.
See item no. 14.

Dance, civet cat: the Tonga and child labour in Zimbabwe.
See item no. 253.

Socio-economic factors in food production and consumption: a study of twelve households in Wedza communal land, Zimbabwe.
See item no. 325.

The dynamics of the social relations of production and reproduction in Zimbabwean communal areas.
See item no. 363.

The Tribal Trust Lands of Rhodesia – problems of development.
See item no. 561.

Zimbabwe's agricultural 'success' and food security in Southern Africa.
See item no. 581.

Agroforestry for Shurugwi, Zimbabwe: report of an appraisal exercise for agroforestry research and extension.
See item no. 594.

The Native Land Husbandry Act of 1951 and the rural African middle class of Southern Rhodesia.
See item no. 601.

Development in rural Tribal Trust Lands: an overview.
See item no. 604.

The Native Land Husbandry Act of Southern Rhodesia.
See item no. 609.

A participatory model of agricultural extension: the case of vleis, trees and grazing schemes in the dry South of Zimbabwe.
See item no. 611.

Livestock populations and household economics: a case study from Southern Zimbabwe.
See item no. 621.

Zimbabwe national household survey capability programme (ZNHSCP): reports on demographic socio-economic survey, 1983/4.
See item no. 710.

Commercial farming sectors

639 The Goldbergs of Leigh Ranch.
W. E. Arnold.   Bulawayo: Books of Zimbabwe, 1980. 140p. (Men of Our Time, no. IV).

This biography deals with the life of the Goldbergs, one of the major white Rhodesian farming families, who owned and ran a large ranch of some 24,000 acres north of the Upper Sabi Valley. Written from a classic racist 'Rhodie' viewpoint, it is nonetheless of some interest in providing details on the development of white commercial farming from 1912 onwards. A number of similar books on individual white farmers or farms have been produced, and although lacking in literary merit, they provide material on many aspects of large-scale commercial farm practice including attitudes towards labour, the role of white men and women, and agricultural techniques. Charlotte Truepenny's *Our African Farm* (London: Victor Gollancz, 1965) is another such account, and books on life on large ranches include Wilfrid Robertson's *Rhodesian rancher* (Glasgow, London: Blackie and Sons, 1935), and D. M. Somerville's *My life was a ranch* (Salisbury: Kailani Books, 1976) which describes the remote and wild Devuli ranch in the Sabi valley. The history of one of the wealthiest European commercial farming areas in Zimbabwe is described in *Echoes of Enterprise: a history of the Enterprise district* (Highlands, Zimbabwe: Enterprise Farmers' Association, [1988]), by Kathie Macintosh.

640 Crop production of large-scale commercial agricultural units.
Central Statistical Office.   Salisbury: Central Statistical Office, 1981. 21p.

This government report on the commercial farming sector at independence surveys crop production, but also includes data on labour employees, construction work and equipment.

641 Idioms of accumulation: rural development and class formation among freeholders in Zimbabwe.
Angela Cheater.   Gweru: Mambo Press, 1984. 199p. (Zambeziana Series on Culture and Society in Central Africa, no. 16).

Angela Cheater's research on black agricultural issues has made a significant contribution to knowledge about this diverse sector. In this book, based on research in Msengezi Purchase Area, ninety-six kilometres west of Harare, she studies the different ways in which rural households in a small-scale freehold area attempt to accumulate capital and assets from their agricultural activities. She undertook two periods of research, one before independence and one shortly after, and completed a total enumeration of land-owners and their production and assets. She identifies two main types of accumulation: a modern 'idiom' based on investment in capital equipment and hired labour, and a traditional style based on the use of extended family labour. Both styles were potentially effective: the former being practiced usually by those with formal education and work experience in the urban sector (some of these being professionals), and the latter by farmers with large, traditional extended families. The former idiom was difficult to accomplish without an outside income such as a pension or remittances from urban-based children, but tended to carry more prestige than the traditional idiom. This study is also an excellent source of information on the nature of small-scale agricultural systems in Zimbabwe.

642 **Modern plantation agriculture: corporate wealth and labour squalor.**
Rene Loewenson. London: Zed Press, 1992. 160p.

This study of plantation agriculture is not confined to Zimbabwe, but it forms the main case study after consideration of the phenomenon in Asia, Africa, Central and South America. The author highlights the paradox so often encountered in this form of agricultural production in the Third World: the high technology, highly productive farming system alongside a frequently poorly paid workforce living in poor conditions. One of her central theses is that analyses of these agricultural systems in Zimbabwe, and elsewhere, often claim they are highly efficient, but no account is taken of the toll on the labour force's health and wellbeing. The author formerly lectured in the School of Medicine in the University of Zimbabwe, and is now an occupational health specialist with the Zimbabwe Congress of Trade Unions. Plantation agriculture is also discussed in *The state and agribusiness in Zimbabwe: plantations and contract farming* (Leeds, England: African Studies Unit and Department of Politics, University of Leeds, 1989. [Working Paper no. 9]), by Lloyd Sachikonye. This study, based on the author's doctoral thesis, also discusses plantations which use outgrowers who produce crops for central processing.

643 **Women: the silent farm managers in the small-scale commercial areas in Zimbabwe.**
Dennis Mungate. *Zimbabwe Agricultural Journal*, vol. 80, no. 6 (1983), p. 245-49.

The importance of women as agricultural producers in Zimbabwe has long been overlooked by policy-makers and practitioners, despite the ever increasing body of research work which shows the centrality of their role. In this paper the author emphasizes how crucial it is for women to be included in extension workers' agendas. In particular he points out that despite the fact that it is has been traditional to exclude women from activities involving cattle since these tend to be a male preserve, in fact some women do have cattle because mothers can get cattle from brideprice payments for their daughters, and thus changes in grazing practices need women's involvement too. Angela Cheater has also written on women and agriculture in small-scale commercial areas in 'Women and their participation in commercial agricultural production: the case of medium-scale freehold in Zimbabwe', *Development and Change*, vol. 12, no. 3, (1981), p. 349-77.

644 **Approach to farming in Southern Rhodesia.**
C. T. Tracey. Salisbury: Ministry of Agriculture and Lands, 1945. 416p.

The author was a farmer in Chakari, and prepared this guidebook to large-scale commercial farming for ex-servicemen from the Second World War whom the Ministry of Agriculture wished to encourage to settle and farm in Southern Rhodesia. It is essentially a training text and discusses issues such as soils, tillage, cattle and other livestock, conservation, crops, veterinary matters and 'native' labour.

Zimbabwe: politics, economics and society.
See item no. 14.

Gold regions of Southewastern Africa.
See item no. 122 (Silver Series: vol. 5).

The Native Land Husbandry Act of 1951 and the rural African middle class of Southern Rhodesia.
See item no. 251.

White farmers in Rhodesia, 1890-1965: a history of the Marandellas District.
See item no. 376.

White farmers, black tenants and landlord legislation: Southern Rhodesia 1890-1930.
See item no. 558.

Formal and informal rights to land in Zimbabwe's black freehold areas: a case study from Msengezi.
See item no. 563.

Zimbabwe livestock in large-scale commercial agricultural units 1981.
See item no. 615.

Agricultural and plantation workers in Rhodesia: a report on conditions of labour and subsistence.
See item no. 675.

Black farmers and white politics in Rhodesia, 1930-72.
See item no. 702.

African farmers in Rhodesia: old and new peasant communities in Karangaland.
See item no. 876.

Industry, Mining and Energy

645 Some aspects of the Kariba hydroelectric project in the Central African Federaton.
Harm Jan de Blij. *Journal of Geography* (USA), vol. 56, (Dec. 1957), p. 413-28.
Kariba dam was one of the great engineering projects of its era, with enormous economic significance for the two Rhodesias. It remains an important supplier of hydro-electric power to both Zimbabwe and Zambia. Its construction had major implications for the people, primarily the Tonga, who were flooded out by the lake. Wildlife also suffered. This treatment of the scheme focusses on its economic and technical features, and is a useful non-engineering reference for those details. A much more lively account is Frank Clements' *Kariba: the struggle with the river god* (London: Methuen, 1960), which addresses the issue, familiar to all Zimbabweans, of the threat the dam and the lake posed to the Zambezi serpent god, Nyaminyami, and the claim that the difficulties encountered in its construction were due to the god's retaliation. The human and ecological consequences are also considered.

646 Gold mines of Rhodesia 1890-1980.
D. J. Bowen. Salisbury: Mardon Printers, [1980]. 106p.
This account of the great gold mines of Rhodesia was sponsored by Thompson Newspapers and is written for the layperson: all of the previous accounts had been appraisals written for the mining fraternity in technical journals. A useful glossary of technical terms is included. After an introduction on traditional mines from the pre-colonial era and discussion of the mining operations of the British South Africa Company, individual mines are described in detail. Information is provided on their discovery, the companies involved in exploitation, problems encountered in development, and anecdotes about people associated with the mining operations. Bowen has also written a similar publication on twenty-one mines in Mashonaland, *Gold mines of Mashonaland 1890-1980* (Salisbury: Mardon Printers, [1980]). The Mashonaland goldfields were also described by A. R. Sawyer, an early white prospector who visited Rhodesia in 1893, in *The goldfields of Mashonaland* (London: John Heywood, 1894). Most of the gold mines known today had in fact been discovered and exploited to some

degree by Africans. A technical and economic history of their mining which contains many technical details and a useful map has been written by Roger Summer, who was the Senior Keeper of Antiquities at the National Museum of Rhodesia: *Ancient mining in Rhodesia and adjacent areas* (Salisbury: Trustees of the National Museum of Rhodesia, 1969 [Museum Memoir, no. 3]). The role of gold mining in the pre-colonial economy is discussed in Ian R. Phimister, 'Alluvial gold mining and trade in nineteenth-century South Central Africa', *Journal of African History* (UK), vol. 15, no. 3 (1974), p. 445-56.

647 **The mining industry in Zimbabwe: labour, capital and the state.**

John Bradbury, Eric Worby. *Africa Development* (Senegal), vol. 10, no. 4 (1985), p. 143-69.

In this article the authors use the mining industry as a case study to examine how relationships between the state, labour and capital altered in the post-independence era. They argue that the state faces a number of constraints in challenging the position of capital in the economy, and that this is particularly well illustrated by the mining sector where state policies have tended to become subordinate to the needs of foreign capital.

648 **Review of Zimbabwe's mining industry in the Chamber's 50th year.**

Chamber of Mines. Harare: Chamber of Mines, 1989. 2 vols.

This glossy anniversary publication celebrating fifty years of the Chamber of Mines in Zimbabwe provides a comprehensive overview of the country's mineral resources, with each mineral discussed separately. On the non-ferrous metal industry see Paul Jourdan, 'Non-ferrous metal industry of Zimbabwe', *Raw Materials Report* (Sweden), vol. 4, no. 2 (1985), p. 28.

649 **Zimbabwe: energy planning for national development.**

Edited by R. H. Hosier. Uppsala, Sweden: Beijer Institute and Scandinavian Institute of African Studies, 1986. 206p. (Energy, Environment and Development in Africa Series, no. 9).

This volume is the key reference on energy issues in Zimbabwe. It covers energy accounting, rural energy problems and woodfuel consumption, and industrial energy needs and issues. A number of policy recommendations are made. Other titles in the same series on energy issues in Zimbabwe are *Zimbabwe: industrial and commercial energy use* (Sweden: Beijer Institute and Scandinavian Institute of African Studies, 1988 [Energy, Environment and Development in Africa Series no. 10]), and *Energy for rural development in Zimbabwe* (Sweden: Beijer Institute and Scandinavian Institute of African Studies, 1988 [Energy, Environment and Development in Africa Series, no. 11]), both also edited by Hosier. The first of these two examines industrial energy consumption and the commercial fuel supply sectors in Zimbabwe. It contains six multi-authored chapters dealing with secondary industry, commerce, the transport sector, the informal sector, and economic modelling of energy consumption. Many useful tables are included. The second volume deals in detail with woodfuel issues, soil erosion, cooking stoves and household energy uses. The research reported in these volumes was originally carried out as part of the Zimbabwean Energy Accounting Project, a joint undertaking by the Beijer Institute and the Ministry of Water and Energy Resources and Development of Zimbabwe. Hosier has also contributed an overview of all aspects of Zimbabwe's energy sector to *Energy and development in Southern Africa: SADCC country studies, Part II* (Uppsala, Sweden: The Beijer

Institute, 1984. [Energy, Environment and Development in Africa Series, no. 4]), edited by Phil O'Keefe and Barry Munslow.

650 **Industrial development in Zimbabwe: the case of women in manufacturing industry.**
E. M. Jassak, K. O. Jirira. Harare: Zimbabwe Institute of Development Studies, 1987.

This study of women in Zimbabwe's manufacturing industries was commissioned by the Ministry of Community Development and Women's Affairs. It provides a comprehensive discussion of the types of jobs women perform in the manufacturing sector, and the potential for expanding their role. Also on women in industry see Patricia Made and Birgitta Wagerstrom, *Zimbabwean women in industry* (Harare: Zimbabwe Publishing House, 1985), which focusses on the need to improve the conditions under which women work, covering themes like equal pay for equal work, sexual harrassment, education and training, and trade unions. The discussion is illustrated with photographs, and case-studies of specific workers.

651 **South Africa and the political economy of minerals in Southern Africa: the case of Zimbabwe and chromium.**
Owen Ellison Kahn. In: *South Africa: the intensifying vortex of violence*. Edited by Thomas M. Callaghy. New York: Praeger, 1983, p. 69-106.

Zimbabwe is an important producer of chrome, which is considered a strategic mineral. South Africa, however, has a larger chrome-producing industry and this is one of the many factors which has tempered the opposition of the United States, and other western nations, to apartheid. The Organisation for Economic Cooperation and Development (OECD) hoped that an independent Zimbabwe would be a significant competitor to South Africa in production of this mineral. In this paper the author examines the political context of chrome production in Southern Africa, and contends that Zimbabwe has been unable to fulfil the competitive role hoped for by the OECD.

652 **Investment sanctions and Zimbabwe: breaking the rod.**
Thomas Lines. *Third World Quarterly*, vol. 10, no. 3 (1988), p. 1182-1216.

A common approach to the issue of imposing sanctions against South Africa by the countries of the Southern African region is to assert that countries like Zimbabwe stand to lose economically far more than they could gain politically. This paper provides a useful antidote to this generalization by providing detailed discussion of supportable ways in which Zimbabwe could avoid dependence on South Africa in the field of metals and the mining sector.

653 **Gold mining in Southern Rhodesia 1919-53.**
Ian R. Phimister. *Rhodesian Journal of Economics*, vol. 10, no. 1 (1976), p. 21-44.

In this account of the economic history of colonial gold mining 1919-53 Phimister details the gradual decline in output from the end of the First World War, and the later fall in employment and share in export earnings. Phimister is the leading historian of Zimbabwe's mining industry. Other relevant articles by the same author include 'The reconstruction of the Southern Rhodesian gold mines 1903-10', *Economic History Review* (UK), vol. 29, no. 3 (1976), p. 465-81; 'Pre-colonial gold mining in Southern Zambezia: a re-assessment', *African Social Research* (Lusaka), vol. 21 (1976), p. 1-30, which discusses Shona gold mining; and 'Structure and development of the Southern Rhodesian base mineral industry 1907 to the Great Depression', *Rhodesian Journal of Economics*, vol. 9, no. 2 (1975), p. 79-88.

654   **The entrepreneurial milieu: enterprise networks in small Zimbabwean towns.**
Jesper Rasmussen.   Roskilde, Denmark: Roskilde University, Department of Geography, 1992. 299p. (Research Report, Roskilde University, Department of Geography; Centre for Development Research, Copenhagen, no. 79).

This study subjects the economics of industrial business enterprises in small urban settlements in the rural areas to close scrutiny. The main focus is on the more signficant small businesses, particularly those in the building sector, rather than micro-enterprises. The economic dynamics of such businesses are detailed, including the way in which their development is influenced by the socio-cultural settings of small rural towns. The author concludes that these enterprises can play a role in the development of a local industrializing process, particularly if government policy avoids the many pitfalls of the usual approach to small-scale enterprises, and focusses on issues like encouraging sub-contracting via incentives. The research was conducted whilst the author was based at the Department of Rural and Urban Planning at the University of Zimbabwe during the late 1980s, and was financed by the Danish Research Council for Development. An article based on this research, 'Small urban centres and the development of local enterprises in Zimbabwe', appeared in *Small town Africa* (Uppsala, Sweden: Scandinavian Institute of African Studies, 1990. [Seminar proceedings no. 23]), edited by Jonathan Baker, p. 130-42.

655   **Zimbabwe.**
Roger C. Riddell. In: *Manufacturing Africa: performance and prospects of seven countries in sub-Saharan Africa.* Edited by Roger C. Riddell. London: James Currey; Portsmouth, New Hampshire: Heinemann, 1990, p. 337-411.

This is the most detailed and comprehensive survey of Zimbabwe's manufacturing sector published outside of consultancy and agency reports, which is virtually book-length despite only being one chapter in an edited collection. Riddell provides not only a wealth of very detailed information and statistics on the nature of this economic sector, but also carefully considered policy recommendations for its future expansion which draw on the empirical nature of local successes in manufacturing. The study begins with a discussion of sources of industrial growth, trends in manufacturing exports and imports, and international comparisons of competitiveness. Riddell then turns to case study material on specific firms drawing on field research conducted in 1987. The importance of agro-industrial linkages are discussed next. The macro-economic context of industrialization, from government-imposed conditions such as foreign exchange constraints, to drought, are detailed. Particularly illuminating is Riddells' analysis of manufacturing policies, in which he demonstrates that the World Bank's recommendations have been built on poor data and, worse, have deliberately misrepresented industrial performance for ideological reasons. In this he concurs with Stoneman's analysis (see item 501). Riddell's own recommendations for the sector are sophisticated and considered, acknowledging that some elements of government intervention needed to change to allow further expansion, but also firmly rejecting the option of laissez-faire liberalization and the fixation on 'getting the price right', having shown in his case studies that local businessmen were aware that other factors were more important than prices in determining industrial performance. Another major study by Riddell on Zimbabwean industry is *Industrialisation in sub-Saharan Africa: country case study: Zimbabwe* (London: Overseas Development Institute, 1988. [ODI Working Paper no. 25]).

656 **The mining industry of Southern Rhodesia 1961.**
Prepared for Seventh Commonwealth Mining and Metallurgical Congress. Salisbury: Seventh Commonwealth Mining and Metallurgical Congress, 1961. 138p.

This publication is largely aimed at the mining fraternity. It describes the distribution of mineral occurrences in Southern Rhodesia, and the processes used for extraction. Financial details on exploitation are covered, including information on the availability of government assistance. An earlier publication of a similar type is *The mining industry of Southern Rhodesia* (Third Empire Mining and Metallurgical Congress, 1930), compiled by N. H. Wilson.

657 **Zimbabwe Electricity Supply Authority. Committee of Inquiry into Parastatals.**
Under the chairmanship of L. G. Smith. Harare: Government Printer, 1988. 301p.

This report from the parastatal inquiry committee provides excellent reference material on the history and operations of Zimbabwe's public electricity supply.

658 **Industrialisation and self-reliance in Zimbabwe.**
Colin Stoneman. In: *Industrialisation and accumulation in Africa.*
Edited by Martin Fransman. London: Heinemann, 1982, p. 276-95.

Stoneman is one of the leading authorities on the manufacturing industry in Zimbabwe. He is not a proponent of the free-market liberalized economic strategies which the IMF and World Bank have been forcing African economies to adopt, and strongly opposed their adoption in Zimbabwe. Zimbabwe had a relatively sophisticated industrial sector at independence, in part due to its central role in the 1953-63 Federation of Rhodesia and Nyasaland and the strong protectionism afforded by sanctions during UDI. Sanctions, however, also damaged the industrial base in some ways, for example by preventing technological progress and investment in some types of capital stock. Whilst independence necessarily ended the extreme protectionism of the UDI period, Stoneman believed that many industries should still be afforded some protection against outside competition, if Zimbabwe was to retain its relatively diverse economic base. This paper provides an overview of the industrial base, and discusses the policies needed to foster self-reliance in that sector. Similar themes are discussed in his paper in item 5, and another overview of manufacturing at independence by David Wield is found in item 12. For a really comprehensive source on Zimbabwe's manufacturing industrial base see United Nations Industrial Development Organization, *Study of the manufacturing sector in Zimbabwe* (Vienna: UNIDO, 1985, 3 vols.).

659 **Location of manufacturing industry in Zimbabwe: a geographical investigation.**
Daniel Tevera. PhD thesis, University of Cincinatti, Cincinatti, Ohio, 1984.

This research study examines the patterns of manufacturing industry inherited by Zimbabwe, and assesses them in terms of the needs of the independent state. Much of the industry is located in Bulawayo and Harare, and the author recommends that incentives should be established to encourage decentralization to other smaller towns. He favours the setting up of growth centres, and presents first-hand data on the nature of industrial location decisions, and attitudes towards relocation to growth centres.

660 **Technological capability and industrialisation: effects of aid and sanctions in the United Republic of Tanzania and Zimbabwe.**
Susumu Watanabe. *International Labour Review*, vol. 126, no. 5 (1987), p. 525-41.

The mix of local and imported technology used for manufacturing production is of great significance, with ramifications for self-reliance, international competitiveness, production capacity and labour to capital ratios. This research study is based on field visits to manufacturing companies in Zimbabwe and Tanzania, and provides details on the nature of manufacturing technologies, as well as discussion of how imports can both assist and hinder industrial development. The impact of sanctions on Zimbabwean industrial technology is also examined. For another discussion of technology issues in industry see Raphael Kaplinsky (item 13).

661 **Prospects and problems of industrial decentralization in Zimbabwe.**
Lovemore Mondiwa Zinyama. In: *Geographical perspectives on development in Southern Africa*. Edited by Geoffrey Williams, Adrian Wood. Australia: Commonwealth Geograpical Bureau at James Cook University of North Queensland, [1986], p. 122-36.

Industrial production in Zimbabwe is concentrated in Harare and Bulawayo, and this paper considers the case for widening the geographical spread of industry by encouraging industries to locate in other urban areas. This would probably require government incentives. This issue has been covered in detail in a PhD thesis by Tevera (see item 659).

From Rhodesia to Zimbabwe: behind and beyond Lancaster House.
See item no. 5.

Zimbabwe's inheritance.
See item no. 12.

Zimbabwe's prospects: issues of race, class, state and capital in Southern Africa.
See item no. 13.

Zimbabwe: politics, economics and society.
See item no. 14.

Zimbabwe: towards a new order – an economic and social survey. vol. 1.
See item no. 15.

Gold regions of Southeastern Africa.
See item no. 122.

Zimbabwean women in industry.
See item no. 359.

Report of the Commission of Inquiry into the distribution of motor vehicles.
See item no. 409.

Zimbabwe at work, 1989.
See item no. 492.

The World Bank and the IMF in Zimbabwe.
See item no. 501.

Studies in the history of African mine labour in colonial Zimbabwe.
See item no. 688.

Chibaro: African mine labour in Southern Rhodesia 1900-33.
See item no. 690.

Finance and Banking

662 **Changing patterns of banking in Rhodesia since 1960.**
J. Askes. *Rhodesian Journal of Economics*, vol. 5, no. 3 (1971), p. 16-21.

This article provides a brief overview of the development of banking in Rhodesia, and how this sector changed during the 1960s. For an analysis of formal credit institutions from 1965 to 1973 see R. Cole's 'The finance houses in Rhodesia', *Rhodesian Journal of Economics*, vol. 7, no. 4 (1973), p. 207-16.

663 **Sixty years north of the Limpopo: the story of the coming of the Standard Bank of Rhodesia and Nyasaland, with some account of its early days there.**
James A. Henry. Salisbury: Standard Bank of South Africa, 1953. 45p.

This is basically a publicity publication for the Standard Bank, describing its expansion from its original establishment in Southern Rhodesia in 1892, to its important financial role in 1952. It contains some details of bank loans for major infrastructural projects, including for the railways. The Standard Bank has also produced a pictorial essay of its history in Rhodesia, *Three quarters of a century of banking in Rhodesia* (Salisbury: Standard Bank, 1967).

664 **The question for Zimbabwe.**
Leonard Maveneka, Anthony Martin. *Southern African Economist*, vol. 2, no. 6 (1989/90), p. 7-12.

This article describes Zimbabwe's banking and finance sector, emphasizing its relative sophistication compared to other SADCC countries and the role it could play in servicing their economies. However this could not be easily achieved because of problems like Zimbabwe's foreign exchange controls and inconvertible currency.

665 **Towards financial independence in a developing country: an analysis of the monetary experience of the Federation of Rhodesia and Nyasaland, 1952-63.**
R. A. Sowelem.   London: George Allen & Unwin; Atlantic Highlands, New Jersey: Humanities Press, 1967. 329p.

The major study of banking and finance in the Federation of Rhodesia and Nyasaland, this is a rather technical account. It is of use as a historical reference on monetary policy and banking in Southern Rhodesia at this time.

Zimbabwe: towards a new order – an economic and social survey. vol. 1.
See item no. 15.

Zimbabwe: towards a new order – an economic and social survey. vol. 2.
See item no. 16.

Transport

666 **Railways of Zimbabwe: the story of the Beira, Mashonaland, and Rhodesian railways.**
Anthony H. Croxton, with additional material by Anthony H. Baxter. Newton Abbot, England: David & Charles, 1982. 2nd ed. 315p.

This is a useful source for details on the chronology of the development of Zimbabwe's railway system up to 1980. The text, which is well illustrated with photographs, is rather adulatory about Rhodes' vision of a Cape to Cairo railway, and its role in the growth of Rhodesia's railways. This second edition of the book, which first appeared in 1973, contains three extra chapters which deal with new locomotives and the conversion to diesel, and Baxter contributes a discussion of the problems faced by the railways in the late 1970s due to sanctions and closure of the Zambian border. A popular treatment of the history of the railways, *The trailmakers: the story of Rhodesian railways* (Salisbury: Illustrated Life Rhodesia, 1973) was published as a supplement to *Illustrated Life Rhodesia*, 31st May, 1973. This is in a magazine format, with many photographs and details of personalities involved in the development of railways.

667 **The history of the construction and finance of the Rhodesian transport system.**
Emile Beaumont D'Erlanger. London: Burrup, Mathieson & Co., 1938. 63p.

The Beira railway, on which this account focusses, was Rhodesia's main transit route to the sea prior to South African-backed destabilization of Mozambique. This short book provides interesting historical reference material on the planning, financing and administration of this railway from 1891 to the 1930s. The author's father was involved in railway investments with Cecil Rhodes.

668 **Steam locomotives of Rhodesian railways: the story of steam 1892-1979.**
E. D. Hamer. Bulawayo: Books of Zimbabwe, 1981. 194p.

This publication is aimed at the many afficionados of steam locomotives. It provides a detailed history of the various types of locomotives which have worked in the territory, from the small green steamers of the narrow guage Beira railway to the modern Beyer-Garratt locomotives of the National Railways of Zimbabwe. Also included are sections on preserved engines, and railway philately. There are many photographic illustrations.

669 **Transport in Southern Africa.**
T. L. Kennedy. Braamfontein, South Africa: South African Institute of International Affairs, 1988. 116p. maps.

The transit trade routes used by Zimbabwe since independence have been seriously affected by South African-inspired destabilization of the Southern African region, particularly the activities of the Mozambique National Resistance. As a consequence Zimbabwe's freight route patterns deviate significantly from those which would be determined by economic and geographic factors, and from those prevalent in the colonial era. In particular, an artificial dependence on South African routes has been fostered. This comprehensive report describes the various road and rail routes used for trade by Southern African countries, including Zimbabwe, with appendices on SADCC transport projects. It is an excellent source for technical details, but less useful for analysis of the patterns, paying insufficient attention to the artificial nature of the region's dependence on South African railways. The author is a consultant on transport in Southern Africa. Good coverage of South Africa's political and economic manipulation of freight routes for Zimbabwe is found in Hanlon (see item 469).

670 **The birth of an airline: the establishment of Rhodesia and Nyasaland airways.**
J. McAdam. *Rhodesiana*, vol. 2, (1969), p. 36-50.

This is a concise historical treatment of the development of commercial air travel in Central Africa, from 1920 to the 1960s.

671 **Problems of public transportation in Zimbabwe.**
Lan W. Situma. *African Urban Quarterly*, vol. 2, no. 1 (1987), p. 49-61.

There is very little written on public transport in Zimbabwe. In this article, the author, an urban transport planner, provides a useful overview of the development and nature of public transport, highlighting the overcrowding of the facilities. The causes of the problems in this sector are examined.

672 **Air Zimbabwe Corporation. Committee of inquiry into parastatals.**
Under the chairmanship of L. G. Smith. Harare: Government Printer, 1986. 130p.

Air Zimbabwe was one of a number of parastatals on which Smith chaired government inquiries. This is a useful source on the company, and its many operating problems. Recommendations for policy changes are made.

673 **National railways of Zimbabwe. Committee of inquiry into parastatals.**
Under the chairmanship of L. G. Smith.   Harare: Government
Printer, 1987. 254p.

The National Railways of Zimbabwe was one of the parastatals reviewed by a
committee established to overhaul the organization and administration of these bodies
in the latter part of the 1980s. The recommendations contained in this report relate to
these issues, one of the main focusses being the need to speed up black advancement.
However the report is also very useful as a recent reference on the railway system in
general as it contains much detailed background information. There are six chapters
covering the history of the railways and the National Railways of Zimbabwe Act, the
function of the Board and Ministry of Transport, problem areas in the railways, the
financial situation, racism in the railways, and a summary of recommendations.

A decade of development Zimbabwe 1980-90.
See item no. 1.

The Cape-to-Cairo dream: a study in British imperialism.
See item no. 140.

Labour, Wages and Incomes

General

674   **The rural labour market in Zimbabwe.**
J. Adams.   *Development and Change*, vol. 22, no. 2 (1991),
p. 297-320.
Adams discusses the nature of wage labour in the rural areas of Zimbabwe. Also by the same author, see 'Female wage labour in rural Zimbabwe', *World Development*, vol. 19, no. 2/3 (1991), p. 163-177.

675   **Agricultural and plantation workers in Rhodesia: a report on conditions of labour and subsistence.**
Duncan G. Clarke.   Gwelo: Mambo Press, 1971. 300p. (Mambo Occasional Papers, Socio-economic Series, no. 6).
This is a major study of the characteristics and conditions of black labourers in the commercial farming sector. The author provides a wealth of detail and data for the serious researcher. Topics covered include the low wages and poor conditions for labourers on large farms, state policy towards agricultural labour, and labour relations and management in this sector. Also see 'Farm-workers' wages and conditions of employment 1940s-1970s', *Rhodesian Science News*, vol. 8, no.7 (1974), p. 206-11, also by Clarke; B. H. G. Duncan, 'Wages and labour supply position in European agriculture', *Rhodesian Journal of Economics*, vol. 7, no. 1 (1973), p. 1-13; and G. L. Chavunduka, 'Farm labour in Rhodesia', *Rhodesian Journal of Economics*, vol. 6, no. 4 (1972), p. 18-25.

676 **Contract workers and underdevelopment in Rhodesia.**
Duncan G. Clarke. Gwelo: Mambo Press, 1974. 132p. (Mambo
Occasional Papers, Socio-economic series, no. 3).

This study provides an overview of the history of contract labour in Rhodesia, and
analyses the impact of this system on the contract workers and the wider economy,
including the effect on the peasantry. The shortage of local blacks for commercial farm
work at prevailing conditions for many decades led to recruitment in neighbouring
territories. The official recruiting body was the Rhodesian Native Labour Supply
Commission and its policies over the years are considered in detail. Clarke stresses the
relationship between the use of foreign labour and low wages, and thus the link
between the system and peasant underdevelopment. The later policy of labour
internalization is also examined.

677 **Domestic workers in Rhodesia: the economics of masters and servants.**
Duncan G. Clarke. Gwelo: Mambo Press, 1974. 88p. (Mambo
Occasional Papers, Socio-Economic Series, no. 1).

Clarke was commissioned to write a number of reports on aspects of Rhodesia's
economy by the Catholic Bishops' Conference on Justice and Peace Commission. This
short book was the first in the series in which he details the vulnerability of domestics
who were usually separated from their families, and were paid partly in kind. They
were the lowest paid group after agricultural labour, and their relationships with their
employers were governed by 19th century masters and servants legislation. This
legislation gave immense powers to employers, and made it illegal for employees to
end their contracts, no matter how badly they were treated. The study includes twelve
case histories of servants from interviews conducted in 1973.

678 **International labour supply: trends and economic structure in Southern
Rhodesia/Zimbabwe in the 1970s.**
Duncan G. Clarke. Geneva: International Labour Office, 1978. 120p.

Zimbabwe has a long history of drawing on labour pools in surrounding countries,
particularly Mozambique and Malawi. For long periods foreign migrant labour made
up the majority of the agricultural labour force, and by enlarging the supply of labour
helped to keep wages low. However by the 1970s the deteriorating conditions in the
Tribal Trust Lands had facilitated some degree of labour internalization. Clarke
discusses the background to foreign labour use, and the current trends.

679 **Unemployment and economic structure in Rhodesia.**
Duncan G. Clarke. Gwelo: Mambo Press, 1977. 81p. (Mambo
Occasional Papers, Socio-Economic Series, no. 9).

In this report for the CBCJPC (Catholic Bishops' Conference on Justice and Peace)
Clarke examines the unemployment problem in the 1970s, and emphasizes the
dependence of the black rural peasantry on wage employment. He also evaluates
proposals to improve the employment situation. A shorter report on unemployment
for the CIIR by Clarke is *The unemployment crisis* (London: Catholic Institute for
International Relations, 1978. [From Rhodesia to Zimbabwe, no. 3]).

680   **National manpower survey 1981.**
Government of Zimbabwe, Ministry of Manpower, Planning and
Development.   Harare: Ministry of Manpower, Planning and
Development, 1981. 3 vols.

This major report is a useful source of data on, and discussion of, Zimbabwe's
workforce at independence, which stresses the constraints imposed by skill shortages.
Volume one contains discussion papers, whilst volume two contains statistical tables
and an explanation of the survey itself. Volume three contains the main findings on the
nature of the workforce, earnings, vacancies, education and training institutions, and
the skills of Zimbabweans abroad. Another source on the topic of manpower is
International University Exchange Fund, *Zimbabwe manpower survey* (Geneva:
International University Exchange Fund, 1979, 3 vols.) which draws on the papers and
speeches given at a Patriotic Front seminar in Dar es Salaam in 1978. Contributors
included Colin Stoneman, Rob Davies, Bernard Chidzero and Duncan Clarke.

681   **Black industrial workers in Rhodesia: general problems of low pay.**
Peter S. Harris.   Gweru: Mambo Press, 1974. 71p. (Mambo
Occasional Papers, Socio-Economic Series, no. 2).

In this short book Harris discusses the problems created for both workers and the
economy as a whole because of persistent low pay for Africans. The poverty of the
average black worker makes it difficult to support their families, and a host of social
welfare problems result. In addition they are unable to pay economic rents, causing
problems in housing delivery for the workforce, and cannot provide real demand for
many types of goods which the economy could produce. Harris discusses institutions
for changing this situation, and the importance of the labour movement.

682   **Industrial workers in Southern Rhodesia 1946-72: working class élites or
lumpen-proletariat?**
Peter S. Harris.   *Journal of Southern African Studies*, vol. 1, no. 2
(1975), p. 139-61.

The post-war period saw rapid growth in the industrial sector in Southern Rhodesia,
and a concomitant increase in the industrial labour force. African wages also increased
and this has usually been interpreted as evidence that labour stabilization was
occurring, necessitating higher wages to cover family costs. Harris strongly challenges
this view, providing evidence that the wages of most black industrial workers in this
period remained woefully inadequate to cover minimum family unit costs, and that the
continued retention of rural-urban linkages as security meant these workers were not
fully proletarianized. He argues that wage increases were caused by the inability of the
peasant sector to absorb the pace of the new demands for labour smoothly. As a
challenge to the labour aristocracy thesis, this study can usefully be compared with
Osmond Stuart's work on social change in Bulawayo (see item 158). A short paper by
the same author which gives useful insights into the ways in which Africans were
excluded from certain types of jobs by legislation, and more often customary practice,
is 'Job reservation: Rhodesian style', *South African Labour Bulletin*, vol. 1 (1975)
p. 46-52.

Labour, Wages and Incomes. General

683 **Ten popular myths concerning the employment of labour in Rhodesia.**
Peter S. Harris. *Rhodesian Journal of Economics*, vol. 8, no. 1 (1974), p. 38-48.

European employers often clung to certain economic notions about their African labour force which they used to justify low wages and racial inequality in general. Whilst these were usually easy to refute, this brief paper is useful in providing an overview of their attitudes. These include the idea that workers are poor because they waste their money, not because they are paid too little, and that employment is a privilege rather than a right. The Rhodesian Front often claimed that every European immigrant generated seven African jobs, and this was used as justification for further immigration. The latter theory was specifically attacked by Duncan Clarke, in 'The assumed employment generating capacity of European immigration in Rhodesia', *Rhodesian Journal of Economics*, vol. 4, no. 2 (1970), p. 33-42. For a discussion of concepts applied to the migrant labour system in the early colonial years see John M. Mackenzie, 'African labour in the chartered company period', *Rhodesian History*, vol. 1 (1970), p. 43-58. They included the backward sloping labour supply curve; the civilizing impact of wage labour; the use of taxes to induce labour into the wage economy; and the relationship between land policy and labour supply. A criticism of such an approach to mine labour is Charles van Onselen's 'Black workers in Central African industry: a critical essay on the historiography and sociology of Rhodesia', *Journal of Southern African Studies*, vol. 1, no. 2 (1975), p. 228-46.

684 **Income-generating projects: a report on forty-seven project groups of the Association of Women's Clubs.**
Annemiek Jenniskens. Harare: The Association of Women's Clubs, 1989.

Income-generating projects for women are very popular with non-governmental organizations, and the numbers have burgeoned since independence. This publication describes various projects, and discusses their prospects.

685 **Supply, control and organization of African labour in Rhodesia.**
Luke Malaba. *Review of African Political Economy*, vol. 18, (1980), p. 7-25.

Malaba provides an overview of the legislation and institutions used to control black labour from the 1930s to the 1970s. In many ways these controls hindered associations between African workers and the liberation movements. The author discusses how this might cause future political problems. The lack of transformation of colonial labour processes, and the way in which this is hindering social transformation is discussed in Nelson P. Moyo's 'The state, planning and labour: towards transforming the colonial labour process in Zimbabwe', in *Markets within planning: socialist economic management in the Third World* (London: Cass, 1988. p. 203-17), edited by E. V. K. Fitzgerald and M. Wuyts.

686 **Chibaro: African mine labour in Southern Rhodesia 1900-33.**
Charles van Onselen. London: Pluto Press, 1976. 326p.

The most detailed study of mine labour in Rhodesia at the beginning of the twentieth century. Van Onselen is a South African, and was educated at Rhodes University, Grahamstown. He now lectures at the University of Witwatersrand in Johannesburg. This book is based on his 1974 PhD thesis from Oxford University. 'Chibaro' means forced or slave labour. The Rhodesian Native Labour Bureau, which recruited labour in the region for the mines and other employers, always sent migrants to the harshest mines where mortality rates could approach ten per cent per year, and 'chibaro' was the term the workers applied to this work. This study is a searing indictment of the employers' exploitation of the mine workforce in this period. Van Onselen has written a number of related articles; see his 'The role of collaborators in the Rhodesian mining industry, 1900-35', *African Affairs* (UK), vol. 72 (1973), p. 401-18; 'Worker consciousness in black miners, Southern Rhodesia, 1900-1920', *Journal of African History* (UK), vol. 14, no. 2 (1973), p. 237-55; and 'The 1912 Wankie colliery strike', *Journal of African History* (UK), vol. 15, no. 2 (1974), p. 275-87.

687 **Origins and aspects of African worker consciousness in Rhodesia.**
    Ian R. Phimister. In: *Essays in South African labour history*. Edited by
    E. Webster.   Johannesburg: Ravan Press, 1978, p. 47-63.
In this article Phimister assesses the history of the development of class consciousness amongst African workers in Rhodesia. See also his 'Coal, crisis and class struggle; Wankie colliery 1918-22', *Journal of African History*, vol. 33, no. 1 (1992), p. 65-86.

688 **White miners in historical perspective: Southern Rhodesia 1890-1953.**
    Ian R. Phimister.   *Journal of Southern African Studies*, vol. 3, no. 2
    (1977), p. 187-102.
This article discusses the nature of the white mining labour force, and its organization, from the beginning of the colonial period to the establishment of the Federation of Rhodesia and Nyasaland.

689 **Studies in the history of African mine labour in colonial Zimbabwe.**
    Edited by Ian R. Phimister, Charles van Onselen.   Gweru: Mambo
    Press, 1978. 150p. (Zambeziana: Series on Culture and Society in
    Central Africa, no. 6).
This collection of essays focusses on the plight of the African mine-worker in colonial Rhodesia, emphasizing the harshness of the mining regime. On conditions for mine labourers up until 1974 see Duncan Clarke's 'African mine labourers and conditions of labour in the mining industry in Rhodesia 1940-74', *Rhodesian Journal of Economics*, vol. 9, no. 4 (1975), p. 177-218.

690 **Skilled labour and future needs.**
    Colin Stoneman.   London: Catholic Institute for International
    Relations, [1978]. 53p. (From Rhodesia to Zimbabwe, no. 4).
A review of the availability of skilled labour commissioned by the CIIR in its *From Rhodesia to Zimbabwe* series. The author evaluates the current supply in relation to an estimate of what will be needed in an independent Zimbabwe.

691 **Manpower inventory study of Zimbabwe.**
    Whitsun Foundation.   Harare: Whitsun Foundation in conjunction
    with Faculty of Social Studies, University of Zimbabwe, 1980. 2 parts.
This major study by the Whitsun Foundation with the Faculty of Social Studies at the University provides the most detailed analysis and information on the manpower and employment situation at independence, and is a key reference. It also assesses the

expected future needs for skilled personnel and other employees in independent Zimbabwe. The first part of of this study provides a massive data bank on manpower in the country and is divided into three volumes, totalling 658 pages in all. Tables on employment in every sector and industry, by race, are provided. The second part of the study looks at skilled manpower in the manufacturing and public sectors, and was published in 1982.

Socio-economic review of Zimbabwe 1980-85.
See item no. 4.

Zimbabwe since independence: a people's assessment.
See item no. 7.

Zimbabwe: towards a new order – an economic and social survey. vol. 2.
See item no. 16.

African unemployment and the rural areas of Rhodesia.
See item no. 258.

Stabilisation policies and the health and welfare of children: Zimbabwe 1980-85.
See item no. 334.

African women in urban employment: factors influencing their employment in Zimbabwe.
See item no. 362.

Labour supplies in perspective: a study of the proletarianization of the African peasantry.
See item no. 481.

The urban poverty datum line in Rhodesia: a study of the minimum consumption needs of families.
See item no. 522.

Report of the commission of inquiry into the agricultural industry.
See item no. 580.

Crop prices and wage policy in the light of Zimbabwe's development goals.
See item no. 606.

Education, race and employment in Rhodesia.
See item no. 719.

Informal sector

692 **One dollar workplaces: a study of informal sector activities in Magaba, Harare.**
Veronica Brand. *Journal of Social Development in Africa*, vol. 1, no. 2 (1986), p. 53-74.
The informal sector tends to be characterized by very low incomes, but its flexibility is suited to the needs of women with the responsibilities of domestic work, and perhaps little education. This economic analysis of informal sector positions in one area of Harare found that many workers were women. The study included consideration of the aspirations of these workers, and found that a significant number would stay in the informal sector even if other opportunities were available to them.

693 **The informal sector: a solution to unemployment?**
Rob Davies. London: Catholic Institute for International Relations, 1978. 30p. (From Rhodesia to Zimbabwe, no. 5).
A discussion of unemployment and the characteristics of the informal sector shortly before independence, commissioned by the CIIR in its *From Rhodesia to Zimbabwe* series. The development of the informal sector in Rhodesia was curtailed by greater restrictions on urban residence without formal employment than was the case in other African countries. Davies points out that the dichotomy suggested by the use of the terms 'formal' and 'informal' sectors is false, since the two are interrelated. He recommends that a future Zimbabwean state should eradicate the concept of the informal sector from its employment policies, and incorporate the sector into the core economic structures of an independent Zimbabwe.

694 **A survey of small-scale industries in the informal sector.**
Economics Department, University of Zimbabwe. Harare: University of Zimbabwe, 1981. 38p.
This is a useful survey of one element of the informal sector in 1980-81, which provides useful data on this important part of the urban economy. The urban areas covered are Harare and Bulawayo.

695 **Formal/informal sector articulation in the Zimbabwean economy.**
Anthony Leiman. *Journal of Contemporary African Studies*, vol. 4, no. 1/2 (1984/5), p. 119-37.
The relaxation of restrictions on movement to the urban areas at independence has enabled the informal sector to grow rapidly. Although sometimes described as though quite separate from the formal sector, in fact the two sectors are closely linked. This article describes the nature of these linkages, and the way in which conflict can arise from competition and other aspects of the relationship. On government policies towards the informal sector see Thandika Mkandawire's 'The informal sector in the labour reserve economies of Southern Africa with special reference to Zimbabwe', *Africa Development* (Senegal), vol. 11 (Jan./Mar. 1986), p. 61-81.

Labour Movement
and Trade Unions

696 **Race and politics in Rhodesian trade unions.**
   C. M. Brand. *African Perspectives*, (1976), no. 2, p. 55-80.
Two aspects of trade unionism are covered in this paper. A useful overview of the history of the development of the trade union movement is provided, including discussion of white, black and multiracial unions. There is also an assessment of the achievements of African trade unions after the Second World War. The author suggests that these experienced little success in increasing real wages, but did achieve some advances in the organization of labour and in conditions of service.

697 **The politics of factory organization: a case study in independent Zimbabwe.**
   Angela Cheater. Gweru, Zimbabwe: Mambo Press, 1986. 156p.
   (Zambeziana: Series on Culture and Society in Central Africa, no. 18).
A detailed case study of a textile factory located in a rural area, employing over 500 workers. Cheater shows that three years after independence the multi-ethnic workforce still preferred to negotiate with local management, and distrusted both the national trade union movement and the state. Details are provided on production in the factory, and at home in the company village.

698 **Trade unionism in the rise of African nationalism: Bulawayo 1945-63.**
   J. Hyslop. *African Perspectives, New Series*, vol. 1, no. 1 & 2 (1986), p. 34-67.
This study traces the relationship between trade unionism and African nationalism in Bulawayo. Hyslop's contention that Bulawayo workers and trade unions were at the roots of African nationalist development challenges previous interpretations which argued that urban workers had little role to play in the nationalist movement.

699 **The trade union movement in Southern Rhodesia, 1910-24.**
Elaine Lea. *Rhodesian Journal of Economics*, vol. 8, no. 4 (1974), p. 215-37.
This short article deals with the early history of trade union organization in Southern Rhodesia.

700 **The state and the workers' movement in Zimbabwe.**
Bruce Mitchell. *South African Labour Bulletin*, vol. 12, no. 6/7 (Aug./Sept. 1987), p. 104-22.
Despite its socialist rhetoric during the 1980s, the Zimbabwean government was not supportive of workers' movements and frequently opposed claims for better conditions and improved representation. This paper examines the ways in which the government had undermined trade unions since independence, and discusses a particular incident when fourteen workers associated with a workers' campaign were detained by the state. For another article on trade unions by the same author see item 13.

701 **An evaluation of workers' real participation in decision-making at enterprise level.**
Dorothy Mutizwa-Mangiza. *Zambezia*, vol. 18, no. 1 (1991), p. 35-48.
At the time of independence there was much hope that labour relations within firms would be transformed, and that one feature of this would be improved participation by the workforce in decision-making. This paper considers the extent to which these hopes have been realized, and appears in a special issue of Zambezia which is devoted to labour issues in Zimbabwe. The other papers are 'Industrial organization and the law in the first decade of independence' and 'We are taken as shovels, used and put aside . . .': anthropological perspectives on the organization of work and workers in Zimbabwean industry in the first decade of independence', both by Angela Cheater; 'Labour relations in a Zimbabwean parastatal' by Mark Shadur; and 'Industrial democracy in Zimbabwe?', by Genius J. Maphosa.

702 **Black farmers and white politics in Rhodesia, 1930-72.**
Oliver B. Pollak. *African Affairs*, vol. 74, no. 296 (1975), p. 263-77.
A useful analysis of farmers' vested interests in the African Purchase Areas where Africans could buy freehold farms, this study shows how the relevant union, the African Farmers' Union, attempted to improve the conditions for accumulation for their members. The research included interviews with past AFU presidents, Aaron Jacha and William Kona. Pollak taught at the University of Rhodesia from 1971 to 1974, and gained his doctorate from the University of California, Los Angeles during that time, going on to teach there and in the History Department of the University of Nebraska.

703 **The impact of the Second World War on African labour organization in Rhodesia.**
Oliver B. Pollak. *Rhodesian Journal of Economics*, vol. 7, no. 3 (1973), p. 121-38.
The Second World War led to expansion in the urban economy, and increasing numbers of longer-term black urban workers. Pollak analyses the impact of this period

on the workforce and shows how a shift towards organized labour was begun, partly in response to a degree of labour stabilization and inflation which affected living standards. The 1948 African General Strike and 1954 railway strike are major themes, and the research included interviews with a number of trade union leaders from that period.

704 **Labour in post-independence Zimbabwe.**
South African Labour Bulletin, vol. 12, nos. 6 & 7, (Aug./Sept. 1987). (Special double edition.)

The wide variety of scholarly articles and documents relating to labour issues in Zimbabwe reproduced in these special editions provide a fairly comprehensive and detailed view of the state of labour relations and workers' movements seven years after independence. The relative weakness of the trade unions is an important theme, and the co-operative movement is shown to have developed to only a very limited degree. The academic analyses include Brian Wood on the roots of trade union weakness, Mark Shadur on workers' committees and a case study of the Dairy Marketing Board, Bruce Mitchell on the relationship between the state and workers' movements, and Roger England on co-operatives and class struggle. Documents related to labour issues include workers' committees' guidelines, and interviews with various workers and with Morgan Tsvanginai, the General Secretary of the Southern African Miners' Federation which co-ordinates mine union activities in the region. There have been other special issues of the *Bulletin* which dealt with economic development and workers' issues in Rhodesia: vol. 1, no. 9 (1975), vol. 2, no.7 (1976), and vol. 3, no. 6 (1977), on African workers and union formation. These special issues were edited by Duncan G. Clarke.

Zimbabwe's prospects: issues of race, class, state and capital in Southern Africa.
See item no. 13.

An economic and social history of Zimbabwe 1890-1948: capital accumulation and class struggle.
See item no. 155.

'Good boys', footballers, and strikers: African social change in Bulawayo, 1933-53.
See item no. 158.

Zimbabwe: the political economy of transition 1980-86.
See item no. 417.

Statistics

705 **Annual Economic Review of Zimbabwe.**
Harare: Ministry of Finance, Economic Planning and Development,
1981- . annual.
This is a useful government publication providing general statistics on national
economic variables.

706 **Minerals Marketing Corporation of Zimbabwe Annual Report.**
Harare: Minerals Marketing Corporation of Zimbabwe, 1983- .
annual.
The Minerals Marketing Corporation of Zimbabwe plays a central role in the export
and sale of Zimbabwe's minerals. Its annual report is a useful reference on mineral
production and trade.

707 **Quarterly digest of statistics.**
Harare: Central Statistical Office, 1983- . quarterly.
This is a standard statistical source for government figures, covering a wide range of
fiscal and production data, as well as estimates of population, migration, crime,
education, employment, accidents and tourism. The government previously published
a monthly update, *Monthly supplement to the digest of statistics* (Harare: Central
Statistical Office, 1980-83) which contained data on production and trade, and prices.
Estimates of government expenditure are contained in *Estimates of expenditure for the
year ending June 30* (Harare: Government Printer, 1982/3-), and general national
economic data are found in the annual *National Income and Expenditure Report*
(Harare: Central Statistical Office, 1985-). The most detailed information on external
trade is found in the annual *Statement of external trade by commodities* (Harare:
Central Statistical Office, 1980-), although this publication has appeared rather
infrequently in recent years. Industrial production data are found in the *Census of
production (mining, manufacturing, construction, electricity and water supply)*,
(Harare: Central Statistical Office, 1981-/2-).

708 **Quarterly Economic and Statistical Review.**
Harare: Reserve Bank of Zimbabwe, Economic Research and
Statistical Department, 1980- . quarterly.

This periodical contains discussion and analysis of broad economic issues current at the time of publication. However its main purpose is to provide tables of statistics on financial indicators such as liabilities and assets of banks and institutions, government finance, interest rates, balance of payments, and data on national accounts. It also contains data on general economic indicators such as consumer prices, value of retail trade, sales of agricultural products, mineral production, manufacturing production, and construction. It is an important source of data on the economy.

709 **Statistical Yearbook of Zimbabwe.**
Harare: Central Statistical Office, 1985- . occasional.

A very useful and comprehensive statistical source on Zimbabwe, the coverage of this yearbook is wide, and includes a commentary on each broad category. The topics covered are physical characteristics and climate, population, health, employment and earnings, social welfare, education, national income and expenditure, public finance, mining, manufacturing and electricity, construction and housing, water supply, agriculture, trade and prices, transport and communications, banking and finance, and tourism.

710 **Zimbabwe national household survey capability programme (ZNHSCP): reports on demographic socio-economic survey, 1983/4.**
Central Statistical Office.   Harare: Central Statistical Office, 1985.
5 reports.

This government survey of the African farming areas in the early years of independence is very useful for baseline data on demographic and socio-economic features of the communal lands in selected provinces at that time. Five provinces are covered in the reports: 'Communal lands of Mashonaland Central Province', 'Communal lands of Mashonaland East Province', 'Communal lands of Mashonaland West Province', 'Communal lands of Masvingo Province', and 'Communal lands of Manicaland Province'.

Education

General

711 **Teaching Rhodesians: a history of education policy in Rhodesia.**
Norman Joseph Atkinson. London; New York: Longman, 1972.
244p.

A valuable study which provides a comprehensive history of western education in Rhodesia from the first missionary impact to the establishment of the University College of Rhodesia. The origins and impact of racial segregation in schools are discussed in detail, and other issues such as the use of Afrikaans, and the role of missionary schools are covered. The beginning of racial integration in schools occurred just before independence, and this is considered by Atkinson in 'Racial integration in Zimbabwean schools, 1979-80', *Comparative Education* (UK), vol. 18, no. 1 (1982), p. 77-89. Atkinson was Professor of Education at the University of Rhodesia.

712 **Education in the new Zimbabwe.**
Edited by Cowden Chikombah, (et al.). East Lansing, Michigan: African Studies Centre and Office for International Networks in Education and Development, Michigan State University, 1988. 192p.

This edited collection of nineteen papers is the proceedings of a conference held at Michigan State University in collaboration with the University of Zimbabwe's Faculty of Education in June, 1986. The conference examined many facets of education in Zimbabwe, including the role of the University, curricular issues, educational planning and technology and audio-visual access. The papers are divided into eight sections: the first and last sections provide an overview and conclusion, and the others cover ways of increasing access to education for children and adults, teacher education, the adaptation of science, mathematics and technical education to the needs of Zimbabwe, schooling for languages in Zimbabwe, and cultural diversity in schools and associated curriculum needs. For an article on teacher education by the same author, see 'Teacher education and development: the case of Zimbabwe', *Rural Africana*, vol. 28/29 (Spring-Fall 1987), p. 121-29.

713 **Socialism, education and development: a challenge to Zimbabwe.**
Fay Chung, Emmanuel Ngara. Harare: Zimbabwe Publishing House,
1985. 148p.

The authors of this book, which examines the links between education and socialist
development in Zimbabwe, both held authoritative positions within the education
sector. Fay Chung was Minister for Education and Emmanuel Ngara was Pro-Vice
Chancellor of the University. In the first part of this study they discuss relevant aspects
of socialism, and go on to consider the need to tie educational policy to development
needs. The move to involve students in production processes as part of their formal
education process, receives much emphasis. The links between education and the
needs of the new Zimbabwe were also discussed from the socialist perspective in a
special issue of *Issue, a Quarterly Journal of Africanist Opinion* (Latin America),
vol. 11, no. 3/4 (1981), in which three papers on Zimbabwe appeared. These were
'African education in Zimbabwe: the colonial inheritance of the new state', by
Chengetai Zvobgo, 'New direction for education in liberated Zimbabwe', by Leonard
Suransky, and 'The role of education in national reconstruction in Zimbabwe', by
P. T. Mudariki. Nathan Shamuyarira, who has held a number of ministerial posts, also
published a paper on this topic: 'Education and socialist transformation in Zimbabwe',
Development Dialogue, vol. 2 (1978), p. 58-72.

714 **Literacy participation in Zimbabwe.**
Inés P. Grainger. Harare: University of Zimbabwe, 1986. 104p.

The National Literacy Campaign in Zimbabwe aimed to bring literacy to the whole
country by 1988. This book is a critical analysis of the progress of the campaign, half-
way through its five-year programme. It was quite clear that the campaign was
nowhere near to achieving its aims, since enrolment levels were far too low. Surveys
indicated that a number of 'demotivating' factors were at work, and the attitudes
leading to this situation are analysed. See also Grainger's shorter paper on the literacy
campaign in which the high drop-out level and low rate of male participation are
discussed: 'The literacy campaign in Zimbabwe', *Journal of Social Development in
Africa*, vol. 2, no. 2 (1987), p. 49-58. Radio has also been used as a medium for a non-
school education programme, and information on this is covered in the Zimbabwe
Broadcasting Corporation's *Radio seminar: radio and communication development*
(Harare: Zimbabwe Broadcasting Corporation, 1984).

715 **The politics of literacy and schooling in Zimbabwe.**
David F. Johnson. *Review of African Political Economy*, vol. 48,
(Autumn 1990), p. 99-106.

There has been a very significant expansion in the number of pupils attending school in
Zimbabwe since independence, and the education sector has been one of the most
important elements in both development and recurrent government expenditure. Some
critics argue that this growth has been achieved at an unwarranted expense in the
quality of education. This article reviews this growth in enrolment. The expansion of
the education sector is shown to have caused strains on the government budget, and
this has been exacerbated by financial pressures exerted by the World Bank, whose
policies are criticized by the author. Some of the increase in urban access to education
has occurred through the re-zoning of township boundaries, allowing black pupils
access to formerly white schools. Johnson contends that the government needs to
employ much more radical measures to transform the educational sector, paying
attention to developing new educational material appropriate to the needs of the

264

independent Zimbabwe, and to altering the nature of staff-pupil relationships within the classroom. The problems associated with Zimbabwe's successes in educational expansion are also considered in 'Zimbabwe's educational miracle and the problem it has created', *International Review of Education*, vol. 34, no. 3 (1988), p. 337-53, by Clayton G. Mackenzie.

716 **A survey of workers' educational activities in Zimbabwe, 1980-81.**
Meshack J. Matshazi, Christina Tillfors.   Uppsala, Sweden:
Scandinavian Institute of African Studies, 1983. 85p. (Research report, no. 69).

An overview of all the educational facilities for workers in existence in Zimbabwe just after independence. The study considers how best these should be utilized to achieve the aims of the new Zimbabwe, and how to build upon the existing infrastructure.

717 **Creating an African middle class: the political economy of education and exploitation in Zimbabwe.**
Tafirenyika Moyana.   *Journal of Southern African Affairs*, vol. 4, no. 3 (1979), p. 324-44.

This study of the political economy of colonial education examines the attempt to create a small African middle class and focusses on the period 1953-70.

718 **The underdevelopment of African education.**
Dickson A. Mungazi.   Washington, DC: University Press of America, 1982. 220p.

Essentially a study of the experience of African Rhodesians who had to go abroad to study, the first part of this work looks at the experiences of those who went elsewhere within Africa to study, and the second part examines the situation with regard to other countries, particularly the USA. The treatment of the material is rather dull. Another rather laboured study on education by the same author is *Education and government control in Zimbabwe: a study of the Commissions of Inquiry 1908-74* (New York: Praeger, 1990).

719 **Education, race and employment in Rhodesia.**
Marshall W. Murphree, Graham Cheater, Betty Dorsey, Buzwani D. Mothobi.   Harare: Association of Round Tables in Central Africa in conjunction with the Centre for Inter-racial Studies at the University of Rhodesia, 1975. 478p.

This major study of African education in Rhodesia was based on a large research study of African school-leavers. The data-base consisted of the entire school-leaving population at fourth form and sixth form levels in 1971, and the study analysed the students' backgrounds, aspirations, expectations, academic achievements and subsequent employment experiences. The researchers then went on to examine the occupational structure into which these students sought to move, with particular reference to the constraints imposed by the racial policies and managerial practices extant at the time. The study was prepared from a basically sociological stance, with inputs from economics, education and management fields. It was published as part of the Association of Round Table's project on race relations set up in 1969 under the directorship of Murphree, who was then Professor of Race Relations at the University of Rhodesia. The main recommendations were to end racism in employment for the sake of economic efficiency and political stability. Apart from the wealth of educational data on the situation in the early 1970s, this volume is particularly useful for its chapters on contemporary management expectations and attitudes. Another study commissioned by the Association of Round Tables focussed on technical training: see *Training for development: an inquiry into the nature and scope of technical training in Rhodesia for African workers in industry with special reference to apprenticeship training* (Salisbury: ARTCA, 1978) by Buzwani Mothobi.

720 **Southern Rhodesia: the effects of a conquest society on education, culture and information.**
Marion O'Callaghan, with a contribution by Reginald Austin. Paris: UNESCO, 1977. 293p.

A major study on the impact of colonialism and a racially discriminatory state on education, culture and information in Rhodesia, which was part of a series commissioned by UNESCO on apartheid and racism in Southern Africa during the 1970s. This useful reference work contains very detailed material and analysis on these aspects of Rhodesian society. There are nine chapters on education, covering the system from primary school to University, and fourteen chapters on general culture, including religion, cultures and population, books and libraries, and censorship. Reginald Austin, who is Professor of Law at the University, considers the impact of Rhodesian policy on the mass media in the last chapter on information.

721 **Planning for education expansion in Zimbabwe.**
Norman Reynolds. In: *Education: from poverty to liberty*. Edited by Bill Nasson, John Samuel. Cape Town: David Philip, 1990, p. 141-56.

Based on a 1986 report by Reynolds and Mary Chirume for the Zimbabwe Promotion Council, this discussion considers how to finance and manage Zimbabwe's expanding education system in as fair a way as possible. The need to find a management system which equalizes differences between communities is emphasized.

722 **Education for employment.**
Roger Riddell. Gweru: Mambo Press in association with Catholic Institute for International Relations and Justice and Peace Commission of the Zimbabwe Catholic Bishops' Conference; London: Catholic Institute for International Relations, 1980. 71p. (From Rhodesia to Zimbabwe, no. 9).

One of the series of studies on different aspects of Zimbabwe's social and economic circumstances commissioned by the CIIR and the JPCZBC. In this volume Roger Riddell, who at the time of independence acted as a consultant and adviser on many policy aspects of the country's social and economic future, describes the nature of the educational sector at independence, focussing on the deficiencies of educational opportunity for the black population. His main recommendation for the future was for a new emphasis on education for employment, and adult literacy programmes. The debate about the nature of education in the future Zimbabwe was also considered in E. W. Rogers' *Education for social reality in Zimbabwe* (Gwelo: Mambo Press, 1979. [Mambo Occasional papers, Socio-economic Series no. 13]).

723 **Correspondence education in Central Africa: an alternative route to higher education in developing countries.**
M. A. Wakatama. Lanham, Maryland: University Press of America, 1983. 535p.

The role and development of correspondence education in Rhodesia is considered in this book written by the first Rhodesian African to head a teachers' college with an all-white staff in Rhodesia, and the first to teach at the University of Rhodesia. Wakatama went on to lecture at the University of Zambia and in the USA. This study of correspondence education is based on his doctoral thesis, and although it covers the whole of Central Africa, much of the case study material is drawn from Zimbabwe. The period covered is up to 1980.

724 **Adult literacy programme: an appraisal of the adult literacy organization of Rhodesia and a plan to mount a national adult literacy training programme.**
Whitsun Foundation. Salisbury: Whitsun Foundation, 1978. 62p. (Project 2.09).

This is a study and analysis of the adult literacy programme as it existed before independence, which also discusses proposals for a new scheme. A very significant body of relevant data on education is presented in nineteen appendices.

725 **Education in Zimbabwe: past, present and future.**
Zimbabwe Foundation for Education with Production. Harare: Zimbabwe Foundation for Education with Production, 1986. 152p.

This collection of papers from a seminar sponsored by the Ministry of Education and the Dag Hammarskjold Foundation in 1981 focusses on the development of new educational programmes for a socialist Zimbabwe, and other socialist nations. It includes information on programmes current in Zimbabwe just after independence. The publishers, ZIMFEP, promote the system of education with production, which is also discussed in Ben J. Siyakwazi's 'Education for production in primary schools in Zimbabwe', *Rural Africana*, vol. 28/29 (1987), p. 29-34.

726 **Transforming education: the Zimbabwean experience.**
Rungano J. Zvobgo. Harare: College Press, 1986. 148p.

This books provides a general history of education and an overview of present-day problems. The changes during the early years of independence are dealt with in each sector of education, including the literacy campaigns, and possible solutions to continuing and new problems are suggested.

A decade of development Zimbabwe 1980-90.
See item no. 1.

Socio-economic review of Zimbabwe 1980-85.
See item no. 4.

Zimbabwe: a land divided.
See item no. 8.

Zimbabwe: a country study.
See item no. 11.

Zimbabwe's prospects: issues of race, class, state and capital in Southern Africa.
See item no. 13.

Zimbabwe: politics, economics and society.
See item no. 14.

Zimbabwe: towards a new order – an economic and social survey. vol. 2.
See item no. 16.

Colonial policy and conflict in Zimbabwe: a study of cultures in collision 1890-1979.
See item no. 152.

Zimbabwe: the political economy of transition 1980-86.
See item no. 417.

Higher education

727 **Final Report of the Advisory Committee on the closure of the University of Zimbabwe.**
Advisory Committee, submitted to the Council of the University.
Harare: University of Zimbabwe, 1989. 116p.
By the end of the 1980s there was much friction between the University and the government, resulting in a number of police actions on the campus. The University was closed several times as a result of the government's anger at criticism by students, and sometimes staff, of specific policies interfering with University independence and of general corruption in the government. This is a major report on the first closure which considers the question of re-opening the campus, and contains many fascinating interviews, appendices and documents.

728 **Development in Zimbabwe: the role of the university.**
Centre for International Development Studies. Oslo: Centre for International Development Studies, University of Oslo, [1983]. 125p.
The role of the different faculties in development in Zimbabwe is considered in this publication, which consists of a series of ten lectures given by University of Zimbabwe staff members in Oslo on that topic. It also contains information on the different faculties in the university, and the current directions and trends of research and teaching within them.

729   **The University of Zimbabwe: university, national university, state university or party university?**
Angela Cheater.   *African Affairs*, vol. 90, no. 359 (1991), p. 189-205.
This essay is a damning indictment of government action against the university in the post-independence era. Cheater is particularly critical of the University of Zimbabwe Amendment Act of 1990 which increased the potential for government control of the institution. She discusses the opposition to this act by the teaching body and its union, and by the students. The students' general opposition to the government and government corruption is also covered.

730   **The role of the university and its future in Zimbabwe.**
Edited by N. T. Chideya (et al.).   Harare: Harare Publishing House, 1982. 64p.
Relationships between the University of Zimbabwe and the government have been extremely strained, and the university has been closed on a number of occasions. Government interference in university matters became a major issue at the end of the 1980s, with a new Act which undermined university autonomy. With hindsight, this publication which emerged from a conference at the university in September 1981, was overly optimistic about the university's future role in independent Zimbabwe. The papers included are an opening speech by Mugabe; Asavia Wandira's 'The University in times of change'; Ralf Dahrendorf's 'The role of the University in development: some sociological and philosophical considerations'; Hasu Patel's 'The relationship between the University and government'; Herbert Murerwa's 'University reform: changing the University to meet new needs'; Dietrich Goldschmidt's 'University curriculum and research'; Phillip Altbach's 'The University in the Third World: comparative perspectives'; and by Walter Kamba, the Vice-Chancellor during much of the period of deteriorating relationships with the government, 'The University: from this time on'.

731   **A non-racial island of learning: a history of the University College of Rhodesia from its inception to 1966.**
Michael Gelfand.   Gwelo: Mambo Press, 1978. 376p. (Zambeziana: Series on Culture and Society in Central Africa, no. 4).
This study looks at the nature of the University in its first ten years. For most of this decade the Federation of Rhodesia and Nyasaland was in existence, and the University was claimed to be one of the 'few enduring and worthwhile achievements of the federal period'. Non-racialism was enshrined in its Charter even after the UDI, despite fierce opposition. Nevertheless, the early UDI years were characterized by many resignations and deportations from the University because of opposition to the racist state. This is a rather prim account of that time, and the important issues of principle involved in the university's opposition to the state are not fully addressed. For a short account of the University's establishment by a previous Vice-Principal, see *The building of a university in Central Africa* (Leeds, England: Leeds University Press, 1962), by Basil A. Fletcher. The story of another centre of higher education, which was meant to promote the concept of common citizenship and non-racialism is *Laboratory for peace: the story of Ken and Lilian Mew and Ranche House College, Salisbury* (Salisbury: Louis Bolze, 1984), by Rowland Fothergill. The author was educated in Rhodesia and later became a journalist and editor of a number of local papers. This account of Ranche House College, which was an offspring of the Capricorn Africa Society, is written in journalistic style.

732 **Planning for education for social development in Zimbabwe: an assessment of the University of Zimbabwe's students and lecturers.**
Saliwe Moyo Kawewe.   PhD thesis, University of St. Louis, St. Louis, Missouri, 1985.

This thesis explores whether shifts have occurred in university curricula to accommodate the needs of the students, who are primarily from rural areas, and to provide the skills necessary to carry out 'national reconstruction tasks'. The conclusion is that curricula have not been modified in response to these new forces.

733 **Student protest in Salisbury.**
Saul Ndhlovu.   *Africa Today* (USA), vol. 21, no. 2 (1974), p. 39-42.

There was much opposition to the Smith regime, and to racial discrimination in general at the university. This paper considers the nature of student protest at this time. Other accounts include Paul Nursey-Bray's 'Rhodesia: a university in crisis', *Mawazo* (Uganda), vol. 1, no. 2 (1967), p. 39-46; and Peter B. Harris' 'Pragmatism versus protest at the University College of Rhodesia,' *Universities Quarterly*, vol. 25, no. 1 (1970), p. 71-82.

734 **Report on the faculty of medicine.**
University of Rhodesia.   Salisbury: University of Rhodesia, 1977.
107p.

This is a comprehensive account of the origins and development of the university medical school, including its organization, curriculum, student numbers, examination system and results, staff, and finance. On faculty publications, many of them on health and related cultural issues in Rhodesia, Gelfand has produced a bibliography, *Faculty of Medicine publications 1963-77* (Salisbury; University of Rhodesia, [n.d.]).

Research and Technology

735 **Zimbabwe and the CGIAR centres: a study of their collaboration in agricultural research.**
K. J. Billing.   Washington, DC: Consultative Group on International Agricultural Research, World Bank, 1985. (Study paper, no. 6).
A very useful source on agricultural research in Zimbabwe, this study was part of a worldwide assessment of the impact of the World Bank's International Agricultural Research Centres. Apart from detailed coverage of research on crop varieties and their yields, there is also a section describing the wide variety of public and private institutions involved in the agricultural sector including veterinary services, land resettlement and marketing boards. Although generally positive about the impact of agricultural research, the report makes the common criticism that CGIAR research neglects the small-scale peasant sector.

736 **Pasture research in Zimbabwe 1964-84.**
J. N. Clatworthy. In: *Pasture improvement research in Eastern and Southern Africa*. Edited by Jackson A. Kategie.   Ottawa: International Development Research Centre, 1985, p. 25-58.
At a workshop held in Harare in September 1984 natural scientists from the region reviewed the state of pasture improvement research in their countries. This report includes details on research methods current in Zimbabwe, the ways in which research findings are translated into policy, and policy implementation. Since overgrazing and cattle stocking rates are highly significant and politicized topics in Zimbabwe, the use and abuse of rangeland is an important research issue. For a technical text on grassland resources, see *Grasses in Southern Africa: Zimbabwe region* (Salisbury: M. O. Collins, 1976), by Lucy K. A. Chippindall and A. O. Crook. Other information on Zimbabwe's rangelands is contained in the overview papers in *Rangeland potential in the SADCC region* (Harare: Ministry of Lands, Agriculture and Rural Resettlement, 1989), edited by A. R. Maclaurin and Barbara V. Maasdorp, the proceedings of a workshop held in Bulawayo in 1987. This book focusses on rangeland resources and development programmes, and the potential of small-scale stock schemes. It also

271

contains two papers specifically on Zimbabwe – an update of the above paper by Clatsworthy, and 'Zimbabwe: rangeland resources and potential' by B. Mombeshora and A. R. Maclaurin.

737 **Zimbabwe research index: register of current research in Zimbabwe.**
Compiled by Librarian, Scientific Liaison Office. Harare: Government Printer, 1985.

This index lists research projects undertaken in Zimbabwe in all fields of science, technology and the humanities. Information is gathered by questionnaires, and where there is a low response rate, as from industry, there are omissions in the record. Research projects are listed by subject, and cross-referenced between subject. It includes listings of research workers, research organizations and subjects. The index was intended as an annual publication but has appeared much less frequently: the 1986 issue covered the years 1983-85 and is the most recent one available. It replaces the Rhodesian Research Register which appeared from 1970-78.

738 **Appropriate rural technology in Zimbabwe.**
Colin Relf. Geneva: International Labour Organization, 1984. 79p.
(World Employment Programme, Technical and Employment Branch, Technical Report).

This concise but comprehensive survey of simple technologies used in the rural sector in Zimbabwe was commissioned by the International Labour Organization. The survey starts with a discussion of existing technologies and recent developments in the following rural sectors: building materials and techniques, water supplies, sanitation, food processing and preservation, cooking systems, furniture and household items and small-scale industrial production such as metal fabrication and carpentry. Agricultural technologies and techniques are also covered, with discussion of cultivation methods such as minimum tillage. There are a number of constraints to the rapid development of appropriate small-scale technologies including finance, information flows, and training, and these are analysed in turn. Recommendations for assisting the spread and uptake of appropriate technologies are discussed, including the subsidization by government of materials for products which have important welfare implications, like the successful Blair pit latrine developed in the Blair laboratories in Harare. This publication is a useful start for those interested in appropriate technology issues in Zimbabwe. A short article on the role of intermediate technology in agricultural development in the African farming areas is W. J. Ascough, 'Intermediate technology as a potential aid to a more productive subsistence agriculture', *Rhodesian Agricultural Journal*, vol. 76, no. 3 (May/June 1979), p. 135-37.

739 **Agricultural research in Zimbabwe.**
R. C. Smith. *Zimbabwe Agricultural Journal*, vol. 79, no. 1 (1982), p.29-31.

Zimbabwe has a reputation for successful agricultural research, and significant resources have been devoted to the personnel and institutions involved. However the vast majority of the research work has been directed at the crops and techniques of the large-scale commercial farming sector, the needs of the small-scale, black farmers being largely ignored. Some redress is now being made, although the 'scientific' approach to agricultural problems is often misguided since the root causes of problems are frequently socio-political. This article provides an overview of the various organizations involved in local agricultural research for the years 1950-82, and discusses their structure, budgets and research work. H. Weinmann has also produced two studies on the history of agricultural research in Zimbabwe: *Agricultural research in Southern Rhodesia, under the rule of the British South Africa Company, 1890-1923* (Salisbury: University of Rhodesia, Department of Agriculture, 1972. [Occasional Paper no. 4]), and *Agricultural research and development in Southern Rhodesia 1924-50* (Salisbury: University of Rhodesia, 1975. [Series in Science no. 2]).

740 **The research environment in Zimbabwe: a study of the state and conditions of experimental research in the agricultural, engineering, life and physical sciences in Zimbabwe.**
Haile Tebicke. Sweden: Sarec Documentation, 1987. 43p. (Research Surveys).

This survey of the research environment in Zimbabwe was prepared as part of a series by the Swedish Agency for Research Co-operation on research in African countries. The study contains information on various aspects of scientific research in Zimbabwe, including an examination of the infrastructure available to implement research programmes, the personnel able to undertake research, the availability of postgraduate programmes and the internal and external institutional links.

741 **Research Register 1986.**
University of Zimbabwe. Harare: University of Zimbabwe, 1986. [n.p.].

This useful register details all ongoing research within the University alphabetically by faculty, and within faculty by department and researcher's name. Each entry includes details of the research, the source of funds, expected completion date, and other publications of the researcher involved. This 1986 register was the fourth time the exercise had been published, and presumably there will be regular updates.

Zimbabwe's prospects: issues of race, class, state and capital in Southern Africa.
See item no. 13.

Rural water supply and sanitation in Zimbabwe: recent policy developments.
See item no. 312.

Report of the commission of inquiry into the agricultural industry.
See item no. 580.

Literature

Literary analysis

742 **Settler myths and the Southern Rhodesian novel.**
Anthony J. Chennells. PhD thesis, University of Zimbabwe, Harare, 1982.

A major study of this genre up to 1978. Chennells maintains that novels written about Southern Rhodesia by whites form a discrete body of literature which deal with concerns peculiar to the white settlers. He shows how these concerns are embodied in a number of fixed perceptions or myths about the country and its indigenous population. He also demonstrates how these novels helped to develop an awareness of a distinct 'Rhodesian' identity. The work covers a very wide range of writing, including some novels of literary merit, and others which are stylistically poor, and which frequently express very racist views. See also the author's article, 'The treatment of the Rhodesian war in recent Rhodesian novels', *Zambezia*, vol. 5, no. 2 (1977), p. 177-202, which discusses four titles: *The day of Chaminuka, The mercenaries, A time of madness*, and *The massacre of Umtali*. Rhodesian settler fiction from 1952-80 is also considered in David Maugham-Brown, 'Myths on the march: the Kenyan and Zimbabwean struggles in colonial fiction', *Journal of Southern African Studies*, vol. 9, no. 1 (1982), p. 93-117.

743 **Images of women in Zimbabwean literature.**
Rudo Gaidzanwa. Harare: College Press, 1985. 101p.

This book looks at the portrayal of women in Zimbabwean fiction written in Shona, Ndebele and English. The author explores the use of images of women as mothers, wives, single people, divorcees and widows, and in urban or rural residence. A historical analysis examines the social, economic, political and psychological factors which affect the way women are perceived. The author concludes that the literature tends to take a punitive and moralistic attitude towards women.

744 **Power, popular consciousness and the fictions of war: Hove's *Bones* and Chinodya's *Harvest of Thorns***

Elizabeth A. W. Gunner. *African Languages and Culture*, vol. 4, no. 1 (1991), p. 77-85.

The genre of literature relating to Zimbabwe's war for independence has been an important element of the country's post-1980 fiction. In this paper, Gunner analyses two of the major contributions to the genre.

745 **The rise of the Shona novel.**

George P. Kahari. Gweru: Mambo Press, 1977. 407p.

A comprehensive study of the quantitative and qualitative growth of the Shona novel and related genres from 1956 to 1990, this is an important contribution to local literary analysis by Professor Kahari. Other titles by the same author which address aspects of Shona fiction include *Plots and characters in Shona fiction* (Gweru: Mambo Press, 1990), *Aspects of the Shona novel* (Gweru: Mambo Press, 1986), and a paper on missionary influences in Shona literature in *Christianity south of the Zambezi* (see item 283). An analysis of the history of writing in Shona, including technical aspects of phonemizing the language so that it could be written down, is George Fortune's '75 years of writing in Shona', *Zambezia*, vol. 1, no. 1 (1969), p. 55-67.

746 **The search for Zimbabwean identity: an introduction to the Black Zimbabwean novel.**

George P. Kahari. Gweru: Mambo Press, 1980. 160p.

An analysis of eight novels published between 1966-78, which the author believes to be the only significant novels published in English by black Zimbabweans up to that time. The novels are Solomon Mutswairo's *Feso* and *Mapondera: soldier for my country*; Stanlake Samkange's *On trial for my country*, *Year of the uprising*, and *The mourned one*; Ndabaningi Sithole's *The polygamist*; W. Katiyo's *Son of the soil*; and Charles Mungoshi's *Waiting for the rain*. Common themes are the feelings of alienation and culture conflict which have shaped Zimbabwean identity. Kahari is Professor in the Department of African Languages at the University of Zimbabwe, and has been the Zimbabwean Ambassador to Germany. Other published analyses of the writings of Zimbabwean writers by the same author include *The novels of Patrick Chakaipa* (Salisbury: Longman, 1972) and *The imaginative writings of Paul Chidyausiku* (Gweru: Mambo Press, 1975).

747 **Teachers, preachers, non-believers: a social history of Zimbabwean literature.**

Flora Veit-Wild. London: Hans Zell Publishers in association with Baobab Books, Harare, 1992. 408p. bibliog. (New Perspectives on African Literature Series, no. 6).

This is the most comprehensive guide and analysis to black Zimbabwean writers and writing available. Veit-Wild covers the processes and forces shaping black writing from its inception to the later 1980s, combining historical analysis with illustrative material from writers' lives and texts. Several major sections on specific writers are included. The first part of the study covers the pioneers of black writing, typified as the teachers and preachers of the title. Special studies of Lawrence Vambe, Solomon Mutswairo, Stanlake Samkange and Ndabezinhle Sigogo are provided after discussion of the general trends in their writing, and the influences of rural life, modernization, education and African newspapers. The 'non-believers', the more radical writers of the 1970s typified as a 'lost generation' are covered in part two. Their work reflects the greater influence of township living, acculturation, and politicization at school. The influence of the Literature Bureau and Mambo Press on writing during this period is also discussed in this section, and a chapter is devoted to the work of Charles Mungoshi. The final section considers trends in post-independence writing, including specific analysis of Chenjerai Hove's *Bones*, Shimmer Chinodya's *Harvest of thorns*, and Tsitsi Dangarembga's *Nervous conditions*. Veit-Wild has also produced a study of specific aspects of Zimbabwean writers' lives, *A survey of Zimbabwean writers*: *educational and literary careers* (Bayreuth, Germany: Bayreuth University, 1992. [Bayreuth African Studies Series, no. 27]). She has made a particular study of Dambudzo Marechera's literary works: see 'Words as bullets: the writings of Dambudzo Marechera', *Zambezia*, vol. 14, no. 1 (1987), p. 113-20. A ten-page bibliography on Marechera is included in the same journal issue.

748 **Zimbabwe fiction in English.**
R. Zhuwarara. *Zambezia*, vol. 14, no. 2 (1987), p. 131-46.
The author categorizes post-independence fiction in English into two types. The first deals with the colonial era and is concerned with issues raised by the social and political changes wrought by colonialism, which he feels is typified by the work of authors such as Chinodya and Ndhlala. The second type deals with the liberation war (see for example Hove, item 230). A brief outline of pre-independence fiction in English is also included.

749 **Those years of drought and hunger.**
Musaemura Bonas Zimunya. Gweru: Mambo Press, 1982. 129p.
This is an analysis of various literary themes common to African writing in English in Zimbabwe, which is based on the author's 1979 MA thesis for the University of Kent, England. The writers and books discussed are Stanlake Samkange, *On trial for my country*, *Year of the uprising* and *The mourned one*; Geoffrey Ndhlala, *Jikinya*; Charles Mungoshi, *Coming of the dry season* and *Waiting for the rain*; Wilson Katiyo, *A son of the soil*; and Dambudzo Marechera, *House of hunger*. Zimunya is a lecturer in the Department of English at the University of Zimbabwe.

Historical dictionary of Zimbabwe.
See item no. 3.

Figurative language in Shona discourse: a study of the analogical imagination.
See item no. 274.

Fiction

750 **Young women in the liberation struggle: stories and poems from Zimbabwe.**
Edited by Kathy Bond-Stewart, assisted by Leocardia Mudihu, photographs by Biddy Partridge. Harare: Zimbabwe Publishing House, 1984. 67p.

This contribution to the abundant literature on the war years brings together a collection of short stories and poems describing the personal experiences of women ex-combatants. In some cases the writing is emotionally charged or ideologically revealing. In others the authors provide straightforward accounts of their involvement in the struggle. An expanded version of this publication, also edited by Bond-Stewart, was published three years later as *Independence is not only for one sex* (Harare: Zimbabwe Publishing House, 1987). It contains several life histories of both prominent and ordinary Zimbabwean women.

751 **Nothing is impossible.**
Samuel Chimsoro. Harlow, England: Longman, 1983. 186p.

The title of this book reflects its upbeat message about the opportunities presented by modernization, a significant departure from the negative portrayal of social change in many other novels by black Zimbabwean authors. This is the story of the ambitious Simbai, who succeeds through hard work in moving from farm labourer through education, to hotel worker. When racial discrimination prevents advancement in this job, he sets up business in Machipisa business centre in a Salisbury township. His business success is presented as a testament to the versatility and vitality of Zimbabweans.

752 **Dew in the morning.**
Shimmer Chinodya. Gweru: Mambo Press, 1982. 287p.

Particularly notable for its sensitive and poetic depiction of rural scenes and peasant life, the impact of new cultural and economic forces on traditional life is addressed in this novel. The issues considered are common to many African novels on conflict between city and country, but this novel presents a more positive view than some others of its type. The story line is rather diffuse, but centres on a woman, Masiziva, who is building a house in a rural area, whilst her husband is away working in town. Her children are sent with him in order to gain access to education, and Masiziva is left alone. Other works by the same author include *Farai's Girls* (Harare: College Press, 1984), in which Chinodya's subject is a boy growing up during the liberation war, and his sexual awakening through various relationships with women. Chinodya has also written a novel about the liberation struggle, *Harvest of Thorns* (Harare: Baobab Books; London: Heinemann, 1989 [African Writers Series]), which addresses the tensions between Christianity and commitment to the armed liberation struggle, through the story of Benjamin Tichafa and his experiences in the war and in Mozambique. Chinodya is also a published poet.

753 Nervous conditions.

Tsitsi Dangarembga.   London: Women's Press, 1988; Harare: Zimbabwe Publishing House, 1989. 180p.

Not only is this one of the best post-independence novels from Zimbabwe, but it is also the first to be published by a black Zimbabwean woman. Its strongly feminist perspective was probably the reason why it was originally rejected by local publishers, and was first published abroad. The novel deals with many issues, including patriarchy, culture clash and alienation through education. The story, told in the first person, concerns Tambudzai, an adolescent rural girl whose wealthy uncle finances her education at a prestigious multiracial convent. Her transformation into a young woman determined to experience true emancipation is particularly influenced by her friendship with her rebellious cousin, Nyasha, whose earlier education and life in Britain leads her into constant conflict with traditional Shona family mores, and an eventual nervous breakdown. Other influential women include Tambudzai's traditional mother and a non-conformist aunt. Some of the novel's themes draw on Dangarembga's own life, as she spent some of her childhood in Britain, returning to secondary education in Zimbabwe. After a brief period as a teacher, she went to Cambridge to study medicine, but returned to Zimbabwe at independence before completing her studies. She has since studied at the University of Zimbabwe, and in 1989 began a course on film in Berlin.

754 King Solomon's mines.

Henry Rider Haggard.   Oxford, New York: Oxford University Press, 1989. 320p.

Haggard's famous novel about vast gold wealth in a remote African territory was based on myths about the Zimbabwe ruins and their supposed connection with King Solomon. Haggard had never been to Zimbabwe when the book was written, although he visited from South Africa many years later. This story has been filmed on a number of occasions, including one truly awful version produced since Zimbabwean independence, using Zimbabwe locations. The story's popularity meant that it had a wide and unfortunate influence on popular perceptions of Africa, promoting many misconceptions about African cultures. It has been translated into both Ndebele and Swahili, and has appeared in many editions since it was first published by Cassell in 1885.

755 Muzukuru: a guerilla's story.

Paul Hotz.   Johannesburg: Ravan Press, 1990. 377p.

This is a fictional account of the war based on interviews with former guerillas. It is the story of a coloured man who becomes a guerilla after serving with Smith's army and being captured by ZIPRA fighters. Although evocative of the guerilla experience, the writing is rather poor.

756 Bones.

Chenjerai Hove.   Harare: Baobab Books, 1990. 2nd ed. 112p.

Hove is one of Zimbabwe's most brilliant post-independence writers. This is his first novel in English, which won the Zimbabwean Book Publishers' Association prize for literature 1988-89 and the Noma Award for Publishing in Africa 1990. The story concerns Marita, a farmworker, whose only son leaves her to join the liberation fighters. Hove's writing is sensitive and poetic, and he tempers his account of her suffering and eventual death at the hands of the security forces with a sense of hope for the future.

757   **A son of the soil.**
Wilson Katiyo.   London: Rex Collings, 1976. 147p.
The story of an African boy growing up in colonial Rhodesia against a background of racial discrimination and institutionalized violence. The story, which is clearly based on the author's life, deals with Alexio, his burning desire for education, and his experiences which include an encounter with the Special Branch. The sequel to this novel, *Going to heaven* (London: Rex Collings, 1979) continues the autobiographical similarities as Alexio manages to leave Rhodesia and go to Zambia, and thence to England, where he continues his studies. The novels contain many insights into the experiences of being black in racist Rhodesia, and African in England.

758   **Shona folk tales.**
Edited by Clive Kileff, collected by A. L. Hodza.   Gweru: Mambo Press, 1987. 150p.
This is a collection of fifteen Shona folk tales which have been translated into English. Other books with traditional folk tales drawn from Ndebele culture are Phyllis Savory's *Matabele fireside tales* (Cape Town: Howard Timmins, 1962), and *Matabele folktales* by R. W. Lamplough (Cape Town: Oxford University Press, 1968).

759   **The grass is singing.**
Doris Lessing.   London: Michael Joseph, 1950; New York: Popular Library, 1976; Glasgow: Paladin, 1989. 206p.
First published in 1950, *The grass is singing* is one of the great novels about white settlers in Southern Africa, which evokes the atmosphere and landscape of the veld and the tensions of white society with style and feeling. Although Lessing left Southern Rhodesia in 1949, some of her novels retained Rhodesian themes, and her writing was always sensitive to the conflicts and tensions between settlers and Africans, and aware of the human costs of colonialism. This fiction includes *African stories* (London: Michael Joseph, 1964); *This was the old chief's country* (London: Michael Joseph, 1951. reprinted, 1973); *The sun between their feet* (London: Michael Joseph, 1973); *Martha Quest* (London: Michael Joseph, 1952; St. Albans, England: Panther, 1969); *Five* (London: Michael Joseph, 1953; St. Albans, England: Panther, 1969); *A proper marriage* (London: Michael Joseph, 1954; St. Albans, England: Panther, 1969); *A ripple from the storm* (London: Michael Joseph, 1958; New York: Simon & Schuster, 1966); and *Landlocked* (London: Michael Joseph, 1965; St. Albans, England: Panther, 1969). Her return to Southern Rhodesia in 1956, and four visits to independent Zimbabwe in the 1980s and 1990s are recounted and critically discussed in *Going home* (London: Michael Joseph, 1957; St. Albans, England: Panther, 1968) and *African laughter: four visits to Zimbabwe* (London: Harper Collins, 1992). One of the great novelists of the 20th century, Doris Lessing was born in Iran, and went to Southern Rhodesia at the age of five, leaving for England when she was thirty. She became a communist, and this influenced her writings, but later her political views became more detached from Marxism. Analyses which focus on her writings with Rhodesian settings include Murray C. Steele, *'Children of Violence' and Rhodesia: a study of Doris Lessing as historical observer* (Salisbury: Central Africa Historical Association, 1974. [Local Pamphlet Series, no. 29]); Mary-Ann Singleton, *The city and the veld: the fiction of Doris Lessing* (Cranbury, New Jersey: Bucknell University Press, 1976); and

Literature. Fiction

Michael Thorpe, *Doris Lessing's Africa* (London; Ibadan: Evans Brothers, 1978). See also Dee Seligman, *Doris Lessing: an annotated bibliography of criticism* (Westport, Connecticut: Greenwood Press, [1981]).

760 **Woman in struggle.**
Irene R. R. Machamba.   Gweru: Mambo Press, 1986; Harare:
ZIMFEP, 1984. 50p.
This novel explores the awakening consciousness of a young girl growing up in colonial Rhodesia. An awareness of the political aspects of women's oppression develops from her association with a guerilla fighter. The unsubtle message of the story is that women's liberation in Rhodesia can only be attained through freedom from colonial oppression.

761 **Black sunlight.**
Dambudzo Marechera.   London: Heinemann, 1980. Reprinted 1982.
117p.
Marechera was a brilliant writer, whose use of language was rich and poetic, but his vision of life both within and outside Zimbabwe was generally angry, if not bleak. In this novel he relentlessly catalogues the collapse of African society well after the onset of colonialism, through the eyes of a black press photographer. His earlier collection of short stories, *The House of Hunger* (London: Heinemann, 1978; Harare: Zimbabwe Publishing House, 1982) won the Guardian Fiction Prize.

762 **Mindblast; or the definitive buddy.**
Dambudzo Marechera.   Harare: College Press, 1984. 128p. (Modern
Writers of Zimbabwe).
Marechera who had been in exile in England returned to Zimbabwe after independence and his views on the transitional state were expressed in a number of poems, stories and plays. This book is a collection of such work. Marechera died in 1987, and a posthumous publication of his writing from his exile period, compiled and edited by Flora Veit-Wild, is *The black insider* (Harare: Baobab Books, 1990). This contains a short account of the author's period in England by the editor. Veit-Wild has also compiled a poetry collection, *Cemetery of Mind* (Harare: Baobab Books, 1992), and further posthumous publications of Marechera's work are planned.

763 **Waiting for the rain.**
Charles L. Mungoshi.   London: Heinemann Educational; Atlantic
Highlands, New Jersey: Humanities Press, 1975. 180p.
Mungoshi was born near Enkeldoorn (Chivhu), in 1947, and educated in mission schools. He became editor of the Literary Bureau, and is currently Literary Director at Zimbabwe Publishing House, and writer-in-residence at the University of Zimbabwe. He is one of Zimbabwe's most important contemporary writers. Some of his fiction was banned during UDI. This novel, and its sequel, *Coming of the dry season* (Oxford: Oxford University Press, 1972; Salisbury: Zimbabwe Publishing House, 1981) focusses on a number of members of an African family whose kinship bonds are slowly unravelling. The common theme of the difficulties of dealing with an alien western culture is expressed, and the conflicts between those with western educational qualifications and attitudes, and adherents to modes of traditional advancement. Mungoshi has also published collections of short stories, *Some kinds of wounds and*

other short stories (Gweru: Mambo Press, 1980) and *The setting sun and the rolling world: selected short stories* (London: Heinemann, 1987; London: Heinemann International, 1989. [African Writers Series]). The latter was shortlisted for the Commonwealth Writers' Prize.

764 The contact.

Garikai Mutasa.   Gweru, Zimbabwe: Mambo Press, 1985. 125p.

This is a good example of the heroic-style novels of the liberation war which depict the liberation forces as invincible. The story illustrates well the gulf of understanding between white and blacks involved in the war. In a similar heroic vein is *A fighter for freedom* (Gweru: Mambo Press, 1983) by Edward Chipamaunga, which depicts the war experiences of an indomitable guerilla fighter, Tinasha.

765 Mapondera: soldier of Zimbabwe.

Solomon Mangwiro Mutswairo.   Harare: Longman Zimbabwe, 1978. 116p. (Also published as *Mapondera: soldier of fortune*, (Washington, DC: Three Continents Press, 1983).

Anger at dispossession of the land by Europeans is the main theme of this novel, which recounts the story of the last great fighter against Rhodes in the 1896 rebellion. Regarded as a hero today, the colonial powers perceived Mapondera as a bandit. The celebrated spirit medium Nehanda is also featured in the tale. Mapondera's stand has also been described in a non-fictional account by David Beach in *Mapondera: 1840-1904* (Gweru: Mambo Press, 1989).

766 Zimbabwe: prose and poetry.

Solomon Mangwiro Mutswairo.   Washington, DC: Three Continents Press, 1979. 2nd ed. 276p.

This volume contains an English translation of Mutswairo's novel *Feso*, which came to have a symbolic significance for the nationalists as it was proscribed reading during UDI. It deals with 17th century African migrations, but its allegorical content made it attractive to the African nationalist movement. *Feso* was first published in Shona in 1957. The rest of the volume consists of twenty-five poems by the main author, and Luke Chidavaenzi, Dintweng Kousu and Herbert Chitepo, all of whom were representatives of a cosmopolitan literati who were associated with the liberation movements.

767 The southern circle.

Geoffrey Ndhlala.   Harlow: Longman, 1984. 260p.

Rugare, the son of Masutu, and grandson of Zengeza is the narrator of this story. He portrays a traditional rural life which is idyllic, but gradually deteriorating under the impact of external forces. The unsavoury influences of urban life and its undermining of kinship values are explored, as Rugare and Masutu are forced to migrate to obtain education. His desire for alcohol and women prevent the well-educated Rugare from helping his father who loses his urban job, and becomes destitute. The liberation struggle provides the background for another novel by Ndhlala, *Jikinya* (Salisbury: Macmillan, 1979).

768   The non-believer's journey.

Stanley Nyamfukudza.   London: Heinemann (African Writers Series); Salisbury: Zimbabwe Publishing House, 1980. 128p.

In this novel the relationship between a dying Rhodesia and an emerging Zimbabwe is outlined, through the detached eyes of Sam, a university graduate teacher who maintains a deep scepticism about the beliefs and aspirations of his people. The possibility that independence will be followed by the betrayal of the ideals for which the struggle is being fought feeds his doubts. This novelist's pessimism about independence can be compared with the similar sentiments expressed in the writings of Mungoshi (see item 763) and Marechera (see item 762) from the same period.

769   Black fire: narratives from Zimbabwean guerillas.

Michael Raeburn.   Harare: Zimbabwean Publishing House, 1986. 182p.

Originally published as *Black fire: accounts of the guerilla war in Rhodesia* (London: Julian Friedmann Publishers, 1978; Gweru: Mambo Press, 1981), this book contains five stories about the war based on real events, which draw on the contacts the author made with guerilla fighters. The authors attempt to illustrate the war as experienced by the guerillas. There is also a historical analysis of the military background to the war. The author went to school and university in Rhodesia. He went on to study film in France and made a film of Doris Lessing's '*The grass is singing*' in 1980. See also item 771.

770   On trial for my country.

Stanlake John William Samkange.   London: Heinemann Educational; Atlantic Highlands: New Jersey: Humanities Press, 1967. 150p.

(African Writers Series, no. 33).

Professor Samkange (1922-88) was born in Chipata, Zambia. He attended Waddilove Institution near Marondera in Zimbabwe, before going on to Adams College and Fort Hare in South Africa. He was active in nationalist politics in the 1950s, and then went to America where he earned his doctorate in history at the University of Indiana, going on to teach at a number of American universities. He returned to the nationalist politics in the mid-1970s, and was one of the African members of Parliament elected in the 1979 elections, as a United African National Council candidate, but left the political scene in 1980 to found the Harare Publishing House. Major themes of his fictional output are the moral outrage of Zimbabwean peoples at the dispossession of their land by the colonial powers and the moral superiority of the pre-colonial past to western 'civilization'. The trial of the title of this book is an imaginary historical one in which Lobengula, Matabele Thompson, the Reverend Helm, Jameson and Cecil Rhodes are the witnesses. The aim of the trial is to determine whether Lobengula was guilty of being a 'sellout' or was a 'victim of unscrupulous men', the verdict being that he was betrayed in a most unprincipled fashion. Ian Smith is given a similar fictional trial in Samkange's *On trial for that UDI* (Harare: Harare Publishing House, 1986). In *The Mourned One* (London: Heinemann Educational, 1975; Atlantic Highlands: New Jersey: Humanities Press, 1976), which has been compared to *Things Fall Apart*, Chinua Achebe's famous story of cultural conflict in West Africa, the negative influences of westernization are examined through the story of Ndatshona, who is awaiting execution on an accusation of rape. Shona culture, the nature of missionary school, and the influence of urbanization are dealt with through his experiences. The narrative is critical of missionaries, as well as African attempts to emulate European behaviour and attitudes. *Year of the Uprising* (London: Heinemann Educational, 1978) focusses on the injustices of land alienation, the bitter resentment of the African dispossessed, and their attempts at resistance. A study of Samkange and his family is being prepared by Terence Ranger.

771 Jit.
Michael Raeburn.   Harare: Anvil Press, 1991. 111p.

This is the book of a popular locally-produced film, which was written and directed by Raeburn. The subject of the book is something of a contrast to the generally sober analysis of the impact of urbanization and culture clash by most Zimbabwean writers, being a street-wise youth whose adventures and romance are enlivened by the frequent interference of his jukwa, the mischievous beer-drinking spirit of his great-grandmother.

772 Pawns.
Charles Samupindi.   Harare: Baobab Books, 1992. 199p.

This novel about the guerilla war provides a marked contrast to the typically heroic perspective characteristic of many of the earlier accounts by black writers. Samupindi's story of a young man called Fangs is told largely in flashback from his desperate position as an unemployed ex-combatant on the streets of Harare, and includes harrowing details of hunger, boredom and disease in the Mozambiquan base camps, as well as the horror of violent deaths in battle. Another novel of this type about three young combatants' experience of the war is Isheunesh Valentine Mazorodze's *Silent journey from the east* (Harare: Zimbabwe Publishing House, 1989).

773 Trooper Peter Halket of Mashonaland.
Olive Schreiner.   London: T. Fisher Unwin, 1897. 264p.

Olive Schreiner was an important South African novelist, and had been a special friend of Rhodes in Cape Town. However, Rhodes' exploits in Southern Rhodesia with the British South Africa Company caused a distancing between them. Whilst a number of African writers have condemned the process of early European settlement through the medium of fiction, this novel, which falls in that genre, is unusual in that its author was white. The story tells of a young soldier's encounter with a stranger, whom he regales with tales of his brutal military and sexual exploits amongst the African population. Only gradually does he come to realize that the stranger is Jesus Christ. The story is a searing indictment of Rhodes and the British South Africa Company.

774 The polygamist.
Ndabaningi Sithole.   New York: Third Press, 1972. 178p.

This novel is notable more for its author, the founder of ZANU, than for its theme of culture clash which is a common one in Zimbabwean fiction. The polygamist of the title is Dube who has seven wives, one of whom is unhappy with her status and the practice of polygamy. The tensions arising from this situation are intensified when Dube's son returns home. Educated in a mission and armed with new western values and morality, the son believes that monogamy is a superior form of marriage. Sithole also wrote a fictional account of the liberation struggle up to the mid 1970s, *Roots of a revolution: scenes from Zimbabwe's struggle* (Oxford, London, New York: Oxford University Press, 1977). For biographical notes on the author see item 395.

775 Children of wax: African folk tales.

Alexander McCall Smith. Edinburgh: Canongate, 1989. 119p.

This is a collection of twenty-seven Ndebele folk tales collected by the author on two trips to Zimbabwe. The stories were mainly collected from the Matopos area. Many of these tales were told on BBC radio, and the title story has been made into an award-winning animated film.

776 Shangani folk tales: a collection of Shangani folk stories.

C. Stockil, M. Dalton. Zimbabwe: Jongwe Printing and Publishing Company in association with the Literature Bureau, [n.d.]. 2 vols.

Thirty folk tales from the Shangani tradition are reproduced in these volumes in English translation. An early publication on local African folk tales, F. Posselt's *Fables of the veld* (Oxford: Oxford University Press, 1929) reproduced a number of stories which mainly concern animals, collected from Rhodesian Africans.

777 Crossroads.

Spencer Tizora. Gweru: Mambo Press, 1985. 200p.

Set in the late 1970s, this novel is another example of the genre examining the impact of the liberation war, this time from the viewpoint of civilians. It tells the tragic tale of a woman caught up in events, whose imprisonment leads to her insanity and separation from her son. The theme of reconciliation between blacks and whites is tentatively explored, as her son is then adopted by a white woman.

New writing in Rhodesia.
See item no. 783.

Poetry

778 Soko risina musoro. (The tale without a head).

Herbert Wiltshire Tfumaindini Chitepo, translated by Hazel Carter.

London: Oxford University Press, 1958. 63p.

Perhaps more notable for the significance of the author than for its literary importance, this epic poem combined with dialogue was originally published in 1955 in Shona by Chitepo, who later became Chair of ZANU, and was assassinated in Lusaka in 1975. In this format it was translated into English by a renowned lecturer in Bantu languages at the School of Oriental and African Studies, University of London. The blank verse and dialogue centre on the accusations made at the court of Mutasa, the Manyika king, who is in a state of crisis because of an unsuccessful offering for rain. Carter also provides copious notes and background information. An analysis of this poem may be found in *Herbert Chitepo's Epic*, *Soko Risina Musoro*: *a critique* (Longman: Zimbabwe, 1988) by George Kahari.

779 **Poetry in Rhodesia.**
Edited by D. E. Finn. Salisbury: College Press, 1968. 80p.

This anthology of Rhodesian poetry was aimed primarily at secondary schools and a general readership, and updated an earlier anthology by W. T. Miller and John Snelling. The poets included are mainly but not exclusively whites, and very brief biographical notes on the poets are provided. There is also a section which provides annotations and explanatory notes for the poems. A short collection of poems by a Rhodesian white which address landscape themes and are evocative of Zimbabwean scenery is *A book of verse from Rhodesia* (Ditchling, England: Ditchling Press, [1957]), by Noeline Barry.

780 **Shona praise poetry.**
Edited by G. Fortune, compiled by A. C. Hodza. Oxford: Clarendon Press, 1979. 401p.

This major study of Shona praise poetry is the result of extensive research by both authors, who were lecturers in the Department of African Languages at the University of Rhodesia when the book was published. Hodza collected the poetry through intensive field work with Shona contributors. In some cases he obtained entire poems, but mainly he collected fragments which he painstakingly assembled together, sometimes contributing lines of his own where gaps had to be filled. Fortune then edited and translated the collection, and made extensive annotations to both the originals and the translated versions. His introductory essay also provides a useful contextual setting for an appreciation of praise poems and their role in Shona society. In an earlier paper Fortune analysed the ways in which Shona poetry changed over time: see 'Shona traditional poetry', *Zambezia*, vol. 2, no. 1 (1971) p. 41-60.

781 **Poetry in Rhodesia.**
R. Graham. *Zambezia*, vol. 6, no. 2 (1978), p. 187-215.

Covering the period 1900-78 this study of poetry in Rhodesia covers a wide range of styles from settler poetry to African protest poetry.

782 **And now the poets speak.**
Compiled by Muderveri Kadhani, Musaemura Zimunya. Gweru, Zimbabwe: Mambo Press, 1981. 178p.

This is a collection of poems in English by black Zimbabweans on the war of liberation, and the continuing struggle for equality and justice. It resulted from a call, shortly after independence, for poems on the 'revolution' which elicited a huge response, and includes poems by Canaan Banana, the country's first President, and Zimunya, one of Zimbabwe's best known poets.

783 **New writing in Rhodesia.**
Compiled and introduced by T. Mcloughlin. Gweru: Mambo Press, 1976. 246p.

This selection of poems, short stories and drama contains the work of African writers from the late 1960s and early 1970s. Many of the poems had previously been published in *Two Tone*, a Rhodesian poetry magazine.

784 **Insights: criticism of Zimbabwean and other poetry.**
T. O. Mcloughlin, F. R. Mhonyera.   Gweru: Mambo Press, 1984.
132p.

This book is aimed at a student market. It discusses and analyses Zimbabwean poetry, and provides information and guidance for students on the practice of poetry analysis.

785 **Zimbabwean poetry in English: an anthology.**
Compiled and introduced by K. Z. Muchemwa.   Gwelo: Mambo
Press, 1978. 150p.

This is a popular anthology of selected poems by African writers from the time of the first contact with the English, up to 1978. The compiler charts the broad outlines of the history of this poetry. He establishes two major periods of thematic and stylistic development in African poetry: 1950-68 and from 1968 onwards. The quality of the poetry in the second period is generally far higher and includes work by Chinodya.

786 **Mambo book of Zimbabwean verse in English.**
Colin Style, O-lan Style.   Gweru: Mambo Press, 1986. 417p.

This is an important contribution to the study of poetry from Zimbabwe, which took sixteen years to compile and publish. The authors have brought together a major collection of poems, divided into two sections. The first comprises traditional Shona and Ndebele poems in translation, and the second an anthology of English verse by more than eighty poets of all races. This anthology is organized into three periods: before 1950, 1950 to 1972 and 1973 to the mid-1980s. There is also an introductory essay which discusses the collection and the development of Zimbabwean poetry, and the contribution of two local poetry journals, *Two Tone* and *Zimbabwean Poetry*.

787 **Patterns of poetry in Zimbabwe.**
Flora Wild.   Gweru: Mambo Press, 1988. 152p.

Seven major Zimbabwean poets are featured in this book, which reproduces a selection of their poetry and provides a critical assessment of each work. The poets covered are Hove, Zimunya, Mungoshi, Seyaseya, Rungano, Chimedza and Marechera.

788 **Thought tracks.**
Musaemura Bonas Zimunya.   Harlow, England: Longman, 1982.
132p.

This collection of Zimunya's poetry addresses a number of different themes. The liberation war is an important topic, and there are also poems on the Zimbabwe ruins and other images of Zimbabwe. Zimunya is a lecturer in English at the University of Zimbabwe, and an important local poet. Another collection of his poems which is divided into rural and urban themes is *Country dawn and city lights* (Harare: Longman Zimbabwe, 1985). He has also contributed to the debate on the one-party state (see item 417).

Gold regions of Southeastern Africa.
See item no. 122 (vol. 6).

Young women in the liberation struggle: stories and poems from Zimbabwe.
See item no. 750.

Mindblast; or the definitive buddy.
See item no. 762.

Zimbabwe: prose and poetry.
See item no. 766.

The Arts

789 **The soul of mbira: music and traditions of the Shona people of Zimbabwe.**
Paul F. Berliner.   Los Angeles, Berkeley, California: University of California Press, 1981. 312p.

This is a thorough study of the mbira and mbira music, which is firmly located within the context of broader cultural issues. The mbira became one of the symbols of African nationalism, when the Rhodesian government tried to prevent it being played. Many technical details are discussed, in fairly non-technical language. The musical selections discussed are keyed to field recordings which are available on record as *The soul of mbira: Shona mbira music* (New York: Nonesuch Records). The author is Professor of Ethnomusicology at Northwestern University, Massachusetts. He not only plays the mbira, but has performed at spirit possession ceremonies. The book contains an appendix on building and playing a Shona karimba. A short, and more technical piece on the mbira is Andrew Tracey, 'The original African mbira?', *African Music Society Journal*, vol. 5, no. 2 (1972), p. 85-104.

790 **Trends in Zimbabwean theatre since 1980.**
Stephen Chifunyise.   *Journal of Southern African Studies*, vol. 16, no. 2 (1990), p. 276-89.

There has been tremendous growth in theatre in the post-independence era. Much of this has been in small-scale productions, at the grass-roots level. Drama is also often used for educational purposes. The author discusses this growth and analyses the nature of new drama. He also indicates that the media have generally not responded positively to the new directions in theatre.

791 **A guide to the rock art of Rhodesia.**
C. K. Cooke.   Salisbury: Longman Rhodesia, 1974. 64p.

This guide is intended for the tourist, rather than the serious student of rock art. The rock paintings and caves described have been chosen for their accessibility from major urban centres, rather than their artistic merit, and those deep in the communal areas were omitted. Twenty-two caves and shelters are described, by region, with details on how to get to them. There are photographs to illustrate the art in each cave. A more detailed and scholarly approach is found in Cooke's volume, *Rock art of Southern Africa* (Cape Town: Books of Africa; San Francisco, California: Tri-Ocean Books, 1969), which discusses over 1500 sites, most of them in Zimbabwe.

792 Shona male and female artistry.

W. J. Dewey. *African Arts*, vol. 19, no. 3 (1986), p. 64-73.

This paper discusses the different material culture artefacts made by Shona men and women. Male artists, who routinely claim to be inspired by dreams, tend to make artefacts connected with ritual. Women's artefacts are not for ritual purposes, and they believe that their ability is inherited, self-taught or learnt from relatives.

793 The material culture of Zimbabwe.

H. Ellert. Harare: Longman Zimbabwe; Harare: Sam Gozo, 1984. 133p.

This book discusses selected types of material culture in Zimbabwe. It deals mainly with artefacts in daily use, either in the past or the present. Details are provided on golden artefacts, houses, wooden craftwork, weapons and tools, musical instruments, pre-colonial textiles, pottery and ceramics, basketware and allied craftwork, traps and hunting equipment, pipes and smoking, games and pastimes, and the ndoro: the flattened whorl of a mollusc shell which traditionally symbolized wealth and authority. The book does not cover clothes, charms, soapstone carvings and body ornamentation.

794 The painted caves: an introduction to the prehistoric art of Zimbabwe.

Peter Garlake. Harare: Modus Publications, 1987. 100p.

This is an excellent guide to the rock art of Zimbabwe, which is designed for the layman, but goes beyond the merely descriptive. Garlake explains the history and technology of rock painting, and the symbolic conventions adopted by this art form. From this he provides an interpretation of the paintings, and discusses the most common themes denoted by them. A catalogue of the main caves and their art is provided, and directions to the sites.

795 Mental colonisation or catharsis? Theatre, democracy and cultural struggle from Rhodesia to Zimbabwe.

Preben Kaarsholm. *Journal of Southern African Studies*, vol. 16, no. 2 (1990), p. 246-75.

The contribution of drama to socio-political developments before and after independence is discussed in this paper. The increase in the production of community-based theatre is described, and the role of the Zimbabwe Foundation for Education with Production is considered. This private organization has been active in promoting grassroots theatre which can play an important part in education.

796 **Shona urban music: a process which maintains traditional values.**

Robert Kaufmann. In: *Urban man in Southern Africa*. Edited by Clive Kileff, W. Pendleton. Gweru: Mambo Press, 1975, p. 127-44.

As the title suggests, in this article the author argues that the playing of Shona music in the urban areas has helped to perpetuate traditional cultural values amongst Shona urban residents. The music has not however remained static, and the discussion includes consideration of the way in which new elements have been absorbed into the music. Types of music discussed include mbira, drums, jazz guitar, and early rock music.

797 **Shona sculpture.**

Fernando Mor. Harare: Fernando Mor, 1987. 160p.

In the 1980s Shona sculpture became one of the most important forms of sculpture in the world. This volume, written by Mor whilst he was Italian Ambassador to Zimbabwe, introduces the art form and its practitioners to the foreign public. The analysis includes an account of its historical and cultural relevance (although the history is sometimes inaccurate), descriptions of the sculptures' aesthetic qualities and the artists' motivations, with short biographies of some of the sculptors. The book is illustrated with 100 colour plates. Other writings on the same topic include J. Kuhn, *Myth and magic: the art of the Shona of Zimbabwe* (Cape Town: D. Nelson, 1978) and M. I. Arnold, *Zimbabwe stone sculptures* (Bulawayo, Zimbabwe: Books of Zimbabwe, 1981). Arnold has also written relevant essay reviews: see 'Shona sculpture', *Zambezia*, vol. 7 (1979), p. 111-14, and 'Contrasting views of Shona sculpture', *Zambezia*, vol. 10 (1982), p. 49-57.

798 **Songs that won the liberation war.**

Alec J. C. Pongweni. Harare: College Press, [1983]. 166p.

Song has been an important cultural element in the liberation movements of Southern Africa. This is a scholarly study of songs associated with the struggle for independence in Zimbabwe by a lecturer in English at the University of Zimbabwe. The text of each song is reproduced in the original language, and also in English. The author provides a discussion of each song and its message and role, and categorizes them into groups such as conscientization songs which aim to heighten political consciousness, and appeals to ancestral spirits. The introduction on the changing role of song in Zimbabwean culture, and on common song structures and themes, provides a guide to a deeper appreciation of this medium. On similar themes, see P. Berliner, 'Political sentiments in Shona song and oral literature', *Essays in Art and Science*, vol. 6, no. 1 (1977), p. 1-29, and Jessica Sherman, 'Songs of Chimurenga', *African Perspectives*, vol. 16 (1980), p. 80-88.

799 **African ingenuity: a description of a toy motor car made from scrap wire by an unknown African child.**

A. P. D. Thomson. *NADA*, vol. 9, no. 4 (1967), p. 10-14.

The wire toys made by African children in Zimbabwe are familiar to anyone who has visited the country, and they are now also produced for a mainly European handicraft market. As the title of this paper suggests, they are most ingenious in their use of locally available, often scrap, materials and are often complex in their manufacture, with moving parts. The article describes one of these toys and includes illustrations.

800 **Roots rocking in Zimbabwe.**
Fred Zindi. Gweru: Mambo Press, 1985. 98p.

Zimbabwean rock music has been one of the country's most successful exports in recent years, with an appreciative international audience for the music of local musicians like the Bundu Boys, and Thomas Mapfumo. This book describes the development of contemporary music in Zimbabwe, from the beginnings of recorded music in the country in the early 1950s, to 1985. Zindi maintains that traditional music was only revived by the efforts of artists like Mapfumo in the early 1970s. An in-depth profile of Mapfumo is included, as well as biographies and interviews with other musicians. The author is a writer and recording artist.

801 **Zimbabwean drama: a study of Shona and English plays.**
R. M. Zinyemba. Gweru: Mambo Press, 1986. 112p.

A study of the growth and development of Zimbabwean drama. Dramatic expression is rooted in Shona society, and its social relevance is examined here. Different types of drama are discussed, including religious plays, comedies, and tragedies, as well as political satire. Many examples from local plays are used to illustrate the points made.

Zimbabwe: a land divided.
See item no. 8.

The story of REPS: the history of Salisbury's repertory players 1931-75.
See item no. 802.

The history of Rhodesian entertainment 1890-1930.
See item no. 805.

Sports and Recreation

802 **The story of REPS: the history of Salisbury's repertory players 1931-75.**
Robert Cary.   Salisbury: Galaxie Press, 1975. 240p.

The 500-seater REPS theatre is housed in a shopping centre close to the University of Zimbabwe. The company of players and the plays they produced catered almost exclusively to the white population during the period covered, and to some extent this remains true today. This account of the history of REPS is anecdotal in style, and littered with comments about white personalities and the snobbery of theatre-goers. There is a listing of all the plays REPS had produced by 1975, and their authors, producers and leading performers.

803 **Outdoor recreational patterns and preferences amongst the residents of Harare, Zimbabwe.**
Graham Child, Robin Heath.   Harare: University of Zimbabwe Publications, 1989. 95p. (Supplement to *Zambezia: Journal of the University of Zimbabwe*).

This book details the results of the Harare sample of a wider national survey on recreational preferences, which is intended to help in the planning of future tourism facilities. Discussion of the general survey is found in Robin Heath, 'The national survey of outdoor recreation in Zimbabwe', *Zambezia*, vol. 13 (1986), p. 25-42. An earlier study of white recreational patterns in Salisbury is P. A. Hardwick's *Aspects of recreation amongst Salisbury's non-African population* (Salisbury: University of Rhodesia, 1978. [Supplement to *Zambezia*]).

804 **The story of Rhodesian sport: Volume 1889-1935.**
J. de L. Thompson, foreword by Ian Smith.   Bulawayo: Books of Rhodesia, 1976. 423p. (Reproduction of *A history of sport in Southern Rhodesia, Volume 1*).

This history and guide to sport in colonial Rhodesia is reprinted from a study published in 1935. Two further volumes were meant to bring the history up-to-date, but they have not yet appeared. The coverage is unfortunately very Eurocentric, with no mention of any African sport. Even soccer is excluded. However polo, cricket, rugby, game fishing and similarly popular white activities are covered in detail.

805 **The history of Rhodesian entertainment 1890-1930.**
Charles T. C. Taylor. Salisbury: M. O. Collins, 1968. 186p.

This is a largely anecdotal treatment of evening entertainments geared to a mainly white audience which developed from 1890 onwards. The main type of productions were theatrical, and often amateur. The author, who lived in Rhodesia from 1927, was chairman of the Southern Rhodesian Drama Association for several years.

806 **Gardening in Zimbabwe: a comprehensive guide to gardening in Zimbabwe.**
Philip Wood. Harare: Modus Publications, 1989. 3rd ed. 200p.

This volume provides detailed information on gardens and gardening, with sections on different features such as shrubs, flowers and lawns.

Handbook and guide to Rhodesian waters.
See item no. 31.

'Good boys', footballers, and strikers: African social change in Bulawayo, 1933-53.
See item no. 158.

Libraries, Museums and Archives

807 **Guide to the historical manuscripts in the National Archives of Rhodesia.**
T. W. Baxter, E. E. Burke. Salisbury: National Archives of Rhodesia, 1970. 262p.

The National Archives are the outstanding reference source for historical research on Zimbabwe. They are the major repository for official records from the colonial era as well as more modern documents. Cape Town, Oxford and London also hold less important collections. This guide provides some analysis and description of the historical collection prior to 1970. Baxter also produced a general guide to documents from the British South Africa Company period, *Guide to the Public Archives of Rhodesia, 1890-1923. Vol. 1.* (Salisbury: National Archives of Rhodesia, 1969), which updated V. W. Hiller, *A guide to the public records of Southern Rhodesia under the régime of the British South Africa Company, 1890-1923* (Cape Town: Central African Archives and Longmans Green, 1956). Also by Hiller, *Central African archives: an historical account, 1935-47, for Southern and Northern Rhodesia and Nyasaland* (Lusaka: Government Printer, 1947) provides a historical analysis of regional archives. J. D. Pearson, Noel Matthews and Doreen M. Wainwright's, *A guide to the manuscripts and documents in the British Isles relating to Africa* (London: Oxford University Press, 1971) is useful for those wishing to trace non-government records in England which are not available in the Public Records Office.

808 **Catalogue of the C. M. Doke collection on African languages in the library of the University of Rhodesia.**
Catalogued and arranged by E. A. Daniels, J. T. Phehane. Boston, Massachusetts: G. K. Hall, 1972. 546p.

Doke was a missionary who travelled widely throughout Southern Africa. He became interested in African languages and amassed a major collection of material on regional languages, as well as publishing a number of articles and books. The collection, excluding Doke's own works, was passed to the University of Rhodesia in 1964. This catalogue of some 7,000 entries covers his collection and his own publications, by author and then by subject.

809 **Directory of libraries in Zimbabwe 1987.**
Compiled by S. R. Dube, R. G. S. Douglas. Harare: National Archives of Zimbabwe, Government Printer, 1987. 28p.
This library directory contains 243 entries and covers four categories of libraries. These are public and subscription libraries, the University of Zimbabwe main and branch libraries, and special government libraries with 'other' special libraries. Each entry provides detailed information including the name of the library, the date of establishment, staff, the authority that runs it, funding sources, hours of opening, how to use it and membership, subject fields covered, numbers of items and collections, the nature of the catalogue and classification system, periodicals taken and co-operative services. Another source on librarians is *Who's Who in librarianship and information work in Zimbabwe*, compiled by B. L. B Mushanga (Harare: Government Library Service, National Archives, 1981).

810 **Libraries and library automation in Zimbabwe: a brief overview.**
Alan Hopkinson. *African Research and Documentation*, vol. 51, (1989), p. 19-22.
This brief article provides an overview of libraries in Zimbabwe, including the libraries of private companies and organizations, and discusses the possibilities for automation.

811 **Rhodesia before 1920.**
National Gallery of Rhodesia and National History Association of Rhodesia. Salisbury: National Gallery of Rhodesia and National History Association of Rhodesia, 1975. [n.p.].
This book was prepared as a guide to a major exhibition of 1500 historical artefacts at the National Gallery in Salisbury. The items exhibited are illustrative of all aspects of the local white economy of that time: agriculture, mining, transport, railways, telecommunications, medicine, education, the army and police, journalism and banking. African culture was only given slight coverage. The text gives a brief history of all the items, and there are many photographs.

812 **Catalogue of the Godlonton collection of Rhodesiana in the library of the University of Rhodesia.**
Compiled by J. T. Phehane. Salisbury: University of Rhodesia, 1972. [n.p.].
The Godlonton collection of Rhodesiana, which has now become the Zimbabweana collection, is a superb reference library, housed in the main library of the University of Zimbabwe in Harare. It endeavours to collect all published work on Rhodesian and Zimbabwean topics, and was a major source of information for this bibliography. Phehane's catalogue is now rather out of date, but is of use in indicating the strength of the collection prior to 1972.

813 **Periodicals in Rhodesian libraries.**
A. L. A. Phillips.   Salisbury: University College of Rhodesia, 1968. [n.p.].

This catalogue details about 5,000 periodical titles held in seventy-two libraries. Periodicals are broadly defined, and include all serial publications, memoirs, year books, and proceedings of academies, government departments and other organizations. Newspapers and reports are excluded. The entries are listed alphabetically.

Mass Media

General

814 Publishing in Zimbabwe.
Laura Czerniewicz. *African Book Publishing Record*, vol. 16, no. 4
(1990), p. 235-38.
This paper provides a brief overview of the book publishing industry in Zimbabwe.

815 None but ourselves: masses versus media in the making of Zimbabwe.
Julie Frederikse, photographs by Biddy Partridge. Harare: Zimbabwe
Publishing House, 1982. 368p.
This well-illustrated volume on the war and Mugabe's electoral success is hard to
categorize, being written in a popular style and yet containing much material of
political significance and research value. By documenting the biassed reporting and
treatment of the black forces involved in the war by the media, and within education, it
attempts to explain why reaction to Mugabe's success was so polarized, with the local
white community and many international agencies stunned by what they had been led
to believe was an unlikely outcome. The text consists of many oral interviews, plus
selections from newspapers and magazines, and appeals to both an academic and
general audience. See also Elaine Windrich, *The mass media in the struggle for
Zimbabwe* (*censorship and propaganda under Rhodesian Front rule*) (Gweru: Mambo
Press, 1981. [Occasional Papers: Socio-economic Series no. 15]), which covers the
period from 1962 to 1979, and *Rhodesia: the propaganda war* (London: Catholic
Institute of International Relations, 1977) by the Catholic Institute of International
Relations.

816 **The Rhodesian press: the history of the Rhodesian printing and publishing company ltd.**
William Daniel Gale. Salisbury: Rhodesian Printing and Publishing Co., 1962. 225p.

In 1962 when this historical account was published, this printing firm was playing a key role in the Southern Rhodesian news media, publishing the *Rhodesia Herald*, *Buluwayo Chronicle*, *Sunday News*, *Sunday Mail* and *Umtali Post*. South Africa's Argus Company, often known as the Argus Group, published Rhodesia's early newspapers, the first being a mimeographed publication produced singlehandedly by Kingsley Fairbridge in 1891. These were sold to the Rhodesian Printing and Publishing Company in 1927, although South African influence in this medium remained very high through shareholdings. This book gives a historical account of the company, detailing all publications and editors up to the 1960s, in the context of social and political developments in the colony. The government now has a controlling interest in the Argus group papers, which are overseen by the Zimbabwe Mass Media Trust.

817 **Reporting Southern Africa: western news agencies reporting from Southern Africa.**
Phil Harris. Paris: UNESCO, 1981. 168p.

This book studies the complex role played by the mass media in response to racist governments in Southern Africa, including Rhodesia. Harris explores the way governments control the news, and the ways in which the media have supported or opposed racism.

818 **Rhodesia: little white island.**
John Parker. London: Pitman, 1972. 166p.

In this book, the author gives a personal account of increasing censorship of the press under the Rhodesian Front during the 1960s. Parker was a journalist who arrived in Rhodesia in 1955, and was imprisoned for a short time during UDI before returning to England. A similar, but very rambling journalistic account of Rhodesian censorship is Eugene Wason's *Banned: African Daily News, Southern Rhodesia 1964* (London: Hamish Hamilston, 1976). Wason was editor of the *African Daily News* in 1964, when it was closed down by the Rhodesian Front for political reasons. Also on censorship in this period is an article by Malcolm Smith, who was editor of the *Rhodesia Herald* from 1963 to 1967, 'Censorship in Rhodesia: the experience of a Salisbury editor', *Round Table* (UK), vol. 59 (Jan. 1969) p. 60-67. A listing of books banned during UDI, which was regularly updated, is *Catalogue of banned books, periodicals, records etc.* (Salisbury: Board of Censors of Rhodesia).

819 **The politics of the mass media: a personal experience.**
E. T. M. Rusike. Harare: Roblaw, 1990. 111p.

This personal account of Zimbabwe's newspapers after independence, and the issue of government interference is written by the former Chief Executive of Zimbabwe Newspapers (which publishes the main dailies), and contains many significant insights into the nature of the media during the 1980s. Unlike many other commentators Rusike is not particularly concerned about the government's financial control of Zimbabwe Newspapers, but is strongly critical of the Ministry of Information's role in the Zimbabwe Mass Media Trust which is presented as a major threat to press freedom. The account includes details of the removal of the editor of the *Bulawayo*

Chronicle which was instrumental in the author's decision to resign from Zimbabwe Newspapers. Rusike was born and educated in Zimbabwe, but moved to Zambia in 1960, becoming a newspaper and radio journalist. He worked in ZANU's publicity and information department in Tanzania and Malawi, and then went to Britain in 1970 where he completed his education at Bristol University. He returned to Rhodesia in 1977 and lectured at the university in political science until independence. He subsequently spent three years with the Public Service Commission, before joining Zimbabwe Newspapers. After his resignation he became Group Managing Director of Modus Publications which publishes the *Financial Gazette*.

Racial conflict in Rhodesia: a socio-historical study.
See item no. 265.

Southern Rhodesia: the effects of a conquest society on education, culture and information.
See item no. 720.

Newspapers, magazines and general periodicals

820 **Beira Corridor Group Bulletin.**
Harare: Beira Corridor Group, May, 1987- . [bimonthly].
The Beira Corridor Group is a private enterprise which promotes the use of the Beira corridor as Zimbabwe's shortest route to the sea. The bulletins report on the security of the corridor, investment in the transport links and port, and the freight carried.

821 **Bulawayo Chronicle.**
Bulawayo: Zimbabwe Newspapers Ltd., 1894- . daily.
The Chronicle is the major daily newspaper after the *Herald*, and in contrast to that paper, is frequently strongly critical of the government, and has had several changes of editor since independence. The other daily is the *Mutare Post*.

822 **Financial Gazette.**
Harare: Modus Publications, 1969- . weekly.
The *Financial Gazette* is one of Zimbabwe's most important newspapers, being independent of government influence. It frequently contains cogent criticism of government policies. It mainly represents the interests of the business sector and commercial farmers, a constituency which is still mainly, but no longer exclusively, white. The *Gazette* provides good coverage of economic issues, and like London's *Financial Times*, is printed on pink paper. It is fairly conservative in its approach to issues. From October 1992 Modus Publications also published a daily newspaper: *The Daily Gazette*.

Mass Media. Newspapers, magazines and general periodicals

823 Horizon.
Harare: Column Width, September, 1991- . monthly.

Horizon was set up by the editorial staff of *Parade* who had resigned in solidarity when their editor, Andy Moyse, was dismissed in 1991. Its format is somewhat similar to that of *Parade*, and it carries many investigative political and social items, along with a range of popular material.

824 The Insider.
Bulawayo: Insider Publications, 1991- . monthly.

This recent broadsheet publication has an independent stance, and has carried some robust investigative journalism.

825 Moto.
Gweru: Mambo Press, May, 1982- . monthly.

Moto is one of Zimbabwe's most successful magazines and contains diverse material, ranging from popular entertainment, short stories and sport to critical political articles, book reviews and international news. There is also good coverage of social, cultural and religious issues. However it has never been quite as politically incisive as *Parade*, and has not attracted the same amount of controversy. A weekly paper called *Moto* appeared throughout 1980 and 1981, and this was originally a Catholic publication which ran from 1959 until 1974 when it was banned by the UDI government.

826 The Outpost: magazine of the Zimbabwe Republic Police.
Harare: Zimbabwe Republic Police, 1911- . bimonthly.

This magazine, containing articles and news relevant to the police force, as well as short stories, was produced throughout most of the colonial period, and has continued in the independence era. It is a potentially useful resource for research, providing an excellent reflection of the attitudes of those involved in law enforcement.

827 Parade.
Harare: Thomsons' Publications, weekly.

Parade is a popular magazine, which like *Moto* carries a wide range of material including popular entertainment, sport and many cultural items. However it has a well-deserved reputation for good political coverage, and is far more analytical and critical than *Moto*. This has led to problems, and in 1991 its editor was sacked. He left with a number of the magazine staff to set up a new magazine, *Horizon*. However *Parade* has retained much of its previous bite and independent stance.

828 Southern African Political and Economic Monthly.
Harare: Southern African Political Economic Series Trust, monthly.

This is a serious, intellectual publication which covers regional political and economic issues from a socialist perspective. It is an excellent source for analysis of both internal events and debates, as well as significant affairs in Zimbabwe's SADCC neighbours. The South African coverage is also very good.

829 **Sunday Mail.**
Harare: Zimbabwe Newspapers Ltd., [1932-]. weekly.
This is the capital city's Sunday paper. Bulawayo's equivalent is the *Sunday News*. Like the three main daily papers, both are owned by Zimbabwe Newspapers Ltd.

830 **Zimbabwe Commercial and Legal Quarterly.**
Harare: Commercial and Legal Publications (Pvt), Oct. 1986- . quarterly.
This periodical contains information and articles directed at the commercial sector, such as commercial opportunities and pertinent legal issues, including recently gazetted legislation and court decisions. A different Zimbabwean company is profiled in each issue, and aid profiles are provided from foreign embassies.

831 **Zimbabwe Herald.**
Harare: Zimbabwe Newspapers Ltd., 1979- . daily.
This is the main national daily newspaper, and is generally regarded as a government newspaper. Its antecedents date back to 1891, when the *Rhodesia Herald* began publication.

832 **Zimbabwe News: official organ of ZANU (PF).**
Harare: Department of Information and Publicity, 1980- . monthly.
This periodical is the official outlet for the ruling party's political viewpoints and policies. Apart from discussions of the political issues of the day, it also contains book reviews and some analysis of international problems – in particular the role of South Africa and apartheid in the region.

833 **Zimbabwe Wildlife.**
Harare: Wildlife Society of Zimbabwe, 1973- . quarterly.
Since the local wildlife is so rich this is a popular local journal which covers the whole range of wildlife issues. The articles are not scholarly in their approach on the whole, but are useful for contemporary information on policy and practice. Reviews of books pertinent to conservation and wildlife issues are also included.

Professional Periodicals

834 **Africa contemporary record: annual survey and documents, 1968-69.**
London; New York: Africana Publishing Company, 1968-69- . annual.
Annual updates on current affairs in African countries are provided in this useful reference source, which utilizes press reports, reproduces significant documents and provides essays on current topics written by authoritative commentators. It is edited by Colin Legum and Marion Doro. Another source for basic reference material, annually updated, is *Africa South of the Sahara* (London: Europa Publications, 1971-). Excellent analysis of current political developments is provided by the fortnightly *Africa Confidential* (London: Miramoor Publications), edited by Patrick Smith, and extracts from newspapers and reports can be found in the *Africa Research Bulletin*, also produced fortnightly.

835 **Central African Journal of Medicine.**
Harare: 1955- . monthly.
This is the main regional periodical for the publication of research on medical issues.

836 **The Farmer.**
Harare: Modern Farming Publications, 1978- . weekly.
This periodical is aimed primarily at the commercial farming sector, and contains both technical and general articles on agricultural topics. It replaces the former *Rhodesian Farmer*.

837 **Journal of Social Development in Africa.**
Harare: School of Social Work, University of Zimbabwe, 1986- . three per annum.
This new journal focusses on social issues in Africa, and has contained many excellent articles on Zimbabwe since it began in 1986.

838   **Journal of Southern African Studies.**
Oxford: Oxford University Press, Oct. 1974- . quarterly.
This important scholarly journal regularly contains academic articles on Zimbabwe, and is particularly strong on historical themes. In the United States of America a similar regionally-focussed journal is the *Journal of Southern African Affairs*.

839   **Kirkia: the Journal of Botany in Zimbabwe.**
Harare: Research and Special Services,
This journal specializes in the botany of Zimbabwe, and carries a variety of articles on topics including African botanical taxonomy, floristics, phytogeography and the history of African botanical exploration.

840   **NADA.**
Salisbury: Ministry of Native Affairs, 1923-1980. annual.
This journal ceased publication at independence, but it is worthy of note because it contained so many articles on culture and ethnography, and the impact of government policy. The contributors were government officials, *NADA* standing for the Native Affairs Department Annual, so the papers were not necessarily academic. The first five volumes were reprinted by Books of Rhodesia, Bulawayo.

841   **Review of the press.**
Oxford: Britain Zimbabwe Society, 1980- . [quarterly].
Although only provided in mimeo format, this regular review of the Zimbabwean press and magazines is currently written by one of the major academic authorities on Zimbabwe, Professor Ranger of Oxford University, and is an extremely valuable reference source. The authorship of the review may change in the near future. It appears three or four times a year, and the topics covered reflect the major issues current in Zimbabwe in the period reviewed. It can be obtained by joining the Britain Zimbabwe Society. Members also receive regular briefings on Zimbabwean coverage in the British newspapers.

842   **Statute Law of Zimbabwe.**
Harare: University of Zimbabwe, 1981- . annual.
This periodical gives details on the laws passed each year, and was previously published as *Statute Law of Rhodesia*. *Statute Law of Southern Rhodesia 1963* (Salisbury: Mardon Rhodesia Printers) detailed all laws in force on, or made before, 30th April 1963.

843   **Zambezia, the Journal of the University of Zimbabwe.**
Harare: University of Zimbabwe Publications Office, 1968- . bi-annual.
This is an important local journal which has a very good record of publishing stimulating and original articles. It publishes on a huge variety of topics, as long as their focus is South Central Africa. It also produces extremely useful scholarly monograph supplements, which are an excellent source for research conducted within the University of Zimbabwe. Up to eight of these supplements are published each year, and they cover the main disciplines of agriculture, commerce, law, education, engineering, humanities, medicine, science, social studies and veterinary science. Not all of these supplements have the same regional focus as the journal however.

Professional Periodicals

844 Zimbabwe Agricultural Journal.
Harare: Research and Special Services Information Services, Ministry of Agriculture, 1980- . bimonthly.

A journal aimed mainly at the commercial farming sector in Zimbabwe, the articles range from the fairly technical to general coverage of new practices. It replaces the *Rhodesia Agricultural Journal* which began publication in 1903. Research and Special Services, a branch of the Minstry of Agriculture, also produce the more technical *Zimbabwe Journal of Agricultural Research* (formerly the *Rhodesian Journal of Agricultural Research*), which covers original research on soil and renewable resources, livestock, crops, forestry, irrigation, hydrology, wildlife and fisheries.

845 Zimbabwe country report.
London: Economist Intelligence Unit, 1993- . quarterly.

The Economist Intelligence Unit's regular publications are a most valuable source for current political events and affairs, and are very strong on economic analysis and data. They are the best extended reference for recent government statistics and forecasts of future economic performance. The current quarterly report devoted to Zimbabwe replaces the previous Zimbabwe-Malawi publication. See also the annual *EIU Country profile: Zimbabwe* (1980-). These are both currently written by Colin Stoneman.

846 Zimbabwe Journal of Economics.
Harare: Zimbabwe Economics Society, 1984- . irregular.

This journal recommenced publication in July 1984, although some volumes had come out before independence. It replaced the *Rhodesian Journal of Economics* which was published quarterly from 1967 to 1976. Prior to that time, the Rhodesian Economics Society published annual proceedings for the years 1959-66. The present journal is dedicated to the discussion of indigenously generated economic issues relevant to development problems in Zimbabwe and Southern Africa in particular, and to developing countries in general. However it has not been published for some time.

847 Zimbabwe Science News: Journal of the Zimbabwe Science Association.
Harare: Zimbabwe Science Association, 1980- . quarterly.

This is an invaluable source on local scientific endeavour and technical material and research. Its scope includes agricultural technology and research, wildlife issues, geology, climatology, ecology, technology and development issues with technical components. It replaced the *Rhodesian Science News* which was published from 1967-79, and the *Zimbabwe-Rhodesia Science News* which ran from 1979-1980. The Zimbabwe Science Association also publishes the *Transactions of the Zimbabwe Science Association*, which has an even longer history since its fore-runners were the *Proceedings of the Rhodesian Science Association* 1899-1960, and the *Proceedings and Transactions of the Rhodesian Science Association 1960-1980*. In its present format the *Transactions* are a series of monographs on special scientific issues.

848 Zimbabwean History: journal of the Historical Association of Zimbabwe.
Harare: Historical Association of Zimbabwe, 1979-81. irregular.

This journal continued from the important and scholarly *Rhodesian History* which published many important articles on local and regional history.

849 **Zimbabwean Journal of Educational Research.**
Harare: University of Zimbabwe, Human Resources Research Centre, 1989- . three times a year.

This journal contains scholarly articles on research findings and policy related to the human resource sector in sub-Saharan Africa. Each volume also carries sections on research in progress in the region, research organizations, and coverage of literary sources. The first issue of each year is devoted to a special topic. Outside Zimbabwe the journal is distributed by Florida State University Learning Systems Institute.

Zimbabwe national bibliography.
See item no. 879.

Encyclopaedias and Directories

850 **A concise encyclopedia of Zimbabwe.**
Edited by Denis Berens, in association with Donatus Bonde and Albert Bruno Plangger. Gweru, Zimbabwe: Mambo Press, 1988. 444p.

This recent encyclopaedia contains broad coverage of standard themes: flora, fauna, history and geography, religion and culture, economics, politics and social life. There are also eight articles focussing on churches, education, international relations, law, literature, publishing, sports and trade unionism. Living personalities, with the exception of political leaders, are not covered. Some statistical tables are included.

851 **Zimbabwe: a handbook.**
John House, Margaret House, with illustrations by Sylvia Bird. Harare: Mercury Press, 1983. 164p.

This general handbook provides introductory coverage of economic, political and social issues, but is less useful than the *Tabex Encyclopedia* (see item 854). Another introductory book is Patricia Cheney's *The land and people of Zimbabwe* (New York: Lippincott, [1990]. [Portraits of the Nations Series]). This assesses economic and social service changes since independence in relation to stated national goals, as well as providing some information on geography, history, culture and the arts. It is presented in a glossy format, but is too insubstantial to be of much use.

852 **Women's organizations in Zimbabwe.**
Olivia N. Muchena. Salisbury: Centre for Applied Social Sciences, University of Zimbabwe, 1980. 34p.

Muchena provides a listing of women's organizations in Zimbabwe at independence, and discusses their activities, and how these might be enhanced.

853 **Zimbabwe NGO activities.**
Compiled and edited by Anna C. Mupawaende, Joyce Kazemba,
Claudette Monteiro, Anni Holmes, Jester Tshuma. Harare:
Zimbabwe NGO Co-ordinating Committee, 1985. 27p.

This book details the activities and addresses of twenty-four non-governmental
organizations in Zimbabwe during the UN Decade for Women 1976-85. Particular
reference is therefore made to NGOS related to women.

854 **Tabex Encyclopedia Zimbabwe.**
Harare: Quest Publishing, 1987. 431p.

This is a very thorough encyclopaedic treatment of Zimbabwe, which was sponsored by
Tabex, the leading locally-owned group of tobacco purchasing and processing
companies. Its coverage includes settlements, flora, fauna, minerals, economic sectors,
major companies and parastatals, places of interest, sport, and organizations in
Zimbabwe. People with 'international reputations' or who had a significant role in the
country's history and development are also covered, although few of the pre-
independence politicians are mentioned. It is the best local encyclopaedia available.

855 **The Rhodesian stamp catalogue.**
Rhodesian Philatelic Agency. Salisbury: Rhodesian Philatelic
Agency, 1975. 118p.

This publication is aimed at the serious philatelist, and provides comprehensive
information on all stamps issued in Rhodesia from 1892 to 1975. The stamps of
Northern Rhodesia from 1925-63 are also covered.

856 **Zimbabwe directory of development consultants.**
Swedish International Development Authority. Harare: ZI
Publications in association with Nehanda Publishers, 1989. 186p.

This is the first attempt to publish a list of consultants on Zimbabwe. It concentrates on
consultants based in Zimbabwe, but some in neighbouring SADCC countries are also
listed. The directory covers consultancy firms, consultants within them and individual
consultants who are freelance or employed in agencies.

857 **Catalogue of the parliamentary papers of Southern Rhodesia and
Rhodesia, 1954-70.**
Norman Wilding. Salisbury: University College of Rhodesia,
Department of Political Science, 1970. 161p.

Guidance on and a listing of parliamentary papers for research purposes are included
in this catalogue. It is the first part of a two-part publication, the second part covering
the papers for the Federation of Rhodesia and Nyasaland, 1954-63. The catalogue is
indexed by institution, and individuals. For the period prior to 1954 see Francis M. G.
Willson and Gloria C. Passmore, *Catalogue of the parliamentary papers of Southern
Rhodesia, 1899-1953* (Salisbury: University College of Rhodesia, Department of
Political Science, 1965).

858　**1983 non-government schools and colleges address list.**
Zimbabwe Government.　Harare: Ministry of Education and Culture,
1983. 138p.

This publication lists all non-government schools and colleges alphabetically, by region
and type of school, as of 1983.

VOICE directory of social services in Zimbabwe 1983.
See item no. 345.

Consolidated index to the Zimbabwean law reports, 1964-83.
See item no. 425.

Spectrum guide to Zimbabwe.
See item no. 483.

Zimbabwe agricultural and economic review.
See item no. 491.

Doing business in Zimbabwe.
See item no. 495.

Directory of co-operative products and services: Zimbabwe.
See item no. 518.

Directory of libraries in Zimbabwe 1987.
See item no. 809.

Bibliographies

859 **Zimbabwean periodicals: a bibliography.**
Pamela Barry.   Harare: National Archives, 1988. 56p. (National
Archives of Zimbabwe. Bibliographical Series, no. 4).
This is the best guide to periodicals produced in Zimbabwe. Entries are listed
according to the Dewey Decimal Classification system, and indexed by subject, and
author or title. Government publications are indexed separately.

860 **Zimbabwe: history, politics, economics, society: a selected bibliography.**
Goswin Baumhögger, with the assistance of Andrea Kersebaum,
Reiner Rademache and Ulf Engel.   Hamburg: Institute of African
Studies, African Documentation Centre, 1984. 266p.
This bibliography covers selected publications on Zimbabwe in English and German
for the period 1970-84. There is a total of 1665 entries of mongraphs, periodical
articles, contributions to collected works, and non-conventional literature. Thirty-six
title entries of annual or more frequently published periodicals which contain material
on Zimbabwe are also included. Theses and dissertations are not covered. Short
annotations in German are provided. The main criteria for entries are that the items
had been indexed by the African Documentation Centre, and that the item should be
available in libraries in the former West Germany, usually the library of Hamburg's
Institute of African Studies. Another selected bibliography on Rhodesian politics,
economics and social change which covers the period 1953-76, and details books,
articles and documents, is 'Bibliography on Rhodesia', *Africana Journal* (New York),
vol. 9, no. 1 (1978), p. 5-42 and vol. 9, no. 2 (1978) p. 101-12, by Patrick O'Meara and
Jean Gosebrink.

861 **Bibliography of African law with special reference to Rhodesia.**
T. W. Bennett, Sally Phillips. Salisbury: University of Rhodesia, 1975. 291p. (Library Bibliographical Series, no. 4).
This is a major reference for sources on African law up to the mid-1970s, compiled by a lecturer in the law department and the law librarian at the University of Rhodesia. It contains 1,579 entries and is indexed by author.

862 **Bibliography on peoples of Zimbabwe.**
Michael F. C. Bourdillon, Angela Cheater. Harare: Department of Sociology, University of Zimbabwe, 1983. Computer database and printout.
This bibliography is computerized and has been prepared by two of the principle lecturers in the Department of Sociology at the University of Zimbabwe.

863 **Southern Rhodesia: bibliography. The development of Southern Rhodesia from the earliest times to the year 1900.**
Olive Carpenter. Cape Town: School of Librarianship, University of Cape Town, 1946. 18p.
Of particular interest to those researching pre-colonial topics on Zimbabwe, this bibliography surveys books and journal articles on the pre-1900 period. It also includes references to some British parliamentary papers on settlement in Rhodesia at the very end of the era covered. The bibliography is organized by historical period, with items arranged alphabetically by author.

864 **An archaeological bibliography of Rhodesia from 1874.**
Compiled by Cranmer Kenrick Cooke, on behalf of Commission for preservation of natural and historical monuments and relics. Salisbury: Historical Monuments Commission, [1969].
This is an update of an earlier archaeological bibliography by Roger Summer and Cranmer Cooke, published in 1959. The entries are listed in alphabetical order by author.

865 **Rhodesia/Zimbabwe. A bibliographic guide to the nationalist period.**
Marion E. Doro. Boston, Massachusetts: G.K. Hall, 1984. 247p.
This is a significant and well-researched work, which is of immense value to scholars. It provides an excellent guide to research resources and themes relating to African nationalism from 1960 to 1980, and the socio-economic conditions of the pre-1960 period. The author holds the Chair of the Department of Government at Connecticut College, USA. The research for this bibliography was conducted in libraries in London, Oxford, Zimbabwe and America. The references include books, many journal entries, government documents such as US congressional hearings and House of Commons debates, magazines, and papers. Some of the major entries are annotated. There is extensive discussion of the nature of the sources on Africa and Rhodesia. This is followed by sections on the socio-economic and political context, history and peoples, UDI and the search for a settlement, and US foreign policy. Useful appendices include details on the independence election results, economic indices in 1970, and African franchise qualifications in 1970.

866   **Zimbabwean political materials published in exile, 1959-80: a bibliography.**
Compiled by I. J. Johnstone.   Harare: National Archives, 1987. 31p.
(National Archives of Zimbabwe Bibliographical Series, no. 3).

This is an important bibliographical source for historical research on Zimbabwean politics and the liberation struggle, covering material produced by Zimbabweans, or solidarity movements for Zimbabwe, which was not available within the country and is therefore not necessarily in the national archives. The bibliography covers letters, poems, memoranda, reports, speeches, broadcasts, posters, tapes, records, photographs, and some oral history where there are transcripts of interviews, with information on where the material can be found if it is not in the archives. Full-scale books are not included, nor articles by Zimbabweans in non-Zimbabwean serials and monographs. Particularly significant broadsheets are covered. The main bibliography is divided into three sections: pamphlets and leaflets, serials, and posters and miscellaneous, and there are two appendices on unverified publications and bogus publications such as enemy propaganda. It includes an index of names and organizations.

867   **Federalism in Rhodesia and Nyasaland.**
J. Gus Liebenow, Robert I. Rotberg. In: *Federalism in the Commonwealth: a bibliographical commentary*. Edited by W. W. Livingston.   London: Cassell, 1963, p. 193-222.

This annotated bibliography on the Federation of Rhodesia and Nyasaland focusses particularly on items for historians and political scientists and covers the literature up to 1961.

868   **Women in Zimbabwe: an annotated bibliography.**
Eve Macnamara.   Harare: Department of Sociology, University of Zimbabwe, 1989. 170p.

This is an absolutely invaluable research tool for any student of women's issues in Zimbabwe. There are 671 entries drawn from books, journals, maganzines, government publications and University and consultancy reports. Only a few of the entries are annotated, and these only briefly. All of the entries are post-independence publications. The scope of the material is very wide, from agriculture to sexuality to women's identity, and items do not have to be specifically on women to be included, as long as they are of some relevance. The contents are organized alphabetically by broad subject categories, and there are author and subject indexes.

869   **A selected bibliography of agricultural extension and agricultural education publications in Zimbabwe.**
D. S. McClymont.   Harare: Institute of Adult Education, University of Zimbabwe, 1981.

This bibliography covers selected publications on agricultural extension and education from 1903 to 1980. In part one these are listed alphabetically by author; in part two the listing is by year of publication sub-divided into five categories: agricultural education and training; general extension articles; extension methods, theory and background; extension policy and management; and extension research.

870 **Women and development in Zimbabwe: an annotated bibliography.**
Olivia N. Muchena. Addis Ababa: United Nations Economic
Commission for Africa, ATRCW, 1984. 50p. (Bibliographic Series,
no. 9).

This bibliography will be of interest to those doing research on women in Zimbabwe. It
is categorized by subject area, and then listed in alphabetical order. The topics covered
are socio-economic conditions for women in rural and urban areas, law, organizations,
education, health, politics and religion. There is an interesting sample of newspaper
articles on women for the period January 1980 to December 1982, a time when the
public debate on women's emancipation in Zimbabwe was at its most fierce.

871 **Rhodesia and international law: a bibliography.**
S. Phillips. *Rhodesian Law Journal*, vol. 17, no. 2 (1972), p. 126-32.

This bibliography deals with publications on issues raised by Rhodesia's illegal
declaration of independence under international law.

872 **Rhodesian literature in English: a bibliography 1890-1974/5.**
J. Pichanick, A. J. Chennells, L. B. Rix. Gweru: Mambo Press, 1977.
249p.

This is the most useful and comprehensive bibliography on this type of literature,
although its coverage ends in 1975. The items covered include novels, short stories,
verse and drama. Biographies, autobiographies, history, reportage and polemic are
excluded. There is a flexible approach to what is considered 'Rhodesian'. For novels
the authors include all fiction published in the country, plus those set, or substantially
set, in Rhodesia. In addition novels by authors of Rhodesian birth are included, unless
they have an international reputation (for example, Doris Lessing), in which case only
those works with a local setting or theme are covered. Only published plays are
mentioned. For the other items the authors searched all locally published periodicals,
except daily and weekly newspapers, plus newsletters and school magazines.

873 **Rhodesia/Zimbabwe: an international bibliography.**
Oliver B. Pollak, Karen Pollak. Boston, Massachusetts: G. K. Hall,
1977. 621p.

This is the major bibliographic work on Zimbabwe for literature up to the mid-1970s.
It contains more than 11,000 items, including books, articles within books, theses and
journal articles. It is multidisciplinary in scope, covering anthropology, ethnology,
religion, sociology, economics, communications, education, fine arts, geography,
history, natural science, political science, and international relations. Items in English,
French, German, Russian and Portuguese are covered, with a few items in some other
languages. Works are organized by subject, with an author index. Excellent
information is provided on bibliographic sources for the study of Zimbabwe, and a
very significant listing of research sources such as bibliographies, periodicals, surveys
and catalogues is included. The authors also wrote the forerunner to this bibliography,
Rhodesia/Zimbabwe (Oxford; Santa Barbara, California: Clio Press, 1979. [World
Bibliographical Series, volume 4]).

874 **From Rhodesia to Zimbabwe: low income housing for Blacks in Salisbury.**
Diana Seager. *Current Bibliography on African Affairs*, vol. 12, no. 3 (1979-80), 313-28.

This bibliography covers publications on low-income housing in Salisbury prior to independence.

875 **Education in Zimbabwe: a bibliography of some major recent publications, reports and other references.**
Michael Sinclair. *Issue: a Quarterly Journal of Africanist Opinion*, vol. 3/4, (1981), p. 64-67.

This is a brief bibliography of sources on education in Rhodesia and early independent Zimbabwe.

876 **Rhodesian geology: a bibliography and brief index to 1968.**
Craig C. Smith, H. E. van der Hyde. Salisbury: Trustees of the National Museum of Rhodesia, 1971. 252p.

The major bibliography available on Zimbabwean geology and mining, although it is now outdated. It contains references to hundreds of books, articles and theses.

877 **Zimbabwean culture: a bibliography.**
Patricia Stevens. Cape Town: School of Librarianship, University of Cape Town, 1950. 47p.

This interesting bibliography aimed to provide comprehensive coverage of publications in English on 'extinct Zimbabwean civilization'. In particular it attempts to assemble literature arising from controversy, such as the Great Zimbabwe controversy. It does not focus only on that civilization and related and comparative material is included. Unfortunately no books or manuscripts from the early Portuguese writers are included, but some in other languages are covered. The bibliography is divided into two parts: the Zimbabwe complex, and Portuguese occupation of Southeast Africa and Monomotapa.

878 **A bibliography of the birds of Rhodesia 1873-1977.**
Michael P. Stuart-Irwin. Salisbury: Rhodesian Ornithological Society, 1978. 241p.

This survey of literature on Rhodesian birdlife is extremely thorough and comprehensive. The material is arranged by family of bird, and then alphabetically by author.

879 **Zimbabwe National Bibliography.**
Harare: National Archives, 1979- . annual.

Under the terms of the Printed Publications Act 1975 one copy of every work published in the country must be deposited in the National Archives in Harare, and this bibliography lists every item thus received in the archives. It includes all books, pamphlets, maps and first issues of new serials such as newspapers and periodicals. The archives contain the bulk of official records relating to the history of Zimbabwe. The citations are arranged according to the Dewey Decimal system, and there are author, title, and publisher indexes. It also lists all government publications. This bibliography replaced the annual *Rhodesia national bibliography* which covered the years 1967-1978, and the *List of publications deposited in the library of the National Archives* which was produced from 1961-1966, both with similar coverage and organization of material, and published by the National Archives. Earlier works are listed in *Rhodesia national bibliography 1890-1930*, compiled by Anne Hartridge (Salisbury: National Archives, 1977) which not only lists the Archives' collections for that period, but also the Rhodesiana collections of the University of Rhodesia, the parliamentary library, the National Free Library of Rhodesia in Bulawayo, and two other legal deposit libraries. Another bibliography covering the period 1930-61 was planned, but this has not yet appeared. Another bibliography with good coverage of early works on Rhodesia is *Rhodesiana library* (Umtali: [n.p.], 1956), which catalogues all the collections of the Rhodesiana library. Items are listed by topic, and although this is a slim volume it contains many interesting historical items.

Historical dictionary of Zimbabwe.
See item no. 3.

A short history and annotated bibliography on soil and water conservation in Zimbabwe.
See item no. 43.

Indexes

There follow three separate indexes: authors (personal and corporate); titles; and subjects. Title entries are italicized and refer either to the main titles, or to other works cited in the annotations. with the exception of journal articles. The numbers refer to bibliographic entries, not to pages.

Index of Authors

A

Abbott, S. C. 579
Abel, N. 594, 621
Abraham, D. P. 106, 115
Adams, J. 674
Adams, R. 544
Addison, J. 342
Adhikari, R. 501
Advisory Committee of the University 727
Africa Watch 397
Afshar, H. 348
Agere, S. 330, 417, 454
Akwabi-Ameyaw, K. 568
Alderson, E. A. H. 122
Alexander, J. 569
Allighan, G. 169
Alpers. E. A. 115
Altbach, P. 730
Aluko, O. 470
Amin, M. 57
Amin, N. 327
Amis, P. 547
Anderson, D. 87
Andrews, C. F. 304
Aquina , Sister Mary
  see Weinrich, A. K. H.
Ardenes, S. 357
Armstrong, A. 420, 431
Armstrong, P. 197
Arnold, G 188
Arnold, M. I. 797

Arnold, W. E. 639
Arrighi, G. 14, 481-82
Aschwanden, H. 233-34
Ascough, W. J. 738
Ashton, H. 370
Asian Association 260
Askes, J. 662
Astrow, A. 14, 414, 417, 419
Atkinson, N. 284, 711
Atmore, A. 121
Atwell, C. A. M. 35
Auret, D. 1
Austin, R. 261
Aylen, D. 34

B

Back, J. H. P. 421
Bailey, M. 187
Baines, T. 122
Baker, B. 70
Baker, C. 215, 220, 406
Baker, H. 122, 135
Baker, J. 553, 654
Baker, P. T. 10
Baker, W. J. 158
Bakere, S. 299
Balarin, J. D. 84
Bampton, I. 421
Banana, Canaan Sodindo 398, 415

Barber, J. 5, 171, 467
Barr, F. C. 184
Barrett, D. 280
Barrett, J. 620
Barry, N. 779
Barry, P. 859
Baskin, L. M. 86
Batezat, E. 13, 348, 359
Batson, E. 522
Baumhögger, G. 371, 860
Baxter, A. H. 666
Baxter, T. 100, 807
Beach, D. N. 99, 110-12, 114, 122-23, 139, 146, 284, 295, 765
Beattie, J. H. 296
Beit, A. 130
Bell, M. 622
Bell-Cross, G. 65
Benetta, J-R. 280
Bennet, K. E. 25
Bennett, J. A. 430
Bennett, N. 124
Bennett, T. W. 432, 861
Berens, D. 850
Berkeley, B. 397
Berliner, P. 789, 798
Berlyn, P. 172, 181
Bernardi, B. 305
Bernstein, R. 323
Bessant, L. 628
Best, J. 18
Bethell, A. 122

317

Phillips, A. L. A. 813
Phillips, C. E. 166
Phillips, S. 861, 871
Phillipson, D. W. 56, 95
Phimister, I. R. 13, 43,
    102, 155, 327, 481,
    588, 619, 646, 653,
    687-89
Pichanick, J. 872
Pickard-Cambridge, C. 523
Pinley, E. 71
Pitman, D. 57, 81, 182
Plangger, A. 273, 299
Plowers, D. 70
Pollak, K. 873
Pollak, O. 702-03, 873
Pongweni, A. 274-75, 798
Posselt, F. W. T. 122, 776
Posselt, J. W. 250
Potter, R. B. 523
Pottier, J. 599
Potts, D. 259, 538, 545,
    599, 638
Pratt, C. 167
Preller, G. S. 124
Prescott, J. R. V. 631
Price Waterhouse 495
Priest, C. 72
Prokosch, E. 471
Prothero, R. M. 554, 631
Purves, W. D. 30
Pwiti, G. 96

Q

Quénet, V. 268

R

Radcliffe, K. 90
Raeburn, M. 769, 771
Raftopoulos, B. 417
Rakodi, C. 546
Randall-Maciver, D. 97
Randles, W. G. L. 115
Randolph, R. H. 303
Ranger, T. O. 9, 44, 99,
    102-03, 106, 109, 112,
    114, 135, 139, 156,
    158, 160, 207, 219,
    252, 291, 295, 298-99,
    304, 391, 464, 497,
    563, 770, 841

Ransford, O. 58
Raphael, L. 140
Rasmussen, J. 654
Rasmussen, R. K. 3, 117
Rea, F. 379
Rea, W. F. 277, 290
Redgment, J. 430
Reed, D. 181
Reese, B. 78
Reid-Daly, R. 210
Relf, C. 738
Rennie, J. K. 298, 558
Republic of Zimbabwe 508
Reynolds, N. 552, 721
Reynolds, P. 253
Rhodesian Philatelic
    Agency 855
Rich, T. 174, 220
Richards, H. 122
Richardson, C. 166
Riddell, R. 5, 12, 194, 338,
    496-97, 509, 522, 559,
    655, 722
Rix, L. B. 872
Roberts, N. 622
Roberts, R. S. 452
Robertson, W. 639
Robinson, K. R. 106
Robinson, P. B. 41, 510
Roblaw Publications 483
Roder, W. 560, 610
Rogers, C. A. 329
Rogers, E. W. 722
Rolin, H. 122
Romaya, S. 545
Rorke, M. 122
Rotberg, R. 141, 867
Rouillard, N. 122, 124
Roussos, P. 498
Rubert, S. 3
Rukobo, A. M. 402
Rukuni, M. 323
Rusike, E. T. M. 819
Ruzvidzo, T. 602

S

Sachikonye, L. 402, 407,
    417, 591, 642
Salau, A. T. 523
Salt, B. 104, 850
Samkange, M. 408

Samkange, S. 124, 142,
    254, 408, 746-47, 749,
    770
Sampson, C. 98
Samuel, J. 721
Samupindi, C. 772
Sanders, D. 13, 16, 320,
    322, 334, 338, 340
Sandford, S. 620
Sandura, W. R. 409
Sanger, C. 166
Sato, M. 515
Sattar, E. 227
Sauer, H. 122
Saul, J. 481
Savory, P. 758
Sawyer, A. R. 646
Scandlyn, J. 333, 340
Schatzberg, M. 10
Schlyter, A. 349
Schmidt, E. 192, 364
Schoffeleers, J. M. 298
Scholz, D. 284
Schreiner, O. 773
Schuller, M. 431
Schutz, B. M. 393
Schwab, W. B. 539
Schwartz, K. 30
Scoones, I. 50, 611, 616,
    621
Scully, P. 209
Seager, D. 874
Seidman, A. 499-500
Seidman, G. 105, 348
Seidman, N. 500
Selous, F. C. 122
Seventh Commonwealth
    Mining and
    Metallurgical
    Congress 656
Shabalala, S. 516
Shack, W. 370
Shackley, M. 59
Shadur, M. 701, 704
Shamuyarira, N. 387, 394,
    398, 713
Shaw, T. M. 470, 476
Shaw, W. H. 402
Shenk, J. R. 276
Sherman, J. 798
Shopo, T. D. 417
Shore, M. 141
Sibanda, A. 13, 428

Index of Titles

342

African township,
Salisbury 536
Two nations: aspects of the
development of race
relations in the
Rhodesias and
Nyasaland 263

U

US military involvement in
Southern Africa 203
UDI: the international
politics of the
Rhodesian rebellion
176
Ukama: reflections on
Shona and western
cultures in Zimbabwe
243
Unconsummated union:
Britain, Rhodesia and
South Africa 1900-45
468
Under the skin: the death of
white Rhodesia 173
Underdevelopment of
African education 718
Unemployment and
economic structure in
Rhodesia 679
Unemployment crisis 679
Unholy wedlock: the failure
of the Central African
Federation 161
United Nations and
economic sanctions
against Rhodesia 191
United Nations and
Rhodesia: a study in
international law 195
United Nations,
international law, and
the Rhodesian
independence crisis
475
University of Zimbabwe:
university, national
university, state
university or party
university 729
Unsettled land: the politics

of land redistribution
in Matabeleland 1980-
90 569
Unwanted pregnancies and
baby dumping: whose
problem 316
Urban and regional change
in Southern Africa 637
Urban commitment and
involvement amonst
black Rhodesians 537
Urban development in the
main centres 535
Urban food distribution
and household
consumption: a study
of Harare 526
Urban low income housing
in Zimbabwe 543
Urban man in Southern
Africa 533, 796
Urban poverty datum line
in Rhodesia: a study of
the minimum
consumption needs of
families 522
Urbanisation in the
developing world 527
Urbanisation in the socialist
Third World: the case
of Zimbabwe 527
Urbanization and socialism
in Zimbabwe: the case
of low-cost housing
547
Use of dambos in rural
development, with
reference to Zimbabwe
622
Utility of a combined
periodic service and
regulated market
system in the
development of
economic hinterlands:
the case of
Zimbabwe's Tribal
Trust Lands 552

V

Vakaranga: an African
religion 240

Valiant years 04
Valley of the Ironwoods: a
personal record of ten
years served as District
Commissioner in
Rhodesia's largest
administrative area,
Nuanatsi, in the
southwestern lowveld
449
Victoria Falls: a handbook
to Victoria Falls, the
Batoka Gorge and part
of the Upper Zambesi
River 56
Victoria incident and the
Anglo-Matabele war of
1893: a study of early
colonization in Central
Africa, and the
African response 129
Vision splendid: the future
of the Central African
Federation 166
VOICE directory of social
services in Zimbabwe
1983 345
Voting for democracy:
electoral politics in
Zimbabwe 405

W

Waiting for the rain 746,
749, 763
Wankie: the story of a great
game reserve 78
War and politics in
Zimbabwe 1840-1900
123
War history of Southern
Rhodesia 1939-45 122
War in the air: Rhodesian
air force 1935-80 198
Warriors 119
Way of the white fields in
Rhodesia: a survey of
Christian enterprise in
Northern and Southern
Rhodesia 157
We carry a heavy load.
Rural women in

Index of Subjects

Atlases 19

B

Baby-dumping 316
Balance of payments 4, 509
Banana, Canaan Sodindo
    782
    theology 285, 299
Banking 15, 17, 498, 662,
    664, 708-09
Bantu Mirror 265
Batoka gorge 47, 56
Beef 321, 619
Beira and Mashonaland
    and Rhodesia
    Railways 63
Beira corridor 820
Beira Corridor Group 820
Beit, Alfred 130
Beit Trust 130
Belingwe 160
Bibliographies 42, 65, 68,
    371, 734, 808, 859-879
    multidisciplinary 3, 873,
    879
    Rhodesiana 812
Biographies 61, 117, 122,
    126, 128, 130, 135-36,
    141, 159, 163, 165,
    172, 175, 184, 218,
    347, 388-91, 403, 411,
    514, 639, 797
    see also Names of
    individuals
Birds 71-74, 878
Board of Censors of
    Rhodesia 818
Boer War 451
Botanical names 75
    Afrikaans 69
    Lozi 67
    Ndebele 67, 69
    Nguni 67
    Shona 67, 69
    Tonga 67
Botany 839
Botha, Pik 213
Boundaries 18, 145
Boxing 158
Boyd, Lord 174
Bridewealth, see Lobola
    353

Britain 468
    and UDI 108, 154, 171-
    72, 176-77, 181, 398,
    480
    colonial policy 108, 140,
    154, 165, 170, 383, 556
Britain Zimbabwe Society
    841
British Colonial Office 170
British South Africa
    Company 128, 132,
    134, 142, 154, 773
British South Africa Police
    444, 450
Building societies 542, 548
Bulawayo 158, 315, 522,
    538
    architecture 531
    informal sector 694
    pre-colonial 136
    workforce 698
Bulawayo Chronicle 265,
    358, 397, 816, 819
Butterflies 71
Byrd Amendment 471

C

Campfire wildlife project
    83, 507
Campus Crusade 285
Cape-to-Cairo dream 140
Capital 419, 647
    see also Economy,
    Investment
Capricorn Africa Society
    269, 379, 731
Carnegie Endowment for
    International Peace
    471
Carrington, Lord 213
Carter, Jimmy 217
Carving 56
    see also Sculpture
Catholic Commission for
    Justice and Peace 397
Catholic Institute of
    International
    Relations 215, 815
Cattle 350, 563, 616, 618-
    22, 631, 643
    dairy 582

grazing schemes 611, 617
    policy 621, 626
    see also Livestock
Censorship 720, 818
Censuses 223-24
Central African Federation
    see Federation of
    Rhodesia and
    Nyasaland
Central Intelligence
    Organization (CIO)
    175, 386, 397
CGIAR
    see Consultative Group
    on International
    Agricultural Research
Chaminuka cult 240
Changamire kingdom
    see Rozwi
Chidzero Report 15
Chief Conservator of
    Forests 67
Chiefs 235, 294, 305, 363-
    64, 463-64, 466
Children 228-29, 241, 253,
    334, 348, 361, 634, 799
    nutrition 320
Chimurenga
    see Wars (1896-97
    uprising); and Wars
    (independence, 1966-
    79)
Chishawasha 159
Chissano, Joaquim 213
Chitepo, Herbert 204, 386-
    87
Chitnis, Lord 174
Chitungwiza 259, 320, 547
Chiweshe reserve 628
Christ for all Nations 285
Christian Care 507
Christianity 115, 279, 284-
    85, 287, 291, 293, 296,
    314, 332, 415
    and African Nationalism
    395
    relations with state 299-
    300
    Shona 289
Chrome 33, 471, 651
Chung, Fay 13, 398, 402

RENAMO
  see Mozambique
    National Resistance
Research 740
  agricultural 580, 736,
    739, 844
  national 737
  scientific 847
  technical 847
  university 741, 843
Reserves 557, 588, 601
  Chilimanzi 628
  Chiweshe 628
  Matabeleland 631
  Zimutu 628
  see also Communal
    areas; Land
Resettlement
  Dewure scheme 577
  strategic
    see protected villages
  see also Land
Responsible self-
  government 122, 468
Review of African Political
  Economy 416
Rheme Bible Church 285
Rhinos 79
Rhodes, Cecil 122, 124,
  127, 132, 135, 140-41,
  667, 770, 773
  biography 44, 60
Rhodesia and East Africa
  164
Rhodesia Herald 265, 816,
  831
Rhodesian Air Force 197-
  98
Rhodesian Amateur
  Athletic Association
  165
Rhodesian Front 171, 372,
  388
  law 443
Rhodesian Journal of
  Economics 846
Rhodesian Native Labour
  Bureau 690
Rhodesian Pioneers' and
  Early Settlers' Society
  122
Rhodesian Publicity
  Association 63

Rhodesian Special Air
  Service 197
Riddell Commission 497
Rivers 31, 487
Rock art
  see Art
Rozvi
  see Rozwi
Rozwi 105, 112, 120, 122,
  146, 245
Rudd Concession 121-22,
  134
Rugby 804
Rural development 4, 83,
  207, 552, 600, 603-04,
  608, 614, 641, 649
Rural settlement
  see Settlements
Rural-urban linkages 259,
  526, 536-37, 599
Rural-urban migration
  see Migration

S

Sabi valley 35, 639
  irrigation projects 610
SADCC
  see Southern African
    Development
    Coordination
    Conference
Salisbury 522, 532-33, 537-
  38, 544
  health 331
Sanctions 5, 187-89, 191-
  95, 471, 474, 475, 660
  against South Africa
    472, 652
  busting 187, 190-91, 194,
    198, 471
  oil 190
  railways 666
  retaliation by South
    Africa 490
Sanitation 738
  rural 312, 608
Sarec
  see Swedish Agency for
    Research Co-
    operation
Save valley

  see Sabi valley
Savings clubs 511
Scandinavia
  and UDI 191
Science 737
  periodical 847
Scramble for Africa 140
Sculptors
  biographies 797
Sculpture
  Shona 797
Second World War 451
Security forces 6, 10, 175,
  209, 381, 386, 438, 439
Segregation 711
  policy 163
  urban 523, 528
Selous Scouts 206, 210
Settlement initiatives
  see UDI
Settlements 520, 854
  rural 549-53, 636
  service centres 549-51,
    614
Settler colonialism 63, 107,
  137, 149, 155, 416, 493
Settlers 125, 131, 143, 149,
  154
  guides 61-64
  mentality 122, 125, 153,
    444, 742
  women 352, 357-58, 449
Sexuality 313, 353
Shona 235, 237, 248
  agriculture 588
  culture 90-91, 97, 226,
    229, 235, 240-43, 245,
    248, 252, 256, 287,
    317, 770, 789, 796
  diet 317
  economy 248
  ethnicity 93, 111, 240,
    245, 252
  fishing 85
  health 331
  independent churches
    278, 283
  law 235, 436
  military affairs 121, 123,
    139
  names 275
  politics 248

366

Map of Zimbabwe

This map shows the more important towns and other features.

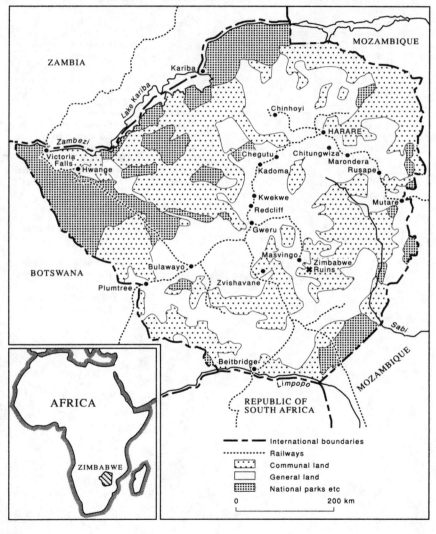